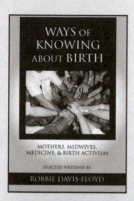

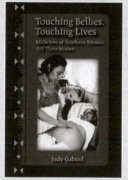

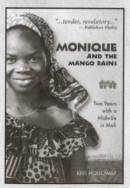

Also from Waveland Press

available in print and ebook formats

Ways of Knowing about Birth
Mothers, Midwives, Medicine,
and Birth Activism
Selected Writings by Robbie Davis-Floyd
ISBN 978-1-4786-3362-4

Touching Bellies, Touching Lives
Midwives of Southern Mexico
Tell Their Stories
Judy Gabriel
ISBN 978-1-4786-2710-4

Monique and the Mango Rains
Two Years with a Midwife in Mali
Kris Holloway
ISBN 978-1-57766-435-2

To order or for more information,
visit waveland.com

Birth *in* Eight Cultures

Birth in Eight Cultures

Brazil • Greece • Japan • Mexico • The Netherlands
New Zealand • Tanzania • United States

Edited by

Robbie Davis-Floyd & Melissa Cheyney

WAVELAND
PRESS, INC.
Long Grove, Illinois

For information about this book, contact:
Waveland Press, Inc.
4180 IL Route 83, Suite 101
Long Grove, IL 60047-9580
(847) 634-0081
info@waveland.com
www.waveland.com

The book cover shows a traditional Mexican bark painting given to Robbie by Marina Rodriguez, a traditional midwife in Cuernavaca, Mexico. It symbolizes "woman holding up the world while giving birth to it." This image places birth within the community/society and thereby within a cultural context, clearly demonstrating the major point of this book: that culture profoundly shapes the practices around, and meanings of, giving birth.

Contents

1

Birth as Culturally Marked and Shaped

Melissa Cheyney and Robbie Davis-Floyd

*Jordan's work is not only a landmark crosscultural study of childbearing,
but also an insightful analysis of methodological issues in anthropology . . .
Brigitte Jordan is midwife to the anthropology of childbirth.*
—*Robert A. Hahn*

How This Book Was Born

I (Robbie) was in my hotel room, preparing to head to yet another fascinating session at the Annual Meetings of the American Anthropological Association (AAA) when there came a knock on my door. Opening it, I was
delighted to find my dear friend and mentor Brigitte (Gitti) Jordan, who had
come to ask me if I would consider updating and revising her renowned book
*Birth in Four Cultures: A Cross-Cultural Investigation of Childbirth in Yucatan, Hol-
land, Sweden, and the United States.* Following its initial publication in 1978, this
classic book had spread around the world and become the catalyst for the creation of not one, but two, new fields: the anthropology of birth and the anthropology of midwifery. Both of these fields are now subfields of the anthropology
of reproduction—which itself only became recognized as a major field of study
after the 1995 publication of *Conceiving the New World Order: The Politics of
Reproduction*, edited by Faye Ginsburg and Rayna Rapp—so, as in much else,
Gitti was way ahead of her time. The third edition of *Birth in Four Cultures* had
come out in 1983, and Gitti was hoping for a fourth. Unwilling at that point in
her long and distinguished career (first in the anthropology of birth and then of
corporations) to do all the hard work of revising and updating the book herself,
she was asking me, quite humbly, if I might be willing.

I stared at her in shock. How could she not know that I would happily
accept this amazing opportunity to revise a book that had so shaped my own

1

Brigitte (Gitti) Jordan. Photo by
Robert Irwin

career for another generation of scholars? Much to my delight, we discussed and argued endlessly over the
wording of nearly every page, until we
had a revision, published in 1993, that
made us both proud and is still to this
day used for teaching.

Now *Birth in Four Cultures, Fourth
Edition*, though still relevant, is
extremely outdated. When I talked to
Gitti about that some months before
she died of pancreatic cancer in 2016,
she repeated various times and in various versions, "Don't try to revise my
work again, just do your own thing."
So I did—in rich collaboration with
my colleague and friend Melissa (Missy) Cheyney, who is simultaneously a
practicing Certified Professional Midwife (CPM), an Associate Professor of
Medical Anthropology, and an outstanding researcher well versed in both
qualitative and quantitative methods. As a medical anthropologist studying
mothers, childbirth, midwives, and obstetricians for over 35 years, I was able
to combine my expertise with Missy's knowledge and skills; we have worked
joyfully together to create this book for you.

The Cultural Marking and Shaping of Birth

The most scientific birth is also the least technological birth.
— Alice Drieger MD

We knew that Gitti's original and most profound point—that "birth is
everywhere culturally marked and shaped"—would remain the central organizing theme of this collection. Cross-cultural comparison remains critical to
reproductive studies because, globally, the medical management of childbirth
has been generally understood to be driven by scientific inquiry and therefore
based on hard fact. As a result, medically managed birth has been (and still is
in most countries) quite commonly seen as the safest, indeed the only, way to
give birth. However, as cross-cultural analyses are so adept at revealing, the
assumed scientific neutrality of medicalized obstetrics is a fiction (Lock 1993,
2001, 2002, 2010; Lindebaum and Lock 2010). Birth *is* everywhere culturally
marked and socially shaped.

In this volume, we look both broadly and deeply at birth in diverse cultures, for *if science were in fact unbiased, and if the management of birth everywhere
were evidence-informed, then births that take place in hospitals would be treated
according to a similar set of standards and protocols that would support normal birth*

physiology. Yet, in fact, there are vast cultural differences in the treatment of birth that reveal the deepest core values of any given society or community; it is *culture* and its concomitant beliefs and values that shape birth practices, not a value-free scientific system alone that somehow transcends culture and belief. Science, like birth, is just as culturally marked and shaped as any other human way of knowing; it is not an unbiased reflection of reality, but a com-plex cultural system that varies regionally, and is increasingly influenced at national and global levels by transnational political and economic interests.

A technocracy, as Robbie has long defined it, is "a society organized around the progressive development and use of high technologies and the global flow of information" (Davis-Floyd 2001, 2018a). Technocratic societ-ies are postindustrial, late modern, capitalistic, hierarchical, socially strati-fied, bureaucratic, institution-laden, and (still) patriarchal to their core. Since its inception in the 1700s, hospital birth went through a long period of indus-trialization, in which hospitals became baby-producing factories and women's bodies were treated like dysfunctional machines on medical assem-bly lines—a process still ongoing in many low-resource countries. In higher-resource countries over the past four decades, biomedical (medicine focused on biology) obstetrics has become technomedical obstetrics: birth has become heavily technocratized via the insistent application of high-tech machines such as ultrasound and electronic fetal monitors; such machines are often unavailable in underresourced nations where the older, industrial-ized model still prevails.[1] As one Argentinean obstetrician working in a large public hospital noted to Robbie:

> Birth is just an assembly line here—we wheel them in, extract their babies, and wheel them out. The doctors are treated like God, but the midwives and nurses do most of the work—we are only there for the last 15 minutes of the birth. But who has time to worry about that? The birth-ing women just keep coming and we just keep getting those babies out—that's why we like cesareans so much—it's so easy and quick and we don't have to wait around! So our national cesarean rate is around 40%, and we are just fine with that.

Over the last century, the industrial or technocratic facility-based manage-ment of childbirth as normative has spread to nearly every corner of the globe. Today we have what can be considered a transnational/global culture of industrialization and technocratization that, along with local cultural vari-ations, shapes the performance of childbirth—often to the point of subsum-

---

[1] There are many kinds of "medicines" and "medical" practices in the world, including those of traditional societies, often referred to as "traditional," "local" or "Indigenous" medicine. *Bio-medicine/biomedical* are terms coined by medical anthropologist Atwood Gaines to specifically index Western-style medicine with its emphasis on human biology instead of on the spiritual practices that often characterize systems of traditional medicine. (See Gaines and Davis-Floyd 2004 for a full explanation.) In this book, we more frequently use the term "technomedicine" to highlight biomedicine's increasing focus on the use of high technology for both diagnosis and treatment.

ing or entirely eliminating the traditional birthways that used to predominate everywhere (Fannin 2003; Davis-Floyd and Cheyney 2009).

Thus, the time is ripe for new cross-cultural reflection. Recognition is growing that technocratic approaches have not lived up to their promises, as they have not significantly improved maternal or infant health outcomes globally, nor have they proven to be economically sustainable in most parts of the world (Gibbons, Belizán, Lauer et al. 2010). As a result, international agencies have for some decades been developing global programs and initiatives aimed at reducing preventable maternal and infant death and suffering, while birth activists and researchers have spurred us to question some of our core assumptions about what women and babies need to survive, thrive, and flourish (UN/WHO 2016). As the chapters in this book vividly illustrate, many pregnant women, physicians, public health professionals, midwives, nurses, and policy makers have begun to reflect critically on what has been gained and what has been lost with the hegemonic spread first of industrial, then of technocratic obstetrics from the global North to the global South. When practitioners of older, industrialized models of birth care in low- and middle-resource countries attempt to emulate the technocratic model of care brought to them by practitioners largely from high-resource countries, there is a tendency to implement only its worst aspects—that is, too many interventions. Chronically understaffed, they tend to leave out the one-on-one compassionate care that is now beginning to transform the technocratic model in the US and other high-resource countries as practitioners in these countries seek to "humanize" their care—a quest generated both by the tremendous pressure applied by birth activists and by the scientific evidence that supports its value.

Compassionate, respectful maternity care is known to be a powerful agent in achieving optimal birth outcomes (World Health Organization 1996, 2014, 2018). While many have assumed that evidence-based maternity care should be primarily technocratic—as in more technology = increased safety—there is a growing awareness that reality is far more complex. Technologies like cesarean section (CS) and synthetic hormones for the augmentation of labor are certainly vital innovations that save many lives annually under certain circumstances. But their routine overuse has been shown to be costly to the system and detrimental to mothers and babies (Miller et al. 2016; World Health Organization 1996). A growing body of evidence indicates that birth is safer in most instances when its normal physiology is understood and supported and when women's emotional states during birth are actively addressed via the care of supportive companions, including doulas (trained labor support companions), family, friends, and practitioners (Peters, Thornton, and de Jonge 2018).

"Too Much Too Soon" and "Too Little Too Late"

Miller and colleagues (2016) set forth a continuum of global maternity care where two extremes exist—what they refer to as *too little, too late* (TLTL) and *too much, too soon* (TMTS) systems. TLTL is used to describe care where a strong push on the part of development agencies and national ministries of health to move birthing people into medical facilities (hospitals and clinics) to give birth combines with inadequate staff, training, infrastructure, supplies, and medications (Austin et al. 2014). The all-too-common result is care that is poor in quality, withheld, or simply unavailable until it is too late. The converse—too much, too soon (TMTS)—is characterized by routine overuse of interventions and hypermedicalization of normal pregnancy and birth. Miller and colleagues (2016) note that TMTS systems often include the unnecessary use of non-evidence-based interventions (such as continuous electronic fetal monitoring [EFM]), as well as the massive overuse of interventions that can be lifesaving but harmful when applied routinely (e.g., episiotomy—cutting the vagina with scissors to open it further to hasten birth, artificial labor augmentation, and cesarean section). As facility births have increased globally, so has the recognition that both TLTL and TMTS systems produce harm, increase costs, and concentrate disrespect, abuse, and violations of human rights in childbirth (Freedman and Kruk 2014; Miller and Lalonde 2015; World Health Organization 2014). While TMTS systems are typically associated with high-resource nations and TLTL with low- and middle-resource ones, due to socioeconomic inequality these extremes may coexist in a given nation and even in the same facility—where wealthy women are placed in special, well-staffed wards with TMTS care, while the poor in the wards on the lower floors have to accept the TLTL care they often receive from overworked and underpaid practitioners.

Conversely, midwifery care—with its reliance on time-honored "low-tech, high-touch" traditions combined with the skilled management of first-line complications and the provision of family planning and contraception—has shown enormous promise for radically improving maternal and infant health globally (Homer et al. 2014; ten Hoope-Bender et al. 2014; Van Lerberghe et al. 2014). These discoveries have opened new conversations around where and with whom women should give birth. Do all women need to go to a hospital and be attended by skilled surgical specialists such as obstetricians, or can some births safely occur attended by midwives in the hospital, at home, or in a birth center? As this book will show, the anthropology of birth can help us move beyond the overly simplistic, global development agency rallying cry of "Every birth a facility birth!" to more nuanced and culturally informed policies that match providers and birth settings to the integral needs (i.e., clinical, psychosocial, spiritual, cultural, etc.) of individual women within their own ethnographic contexts.

The Importance of Ideology: Risk, Fear, and the 1-2 Punch

The cross-cultural study of how societies perform birth can operate not only as a critical lens into much deeper understandings of any given culture but also as a means to a clear understanding of how deeply culture—far more than science—influences childbirth (Davis-Floyd 2003, 2018a, b; Davis-

Floyd and Laughlin 2016; Cheyney 2011). In fact, the science of birth can only be accessed through a practitioner's own interpretive lens—a lens that is always and inevitably influenced by the culture in which that practitioner was socialized. Why does this kind of cultural influence on practitioners matter? It matters because, some years ago, researcher Ellen Hodnett (2001, 2002) clearly demonstrated that *the major factor affecting the outcome of a birth is the attitude/ideology of the practitioner*—and that attitude or ideology will always be heavily culturally influenced.

Around the world, at this very moment, the global culture of technocratic obstetrics—along with its local, socially stratified variations—is influencing the mistreatment of thousands of women as they labor and give birth, and critical care is being withheld from poor women and women of color at the bottom of their social hierarchies. The chronic lack of supplies and/or trained personnel in lower-resource nations affects poor women and members of devalued ethnic groups most, while others, including the wealthy and the middle-class, are being subjected to interventions they do not need and are often harmful. Many of these women, rich and poor, know or suspect they are being violated, yet some do not, as abuses during parturition (labor and birth) are so common that they have become normative in high-, middle-, and low-resource countries alike. (See www.humanrightsinchildbirth.org and www.whiteribbonalliance.org for excellent information on disrespect and abuse during labor and birth.)

Thus, many pregnant people have come to accept disrespect and violations of their autonomy as just "the way things are," and so may not recognize their treatment as a violation of their fundamental human rights. Those who intentionally avoid facility birth because they fear mistreatment and/or unnecessary interventions may face significant consequences for birthing outside the technocratic box. Especially in high-resource countries where hospitals abound, the blaming and shaming of women who give birth in their own homes with a skilled midwife emerges from a global culture of risk avoidance we have collectively created around birth. Once birth becomes viewed as inherently risky, then it appears as if all measures *must* be taken to keep it safe. Yet birth, especially among healthy, well-nourished women, is not necessarily or generally risky business—most babies are born healthy to healthy mothers, no matter what impediments we throw at the birth process. Indeed, the World Health Organization (2018) estimates that a majority of babies globally can be born without major medical intervention.

Nevertheless, *perception is everything.* Once we have internalized the belief that birth is dangerous for everyone (as opposed to the more nuanced and factual perception that "birth is dangerous for a small percentage of women under certain circumstances"), then fear of a bad outcome can become our primary motivation for its medical management. Sadly, the reality is that the technocratic management of birth, especially when too much of it is applied to soon, often makes parturition not safer but far riskier and often more damaging to mothers and babies than it should be, as the chapters in this volume illustrate.

Anthropologist Peter Reynolds (1991) has identified a phenomenon in technocratic societies that he calls "The 1-2 Punch of Mutilation and Prosthesis": Punch 1: Mutilate a natural process with technology, like damming a river to prevent floods, thus also preventing salmon from swimming upstream to spawn; or apply TMTS to birth—perform too many technological interventions too quickly, thereby disrupting the normal physiology of birth. Punch 2: Fix the problems caused by Punch 1 with more technology—take the salmon out of the river to spawn in artificial salmon factories, then put them back into the river below the dam (as has been done in California)—perform a CS to save the baby now in distress from TMTS (as is happening all over the world in what has long been called "the cesarean epidemic"). Reynolds' deeper insight is that *Punch 2 is the point: we frequently believe that we have made natural processes better by interfering in them with technology.* Women often thank their doctors for "saving my baby's life" by performing a CS, when the need for that CS was caused by technological interventions that precipitated the emergency (as in the case, for example, of maternal blood pressure dropping precipitously when an epidural is administered). This 1-2 Punch is closely linked to what we call the *obstetric paradox*—the conundrum that intervening in birth to make it safer and more controllable actually may make it more dangerous, as the interventions themselves often cause harm. In a technocratic society, the potential solution of less intervention and more support for normal processes is often not recognized or explored, as the belief that more technology = greater safety is so deeply ingrained. You will see examples of the 1-2 Punch and the obstetric paradox throughout this book.

The term *obstetric violence* has been introduced into the birth lexicon in the past decade to name, and thus make visible, the mistreatment of laboring women, which occurs most frequently in low-resource countries. Yet obstetric violence also occurs more frequently than previously thought in high-resource nations, often in more subtle ways. This book contains tales of mistreatment, disrespect, and tragedy, where women's rights are violated and they and their babies suffer accordingly, as well as tales of triumph, where women rise up to demand those rights and practitioners rise up to honor them.

It is our hope that this book, like its predecessor, will serve both to teach students about the field of the anthropology of birth and to wake up a new generation of students and consumers, of policy makers and funders, of ministry of health officials and local grassroots organizations to the pervasive cultural and subcultural influences on the processes of childbirth. We hope to inspire a new generation to work to create new kinds of global and local cultures around birth management that encompass respectful, evidence-based approaches to maternity care. These systems must be respectful of childbearers and their families, respectful of the normal physiology of birth and how best to support it, and respectful of the practitioners themselves, who often treat women with disrespect because that is how they themselves are treated by those above them in the technomedical hierarchy.

The Technocratic, Humanistic, and Holistic Paradigms of Birth and the Midwifery Model of Care

Throughout the ethnographic chapters in this volume runs a common thread of the three primary paradigms (or templates) for conceptualizing birth—the technocratic, humanistic, and holistic models—that Robbie (Davis-Floyd 2001, 2018a) has long identified as key ideologies that deeply influence birth practice around the world. Briefly, technocratic practitioners tend to see the body as a machine and birth as a mechanistic process in need of technological interventions. Time is of the essence; impatience tends to prevail; the focus is on the inherent defectiveness of the birthing body-machine and "managing risk" via technology. The patient is viewed as an object and treated accordingly. In the humanistic model, the body is conceptualized and treated as an organism and the woman as a whole, relational being so that the normal physiology of birth, the pregnant person's emotions, and compassionate support from caregivers are considered paramount. Patience is a virtue, along with trust in the birth process and the value of relationships among the patient, her family, and her caregivers. (Robbie has been careful to distinguish between "superficial" and "deep" humanism: it is *superficially humanistic* to paint the birth rooms in pretty colors and allow at least one companion, while still giving TMTS or TLTL care. It is *deeply humanistic* to fully support normal physiologic birth by encouraging eating and drinking at will during labor, freedom of movement, and upright positions for labor and birth—and most of all, to listen to women.) The holistic view of birth as delineated by Robbie is of the body as an energy field in constant interaction with other energy fields. The energy surrounding the birth is seen as having a strong effect on the birth process. Attuned practitioners take care to be aware of and to work with these interactive energy fields—to keep them positive and clear—often relying on intuition as well as professional knowledge and skills.

The "midwifery model of care" (MMOC) that is often discussed in these pages is a combination of the humanistic and holistic models; it can also entail judicious use of technology and technocratic skills. This midwifery model is person-centered: its practitioners uphold the woman as the autonomous and respected protagonist and decision-maker in her care. MMOC practitioners are relationship-oriented, "birth energy" conscious, and utilize both hands-on skills and intuition as a source of *authoritative knowledge* (Davis-Floyd 2018c; Davis-Floyd 2018g). Authoritative knowledge as Gitti (Jordan 1993, 1997) has defined it is the knowledge that counts in a given situation, on the basis of which people make decisions and take actions.

Because this book contains descriptions of cultural birth models that do and do not work well, some stark contrasts between systems emerge. The excellent outcomes achieved by functional and integrated models of care as

The Technocratic, Humanistic, and Holistic Models of Medicine

The Technocratic Model of Medicine	The Humanistic (Biopsychosocial) Model of Medicine	The Holistic Model of Medicine
1. Mind/body separation	1. Mind-body connection	1. Oneness of bodymindspirit
2. The body as machine	2. The body as an organism	2. The body as an energy system interlinked with other energy systems
3. The patient as object	3. The patient as relational subject	3. Healing the whole person in whole-life context
4. Alienation of practitioner from patient	4. Connection and caring between practitioner and patient	4. Essential unity of practitioner and client
5. Diagnosis and treatment from the outside in (curing disease, repairing dysfunction)	5. Diagnosis and healing from the outside in and from the inside out	5. Diagnosis and healing from the inside out
6. Hierarchical organization and standardization of care	6. Balance between the needs of the institution and the individual	6. Lateral, networking organizational structure that facilitates individualization of care
7. Authority and responsibility inherent in practitioner, not patient	7. Information, decision making, and responsibility shared between patient and practitioner	7. Authority and responsibility inherent in each individual
8. Supervaluation of science and technology	8. Science and technology counterbalanced with humanism	8. Science and technology placed at the service of the individual
9. Aggressive intervention with emphasis on short-term results	9. A long-term focus on disease prevention	9. A long-term focus on creating and maintaining health and wellbeing
10. Death as defeat	10. Death as an acceptable outcome	10. Death as a step in a process
11. A profit-driven system	11. Compassion-driven care	11. Healing as the focus
12. Intolerance of other modalities	12. Open-mindedness toward other modalities	12. Embrace of multiple healing modalities
Basic underlying principle: separation	Basic underlying principles: balance and connection	Basic underlying principles: Connection and integration
Type of thinking: unimodal, left-brained, linear	Type of thinking: bimodal	Type of thinking: Fluid, multimodal, right-brained

juxtaposed with the suboptimal, even horrifying, outcomes that result from dysfunctional and dis-integrated models highlight the roles that systems-level factors play in maternal and infant health outcomes. We intend this book to serve both as an educational tool and as a call to action for those readers who have heretofore been unaware of the current global crisis in maternity care or to those who assume that these are not issues in the United States or their own country. An enormous and rapidly growing body of work has documented tragic inequities in birth outcomes for women of color, and especially among Black women, in the US (see, for example, Brownell et al. 2018; Kothari et al. 2017; Malat et al. 2017; Mehra et al. 2017; Villalonga-Olives, Kawachi, and von Steinbüchel 2017) and elsewhere. Pregnant people and their babies are dying and suffering unnecessarily worldwide. There is much work to be done, and we hope some of you will feel called to engage in some aspect of this work, for it is critical to ensuring that all people in all places have access to a safe and fulfilling birth in which they are treated with dignity and respect and where their babies are cared for as sentient beings capable of feeling both pain and comfort.

An Overview of the Chapters in This Volume

In this Introduction, we emphasize a global reality that many, especially in privileged, high-resource countries, understand very little about: there exists a global crisis in maternity care—over 300,000 women die each year from maternity-related causes; perinatal mortality rates in many countries are stunningly high, and these rates are not distributed evenly. Women of color, poor women, and women from subjugated ethnic groups suffer disproportionately relative to their counterparts higher up in social hierarchies. Laboring people all over the world (and not just in low-resource countries) often suffer from both obstetric violence and non-evidence-based maltreatment (Punch 1), leaving them severely traumatized postbirth (McGarry et al. 2017; Ruder, Cheyney and Emasu 2018; Williams et al. 2018). Thousands of birth workers around the world are keenly aware of this global crisis, and there are many international organizations working to alleviate it. These global-level attempts at change are complemented and supported in many countries by local and national birth activist movements focused on the humanization of birth. You will read about such movements in the following chapters, particularly in Brazil, the United States, New Zealand, and Mexico.

Chapters 2–6 contain the heart of the book—comparative ethnographic descriptions of childbirth in eight cultures. *Birth in Four Cultures* was primarily based on Gitti's lengthy fieldwork with a traditional midwife, Doña Juana (her real name), in Mexico's state of Yucatan. Therefore, to honor Gitti, it was clear that we should include in this volume an entire chapter on Mexico. Since one of our primary criteria for selecting chapter authors was that their fieldwork be current, we considered ourselves lucky to find three outstanding scholars presently studying various aspects of Mexican birth—Vania Smith Oka, who has focused on studying hospital birth in Puebla, Lydia Dixon, who has studied Mexico's relatively new class of professional midwives, and Mounia el-Kotni, whose research concentrated on traditional midwives. In comparing all types of births in Mexico, these authors present a comprehen-sive portrait of birth across its three subcultures of maternity care—tradi-tional midwifery, professional midwifery, and obstetrics.

For Chapter 3 we were equally delighted to find three extraordinary scholars currently conducting research in Tanzania—Adrienne Strong, Megan Cogburn, and Summer Wood. Their long-term fieldwork projects took place in different regions of the country—in the major city Dar es Salaam and in the towns/regions of Dodoma and Rukwa. Collectively, their work documents the forced disappearance of Tanzania's ancient tradition of community-based midwifery via policies that include fines for women who give birth at home; the reasons why Tanzania's maternal mortality rate is so high; the systemic dysfunctions in Tanzanian hospitals—including poor infrastructure and a chronic lack of essential supplies; and the massive stress-ors this system places on both its health care practitioners and their patients.

An important contribution of this chapter is that its authors explore mul-tiple sides of the maternity care equation, examining the perspectives of both patients and practitioners on why so many women die of maternity-related causes in their country. Summer's section on the difficulties of obtaining a birth certificate illustrates the extent to which low-resource countries may struggle in the wake of postcolonial infrastructural devastation to perform even the simplest of services. One end result is that birth certificates—some-thing taken for granted in other regions represented in this volume—are often unattainable for the Tanzanian poor. The wealth of information these three authors bring, their comprehensive fieldwork in three separate regions, and their emphasis on three distinct but related issues (the phasing out of home-birth, the dysfunctions of hospital birth, and the complexities of birth registra-tion), inspired us to include Tanzania as a second intracultural comparison chapter along with Mexico.

Both the Mexican and the Tanzanian chapters compare birth across regional or subcultural systems within those countries. The rest of the ethno-graphic chapters each compare birth in two countries, thereby highlighting the vast differences *national* cultural ideologies can make in the treatment of birth. For the sake of achieving both sharp contrasts and blurriness (because "reality" is full of both), we organized comparison chapters with markedly differing systems, and some with significant commonalities.

Chapter 4 contrasts obstetric systems in Japan and Brazil; we selected this pairing not only because their differences are extreme but also because there has been a long-standing exchange program between the two countries run by the Japanese International Cooperation Agency (JICA). This pro-gram supported hundreds of Brazilian midwives to travel to Japan to study its gentle birth model—a model so far removed from the violent Brazilian approach they were accustomed to that these Brazilian midwives experienced profound culture shock both on arrival and on returning home.

Japanese author Etsuko Matsuoka is critical of some of the deficiencies of the Japanese model, which is increasingly focused on birth as a business with a strong "please the consumer" orientation—which, she came to realize as she co-created this chapter, may not be so bad relative to what Brazil has to offer. In fact, there is much to celebrate within the Japanese birthing system. The obstetric violence that Eliza Williamson describes as rampant in Brazilian hospitals, accompanying its high CS rate of 55%, is practically nonexistent in Japan, where birth is regarded as a normal process and labor pain is considered a positive path toward becoming a strong and empowered mother. While midwives attend almost all Japanese births, they attend only about 9% of Brazilian births. Almost the same is true for the United States and the Netherlands; in the US, midwives attend around 12% of births (a rate significantly higher than the 2% they cumulatively attended in 1980 [Davis-Floyd 2018e; Chapter 6, this volume]), while in the Netherlands they attend the vast majority.

The technocratic model is most clearly evident in Greece (Chapter 5), where the national CS rate is just under 70%, while in New Zealand, the midwifery model prevails. There the CS rate is 25%, and midwives are present at 100% of births (even when those births are scheduled cesareans performed by obstetricians). Chapter coauthor Nia Georges describes how, after World War II, Greece rapidly transformed its birthing system from a traditional, home-based model to its current entirely hospital-based and highly interventive model. New Zealand was heading down the same path during the 1970s and 1980s, until its few practicing homebirth midwives organized, creating a highly effective social movement and generating a full-fledged midwifery renaissance. Their brilliance lay in how they got New Zealand's doctors on board: The midwives proposed the concept that *every woman deserved continuity of care during labor and birth*, so therefore there should be a practitioner called a Lead Maternity Carer (LMC), who would agree to care for that woman during pregnancy and pledge to be with her for the birth.

The doctors signed on to this idea because they agreed that continuity of care was important and because they believed that any well-informed mother-to-be would choose a physician as her LMC. However, once the midwives had achieved legislation establishing them as autonomous practitioners and solidifying the idea of the LMC, women voted with their bodies; today a full *92% of women in New Zealand choose midwives as their LMCs*. The obstetricians have by now come to accept this situation as status quo, since they are usually not the ones who have to get out of bed in the middle of the night, and their skills are properly reserved for the high-risk cases where they are truly needed. Around the world, as these chapters demonstrate, it has been shown that knowledgeable, skilled, and relationship-oriented midwives are the optimal care providers for normal, healthy, physiologic births, as midwives commonly know how to support and facilitate that process without the TMTS interventions that characterize technocratic obstetric approaches.

Readers will observe as they move through the chapters that *where auton-omous midwives are the predominant birth practitioners, humanistic models of care prevail*, characterized by the compassionate, patient, person-centered approach of the MMOC. Where obstetricians are the primary providers, the technocratic model of birth is almost always dominant—many impatient high-tech interventions are performed to speed the birth process along (Punch 1), and many cesareans are done to "save the baby" from the prob-lems generated by these interventions (Punch 2). New Zealand, with its many autonomous midwives, has generally embraced the midwifery model of care, while in Greece, highly trained and skilled midwives are restricted to the margins—on the so-called "Gamma" wards where the poor and the immigrant women are placed. Wealthier Greek women seek to establish, and pay extra for, an exclusive, personal relationship with their obstetricians. Obstetricians practicing in the higher-income "Alpha" and "Beta" wards make extra money from the "gifts" that are commonly given by parents who are grateful to receive the continuous care they strongly desire. Poorer women cannot afford these "gifts," which often involve large sums of money and which have become an inextricable part of middle-class Greek birth structure. Most obstetricians are happy to leave the care of the poor to the midwives, who do not expect to receive such gifts. The CS rates in the Alpha and Beta wards are exceptionally high, giving Greece its current CS rate of nearly 70%, while those on the Gamma wards are much lower, as midwives apply both their hands-on skills and caring attitudes, and the 1-2 Punch phe-nomenon does not prevail.

Chapter 6 on the United States and the Netherlands shows that both birthing systems can be considered humanistic, in that laboring women in both countries are often (though not always) at least nominally treated with compassion and respect. In contrast to the United States, the Netherlands has been renowned in birth activist circles since the 1970s as the country with the most optimal obstetric and midwifery systems in the world, long seen as *the* model for others to emulate. Yet the Dutch model has undergone rapid change since 2009, with homebirth rates dropping from 30% to around 12%, so that a practice once considered normative in Dutch society is becoming increasingly marginalized, requiring that a social movement rise up to support it.

This drop in the Dutch homebirth rate did not result from poor outcomes at home but rather from media reports on studies showing that the Dutch had one of the highest perinatal mortality rates (PNMR) in Europe (10/1,000, meaning 10 newborn deaths per 1,000 births). The Dutch were shocked, and it was all too easy, as you will read, for the national media to shine a spotlight on homebirth as the culprit, though this was not supported by evidence. Fur-ther investigation showed that the higher PNMR in the Netherlands could be explained by a number of different factors, including the poorer nutritional and health status of women—Dutch as well as non-Dutch—living in deprived areas, yet the media had done its damage. As a result, more normal, healthy, low-risk Dutch women have been choosing to give birth in the hospital and more midwives have been encouraging them to do so. Birth centers now appear on their way to becoming a comfortable compromise. Nonetheless, the Dutch still have the highest homebirth rate among high-resource countries, where homebirth rates commonly hover around 1%.

In their early drafts of the US/Netherlands chapter, like our Japanese author Etsuko, the Dutch authors Therese Wiegers and Bahareh Goodarzi—a researcher and a practicing midwife—were at first highly critical of their nation's model, and especially of the more medicalized ways in which their system has evolved in the last decade or so. However, after reading what their coauthors Missy Cheyney, Saraswathi Vedam, and Robbie Davis-Floyd had to say about birth in the United States, they revised their opinion of their own system; its comparison with the United States led them to realize that despite recent changes, the Dutch system, while certainly not perfect, still has much worth emulating. Missy, Saras, and Robbie show that in the United States, a for-profit maternity care system, institutionalized racism, and a historically rooted and deeply contentious home–hospital divide function to prevent the vast majority of pregnant women from having access to anything resembling choice in birth place or provider type. Midwives in the Netherlands are fully integrated into the system, as is homebirth, whereas in the US, midwives and birth centers are few, and homebirth remains a highly marginalized choice.

Wanting to provide social science students with a sense of what it is like to conduct fieldwork, we asked all of our chapter authors to write fieldwork stories, which we include in Chapter 7, "Reflective Ethnographic Vignettes: Confronting Yourself in the Field." These stories range from the tragic to the hilarious, from the mistakes we all make to the lessons we have learned from those mistakes. We trust you will find them both entertaining and useful as you undertake your own fieldwork projects, or consider whether anthropology is the field for you.

In Chapter 8 we reflect back on each chapter and discuss the theoretical contributions each set of authors has made to our understandings of the cross-cultural treatment of birth. We conclude with some reflections on where we are headed and the role that the next generation of more diverse students and scholars may play in shaping those paths.[2]

Before We Begin:
Some Quick Notes on Language

Gender Inclusivity

We wish our readers to know that we are aware of the complexities introduced into our language by calls issued by LGBTQAI (Lesbian, Gay, Bisex-

---

[2] Much of the work on the anthropology of reproduction can be found listed in an Annotated Bibliography that we and our colleagues in the Anthropology of Reproduction have been developing for years, available at https://goo.gl/heqkX7.

ual, Transgender, Queer, Asexual, Intersex) communities to make the English language fully inclusive of queer and other nonbinary gender identities—an enterprise that we both support and are trying with various degrees of success to adapt to and to integrate linguistically. We have discussed at length the relative merits of using the terms "women," "woman," "mothers," "fathers," and "pregnant people," and have come to some agreements about the language we will adopt here.

First, we are committed to gender inclusivity in our language, so you will see us use terms like "pregnant person," "childbearer," "clients," and "parents" to avoid the constant gendering of birth and those who give birth and raise a child as feminine. However, because women in general are also marginalized and oppressed to varying degrees in many places around the world, we felt we could not erase the terms "woman," "mother," or "maternity" completely. For us, inclusivity means the use of both gendered *and* gender-neutral terms to refer to those members of society who give birth to new human beings.

Second, because our ethnographic chapters reflect vastly different cultures, we have deferred to individual authors about how to best convey the preferred terms for pregnant people in the communities where they work. For most of the authors who contributed to this volume, this means a consistent use of the terms "woman" and "mother"; we hope readers who identify as queer or nonbinary will not feel "othered" by this usage. We believe a diversity of terms is needed to convey meaning in diverse ethnographic contexts.

"Out-of-Hospital" versus "Community" Birth

We have also struggled over how to refer to births that do not occur in the hospital. The term out-of-hospital (OOH) has long been in use to refer to birth center and homebirth collectively, and Robbie initially preferred this term. Missy, however, prefers the term "community birth" to refer to births that occur at home and in freestanding birth centers—or anywhere outside of hospitals (Cheyney et al. 2019). Missy argues that "out-of-hospital" reifies hospital birth as normative and community birth as "other"—marginal or alternative—just as calling nonallopathic forms of healing "complementary" or "alternative" keeps technomedicine in general hegemonically normative. Hence many complementary and alternative medicine (CAM) practitioners prefer to call their forms of healing "holistic," "integrative," or "functional" medicine to indicate that modalities such as acupuncture, homeopathy, chiropractic, Reiki, and so on are all autonomous healing modalities that may exist outside of biomedicine but are not subservient to or "less than" allopathic/biomedical modalities.

We also note that the Dutch refer to hospital birth as "out-of-home birth," reminding us yet again the degree to which language and culture shape perceptions of normality. Robbie takes issue with the term "community birth" because she, like so many other homebirthers in countries where homebirth is rare, felt so isolated as a homebirther herself—that is, not a part of a community. Yet, as Missy explained to Robbie, this term is not intended to convey that the woman giving birth feels like she has a community of like-minded people or social support or that lots of people were at her birth in the sense of a *communal* birth. It is a space/place term meant to convey that the birth is occurring within a woman's own community in a *geographic* sense. She does not have to leave her community and go to a hospital that may be quite far away from her family and her home. Thus, after multiple engaging discussions, we have settled on "community birth" as our shorthand for what we used to call "out-of-hospital" or "home- and birth-center" birth.[3] We hope you enjoy the pages that follow and find our terminological choices both apt and inclusive.

THOUGHT QUESTIONS

1. What is the global crisis in maternity care as described in this chapter?
2. What ways can you think of to deal with this global crisis? What is already being done?
3. What do women's rights in childbirth consist of? Why do they matter?
4. What do you think of the editors' choices around language? How does language shape the way we see the world? How have Missy and Robbie's linguistic choices begun to shape the ways you see birth?

RECOMMENDED TELEVISION SERIES

Based on the memoirs of British midwife Jennifer Worth, the popular British television series *Call the Midwife* shows a historically accurate (1920s–early 1960s) model of community midwifery care. This series has encouraged many UK women to become midwives, wanting to practice as did the community midwives in the London district of Poplar, where the show is set—tending to women in their own homes with appropriate hospital transport available by ambulance. This kind of community midwifery, which began to decline as birth increasingly moved into the hospital, is experiencing a strong renaissance, due in part to the popularity of the show, which also accurately depicts the value of midwives checking up on women in their homes before and after birth. This series, along with the rich British data on the safety of midwife-attended community birth, has surely played a role in the rise in the UK homebirth rate from 1% to 8% over the past few years.

---

[3] Please note that Chapter 5 presents a different usage of this term "community birth." In New Zealand, a "community midwife" is an autonomous Lead Maternity Carer (LMC) who provides continuity of care throughout pregnancy and the postpartum, and attends her clients' births in hospitals, birth centers, and homes—that is, wherever the woman chooses.

2

Teaching about Childbirth in Mexico

Working across Birth Models

Lydia Zacher Dixon, Vania Smith-Oka, and Mounia El Kotni

As childbirth educator and activist Gayle Peterson once put it, "As a woman lives, so shall she give birth, so shall she die; in like manner and style to her own individual approach to life" (1984:3). More broadly, women's births are microcosms of their overall life circumstances. Mexican women's birth experiences are constrained by much more than individual choice—they are often constrained by its absence. Following in the footsteps of Brigitte Jordan's eloquent description of traditional Maya births in the 1970s in *Birth in Four Cultures*, we examine the process of birth in Mexico today in three different ethnographic contexts—a hospital, a midwife's home, and a birth center—to show how power dynamics, social stratifications, and legacies of inequality come to bear on the ostensibly private, intimate, and individualized experience of giving birth. We paint a picture of the ways in which contemporary Mexican women's births both reflect and reinforce these factors in their lives. Specifically, we look at how senior practitioners teach their students and lower-ranked colleagues how to manage childbirth in different contexts (in and out of hospitals). The practitioners involved in the births presented here share a cultural narrative that views development and modernity as markers of success, yet they justify their methods of achieving these markers in very different ways, and with very different outcomes for their patients.

We show that these differences are due to entrenched systems of inequality that shape how practitioners approach their patients. Indeed, as Davis-Floyd and Cheyney have demonstrated in Chapter 1, differences in how birth is managed in diverse places around the world increasingly have less to do with "specific customs of particular cultures, but instead, are more closely tied to the vast disparities between resource-rich and resource-poor countries." That is, *birth is more a reflection of contemporary global inequalities than traditional practices.*

By comparing three births—one in a hospital, one in a midwife's home, and one that began in a birth center and ended up in a hospital—we also aim to show how social inequalities in Mexico enable professional approaches that are reinforced through educational or teaching moments and to situate these births within broader national and international concerns. Specifically, we look at the interactions between practitioners, students, and the women they are attending, and ask: how do the hierarchies of knowledge and power at work in the moments of birth shape possible outcomes for women? At stake are not only positive birth experiences for women but also how birth is managed in Mexico today. There are pressing national concerns about maternal mortality and national development, as well as growing international concerns about obstetric violence in birth and the need to humanize women's health care.[1]

Our argument is twofold. First, we argue that authoritative knowledge regarding how birth should be managed is contested, reinforced, and reproduced through *teaching moments*, when narratives about what must be done and why are transmitted. As Brigitte Jordan explains, authoritative knowledge is constituted through "an ongoing social process that both builds and reflects power relationships within a community of practice" (Jordan 1997:56). Thus, by looking at the teacher–student relationship across places of birth (hospital, birth center, and home) we can trace what learning processes look like in practice. Second, we argue that the authoritative knowledge reinforced in these cases has important consequences not just for women's health outcomes but also for how gender equity and issues of choice are understood more generally.

Background and Context

Delivery of Care

How birth has been managed, and by whom, has shifted over time in Mexico. Midwives were women's primary caregivers in pre-Hispanic times (Castañeda Nunez 1988) and maintained authority in the field during Spanish colonialism (Leon 1910:227). By the end of the 19th century, the medical practitioners of obstetrics and gynecology had begun to push midwives out of the field of birth in favor of a biomedical approach (Carrillo 1998), a shift that

---

[1] Here we define "obstetric violence" as the overuse of unnecessary practices in birth—such as episiotomies, forceps, forcing women to lie down when they wish to be up and moving; the continuous electronic fetal monitoring that keeps them tethered to the machines and their beds; the denial of food or drink when they are hungry or thirsty; preventing them from bringing a companion to support them; manually stretching the cervix during contractions; performing cesareans; and others—as well as the presence of physical, psychological, or emotional violence (slapping, taunts, humiliations, etc.) targeted at women during their labor experiences.

was part of the broader global push to favor biomedical, Western institutions and approaches to medicine, including birth. Hand in hand with the spread of biomedicine came gendered divisions of labor; while obstetrical training had initially been incorporated into the training of both male medical students and female midwifery students, it came to be considered to be more of a male and medical enterprise and thus no longer within the purview of female midwives (Penyak 2003). Obstetrics and midwifery were eventually divided by gender: men were the obstetricians and women were the midwives. This gendered division continues to this day in the midwifery arena, though Mexican obstet- rics today is more evenly divided between men and women (Penyak 2003).

The vast majority of women in present-day Mexico give birth in public hospitals, attended by physicians. Up until the 1960s, traditional midwives attended the majority of Mexican births; since then they have gone through a rapid nationwide decline. By 2014, 94.6% of births were attended by physi- cians, and only 2.7% by midwives and 2.7% by nurses or other attendants (INEGI 2015). Because until recently midwives were not considered health personnel, there is still a strong division between hospital-attended birth and physicians on one hand, and homebirth and midwives on the other. However, in the nation's rural areas, empirically trained traditional midwives (they call themselves *parteras empiricas* or *parteras tradicionales*; in the international devel- opment community, they are called "traditional birth attendants" [TBAs]) con- tinue to be the primary attendants for births. In 2015, the three states with the highest numbers of midwife-attended births were Chiapas (26.9%), Guerrero (9.3%), and Oaxaca (7.1%), which are also the poorest states and the ones with the highest number of Indigenous and rural populations (CONEVAL 2015).

How do women give birth in Mexican hospitals? Almost half (46%) of all births in Mexico are cesareans (23.2% emergency cesareans; 23.1% sched- uled) and 54% are vaginal births. Data from our research indicate that for vaginal births, there is little or no epidural use in public hospitals, as the sup- ply of epidural anesthesia is reserved for cesareans. We do not have data for private hospitals, as most of them do not share these data publicly. Cesareans in both types of hospitals are primarily carried out under epidural anesthesia. Cesareans are much more common in locations with populations larger than 15,000—where one is more likely to encounter a hospital (INEGI 2015). The cesarean section rate continues to increase, despite Mexico's official rules stating that vaginal births should be prioritized over cesareans (Secretaría de Gobernación 2012). This uneven increase in cesareans in urban regions is of particular concern because it has not corresponded to a simultaneous improvement in birth outcomes; in recent years the proportion of maternal deaths in urban areas has increased, while it decreased in rural areas where cesareans are less common (Cragin et al. 2007). Furthermore, the increases in maternal deaths in urban Mexico are not evenly distributed across the popu- lation. They are far more common among marginalized populations, with the risk for these communities as high as four times greater than the national average (Freyermuth Enciso and Luna Contreras 2014).

Mexican Health Care Systems

Historically, the Mexican health care system has been fragmented in its coverage of the population (Knaul et al. 2005). In response to a hierarchical health care structure, the country reformed its General Health Law in 2003 to create a system to guarantee that marginalized populations receive financial support for health care. This system was named *Seguro Popular* (People's Health Insurance). Its objective has been to diminish the number of families impoverished by health-related expenses (Sosa-Rubí et al. 2011). *Seguro Popular* has been a major contributor to the rise in hospital-attended births. Similarly, *Prospera*—another national program that gives conditional cash transfers to impoverished women in exchange for their and their children's participation in health, nutritional, and educational advancement opportunities (Smith-Oka 2013a)—further incentivizes women to attend public hospitals for their births.

Parallel to the governmental push for women to give birth in hospitals, the past 30 years have also seen a proliferation of formalized professional midwifery education programs across Mexico[2] and the resistance of traditional midwives to the displacement of their practice (El Kotni 2018). Both traditional and professional midwives are central actors in contemporary national debates over the need to reform obstetric care and humanize childbirth treatment. While midwives are often framed as appropriate providers to attend low-risk pregnancies among women in rural, underresourced areas, the midwives themselves are increasingly calling for a reevaluation of their role: midwifery can offer a corrective to the poor outcomes and bad experiences women suffer within the state health care system (Dixon, El Kotni, and Miranda forthcoming).

Modeling Care

Midwifery in Mexico has been highlighted not only as a potential corrective to the overuse of technologies in birth but also as a development tool to bring care to regions without medical providers (United Nations 2008). The CASA (*Centro para los Adolescentes de San Miguel de Allende*—Center for the Adolescents of San Miguel de Allende) Professional Midwifery School in San Miguel de Allende, in the state of Guanajuato, has been cited as an example of a "birth model that works" (Mills and Davis-Floyd 2009:305–336) because of its ability to blend allopathic and traditional methods into a state-sanctioned, professionally licensed model of midwifery education and practice. Indeed, in Mexico, professional midwives have been found to be more competent in their use of evidence-based practices than have general physicians (Walker et al. 2013).

---

[2] Such as, for example, *Nueve Lunas in Oaxaca, Luna Maya in Chiapas, Mujeres Aliadas* in Michoacán, CASA in Guanajuato, etc.

One of the CASA classrooms in San Miguel de Allende, which has classrooms for 1st-, 2nd-, and 3rd-year students. Photo by Robbie Davis-Floyd

CASA students study and gain clinical experience for three years. That experience includes repeated visits to live with and learn from traditional midwives in remote regions in an ongoing effort to record and preserve their knowledge. Graduates are able to go on to work in public hospitals and clinics across Mexico. Government officials of the state of Guerrero and other Mexican states have shown interest in replicating this model of training *parteras profesionales*—professional midwives.[3] While this relatively new breed of professional midwives is indeed finding work in many Mexican states, the number of midwives in this group is still small (see Davis-Floyd 2001). Despite the nationwide push to move birth to the hospital setting—which has been largely effective—professionalized midwifery is also gaining state support.

In a previous publication (Dixon 2015), Lydia has argued that this support for *parteras profesionales* must be understood as a symptom of the larger national push to reduce maternal mortality through investment in practitioners who can attend to women in marginalized regions without physicians or hospitals; Jordan's work emphasized the role midwives played in attending this population (1993). Both the increase in hospital births and the support of professionalized midwifery reflect the national desire to improve maternity care outcomes (widely seen as critical development indicators for Mexico), albeit in distinct ways (Dixon, El Kotni, and Miranda forthcoming). By looking at how birth actually plays out across three settings, then, we can see how broader development ideologies and goals impact practitioner actions, structure the way practitioners teach their students, and ultimately influence women's experiences and outcomes in very different ways.

---

[3] While the graduates of the CASA and Guerrero programs are officially called "*parteras técnicas*," they refer to themselves as "*parteras profesionales*," or professional midwives. However, the term "professional midwife" is contested between groups of midwives, who have differing opinions on the differences between titles such as traditional midwife, empirical midwife, professional midwife, etc. In this chapter, we refer to the midwives by the titles they use for themselves.

A former CASA student, Carolina Alcocer, with one of the traditional midwives with whom she studied, Doña Leonor ("Doña" is an honorific, like Madam or Ma'am, frequently used to honor elders), in front of the midwife's home in a rural area of the state of Guanajuato. Photo by Robbie Davis-Floyd

A birthing room in the CASA Hospital, painted by professional midwives. Photo by Robbie Davis-Floyd

Methods and Sites

We draw here on our combined long-term engagements with women's health in Mexico to analyze the connections between authoritative knowledge, birth practices, and inequality. Our ethnographic data are derived from our individual fieldwork experiences among traditional midwives, professional midwives, physicians, nurses, medical interns, and patients.

Vania Smith-Oka's primary focus is birth as it unfolds in the hospital. She conducted ethnographic studies in three hospitals and one medical school in the city of Puebla between 2008 and 2016. Her methods consisted of detailed observations of 26 labors and births (vaginal and cesarean), unstructured interviews with 71 women in various stages of pregnancy and postpartum time periods, and semistructured interviews with 54 clinicians, 40 interns, and 86 medical students. She also interviewed 12 midwives who were being professionalized via a program in a hospital—she attended workshops, entered the hospital wards alongside the midwives, witnessed their interactions with patients and clinicians, and listened to their concerns about patient care. From 2008 to 2011, her research focused on physician–patient interactions, birth expectations and outcomes, medical perceptions of risk, and obstetric violence. Her subsequent research (2013–2016) aimed to understand how medical students learn the skills and attitudes of medicine from their mentors and peers. She carried out systematic observations of interactions between medical interns and their colleagues, interviewed participants about medical culture, knowledge transmission, and obstetric practices, and also engaged in a social network analysis of interns' key mentors in order to understand how they learn medical culture. She audio recorded most of these interviews.

Lydia Zacher Dixon conducted 17 months of fieldwork, between 2009 and 2012, studying professional midwifery schools in the Mexican states of Guanajuato, Guerrero, and Michoacán. Her larger research project investigated tensions among midwifery schools and between midwives and the government about what forms professionalized midwifery education and practice should take. She conducted observations in midwifery classes, clinical rotations, patient home visits, national conferences, and administrative meetings regarding midwifery education. She observed 10 labors in various phases, and one complete labor and delivery (described below). She had already observed many other labors and deliveries at CASA and elsewhere as an intern and doula (labor support provider) before beginning this research project. In addition, she interviewed 20 students, 11 practicing midwives, 15 school administrators, and four physicians, and she surveyed 38 midwifery students about their experiences and goals. In this chapter, Lydia focuses on the methods of training at the CASA School of Professional Midwifery in San Miguel de Allende, Guanajuato. An interesting facet of the CASA midwives is that despite the many things they share with physicians—a training underpinned by biomedical knowledge, a reliance on Western medicines and technologies, and an ability to officially work within public health spaces—

their approach to care is heavily informed by feminist activism. The midwives at CASA are explicitly trained to view themselves as activists, advocating for women's rights to safe, humanized care in birth and beyond.

Mounia El Kotni has been involved with studying women in the state of Chiapas since 2009. The data she draws on here were collected during 13 months of fieldwork between 2013 and 2015, analyzing the changes brought by national and international health policies in the lives and work of traditional midwives. Mounia conducted multisited ethnography (Marcus 1995) throughout Chiapas, interviewing 40 traditional and professional midwives and 27 medical personnel about the changes occurring in their work. She also spoke with more than 20 mothers about their birth experiences. During her work in Chiapas, Mounia conducted detailed observations during 10 government and NGO trainings for traditional midwives, and participant-observation with five midwives: she stayed with some, participating in their daily activities, and for the one who lived in San Cristóbal de las Casas, she served as an assistant and doula during labor and birth. She also observed six women in labor with a traditional midwife and one labor in a public clinic with medical personnel. Together, these experiences highlight the uneasy relationships between different kinds of practitioners at a time when all birth attendants—traditional or otherwise—are urged to comply with development goals and to work to prevent maternal mortality.

All births are unique, yet many share structural similarities, for example in terms of physiological processes and the presence of an attendant or attendants who claim some level of knowledge and/or authority. We chose these particular births because they paint a nuanced picture of the ways in which authoritative knowledge can structure birth—embodied rigidly by some and more fluidly and collaboratively by others. These narratives also show how birth can be a teaching moment for its practitioners and how different forms of knowledge are taught and transmitted to students and trainees.

Performing Authoritative Knowledge: A Hospital Birth

It was Grace Moya's[4] second pregnancy; her first had resulted in a cesarean two years earlier.[5] She was laboring at one of the public hospitals in

---

[4] We use pseudonyms for our participants throughout, except in the case of one student researcher, Irazu, who gave permission for her name to be used. The names used here, while pseudonyms, reflect the level of formality used in practice for these individuals. This often meant that men and doctors were referred to with their professional titles, while women, nurses and midwives were referred to by first names.

[5] Policy in many public hospitals in Mexico is to allow trial of labor following cesarean birth as long as the cesarean was more than two years prior; however, in the public hospitals where Mounia conducted her research, women were told by their doctors and ultrasound technicians, "once a cesarean, always a cesarean." Thus, we find that there is not a clear or universal approach in practice to trial of labor following cesarean births in Mexico.

Puebla and was the only patient in the delivery ward, so she had the clinicians' undivided attention, an unusual situation for this hospital. She lay on
her back on a gurney, occasionally gripping the railings when contractions
rocked her rounded frame. The two female interns in the ward that morning,
Paola and Evelyn, as well as the most junior male resident, Dr. Marco, managed much of the early labor, checking the fetal heart rate with a handheld
Doppler, as well as the number and spacing of contractions. A senior female
resident, Doctora Valentina, stood to one side, supervising her junior staff.
Two young men, Leonel and Iván, interns from a school of alternative medicine, were supporting Grace through this early labor, playing relaxing music
and using aromatherapy and acupressure to relieve her pain. One of them
told Grace, "Breathe, exhale; remember what I told you." The clinicians were
relaxed. Grace was struggling with pain, her breath catching in her throat.

Doctora Valentina asked Grace if she could examine her dilation, "Bend
your legs so I can see if the baby's head has descended. [There'll be] a minor
discomfort." When the doctor was done, Leonel told Grace, "Breathe. This is
a process. Breathe, breathe properly." Grace cried out desperately, "I can't!"
Leonel told her as he placed his hand on her forehead, "Yes, you can.
Breathe. You are doing very well." After about 30 minutes, Doctora Valentina
asked what the contraction spacing rate was. Evelyn said it was four contractions in nine minutes. Grace was 6 cm dilated and 50% effaced (effacement
refers to the thinning out of the cervix that occurs before or during labor
along with dilation—the opening of the cervix). It was 10:30 A.M. Grace's
labor was slow and the interns, nurses, and residents occasionally wandered
off, sat on one of the gurneys and chatted, or checked their phones idly. Leonel asked Grace, who had been sitting up, to lie down and began to press her
shoulder, telling her, "Breathe. That is important. You tell me when the contraction is over. Does what I am doing relax you or bother you?" Grace
sighed and said, "It relaxes."

Around 11:00 Dr. Molina, an attending physician, came into the ward.
He immediately took charge, telling Grace, as he took the bed sheet off her
body, uncovering her completely, "Let's see; we're going to check you." Evelyn and a nurse hastily held the sheet up to create some privacy. Dr. Molina
put at least three fingers into Grace's vagina, causing her to cry out. He asked,
"Are you in pain? Push, push." Then he told the others (approximately eight
other people suddenly surrounding Grace) in a matter-of-fact voice, "Her pelvis is small. I have just broken her membranes." He turned to Grace and said,
"You are 7 cm dilated."[6] As he pulled off his glove, Dr. Molina said, "Now
that the [amniotic] sac is broken, the baby will descend (*encajar*). Let's give it a
chance." He then turned to Doctora Valentina and told her that as an OB/
GYN she had to "properly learn what labor was like, as it is our daily bread."

Meanwhile Dr. Molina and the residents stood by the nurses' station, chatting and laughing. The interns and the alternative medicine students supported

---

[6] It is scientifically unsound to tell a woman to push before she has reached 10 cm dilation and
feels the actual urge to push.

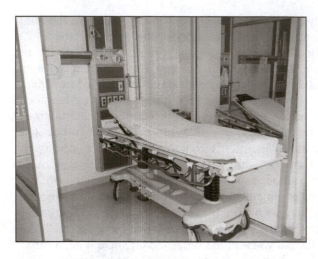

Labor gurney in a Puebla public hospital. Photo by Vania Smith-Oka

Grace during the next 30 minutes of contractions and pain. Grace alternated her position on the gurney between being flat on her back and on her side. She was eager to push, even though she did not feel the urge. Soon, however, she cried out, "I want to poop!" Dr. Molina, the residents, the interns, and a nurse came up to her gurney. Dr. Molina said, "She needs to be examined; she might be *completa* (fully dilated)." Grace was placed on her back, while Dr. Marco put on a glove. He waited for a contraction and examined her, saying to Dr. Molina, "Doc, she is not there yet. She is 8 cm. [The cervix] is still thick." Dr. Molina replied, "Eight. She has advanced. Not long now." They walked away. Grace was crying and clinging to the railing of her gurney. She screamed in pain. Someone told her, "Don't scream; you can hurt your throat." She screamed out once more and then clapped her hand over her mouth.

At 11:30 A.M., Dr. Marco checked Grace's dilation again. She was still 8 cm. Dr. Molina told Dr. Marco, "She should push now," adding, "The cervix continues to be hard." There were 14 clinicians in the ward by this time, most of them waiting around for Grace's birth to be imminent. A while later Dr. Molina put on a glove and told Grace, "Let's see, *hija* (daughter), when you feel pain you will push. I will help you to dilate." As he did this, there were eleven of us standing by the gurney looking on as Grace strained with her legs wide open. At her next contraction, Dr. Molina put his hand into her vagina, saying, "Push! Strongly, strongly, strongly! Hold it. . . ." He repeated this process four times, telling her after each one, "It's over. Breathe. You are 9 cm." He kept his hand in her vagina between each contraction.[7]

---

[7] This process is called manual dilation. Clinically, it is done to facilitate a vaginal birth when there is fetal distress and a birth needs to happen quickly. Alternatively, it may be done to help with a condition called an anterior lip where the cervix dilates unevenly. It is unclear why such a procedure would be performed in this case except for physician convenience. The woman's experience of manual dilation is extreme pain, well above and beyond the normal pain of labor.

Dr. Molina turned to Doctora Valentina and instructed her, "When you feel it, you dilate them manually." He demonstrated to her how to do it. He put his fingers into Grace, palm facing up. His gloves were covered in blood and tissue as he showed the residents how to do this maneuver. Pulling off his glove, he turned to Dr. Marco, ordering, "Touch her." Dr. Marco put on a glove and inserted his hand, telling Grace, "A small discomfort, I'm just going to see." Dr. Molina stood by Dr. Marco, saying, "She is more effaced." He demonstrated on his own hands how to efface the cervix so the baby's head could descend. Grace's contractions were coming very frequently and rocking her body vigorously. Dr. Molina told the residents that this was the only thing they needed to do, "You'll see that once we take out these [membranes] how quickly [the baby] comes out." He boasted how, as a senior resident at another hospital, he would do these dilations to all the patients in the ward, rapidly increasing the number of them in active labor, and making his junior residents work harder at managing them all. On this day, after approximately 20 minutes of these maneuvers, Dr. Molina announced, "She is completely dilated," telling the interns to empty her bladder via a catheter to speed the final process up. It was noon.

Once Grace's bladder was empty, Dr. Molina told her to sit up and put her feet on the side rails, telling her, "I need you to push and to hold the push. This is the last step. Push and hold it, hold on." Grace said, "I am trying, but I can't." He replied, "Do it, don't just try. Push, strongly, strongly, strongly. There comes the head. Push, push!" Evelyn told Grace, "Push, so you cooperate." Grace cried out, "It hurts me!" Dr. Molina snapped, "Of course it does! Who told you that birth isn't painful?"

Dr. Molina boasted to the assembled residents, "How long did we take to dilate her? Not everyone knows how to do this. We saved her three hours of labor." He then gave the order for Grace to be rolled into the delivery room, where she painstakingly shuffled from her gurney to the delivery table. Although she seemed relieved to be moved into delivery, she had had no decision-making power at any point during the labor and delivery. The younger residents and interns placed her legs in stirrups. She was screaming in pain. A female resident cleaned Grace's legs and vaginal area with antiseptic. It was decided that Dr. Marco would attend. He began by cutting an episiotomy, a routine procedure for this hospital and most others across the country. Dr. Molina massaged Grace's abdomen, above the fundus. As the baby's head crowned, every clinician looked on expectantly. Grace's baby girl was born at 12:17 P.M. Grace sighed, "My baby is out." The pediatrician holding the baby placed her gently on Grace's chest. Grace gasped in delight. The baby was then taken by the pediatrics team to clean and measure.

The physicians waited for the placenta to emerge. Dr. Molina smirked and said, "If we'd bet on when the baby would be born, who would have won? They were saying [it would be born] after 2:00 P.M." Turning to Grace, he asked, "How will you *cuidarte* (contracept)?" He added, speaking rapidly, "If you say you will get an operation, we'll pass you over to a BTL (bilateral tubal ligation)[8] right now. . . . If you tell us yes, we'll do it. So, what will it be? Yes or no? Do you want another child? If not, what will you do?" He pointed out that postpartum was the best time for a tubal ligation because the size of the uterus would mean a small incision. He continued, saying, "What do you say? Should I call your husband?" Grace mumbled something and Dr. Molina left the room.

Dr. Marco caught the placenta and told Grace he would start suturing her episiotomy, while a pediatric intern held the baby. Dr. Molina came back a few minutes later and told Grace, "I've spoken with your husband. He's in agreement with the surgery." Grace hesitantly said yes, which Dr. Molina took as a definite and walked out to call for an anesthesiologist and for the surgery room to be readied. A few minutes later Grace quietly told an older nurse that she wanted to talk with her husband. The nurse left to find him in the waiting room. Dr. Marco continued to suture. It was 12:38 P.M. A senior male anesthesiologist walked into the delivery room and demanded that Dr. Marco finish up soon as he had little time before his shift ended.

It soon became evident, however, that Grace was not entirely convinced about getting the surgery. One nurse mumbled to another that they should not let her talk with her husband. Dr. Molina, hearing of Grace's hesitation, told her, "I've already spoken with your husband and he says that if you sign the C-BTL form, he will sign it too. Don't blame the husband. If you don't want to get the surgery, don't sign. But don't put the ball in your husband's court." Grace wailed, "Ay, I don't know!" The older nurse quietly told Dr. Molina of Grace's wish to speak with her husband. Doctora Valentina and Dr. Molina told her to ignore her. The anesthesiologist and an intern went up to Grace to try to convince her. The intern told her, "I'll take the consent forms right now to your husband." Sensing that Grace was relenting, Dr. Molina placed the forms by Grace's face and said, "Full name and signature." Grace signed. Dr. Molina quickly took the papers and said, "*Ya*. It is done." He walked off to tell Grace's husband.

All this took place while Dr. Marco continued to suture Grace's episiotomy. Doctora Valentina peered over his shoulder and criticized his work because his suture ends were too long and would likely bother Grace during recovery. She told him to cut off the ends and to hurry up as the tubal ligation was about to begin. As Dr. Marco rapidly completed the last suture, the nurses and junior residents took Grace's legs out of the stirrups and helped her to shuffle to a waiting gurney to roll her into the adjacent surgery room. The anesthesiologist told Doctora Valentina, who would be performing the tubal ligation, "Do this in 30 minutes. I have to leave by 2:00."

---

[8] Bilateral Tubal Ligation is a permanent form of birth control that involves surgically blocking (through cutting, cauterizing, or removing) the fallopian tubes to prevent fertilization.

Respectful Authority: A Professional Midwife-Attended Birth in a Birthing Room

Professional midwives working at the CASA School and Clinic of midwifery attend births in various locations: at the CASA clinic, in their patients' homes, at government hospitals where they are rotating or working, or in their own homes. Marta, a professional midwife trained at and working for CASA, had built up a strong client base over the years. Women began to come to her house in labor, and after a woman gave birth in her hallway, and another in her daughter's bedroom, Marta decided to build a dedicated space for births on her property. Only a few blocks from the CASA school, and closed off from the rest of her family home, Marta's birthing room provides a comfortable medium for many of her patients who want the feeling of home within close distance to backup medical aid, as well as the care of a midwife with the assurance of professional credentials. The room itself reflected this middle ground in myriad ways through the tools and decorations it contained: an oxygen tank rested in one corner, a set of homeopathic *chochos* (pills) shared a table with sterile packets of syringes and instruments, and a framed image of Jesus looked down upon the single narrow bed made up with colorful blankets.

When Lydia arrived at Marta's home, Anita—a middle-aged woman of short stature with a long rope of black hair—was already in active labor. Olivia, a third-year professional midwifery student, stood behind her and helped her rock her hips in circles as she leaned forward onto the narrow bed. Anita wore a blue hospital gown, a detail that seemed somewhat out of place in this homey atmosphere. Her husband sat quietly in a chair next to the bed; his tightly clasped hands and alert eyes locked on to his wife's face were the only clues to his nerves.

This was Anita's fourth birth. Her two prior children were born with Marta as well; it had been five years since her youngest. She had been seeing a physician for her prenatal care this time (under the free *Seguro Popular* program), but when her physician told her that she would need a cesarean section due to the large size of the baby, she decided to return once more to Marta. Marta agreed that the baby did indeed feel large, but said that she was not concerned about the birth.

While Olivia rubbed Anita's back, Marta reminisced to Lydia about her own days as a student and young professional midwife. She said that she remembered when CASA first opened, and how the local physicians marched in protest against it. Since then, she said, she has been fighting to practice the way she wants to—fighting against the local physicians as well as against state bureaucrats. She thinks women should be able to give birth where they wish, with the practitioners they want.

As Anita's contractions (which Olivia and Marta call *molestias*—annoyances) began to increase in intensity, Olivia suggested that she take a warm shower. There was a small bathroom attached to the birthing room, and everyone waited while she relaxed in the water for a few minutes. When she came out, she said she was worried that the contractions had slowed down. Olivia offered her food, but she was not interested. Marta tried to press her to drink water, but she only took a few sips. This made Marta concerned; she worried that Anita might have a urinary tract infection (UTI), because of her dehydration and pain while urinating. She had sent earlier for lab work to confirm her concern, but it came back negative. Just to be safe, Marta began giving Anita homeopathic pills of blue cohosh and echinacea[9]—remedies that she assured Anita would help to enhance contractions and to reduce the chance of infection.

Olivia listened to the baby's heart tones with a handheld Doppler. As she searched for the heartbeat, she noticed that the baby's back was resting far to one side of Anita's belly, and she asked Marta if she would recommend a *manteada* to better position the baby for labor. The *manteada* is a traditional technique in which a *rebozo*—a shawl—is slung under a woman and rocked in such a way as to gently move her body and encourage the baby to shift position. In this case, they had Anita lie on her back on the bed, while they put the *rebozo* under her middle back. Olivia and Marta each held a side of it and rhythmically pulled it back and forth for a few moments. Then Marta took both sides of the *rebozo* over to one side and did a series of quick jerks to get the baby moving. As soon as she was done, Anita had to get up to use the bathroom, and contractions began to pick up again. While Marta was still concerned that the frequent bathroom trips meant a hidden UTI, she was happy that the *manteada* had helped jump-start labor once more.

The practice of using a *rebozo* to do a *manteada* is common among midwives across Mexico. Here, a traditional midwife teaches a group of students how to do a *manteada* to relieve pain in labor or orient a baby. Photo by Lydia Z. Dixon

[9] The scientific names for these homeopathic remedies are *Caulophyllum thalictroides* and *Echinacea purpure*.

Between her next contractions, Olivia decided to check Anita's cervical dilation to see how far along she was. She got Anita comfortable on her back on the bed, then gently reached in to measure the cervix. "She is at six centimeters, and 70% effaced, with her membranes still intact," Olivia said, confidently. Marta nodded, and then asked her what position the baby was in. Marta was largely letting Olivia run the show but wanted to make sure that Olivia knew what she was doing. In a few months, Olivia was going to take her final exams and graduate, at which point she would be on her own. Marta took her job as an educator seriously. Olivia concentrated as she felt the baby's head. "Slightly posterior, I think," she said. Marta then asked the mother's permission to check her as well, to make sure Olivia's assessment was correct. She confirmed Olivia's findings and told Anita that things were moving along and that she and the baby were both doing great. Then she told Olivia to start an IV drip to keep Anita hydrated, since she had been in labor for two days at this point and hadn't even been able to finish a half a cup of water. Olivia struggled to find a vein in Anita's arm, and Anita—who had been stoic and quiet throughout most of her contractions—cried out in pain at the needle pricks. Throughout, Marta continued to periodically tilt capfuls of the homeopathic doses under Anita's tongue.

After a few minutes, still concerned about the possible UTI, Marta decided to run some antibiotics through the IV as well. This perked Anita up; she said that she remembers her last labor picking up once she received antibiotics. Marta agreed that she had seen this happen sometimes, although she wasn't sure why. Indeed, shortly after the antibiotics made their way through her IV, Anita began to experience noticeably more intense contractions. She was making low noises, and her husband moved toward her, breathing with her and keeping eye contact. The room suddenly felt too crowded for this intimate moment, and Marta suggested that we leave the couple alone to labor for a while.

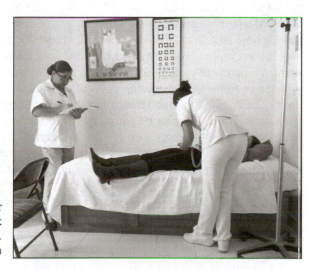

A senior midwife tests her student during a mock prenatal exam at CASA. Photo by Lydia Z. Dixon

Lydia left with Olivia and Marta to drink Nescafe and eat cookies and melon in her office next door. They agreed that sometimes women need time alone with their partners to allow labor to progress naturally. Marta told Olivia that she thought Anita was nearing transition, that she was "perhaps at eight centimeters," because of the frequency and duration of her contractions. Olivia said that Anita was taking it very well if she was indeed in transition—she still had hardly made any noise and continued to breathe calmly in through her nose and out of her mouth. Olivia talked a little about her upcoming year of social service (all professionals in Mexico are required upon graduation to spend a year in "social service," usually working in rural areas), which would send her south to a small town in the state of Chiapas along with four other CASA graduates. She was nervous, but glad to have the company of her classmates. Many students, she said, are sent to far-flung villages where the attending physicians and nurses do not know what to do with a professional midwife in their midst.

Everyone headed back into the birthing room, where we could immediately see that things had picked up in our absence. Anita was lying on her back, with her husband standing over her holding her hands. Marta asked her to turn onto her side, to get the baby into a better position. Then Marta pointed out Anita's toes, which were going back and forth with each contraction; "That's a sign that she is getting close," she whispered.

"Anita, we have to wash *tu parte* (your genitals) because of the infection you may have brought in, so that if your bag of waters breaks you won't have a worse infection," Marta told her. They repositioned her on her back and noticed that her mucous plug had come out. They washed her legs and groin, then Marta had Olivia check dilation and try to break Anita's bag of waters to get things moving faster. Olivia struggled with her instrument, and finally Marta took over. The water broke in an instant, rushing everywhere. Olivia checked the baby's heartbeat and announced that the baby was doing great. "Do what your body asks you to. What does your body want you to do, Anita?" asked Marta encouragingly. Anita didn't answer her, but was breathing more heavily now, laboring hard. Aside from her heavy breathing and low moans, she was still very quiet. The rest of us were the loud ones, offering her encouragement, telling her to breathe, telling her to go with what her body wanted.

Marta rolled up a receiving blanket and tied it tightly around the top of Anita's belly. She explained that it would help the baby descend and "not go back up anymore." Anita began to moan louder, and started repeating "*no puedo, ya no puedo*—I can't, I can't do it anymore." At this, Marta gave Olivia a knowing look. "When they say they can't do it anymore, it means they are almost done," she said. Anita's leg was cramped and causing her pain; she couldn't get comfortable. Lydia massaged her leg to try to ease the muscle cramps as Marta and Olivia prepared to receive the baby. They motioned for Anita's husband to help hold up her leg to get her in a better position for pushing. The mood changed in the room as Anita began to make pushing noises, her feet pressed against our hands for counter-pressure. After only a

few contractions, Anita's baby girl slipped out into the world, caught by
Olivia. The baby was immediately placed on Anita's chest, and she and her
husband smiled and breathed and cried as they examined their daughter.
Olivia checked Anita's placenta when it emerged a few minutes later and
announced that it was intact and there was no vaginal tearing. After the midwives checked the baby and gave the couple a few hours to bond and rest,
they would send the family on its way.

Authority in Birth Transfer:
A Traditional Midwife-Attended Labor
and a Hospital Birth

Doña Gabriela, a Maya-Tsotsil midwife in her late sixties, attended
births in three settings: her home, the expectant mother's home, and the birth
center of an intercultural hospital.[10] Launched by the Mexican government
to provide a space for officially recognized traditional midwives to attend
nonmedicalized births, San Cristóbal de las Casas' birth center was a large
building with two rooms, a bathroom, a *temazcal* (steam bath), a kitchen, and
a garden. The birth center was adjacent to a general hospital, and mostly
used by a group of seven traditional midwives and their patients. When one
of Doña Gabriela's patients, Adelina, went into labor on a Sunday morning,
Mounia met with her and her husband, Doña Gabriela, and Irazu—a master's student conducting research on midwifery—in the hospital's birth center. Doña Gabriela asked Adelina to lie down, felt the baby's position with
her hands, and listened to the heartbeat. "We won't be seeing this baby before
tonight," she told the couple in a reassuring tone.

Adelina and her husband were both in their early thirties, and were
expecting their first child. Although she was herself born in a rural area of
Chiapas, Adelina was raised in San Cristóbal de las Casas, as was her husband. While waiting to build their own house, the young couple lived with
Adelina's in-laws. Throughout her pregnancy, Adelina had been reading
about homebirth and hospital birth on the internet and asking questions of a
friend who was a doula. Her husband, parents, and in-laws supported her
choice of a nonmedicalized birth with a traditional midwife. However,
among her siblings, she would be the only one not undergoing a cesarean section. "My brother says that as soon as I will feel the first contractions, I will
be begging for a cesarean," she told Mounia that morning.

To help with the early contractions, Doña Gabriela instructed the couple
to walk through the birth center, where no other patients or staff were pres-

---

[10] San Cristóbal de las Casas' intercultural hospital is one of three in the country (the other two
are in the states of Nayarit and Puebla). These hospitals constitute an attempt by the Mexican
government to include traditional medical practices so as to make hospitals more welcoming
to Indigenous peoples. For more details, see El Kotni (2016).

ent, while she prepared some medicinal tea for Adelina to drink. Adelina's husband held her by the waist as they cautiously made their way through the corridors and into the garden. "Should we keep walking?" he asked after an hour. "Yes, keep strolling like lovers," Doña Gaby responded jokingly, while everybody laughed. A few hours later, around 1:00 P.M., Adelina's mother, father, sister, and in-laws arrived in a joyful mood. They sat in the kitchen space, making small talk with the couple, who were walking back and forth through the room. Family members heated the chicken soup that they had brought—a typical postpartum meal—and offered it to all present. Adelina's contractions were becoming more frequent, and she would pause in her conversations with her family, holding tight on to a chair and breathing as they passed, while Doña Gabriela would rub her lower back.

After they had eaten lightly, Doña Gabriela sent Adelina and her husband to rest in the labor room—a large room next to the kitchen with a double bed and a birthing chair. Later in the afternoon she joined them, as Adelina's contractions grew in intensity. As evening approached, Adelina, who had felt her first contractions the previous night, grew tired. At each contraction, her mother massaged her back, while her husband held her hand and whispered to her. Talking to her unborn daughter, Adelina would rub her belly between contractions and say, "Come on darling, we are waiting for you. We can't wait to meet you; don't you want to meet us too?" In the other room, the family was becoming nervous, and regularly inquired about Adelina's state.

By 9:00 P.M., as per the hospital rule (even though the birth center was staffed solely by midwives, they had to abide by the nearby hospital's rules), visitors were asked to leave. Only Adelina's husband and mother were allowed to stay. Adelina was now in active labor and trying out different positions through her contractions. One of the positions she tried was kneeling, while her husband was sitting on a chair facing her and supporting her with his arms wrapped around her chest. Doña Gabriela stood behind Adelina and called to Mounia, "Look, you just lift up her skirt when she is having a contraction, to see what is coming out. But you don't undress her fully, not like doctors do." Adelina did not stay long on her knees, and moved to lying down on the double bed. At this point, Adelina had been under the care of Doña Gabriela for almost 12 hours. Doña Gabriela had given her several different sorts of medicinal tea and energetically massaged her belly a few times to help the baby get through the birth canal. As she was administering one such massage, Adelina and her husband provided Doña Gabriela with new information: they had gotten an ultrasound at a private clinic a few days earlier and were told the baby's umbilical cord was wrapped around her neck (called a nuchal cord). After finishing the massage, Doña Gabriela paused for a few minutes. She then looked at Adelina and said, "This baby does not want to come out." She took off her gloves. Adelina repeated that she did not want a cesarean section. Her mother and husband asked Doña Gabriela to seek out a doctor in the adjacent hospital and get a second opinion.

As Doña Gabriela went in search of the physician on call, she instructed all those present to start packing up. The factors accounting for Doña Gabriela's change in attitude are complex. Perhaps Doña Gabriela felt pressured because she had predicted that birth would happen in the early evening, and Adelina was not yet in active labor at night. Even though she was an experienced midwife and had delivered children with a nuchal cord before, Doña Gabriela might have feared that should something happen at the birth, she would be held accountable.

About 15 minutes later, Doña Gabriela came back with a male doctor who asked Adelina's mother, Mounia, and Irazu to wait outside the room, saying, "You, wait for me here. Only the *partera* and the husband are allowed in there." Less than five minutes later, the doctor walked out. Irazu and Mounia asked him about Adelina, and his response took them aback, "She still has a long way to go (*le falta mucho*), at least 8 to 10 hours. She is only two or three centimeters dilated! [If she wants a nonmedicalized birth], you will have to stay here all night and probably tomorrow too!" Adelina's mother asked if they should stay in the birth center then. The doctor answered in a sharp tone, "Take her to the maternity hospital; gynecologists should evaluate her. We don't have gynecologists here." He added that the hospital ambulance was not available, so the family would need to arrange private transportation for Adelina's transfer.

The doctor's authoritative tone left little space for discussion. Doña Gabriela and Adelina complied, frenetically packing up and preparing to leave for the maternity hospital. In a later conversation, Adelina filled in the blanks and described what had happened during the physician's visit,

> He came in and the first question he asked was where we were from. When we replied "San Cristóbal" he scolded us, "So why did you come to give birth here? Why didn't you go straight to the maternity hospital?" And then he did a cervical exam. Honestly, out of the whole birth process, the doctor's attitude was what hurt me most.

Despite the fact that the labor was taking place in a public birth center under the supervision of Doña Gabriela, all those involved (Adelina, her mother, her husband, and Doña Gabriela herself) immediately abided by the instructions of the general doctor (not an obstetrician). The moment Doña Gabriela sought a second opinion from the medical professional, her expert knowledge became subordinate to biomedical authoritative knowledge. While Doña Gabriela performed cervical checks on her patients, she never announced the centimeters of dilation after doing so. She used cervical exams and external checks to assess "how far the baby's head was," as she explained to her patients. When the doctor announced that Adelina's cervix was not dilated enough, she did not publicly contradict or question the doctor's assessment.

However, after Adelina arrived at the maternity hospital and went through another cervical exam, Doña Gabriela was called by the hospital's medical staff and conveyed the news to all the family members gathered in the waiting room that Adelina was in fact seven centimeters dilated. Adelina entered the public maternity hospital but did not like how she was treated there because instead of being rapidly attended to, she was told to wait in the emergency room. So her family decided to transfer her to a private clinic, where Adelina's daughter was born later that night via cesarean section. During a postpartum visit, Adelina was breastfeeding her daughter, a large bandage wrapped around her abdomen, when she said, "Of course, it was not the birth that I had envisioned. But I know Doña Gabriela did her best and took the best decision (to transfer). What really impacted us was that doctor's attitude." Her husband nodded his head in agreement.

In contrast to their experience, the drawing below shows the position that women typically use when giving birth at home in Highland Chiapas, much like the ones Jordan described for Mexico's Yucatan (1993). As women are increasingly encouraged to birth in hospitals, it is replaced with the lithotomy/supine position, as described earlier in Grace's experience.

Authoritative Knowledge Production and Reproduction

The authoritative knowledge that presides in each of the above birth stories is produced through deep, structural inequalities that shape the provider's approach to women and birth. How the individual practitioners come to

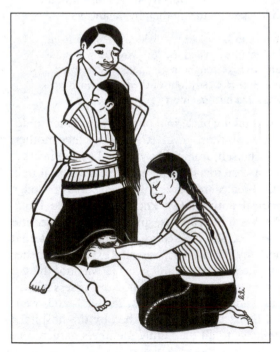

Drawing of a traditional home-birth in Highland Chiapas. Drawn by Alice Bafoin; used with permission

learn their professions, the location/s they can practice in, what they can do, and how they are treated within the health care system all impact the ways that they treat women and understand birth. Physicians and midwives come from very different realities that, in turn, shape what they see as appropriate knowledge and practice.

Physicians in Mexico, as in most parts of the world, are trained to be the experts in medical situations. During interviews with medical students, Vania discovered that 100% of the participants defined a "good" patient as some-one who was cooperative and compliant with their rules. At no point did they perceive their interactions with patients as a collaborative endeavor. They are trained to *become* the authority, and thus during a birth they *are*. Like other Latin American nations, Mexico is marked by a distinct class-based and racial hierarchy, which is often reflected and enacted in medical contexts with impoverished or vulnerable populations (Finkler 2004; Zacher Dixon 2015; Smith-Oka 2013b). Gendered hierarchies also exist but are expressed in ways different from race and class. In medical interactions, there is an assumption of "male" as the normative authority. Despite most physicians in Mexico working in the public sector, medical schools rarely train students to understand structural issues such as poverty as factors in their patients' health or how to provide high-quality care to these patients (Nigenda 2013).

In the hospital birth described above, Grace's labor began gently. Soft music played while clinicians hovered around her, respectfully asking if they could examine her dilation or encouraging her to breathe. Her concerns seemed to be respected: clinicians sat her up when she requested it, rubbed her calves when they hurt, and validated her experience of pain. On the surface this seemed like a gentle labor wherein Grace was the subject of the experience. But as her labor progressed, it became increasingly apparent that she was the *object* of the narrative: the one to whom things were done. Her voice, emerging as screams of pain, was literally shushed by clinicians, alleg-edly to protect her throat from damage.

Several of the clinicians Vania interviewed described birth as a transfor-mative moment that they found deeply moving. For instance, Doctora Valen-tina stated that, "I am more moved when I see [a baby] born on its own than me having to [help] it be born." But little of this awe was evident in their interactions with Grace. To them, her birth was routine, quotidian—some-thing to be measured in centimeters and minutes. Grace's birth is illustrative of many of the normative structures of births in public hospitals across Mex-ico. Grace was talked at and over; she was not consulted about her wishes, concerns, or fears. These authoritative interactions became all the more evi-dent at Dr. Molina's arrival. His entrance markedly sped up Grace's labor and greatly increased the number of interventions she received. Indeed, we see an inverse relationship between the number of procedures and interven-tions she received and her ability to choose or even to be heard. Dr. Molina's boasts showed a lack of concern for Grace's needs; instead the labor became an arrogant competition against time upon which bets could be made. This emphasis on time was particularly puzzling as there was no need for the labor to be faster—after all, the ward was empty. And his forcible manual dilation of her cervix was excruciatingly painful to Grace—far more painful than the normal pain of undisturbed contractions.

Grace's vaginal birth was unusual for this hospital, as increasingly more children are born via cesarean. Despite national and international concerns with the rising "cesarean epidemic," the cesarean rate in Mexico has nearly doubled over the past two decades; cesareans are normalized in many hospitals, private and public, across the country. While perceptions of risk and fear of birth are frequently cited as reasons for cesareans, insurance companies, which provide greater monetary incentives for cesareans, have become recognized culprits, especially in private hospitals (García Vázquez et al. 2012). There is a disjunction between national rhetoric and local practice. Authoritative knowledge present in hospital-based reproductive care can work to constrain patient choice, to reproduce inequality, and to normalize obstetric violence. The inequality between patients and clinicians becomes embedded in institutionalized knowledge and practice in hospital births such as Grace's.

In Adelina's story, the physician, whom neither Adelina nor Doña Gabriela had ever seen before that night, stepped in to make an important decision: to transfer Adelina to a higher level of care. While initially brought in for a consult by a fellow practitioner, the physician swiftly criticized Doña Gabriela's work and Adelina's choice to attempt a nonmedicalized birth. Despite having little training in obstetrics himself (which showed in his incorrect assessment of Adelina's cervical dilation), his status as physician allowed him to perform the cervical exam and to voice critiques, ultimately shaping Adelina's birth outcome. This status was tied to entrenched social hierarchies related to class, Indigeneity, gender, and education. Evidence-based protocols would have indicated that Adelina should not have even been admitted to the birth center until she was in active labor, defined as starting at 6 cm. As in so many cases around the world, this simple step might have prevented Adelina's eventual cesarean section.

In contrast, Marta—the professional midwife—identified strongly with her patient. Both are women, and they had formed a strong relationship over the years through multiple births together. Marta has also spent her professional life fighting against hospitals' and physicians' control over birth, and for a woman's right to humanized birth care. Thus, she sees birth as a process that is both deeply personal and intimate, and deeply political. This orientation shapes the authoritative knowledge that matters to her during labor. Thus, she viewed Anita's body language, needs, emotions, and desires as central indicators as to the progression of labor. She shared information with her patient and sought consent. She commiserated and touched gently. In all of these ways, she showed that the authoritative knowledge in the room was collaborative, inclusive, and respectful; she was knowing *with* her patient. This democratization of knowledge is also evident in the births described by Jordan in *Birth in Four Cultures*, with the difference that among the Maya of the

Yucatan, whom Jordan describes, all the women present who have given birth are considered to have authoritative knowledge; only the first-time expectant mother is regarded as not knowing anything. For that reason, Doña Juana, the *partera tradicional* with whom Jordan worked, would act out the birth for her in advance, and the other women with prior knowledge of birth would pass on that knowledge to the new mom via their actions during her birth.

While in the past in Mexico, the approaches to birth represented in the three stories narrated above—the spaces, technology, and their practitioners—existed on opposite sides of a spectrum of how birth could be performed, over time, they have become increasingly similar in many respects—at least among professional midwives and physicians. Professional midwives can and do work in public hospitals and clinics nationwide, often alongside physicians. Both kinds of practitioners can prescribe medications, and while professional midwives state that they reach first for alternative therapies, they are comfortable using allopathic medications for a full range of concerns during pregnancy and labor. Thus, while physicians and professional midwives come from different ideological approaches to birth, and go through different processes to learn their professions, they are increasingly convergent in some important and tangible ways. These growing similarities make the differences that emerge during labor more visible. How do we make sense of practitioners with access to the same spaces, technologies, and medications treating women so differently? Based on our collective fieldwork experiences and data collection over the years, we argue that *these differences largely come from, and are reinforced by, the passing on of different versions of authoritative knowledge through practitioner training.* Where do these authoritative knowledge hierarchies come from and why does their provenance matter?

As we see it, authoritative knowledge is actively reproduced through interactions among practitioners and between practitioners and students throughout the experiential training and learning that occurs during labor and birth. In the first hospital birth, authoritative knowledge followed the hierarchy of the clinicians—interns at the bottom, then the nurses and residents, and at the peak, the senior physicians. Authoritative knowledge is transmitted from clinicians of higher rank to those of lower rank. Rank is strictly respected in these interactions, which are top-down for most interactions and bidirectional between people of close rank. Questions flow upward from interns to first-year residents, from first-year residents to second-year residents, and so on, and answers/knowledge flow downward. Despite being central to the birth itself, patients are figuratively peripheral, or almost entirely absent, from these interactions, while the physician is figuratively central.

In these interactions, the interns and junior residents underscored what they already believed—that physicians were in charge and patients needed to cooperate. Dr. Molina exemplified this belief in his interactions with Grace and his residents. Knowledge, techniques, and attitudes were transmitted in a purposeful way through overt teaching—as with the technique for manual dilation taught on Grace's body without her consent. In these medical contexts, putting someone more junior on the spot can be a key way to force the person to learn and also a way to highlight his or her inferiority: if the junior person knows what to do, then it is evident he or she has learned, but if the person does not know, then her or she is taught how to do it, all the while reinforcing the learner's location within an implicit and explicit hierarchy. This reinforcement happened when Dr. Molina asked Dr. Marco to examine Grace's dilation. Dr. Marco knew the basics, but he did not know how to dilate or efface the cervix. At that point, Dr. Molina stepped in and taught the assembled residents and interns how to perform this technique and the rationale for doing so. Grace was thus a vehicle for purposefully transmitting knowledge and techniques to the residents—such as how to efface and dilate the cervix. Not considered at all was the lack of clinical indication for the procedure or the extreme pain that the manual cervical dilation caused Grace.

A large portion of knowledge can be transmitted in unintended ways, in what has been termed the "hidden curriculum" (Hafferty 1998; Michalec and Hafferty 2013), defined as the gap between what people are *taught* (through direct means) and what they *learn* (through indirect means). In some cases what is transmitted is the opposite of what is intended. So, while clinicians might *speak about* patient-centeredness as important goals, their *actions* might emphasize measurable outcomes, cost-effectiveness (Hafferty 1998; DelVecchio Good 1995), authority (Michalec and Hafferty 2013), or even attitudes of contempt for patients (Smith-Oka 2013b). These attitudes can be seen in Grace's birth when Dr. Molina disdained her dignity by exposing her naked body, and in his disregard for her right to informed consent in the cases of the manual cervical dilation and the tubal ligation. She was effectively coerced into both these procedures, the ligation at a time often called "The Golden Hour" when women and their partners should be left to bask in the afterglow of birth and bond with their babies. All of these constitute common examples of obstetric violence, as did the attitude and actions of the physician at Adelina's birth, who performed what he thought was expected of him: a cervical exam, although he obviously was not well trained at it. His attitude starkly contrasted with Doña Gabriela's gentle guidance. The physician's attitude clearly indicated that he did not consider her as a medical professional; at no point did he inquire as to her opinion on Adelina's status.

In the professional midwife-assisted birth, Marta guided Olivia with patience and respect. Olivia took initiative with the patient, but checked in with Marta along the way; at other points, Marta asked Olivia questions to test her knowledge or suggested that she try certain things with the patient. Marta told Olivia stories while they worked, and while they waited—stories that highlighted the history of midwifery as a struggling profession, the differences between midwives and physicians, and the importance of advocating for patients. The information that Marta passed on to Olivia in these interactions went far beyond the verbal data—her very form of respectful guidance reinforced the kinds of knowledge that have authority in this setting. Olivia

learned through these interactions, as part of the midwifery "hidden curriculum," that knowledge in birth can and should be collaborative, respectful,
and creative.

Marta was not modeling for Olivia a form of authoritative knowledge
that has, in the past, been associated with (stereotypical) notions of traditional
midwife-attended births. On the contrary, while Marta did use a variety of
alternative medications on her patient, including the traditional Mexican
rebozo technique, she was also quick to use antibiotics and had her oxygen
tank at the ready. This interaction reveals that authoritative knowledge in midwifery is increasingly about mixing the methods at hand, using what works
from the tools available. While notions of tradition and ancestral knowledge
inform midwives' practices, they do not confine them, but rather expand them
into what Davis-Floyd (2018f:221–264) terms *informed relativism*, which she
defines as the primary characteristic of "the postmodern midwife."

Today, midwifery in Mexico is changing rapidly and is working to present itself as a profession that reflects international best practices regarding
women's health—both in terms of improving development outcomes and
improving the quality of women's health care. The Mexican Association of
Midwifery (*Asociación Mexicana de Partería*), founded in 2012, states that midwifery is "based on knowledge proven by scientific evidence or ancestral wisdom" (*Asociación Mexicana de Partería* 2014, translation by Dixon). A key part
of the way authoritative knowledge is reinforced and passed on by teaching,
then, is through how both professional and traditional midwives model to
students when to rely on scientific evidence and when to rely on other forms
of knowledge (empirical, ancestral, intuitive). Arguably, physicians rely on
the same mechanisms for their own teaching, only their "ancestral wisdom"
is embedded not in the ancestral Indigenous wisdom of thousands of years
but in the much more recently established (three centuries or so) "traditional"
practices of the medical profession. In both cases, students must learn when
to follow scientific guidelines and when to tap into practices that have gained
authority through consensus—because "that is how things are done."

Implications for Women's Health Outcomes

Marta, like many Mexican midwives (both professional and traditional),
is savvy about the national push to reduce maternal mortality through
improving birth outcomes. She sees the way to better outcomes through
improved care of women, through what is referred to as *parto humanizado*—
humanized birth. The humanized birth movement, which gained momentum
in Latin America during the First International Humanization of Birth Conference in Brazil in 2000 (Page 2001; Davis-Floyd 2018d; Davis-Floyd and
Georges 2018; Williamson and Matsuoka, this volume, Chapter 4), seeks to
improve the quality of care women receive in birth and is based on the idea
that women's needs and choices should be respected and that birth itself is a

normal, healthy event. This respect also entails a reduction in unnecessary interventions like cesareans or episiotomies, which the midwives are trained to see as procedures of last resort, not of routine. In Grace's case, for example, a humanistic approach would have seen the tubal ligation issue discussed and decided well in advance of the birth, not in the moments that should have been "golden." It is through this respectful approach that women will ultimately have better experiences and better health outcomes, because they have been allowed to labor naturally and have not received more interventions than necessary.

As mentioned above, in recent years birth activists and professionals have begun to talk about infringements on humanized birth as instances of *violencia obstétrica*—obstetric violence. Throughout Latin America, a movement has been growing to regulate and legislate against obstetric violence as both an affront to women's dignity and as a barrier to improving health outcomes such as maternal mortality and morbidity. However, what counts as obstetric violence and how it should be regulated are questions that continue to be debated (Dixon 2015). For many midwives, obstetric violence entails a range of activities, from outright abuse of patients during labor to lack of informed consent for various procedures, to not allowing partners to be present in the delivery rooms. Each of these kinds of violence has become associated with negative outcomes, bolstering arguments for the need to legislate against them. Indeed, in recent years "obstetric violence" has been added to state and national policies legislating violence against women more generally throughout Latin America (Calzada Martinez 2009; D'Gregorio 2010).

Defining and regulating against obstetric violence continues to be tricky because it is not always clear when an intervention or action should be categorized as "violent" or as "lifesaving." Most physicians, in contrast to midwives like Marta, see their interventions in obstetric care as crucial to reducing maternal mortality—in spite of the large body of evidence showing that the use of unnecessary interventions is a major factor in *causing* maternal morbidity and mortality. The "FIGO Guidelines for Mother-Baby Friendly Birthing Facilities" offer a very clear description of the international situation:

> Evidence collected in a variety of settings has documented that the quality of care is related to the quality of maternal and newborn health outcomes, including mortality. . . . Miller et al. (2003) noted that paradoxically high rates of maternal mortality persisted in the Dominican Republic, despite 98% facility delivery by skilled attendants. The results of the study demonstrated that *the lack of quality care and accountability was at the root of unnecessary maternal deaths*. A recent review series on quality of maternal and newborn care found that *improving access to facilities did not guarantee improved maternal outcomes*, and posited that poor quality of care was the most likely explanatory factor. (Bhutta et al. 2014:1; italics ours)

As we mentioned above, a cesarean—which is major abdominal surgery—and its risk factors are rationalized as less dangerous to mother and baby than a vaginal birth. While there is pressure to have a state-sanctioned hospital birth, women like Adelina quite aptly perceive cesarean sections as a direct *consequence* of hospital birth, the ultimate result of the well-known "cascade of interventions" (see Davis-Floyd 2003[1992], 2018b, and Cheney and Davis-Floyd, this volume, Chapter 1). In contrast, choosing a community (home or birth center) birth with a midwife is a political choice, often ill-received by biomedical professionals. A major underlying difference in the care models is how birth is perceived: midwives view it as inherently safe and natural in the vast majority of cases, and physicians view it as inherently dangerous. This conceptual difference structures providers' choices and gives weight to their justifications. Further, the structures are passed on through a myriad of encounters between practitioner and student throughout any given birth in which students are present.

A few of the interns Vania interviewed had heard of the concept of obstetric violence and could discuss it. Yet most knew nothing about it. This finding parallels studies that have analyzed practitioners' reactions to obstetric violence legislation elsewhere; they have found that people often do not know what the term means or what steps to take if they witness it (Calzada Martinez 2009; Faneite and Toro Merlo 2012). Hence, the existence of legislation about obstetric violence—and the activist movements that have advocated for such legislation—may be making the term more familiar, but knowledge about what do to about it, much less how to press legal cases concerning it, has not been disseminated. Currently, the authority of the law does not appear to supersede the authoritative knowledge of the highest-ranking physician within the hospital birthing room.

To understand how authoritative knowledge works to facilitate obstetric violence, we must understand where authoritative knowledge comes from. In the hospital setting, authoritative knowledge emerges from assumptions about the primacy of technology as a sign of modernity. "Modernity" is often embodied by Western technomedicine and gets entangled with entrenched social ideas about gender, class, ethnicity, and nationalism. To be a "good physician" is to embrace technological intervention, to be modern. The problem is that when technologies are used inappropriately during birth—as in cases of unnecessary cesarean births or routine episiotomies—and when these inappropriate interventions lead to poor health outcomes or are experienced as obstetric violence, the technologies themselves and the practitioners wielding them can remain blameless. The technologies and their users represent modernity and progress and are presented as lifesavers and thus are not faulted for poor outcomes—even when they are the cause of those poor outcomes. Rather, blame is shifted back to the women for not acting in a responsible manner, for not taking care of themselves, or for not making correct choices. This process becomes a vicious cycle in which marginalized women experience obstetric violence or have poor health outcomes in hospital settings. As their outcomes are linked to their marginalized status, the image of impoverished women as uneducated, unhealthy, and at risk is reinforced. Thus, these women's choices are further constrained—they themselves are risky and so must be acted upon, while those actions often further increase their risk. Sadly, this *obstetric paradox* characterizes birth around the world, especially for marginalized women.

Despite physicians' reliance on modern technologies and the marked increase in hospital-attended births in Mexico in recent decades, maternal mortality and morbidity remain stubbornly high (*Objetivos de Desarrollo del Milenio* 2015). Women are not just suffering the everyday violations of obstetric violence, they are also suffering serious and sometimes mortal danger during birth from iatrogenic (medically induced) intervention—too many cervical checks can lead to infection; an unnecessary cesarean can lead to an unnecessary death. Birth technologies are, as Jordan (1997:68) states, often used as a resource and justification "for negating and redefining the woman's experience." Thus, these technologies contribute to the reinforcement of the power difference between women and physicians, and to these alarming statistics.

Authoritative knowledge in birth, when wielded by those in power, is often used to justify women's suffering. As Mexico continues to struggle to reduce maternal mortality nationwide as part of its push for national development, it has to grapple with the contradiction illustrated in the FIGO quotation above: increased technology use has not led to the development goal of significantly lower maternal mortality. Indeed, it is because of this seeming contradiction that professional midwives like those at CASA have gained traction. For the state, they offer the possibility to reduce maternal death at a much lower cost than physicians. For women, they provide humane treatment and birth experiences during which the authoritative knowledge does not lead to power abuse.

The Future of Mexico's Approach to Birth

What are the consequences of the differences in models of authoritative knowledge seen in the births we have described here? Will they continue to perpetuate deep differences in how birth is approached and managed, as practitioners pass on their knowledge through micro-practices and "hidden curriculum" interactions with students? Despite the often opposing ways in which technologies, teaching, and patient treatment are addressed in hospitals and with midwives, we argue that there are also emergent similarities between these approaches that may lead to better communication between practitioners and better health outcomes for women.

Many Mexican midwives are joining national conversations alongside physicians about how to improve women's health; their growing legitimacy can be seen both in the spread of professional midwifery as an accepted realm of practice and in the increased political voice of the new Mexican Association of Midwifery. CASA's professional midwifery school graduates have secured jobs in state health clinics nationwide, and the new professional midwifery school based on the CASA model opened by the state of Guerrero has shown that this model of care is appealing to policy makers and institutions alike. Other nonstate training programs for midwives—private schools like *Nueve Lunas* in Oaxaca, *Luna Maya* in Chiapas, and *Mujeres Aliadas* in Michoacán—continue to work to meet the demand for more professionally trained midwives across Mexico and the desire of more women to receive formal training in midwifery. The Mexican Association of Midwifery has become an important site of the dissemination of information about midwifery studies, laws, knowledge repositories, educational opportunities, and national conferences. Midwifery in Mexico is increasingly political, as midwives work with institutions and policy makers alike to highlight the importance of midwives for addressing pressing women's health concerns. Through such politics, traditional and professional midwives and physicians must come together to evaluate problems in the current health care system. These three kinds of practitioners will need to find a shared understanding of what knowledge is important in birth if they are to address national issues around maternal mortality, morbidity, and obstetric violence.

The potential for finding this shared ground seems more possible today than in the past, in part because of the concepts, spaces, and technologies that midwives and physicians increasingly share. Just as professional midwives use biomedical technologies and medications when appropriate, physicians rely on low-tech solutions much of the time. For instance, the physicians and some of the midwives we interviewed relied on hand-held Dopplers to track

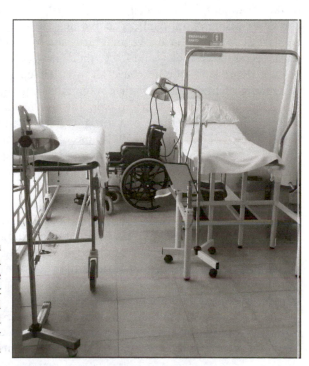

A birthing table that can be placed upright, with a bar for holding onto while pushing in an upright position. Intercultural Hospital in San Cristóbal de las Casas. Photo by Mounia El Kotni

fetal heartbeats or used their fingernails to break the bag of waters. Indeed, Mexican physicians frequently cited their clinical skills and their ability to diagnose their patients with almost no technology as their greatest strength, considering their own skills to be markedly better than those of US physicians, whom they deemed too reliant on technology. In addition, physicians may teach professional midwives, and hospitals are becoming more open to including alternative medicine students and professional and traditional midwives in their institutional structures. For example, intercultural hospitals such as the one in Chiapas (a model that also exists in a handful of other states including Puebla, Nayarit, and Tamaulipas) intend to offer a greater integration of different medical systems so patients can choose the approach that best suits their needs. While hospitals such as these are not without their problems (El Kotni 2016), they provide forms of integration almost unheard of in other biomedical hospitals. Such initiatives might foster increased communication and understanding between practitioners and lead to more fruitful conversations about how best to address national health concerns.

While all these changes are extremely positive and give us hope for the future of births in Mexico, certain deeper structural issues remain that affect many women's birth experiences. Our primary concern is obstetric violence, and though the concept itself has not permeated the national conversation in the same way as other health concerns have (such as maternal mortality for example), obstetric violence remains one of the most significant causes of risk, morbidity, and poor birth outcomes for women across the country. For further examples, being yelled at, demeaned, and commanded during labor can lower women's self-confidence and negatively affect their labor progress, weaken their will to have a vaginal birth and so end up with the violence of an unnecessary cesarean, and lower their self-esteem and contribute to postpartum depression. Studies have shown that episiotomies contribute to a weakening of the perineal walls, potentially leading to increased maternal blood loss, infection, postpartum pain, lowered mother–infant bonding, and/or incontinence (Karaçam and Eroğlu 2003; Lappen and Gossett 2010; Chang et al. 2011). Although WHO has cautioned against their routine use, episiotomies continue to be a routine part of hospital birth care (García Vázquez et al. 2012); very nearly all Mexican women who give birth in hospitals have either "the cut below" or "the cut above"—an episiotomy or a cesarean (Diniz and Chacham 2004). It is only recently, and because of the involvement of midwives in bringing the problem with these procedures to light, that the need for them has been questioned at institutional levels. We believe that while there is still a long road ahead to correct the imbalance of authority and power in hospital births; the very fact that there is recognition of the presence of obstetric violence is an important first step in establishing humane birth treatment for women.

What we have shown here, however, is that despite the convergence of midwives and physicians, of practices, spaces and technologies of birth in Mexico, important differences persist between systems of authoritative knowledge in different birth settings. At their core, these differences are about how practitioners think about issues of risk, choice, and equality. Jordan (1997:58) stated that, "The power of authoritative knowledge is not that it is correct but that it counts." The knowledge that counts as authoritative in each setting thus draws from and reproduces narratives about what counts as risk in birth, what choices women have over their own labors and deliveries, and what kinds of relationships exist between patients and providers. Here we have argued that these differences will continue to be entrenched through training encounters in birth that shape how students come to contextualize birth processes. Through understanding the processes of the transmission of knowledge and attitudes themselves, we can trace how authoritative knowledge becomes embodied, transformed, or enacted in birth encounters. These narratives matter; not only do they affect how women feel about their births, bodies, and babies, but they also have tangible impacts on health outcomes. It is not enough, then, to think about the artifacts and institutions of birth—these alone do not tell us the full story. We must interrogate the systems of knowledge that reflect and perpetuate ways of thinking about women, bodies, and birth and the rationales for acting upon them.

THOUGHT QUESTIONS

1. Why should Mexico, or any country, be concerned about women's experiences of childbirth? What is the role of legislation in managing experiences as well as outcomes?

2. How might the hierarchical system of authoritative knowledge in hospitals change to include patient choice?

3. How can midwives in Mexico become a standard option within the clinic-based birth system, as in the Netherlands, for instance?

4. How can midwives and physicians collaborate to improve birth experiences and outcomes for women in Mexico?

5. How are the experiences of obstetric violence in Mexico similar to or different from other countries discussed in this book?

RECOMMENDED FILMS

Catching Babies is a documentary that traces the lives of midwives and birthing women along the US–Mexico border, focusing on the midwifery school and birth center Maternidad La Luz. Available at http://www.imdb.com/video/wab/vi394570777

El Parto (En comunidades indígenas maya de Chiapas, México) is a short documentary filmed in the 1990s and is about the various stages and rituals surrounding home-birth in Highlands Chiapas. Available at https://www.youtube.com/watch?v=lsT0Fok2TrI&app=desktop

Loba is a documentary that looks at contemporary birth experiences in Spain, Mexico, Cuba, and France. Available at http://lobafilm.com/

3

Choiceless Choice in Tanzania
Homebirth, Hospital Birth, and Birth Registration

Megan Cogburn, Adrienne Strong, and Summer Wood

As in most countries in sub-Saharan Africa, Tanzania's colonial history and postindependence political and economic strategies continue to influence the health care services the state can provide. The country's health sector still generally follows the British organizational system, while broad expansion of basic health care services in rural areas can be traced to *Ujamaa* socialism in the postindependence period. In the 1980s, historical forces began to work in concert with broader global forces in new ways through heightened flows of foreign aid. Starting in the mid-1980s, Tanzania undertook broad economic reforms as a condition of accepting loans and aid from the International Monetary Fund (IMF) and the World Bank, which required reduced spending on health and social services. At approximately the same time, Tanzania became one of the first countries to pledge its support for the Safe Motherhood Initiative (Tanzania Ministry of Health 2008:1), which focused global attention on the magnitude of maternal death as a public health and social problem. In 2000, the United Nations member states, including Tanzania, adopted the Millennium Development Goals, among which maternal, child, and reproductive health care figured prominently. To improve such care, Tanzania has adopted a number of initiatives over the course of the last 35 years, including alternately emphasizing training for local midwives (aka traditional birth attendants/TBAs) and encouraging facility-based births (FCI 2007:76; Tanzania Ministry of Health 1990).

In many high-income countries, women have (at least some) access to formally trained midwives who will assist them if they choose to give birth at home, and if an emergency arises, the woman can take advantage of reliable emergency transportation to reach a health facility adequately equipped to provide interventions she might need. In places such as Tanzania, poor infrastructure, unreliable transportation, endemic disease, and poverty all contribute to making a woman's home a more dangerous place for delivery than would be the case in a wealthy country, should she develop a complication. Therefore, in lower-resource environments, the global community considers increasing the percentage of women who deliver in health facilities to be an important indicator of improved maternal health; the Tanzanian state has also adopted this measure as a marker of development.

Demographic surveys (TDHS-MIS 2016) from Tanzania show that more than half of all births (52%) are attended by a nurse, professional midwife, or assistant nurse, with doctors (MDs), assistant medical officers (AMOs), and clinical officers assisting an additional 12% of deliveries.[1] Just over half of all women living in rural areas deliver in a health facility, compared with 86% of women who live in urban areas. More than one-third (37%) of women still give birth outside of health facilities, predominantly in rural areas. In almost all cases, women give birth vaginally without much biomedical intervention. CS births amount to less than 6% of all births throughout the country. About one-quarter of births are assisted by relatives, friends and/or traditional midwives, who are officially called "traditional birth attendants" (TBAs)—a somewhat derogatory term used by development agencies that wish to preserve the term "midwife" for those who have graduated from professional training programs. Most anthropologists in this field use the term "traditional midwife" to honor these women's important roles in their communities, which often extend far beyond midwifery into other types of healing skills. Following the World Health Organization's definition of a "skilled birth attendant," policy makers and public health practitioners do not consider TBAs to be skilled attendants, and likewise, the statistics generally assume that if a woman gave birth in a health facility, a skilled health care worker attended her.

However, Adrienne's extensive work in Tanzanian maternity wards indicates that women not infrequently give birth alone in these facilities due to staff shortages and the overcrowding that have resulted from the push to promote facility births before there were sufficient facilities and care providers available. In a country of over 55 million people (World Bank 2017), there are just 172 registered obstetricians/gynecologists and of those, only 65 are working in government health care facilities (AGOTA 2017). There are approximately three nurses *and* nurse-midwives (the two categories are combined in the reporting) for every 10,000 people in the country (Ministry of Health 2013:15). This severe shortage of health care personnel, particularly those with expertise in taking care of pregnant women, leads to high workloads and poor patient coverage. With these numbers in mind, we urge you to

---

[1] The cesarean section (CS) rate in Tanzania varies widely by location and women's socioeconomic status, particularly between urban and rural areas. The national CS average is 6% of births, lower than the WHO's recommended 10%–15% (TDHS-MIS 2016:173-4)—meaning Tanzanian women and babies are likely dying from lack of access to CS. The government has worked for several years to train assistant medical officers (non-MDs) to perform CS in order to expand access to this sometimes lifesaving care (see Pereira and Bergström forthcoming).

maintain a healthy skepticism about reported statistics. Less absolute truth than a representation of general trends, these data are fallible and are often merely estimates with significant margins of error.

Despite questionable data quality, it is undeniable that more and more women in Tanzania are giving birth in health facilities, yet large disparities in access persist between urban and rural areas of the country. Urban women are much more likely than rural women to have skilled assistance during childbirth. Likewise, women with secondary education or higher are more than twice as likely to be assisted during delivery by a skilled provider than are women with no education (91% and 42% respectively) (TDHS-MIS 2016). Only 42% of the country's poorest childbearing women are assisted by a skilled provider, in contrast to 95% of the wealthiest women. These num-bers all demonstrate the presence of ongoing barriers to skilled care at birth for women in rural areas, and for those with lower socioeconomic status.

However, what these statistics from the country's 2015 Demographic and Health Survey (TDHS) blur is the experiences of women and health care workers on the ground, an understanding of which can provide insight into *why* disparities persist and what is still needed to provide high-quality, locally accessible and culturally acceptable care for all women. Additionally, while these numbers are an improvement over previous years, the estimated mater-nal mortality ratio (MMR) in the 2015–16 Tanzanian Demographic and Health Survey of 556 deaths/100,000 live births, while lower than that recorded in the 2004–05 TDHS (578), is higher than the ratios reported in 2010 (454) and in the 2012 Population and Housing Census (432). Despite increased efforts, therefore, the MMR in Tanzania has remained relatively stable throughout the last decade, indicating poor progress toward saving women's lives. Why is it that, even though facility births have risen by 13% (from 50% in 2010 to 63% of all births in 2015) in just five years, the same number of women (if not more) continue to die?

Tanzanian Conceptions of the Body

Across many of Tanzania's ethnic groups, there are certain common concepts related to the body, health, and illness. There is a *physical* body, which belongs to an individual, but that individual is also an inextricable part of a broader *social* body, which connects people within a community or ethnic group. People may become ill or experience difficulties during pregnancy and birth, not only as a result of physical problems, but also because of distur-bances in the social body—either of which may manifest in the individual body. Disruptions in either realm can result in various forms of physical health problems, including those related to reproduction, such as infertility (Allen 2002:137–140) or problematic births. For example, in one village Adri-enne visited in 2015, she met a woman from the Fipa ethnic group whose family insisted that her prolonged labor was due to conflict within the family.

Instead of allowing the dispensary nurses (dispensaries are small local facilities, the lowest level of health facility in the Tanzanian biomedical health care system) to call the district ambulance so the woman could go to the district hospital for a cesarean section, her older relatives insisted they take the woman back home so they could resolve the family conflict, thereby resolving her prolonged labor.[2] Disturbances in the social body often entail violations of morals and norms, such as adultery, failure to share resources for the good of the group, or incomplete bridewealth payments. Some families believe that difficulties in birth signal that the woman has been unfaithful to her husband; the remedy is admission of guilt, though this is no longer as common a belief as it once was.

In Tanzania, childbirth has historically been a sacred act. In the Swahili language, the verb "to give birth," *kujifungua*, literally means, "to open oneself." The Swahili phrase for "I am pregnant," *nina ujauzito*, literally translates in English to "I have a heaviness." An opening of oneself up to the sacred dimensions of birth lightens the physical and psychosocial "heaviness" of pregnancy, a process that for generations has taken place in the home. Some Wagogo women in the central region of the country said that in the past, it was the husband's role to make the necessary preparations for a homebirth. The husband would plan with the *mkunga wa jadi* (spelling for the singular, "traditional midwife") ahead of time, making the logistical arrangements, and at times, consult with a diviner to make any necessary spiritual preparations or interventions (Green 2000). Stacey Langwick describes the current decline of practices such as divination for the senders of ailments and afflictions, which have, in the past, been important aspects of maintaining a healthy social body in a community. This decline reflects "a world in which life is increasingly conceived of through modern notions of persons and bodies that are self-contained units rather than relational" (Langwick 2011:156). Nevertheless, as Adrienne's 2015 example above indicates, healthy social relations are still an important aspect of understanding illness or complications during birth for many women and their relatives.

The communal aspects of activities surrounding birth and birth preparations reflect ideas about the social body. As the care of pregnancy and childbirth becomes increasingly enclosed in biomedical health facilities, and the body becomes increasingly seen as separate from the social fabric, some of these sacred elements are lost. Men are excluded from their preparatory roles, while women are opened up to a range of rising responsibilities and tensions. Many of the ways in which communities care for pregnant and parturient women take place in the home. It is important to critically reflect upon what other important social and cultural practices will be lost if birth in Tanzania becomes solely relegated to biomedical health facilities.

---

[2] The baby was lying transverse and the presenting part was the baby's arm. As far as the medical practitioners knew, there was no way to help other than to have a CS, which the woman eventually received after being transported to the district hospital. By the time the CS was performed, more than 12 hours after she had first arrived at the dispensary, her baby had already died.

The Three Regions

In this chapter, we use ethnographic data collected from interactions with women and health care workers to explore the policies and political-economic factors that shape the maternity care system in Tanzania by influencing the services available, impacting the levels of biological risk pregnant women experience, and often disadvantaging certain women. The three sections of this chapter represent three different regions of Tanzania—Dodoma in the center of the country, Rukwa to the southwest, and the main urban center of Dar es Salaam, on the east coast of the country (see map). These

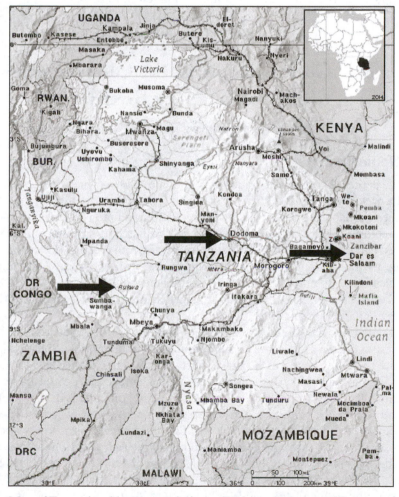

Map of Tanzania with arrows pointing to Dodoma, Rukwa, and Dar es Salaam regions.

three regions encompass the range from small, rural communities (Megan's work in Mpwapwa, Dodoma), to midsized towns that are regional headquarters (Adrienne's work in Rukwa), to a sprawling, cosmopolitan city (Summer's work in Dar es Salaam). Our chapter starts with a look at women in rural communities and how they experience new bans on giving birth at home. In the second section, we explore a government hospital's maternity ward to understand how nurse-midwives' working conditions affect their interactions with their clients and the quality of care they can provide. In the third section, we observe the difficulties of formally registering children by obtaining birth certificates. Finally, we offer some thoughts about the common themes in each of these settings and suggest some innovative approaches to improving access and care for women and their newborns.

Fining Homebirth in Rural Tanzania: Local Consequences of the Global Push for More Facility Births

Megan Cogburn

A Home Birth

A petite, sharply lined traditional midwife, Dolisia, had one good eye and a welcoming smile. When Dolisia and I arrived at the brick home, the mother was laboring on her bed beneath the home's lone window, naked but for a colorful *khanga* (cloth wrapper) loosely gathered around her waist. She looked calm. I could see her contractions, her big round belly tightening, rippling, its mountainous shadow quaking on the wall above the bed. Using petroleum jelly to massage the mother's stomach and feel her internally, Dolisia checked her progress. She determined that the baby was close, and the energy in the room quickened.

Letting her *khanga* fall to the earthen floor, the mother folded up her bed frame and mattress against the brick wall in one strong motion. She prepared a space to deliver, covering the packed dirt with two large plastic feed sacks of the same kind people use to store their annual maize and peanut harvests. Meanwhile, Dolisia removed her own clothing, a blue taffeta dress—probably her finest such garment—and wrapped her body with a swatch of *kitenge* (piece of cloth) from the breasts down. Situating herself on a low wooden stool, she ripped a thin strip of plastic off one of the sacks, tearing it down the middle and discarding the leftovers until she had just three wiry strings in her hands. She went about braiding them together, intermittently rubbing them between the palms of her hands as if trying to start a fire. I found another stool and sat down, forming the third point in a triangle of women framed by the sacks on the floor. Dolisia reworked the braided strings over and over in her hands while the mother quietly labored, lying on her left side, close beside us in the dimming light.

Sometime later the mother squatted over a plastic basin. Her water broke and filled the bowl with a rush. Returning to rest in a position halfway on her side, halfway propped up on her back by her elbows, she indicated by her posture that the baby was near. In seconds, I could see the tip of the head crowning and Dolisia knelt in closer, using her hands and a folded piece of *khanga* to guide the baby's protruding head and gently apply pressure to the mother's perineum. The mother's eyes were closed and her chin pressed down to her chest. She breathed steadily and with evident purpose, neither frantic nor ecstatic, carrying out her labor in line with the culturally valued stoicism and bravery expected of her. Dolisia told the mother to give another strong push, "*Sukuma.*" The baby's head emerged, followed by shoulders and its little curled-up body; it fell into Dolisia's two waiting hands with a plop.

For a nervous second the baby boy did not cry. Dolisia went to work massaging his body and removing the lining of the placental sack that was still around his head, resulting in a strong cry. Still attached to his mother, he was lifted up toward the window and brought back down, quickly, three times in a row, as if falling from the air. "*Phew, phew, phew,*" Dolisia spit into his eyes (to ward off illness, especially eye issues, which are common in infants in rural Tanzania, and to bless the baby), two tiny white ovals opening for the first time in the waning light. Setting the baby down on the plastic sack near his mother, Dolisia received the placenta and placed it in the basin with the other fluids. Using the plastic strings she had prepared, she tied off the cord and cut it with a razor blade that was tucked away in the taffeta folds of her dress on the floor. I walked outside just in time to see the final, fading display of pale evening blues and pinks, and the incoming purples of night.

Research Questions and Methods

I first met Dolisia in a dilapidated classroom at the Ijenji village primary school. She was one of the first participants to arrive for the day's development workshop. She was a representative of her community's group of elderly *wakunga wa jadi*, (spelling for plural, "traditional midwives"), some of the last still delivering babies in local homes. The village leadership had selected Dolisia and 14 other community members to participate in a Community Scorecard[3] intervention aimed at improving outcomes in maternal and newborn health. The main goal of the intervention was to empower the participants to find and implement practical ways they could increase the number of facility births in their own communities. In Tanzania today, roughly 40% of all births take place outside of health facilities (TDHS-MIS 2016). The interna-

---

[3] Community Scorecard is a participatory methodology and tool commonly used in development projects aimed at improving community-based empowerment, specifically related to increased transparency and accountability. In this instance, the project implemented an adapted Community Scorecard approach to see whether communities could address core obstacles to improving maternal and newborn health.

tional development community and Tanzanian government have been trying to change this statistic since the launch of the Millennium Development Goals (MDGs) in 2000 (now transitioned to the Sustainable Development Goals, following the 2015 close of the MDGs). Since then, debate surrounding place of birth remains central to global efforts to combat high maternal mortality rates (MMRs) and improve maternal and newborn health, with the public health community considering homebirth an important target for intervention and more facility births a key indicator of maternal health progress.

Throughout the three-day workshop in Ijenji, questions surrounding the promotion of facility births began to emerge. Two young facilitators from the Clinton Health Access Initiative assisted the participants as they came up with specific social actions set on increasing facility births, as well as indicators of progress related to the early onset of prenatal and postpartum care. They also talked about barriers to facility births, depicted on sets of laminated, colorful cards that the facilitators had taped to the blackboard. One depicted the image of a looming *mkunga wa jadi* standing in the corner of a pregnant woman's home, awaiting delivery for a now illegal homebirth. As the participants discussed this image of traditional midwives as problematic barriers to improving maternal health in their community, I could not help but look at Dolisia, wondering how she felt about being depicted in such a negative way. I began to question some of the intended and unintended consequences of the development-driven push for more facility births. How do these larger policies and regulations aimed at increasing key maternal health indicators intersect with lives at ground level? How do they affect mothers, *wakunga wa jadi*, and the state of maternal health in rural communities? What sociocultural aspects of pregnancy and childbirth are lost, or remain, as the public health community continues to promote health facilities as the only "official" place for women to give birth?

In this section I address these questions and the ways that women encounter and negotiate the push for more facility-based maternal health care in rural central Tanzania. I draw from seven months of multisited ethnography (Marcus 1995) conducted in Mpwapwa District, where I engaged in weekly participant-observation at three dispensaries, as well as in aspects of daily life spent in conversation with mothers, dispensary-based health care workers, and *wakunga wa jadi* in the three communities. I engaged in informal and formal interviews with village leaders and spoke with district and regional medical officers about birth at home and in health facilities. I also conducted three focus groups (one in each village) with mothers and with traditional midwives about the workings of maternity care regulations and fines.

Findings from my research highlight how national maternity care policies aimed at increasing facility births have "complex 'social lives' as people interact with them," and as they, in turn, enter into relations with the communities of mothers, birth attendants, and health care workers in which they are embedded (Latour 2010; Shore and Wright 2011:3). I will show how increased maternity care regulations and bylaws promoting homebirth fines reinforce structural vulnerabilities (Quesada, Hart, Bourgois 2011; Holmes 2013:99) for some of the poorest women, leaving them with limited abilities to enact care preferences and access future health care services. Similar to *structural violence* (violence that is built into societies and institutions that manifests as different forms of social stratification and people's "unequal power and . . . unequal life chances" [Galtung 1969:171]), the concept of *structural vulnerability* reveals how an individual's vulnerable position, such as a woman's during pregnancy and childbirth, is a product of one's position in a hierarchical social order of cultural values, institutions, and "diverse networks of power relationships and effects" (Quesada, Hart, and Bourgois 2011:2).

As in many places around the world, in rural Tanzania a significant amount of social, cultural, and economic capital is required for a woman to achieve her pregnancy care preferences and desired, positive childbirth experiences. Women who are poor, live in remote places, and/or lack access to the necessary social capital,[4] are more vulnerable to the discrimination and lack of care embedded within structural inequalities—which, as I will argue below, the maternity care policies work to exacerbate. Lastly, I will describe the ways that attempts to prohibit the traditional work of *wakunga wa jadi* force them to escort women to health dispensaries for birth rather than attending them at home as they previously had for generations, creating an environment of confusion and secrecy—one that further excludes *wakunga wa jadi* and the women they care for in rural communities from the formal, biomedical health care system.

Women's Encounters with the Push for More Facility Births

A few days following the homebirth I had attended with Dolisia, I received a phone call from Mama Julius, the mother who had given birth. She sounded upset. Dolisia was demanding more money for the delivery, even after Mama Julius had paid her 10,000 Tsh (approximately $5 US), the going rate for a *mkunga wa jadi*. She told me she felt as though Dolisia was trying to take advantage of her, possibly even because of my presence and the small gifts Dolisia knew I had given to Mama Julius following her birth, as is customary. Mama Julius was adamantly opposed to paying more. Even worse, Mama Julius had taken her infant to the local dispensary to register his health card and initiate his care.[5] After the nurses found out that she had a homebirth, they scolded her for being irresponsible and lazy for birthing at home when she should have come to the health dispensary. The nurses then told Mama Julius that a homebirth fine of 15,000 Tsh (approximately $7 US) must be paid in full before they would issue a child health card.

---

[4] Social capital is defined as socioculturally acquired knowledge, relationships, and behaviors that bestow economic and cultural advantages on some in society over others (see Bourdieu 1972).

[5] In Tanzania, national health care for children age 0–5 years is free; however, in order to access this care one needs a child health card. These cards should be issued upon birth and are required for vaccinations and the general health monitoring throughout a child's first five years of life. Legally, they are to be given free; printed in bright red type at the top are the words "not for sale."

Most of the mothers I talked to in Mpwapwa who had given birth at home over the last two to three years had stories and frustrations similar to those of Mama Julius. Homebirth fines and the withholding of child health cards are two examples of the ways in which maternity care policies aimed at increasing facility births take on punitive and improvisational forms as they are translated into and interact with realities on the ground. These new sanctions are the unintended consequences of the global health push for more facility births. In order to meet *international* development recommendations and targets, *local and national* governments fully intend these sanctions to scare women out of giving birth at home and push them to deliver at their local biomedical health facilities.

While the new maternity care policies seek to normalize facility births and punish homebirthers, these homebirth fines and increased regulations also negatively affect women who prefer *not* to give birth at home, but who lack the social and economic capital needed to access a facility birth. A conversation I had one day with my friend Asha illustrated this sad irony. At the age of 28, Asha was preparing for the birth of her fourth child. She was frustrated with how difficult it was to make the necessary arrangements for birth at the health facility. She told me that the "delivery equipment" (*vifaa vya kujifungulia*) required posed significant challenges for women whose husbands were poor, as hers was (see also Allen 2002; Spangler 2011 for similar accounts). In addition to her clothes, health care workers often expect a woman to bring up to five clean or new *khanga*, sterile surgical gloves, water, a plastic basin, and a tarp. When the facility is undersupplied, the woman may also have to purchase all the needles, medications, and other necessary medical supplies. Thus, it was not uncommon for a woman to give birth at home with an inexpensive *mkunga wa jadi*, or to give birth on the way to the hospital. One young woman had recently done so after a nurse turned her away, while in labor, from the local dispensary because the woman lacked the necessary delivery equipment. Sadly, she lost her baby as a result of this delay and talked about opening a case against the nurse. As I pressed Asha further about other comments I had overheard about women preferring to give birth at home, Asha's demeanor changed. Sitting in the sun outside of her red, mud-brick home, Asha looked me straight in the eyes, and pointedly asked, *"Kupenda kujifungulia nyumbani? Haiwezekani!"* "To like to give birth at home? Impossible!"

Asha's dislike of homebirth speaks, importantly, to some of the underlying tensions rural women must face during pregnancy and childbirth. It also challenges my own, perhaps somewhat romanticized, assumptions about homebirths and the existence of strong "cultural" preferences for the homebirth environment. Many women in Mpwapwa historically and currently *do* prefer to give birth at home. The opening vignette describing Mama Julius' homebirth experience highlights many reasons why women choose to give birth at home—choice of birthing position on the floor, the quiet, calm, uncrowded atmosphere of her home, and the presence of an older, experienced *mkunga wa jadi* whom she knows and trusts. But problems arise, as

Mama Julius after her birth at home [left]. Asha standing outside her house [right]. Photos by Megan Cogburn

Asha rightly notes, when the preferences of some particular women become the normalized assumptions about all women—especially when people in positions of power, such as health care workers, use these assumptions to draw conclusions and perpetuate harmful stereotypes that "rural," "back-ward" women just "like" to give birth at home. In an atmosphere where a homebirth is now an illegal act, these false assumptions can negatively affect the social body by creating new conflicts and tensions. They can also lead to physical risk for pregnant women due to the poor quality of the maternity care that women in rural communities are able to access.

Health care workers' judgments about rural women preferring to give birth at home because they are lazy or ignorant become yet another set of structural barrier to quality pregnancy and childbirth care. Regardless of a woman's true preference for home or facility, these social and structural barriers play major roles in deciding where a woman will give birth. For example, Tanzanian regulations now state that all first-time pregnant women and women who have had two or more cesareans or five or more pregnancies, or women who are shorter than 150 cm, are "high-risk" and must deliver at their district hospital instead of their local dispensaries. This policy is meant to capture all women medically considered most at risk for complications during labor and delivery, requiring them to go to facilities with Comprehensive Emergency Obstetric and Neonatal Care (CEmONC), including operating theaters, blood banks, and more highly skilled personnel. While this policy is motivated by the intention of saving the lives of mothers and babies, it poses negative consequences for women living in remote areas. Unreliable roads and transportation, travel expenses, time away from domestic responsibilities, and the unpredictability of labor and birth are just some reasons why women cannot access hospitals for birth and end up making what often becomes the choiceless "choice" of giving birth at home.

Asha's words above encoded her understanding that for many women in her community, births at home alone, births on the way to the hospital, or births with an inexpensive *mkunga wa jadi* were the only options. Moreover, in line with recent studies documenting poor care and abuse in biomedical facilities in Tanzania (Kruk et al. 2014; Mselle et al. 2013), women with whom I talked explained that the district hospital in Mpwapwa was often their last preference for place of birth, even if they had been referred there. Overcrowding and inattentive, rude nurses were reasons women did not like giving birth in the hospital. They were more likely to have positive birth experiences at their local dispensaries where they knew the nurses and had the support of family and friends. Adrienne's section below explores the birthing dynamics in larger Tanzanian hospitals and how these environments impact nursing care and pregnant women's experiences, but, for now, let's turn our attention back to the health dispensaries and women's encounters with new maternity care policies.

Shifting the Focus: Blaming Mothers for Systemic Failures

The following two stories show how policies mandating hospital births and homebirth fines create negative consequences for women who, for a variety of reasons, are least likely to be able to access facility births in the first place. While shadowing a nurse during the antenatal clinic at one of the dispensaries in my field site, I was reminded of the structural vulnerability some women face during pregnancy and childbirth, and the unfortunate ways in which the larger community of policy makers, village leaders, and health care workers blame women for what are actually systemic shortcomings of the Tanzanian health care system.

The nurse was meeting with a 16-year-old girl who was pregnant for the first time and attending her second prenatal clinic. The nurse reminded the girl that she must go to the district hospital in Mpwapwa to deliver because this was her first pregnancy. The nurse then listed all the supplies the girl would need to bring. Knowing the significant cost of the delivery items, as well as the fact that it was rainy season with unreliable public transport and at least a two-hour drive to Mpwapwa town, I later asked the nurse if she really thought this girl would make it to Mpwapwa to give birth. The nurse replied no, that this girl would most likely end up having a homebirth with a *mkunga wa jadi*, adding in an accusatory tone that the girl was young and her home community had "very many *wakunga wa jadi*." By focusing on the girl's age and a possible preference for delivering with a traditional midwife, the nurse shifted the focus away from the structural health disparities—distance to facilities, weak supply

Rainy season view of one of the roads women must walk to get to a facility. Photo by Megan Cogburn

chains, and the unaffordable cost of the supplies that the girl was supposed to buy, all of which made this girl more vulnerable to birthing in her community without professional attendance. Instead, she blamed the girl herself.

The story of Mama Grace, an older mother, also highlights this shift in blame and how the larger community of policies, health care workers, and village leaders punish women for giving birth at home. With her baby girl bouncing on her lap, Mama Grace narrated her numerous, fraught attempts to obtain a child health card for her daughter, the last of six children born 10 months ago. In line with the new policy, nurses at her local health dispensary demanded that Mama Grace pay 15,000 Tsh (roughly $7 US) for the home-birth fine before receiving the child's health card. Because it was before the harvest season, this expense was too great for Mama Grace; most subsistence farmers are very cash-poor before they harvest the year's crop. Moreover, numerous attempts to get assistance from her husband and village leaders proved futile, as both reminded Mama Grace that she knew about the village bylaw and the consequences of giving birth at home. Mama Grace did know about the fines, but she preferred to give birth at her home, with the same *mkunga wa jadi* who had delivered her other children. Also, she was ineligible to deliver at her local dispensary due to her "high-risk" status and was not able to make the two-hour journey by bus to Mpwapwa town when her labor suddenly started. Now faced with the new sanctions, Mama Grace even tried to travel to other nearby health dispensaries to obtain a child health card, but nurses there also wanted money for the homebirth fine before issuing a card, and Mama Grace had none to give. Mama Grace worried about her 10-

month-old child who, lacking a health card, had not been seen by a health care worker or received any infant vaccinations. Expressing the frustration and marginalization she felt, she repeated one phrase several times as we talked—"Never have I had a child without a card!" (*"Sijawahi kukaa na mtoto bila kadi!"*). Sorrowfully, she carried this burden that could be life-threatening in an environment still rife with potentially fatal infectious diseases.

These stories reveal how new top-down maternity care policies interact with social communities with devastating results for certain women living in remote areas. Punitive scare tactics such as homebirth fines and the withholding of child health cards reinforce already unequal access to care, further excluding some of the most marginalized mothers. In the face of new policies and regulations aimed at increasing facility births, they are fined, harassed, shamed and denied health cards for their children following homebirths.

Wakunga wa Jadi: The Ones Who Are There in a Changing Maternal Health Landscape

Mothers are not the only group negatively affected by the global push for facility births. Local birth attendants like Dolisia also feel the burden of increased bylaws and policies that prohibit what once was valued, community-based work. "We do not deliver babies anymore. We always escort [women] to the health facility." These were the words *wakunga wa jadi* spoke repeatedly throughout my interviews about the work they do in their communities today. Their words echo the "official" Tanzanian national policies that state that all local birth attendants must *only* escort laboring women to the

Mother and infant following birth at the health dispensary. Photo by Megan Cogburn

health facility to give birth. Supported by an international development NGO that pays traditional midwives to bring women to health facilities in Mpwapwa, this policy creates an atmosphere of confusion, secrecy, and surveillance. Like the homebirth fines, this policy is exclusionary, pushing local midwives and their clients further to the margins of the formal health system. Moreover, this policy frustrates and confuses the elder generation of *wakunga wa jadi*, who are left filling in the care gaps for a health system that is unable to provide for all women in rural communities. *Wakunga wa jadi* do not refuse the women who still ask them for birth attendance, as they know well that refusal might well result in these women birthing alone.

"When we bring laboring women to the health facility, the nurses are not there," a *mkunga wa jadi* told me one day as we chatted under the shade of a blooming baobab tree in her subvillage. One of the most remote I had visited, this subvillage was a couple of hours' walk or a half-hour *pikipiki* (motorcycle) ride along sandy, bumpy trails to arrive at the nearest health dispensary. This local midwife was frustrated about the nurses' long absences and the negative treatment she and the laboring women she escorted to the dispensary received upon arrival. "'Come back later, come back later,' the nurses just say," without even welcoming them inside or conducting an exam. She described how she has waited with women in active labor outside of the health facility, all the while the nurses telling them to "come back later." "Up until the point when the baby is crowning"—she made a gesture to indicate this by placing both hands in a triangle shape around her face—"the nurses will say 'come back later' and not do anything." Then, after the baby is born, the nurses will ask for *chai* (a bribe or informal payment for their services). She shook her head in frustration and reminded me that all the while she is "the one who has been there [with the mother]."

The fact that *wakunga wa jadi* are the ones who are there, providing vital pregnancy and childbirth care in rural communities, has been used and abused by international development and public health policies throughout the last few decades. In the late 1980s and 1990s, efforts to improve maternal health specifically encouraged the use of local birth attendants like *wakunga wa jadi*, offering them training and homebirth delivery kits and supporting their formal integration into the biomedical health system (Langwick 2011, 2012). Across the globe many of these efforts failed, often because they did not account for existing practices and understandings of the body, social obligations, and structural barriers to health (see Berry 2006, 2010). Today in rural Tanzania, we can point to similar shortcomings. Global recommendations and national policies that prohibit the delivery work of *wakunga wa jadi* fail to account for, or reflect, the lived experiences of women and those who care for them in rural communities. Moreover, these prohibitions work to create an atmosphere of confusion, exclusion, and surveillance of mothers and local birth attendants, who may be afraid to speak out about their real experiences and problems they face. In a setting where acquiring accurate measures of maternal mortality is already highly problematic, this new environment of silencing will only make matters worse.

Concluding Thoughts from the Community

The homebirth I described at the beginning of this section took place in March 2016 in rural Tanzania. Just hours after I first met Dolisia in that dilapidated classroom for the development workshop, I found myself running after her along a sandy path, asking her if it would be okay for me to tag along and watch her work. Amidst small group discussions and the demonstration of cards designed with graphics to show why women should not give birth at home, Dolisia was called out of the meeting to attend to a woman laboring at home and in need of care. The next day we returned to the development seminar, me a bit wiser, slightly more on the inside as I discreetly shared little winks and smiles with the other female participants in the room, all in on the happenings of yesterday's homebirth.

As discussions of indicators and ways to increase facility births continued, the lesson, and irony, for me, could not have been clearer. Contemporary, development-driven maternal health policies have become so concerned with increasing facility births that they have become ignorant of, and blind to, the actual, lived experiences of mothers, and the kinds of maternity care desperately needed on the ground in rural communities. Women everywhere prefer not to travel long distances to receive prenatal care or to give birth; *they want and need care in their own communities* (Davis-Floyd and Cheney 2009); Tanzania is no exception. Moreover, policies that prohibit the traditional work of *wakunga wa jadi* ignore and silence women's voices, ultimately creating a maternal health landscape wherein structural vulnerabilities are reinforced and perpetuated, instead of exposed and mitigated. Such a landscape places the blame on traditional midwives and mothers themselves, instead of on the systemic shortages within the Tanzanian health system that have led to poor-quality childbirth care in health facilities and the continued need for the home-based maternity care of *wakunga wa jadi*, especially in remote communities.

So, then, what happens to the Tanzanian women whose local facility *is* a large hospital or who are able to follow the referral advice of their dispensary health care workers and give birth in a hospital? The next section continues such women's journeys as they reach a hospital and interact with the nurses and doctors there.

"Hospitals Are the Only Place": Shrinking Choices and the Burden of Caring in Resource-Poor Facilities

Adrienne Strong

At the Mawingu Regional Referral Hospital, in the peripheral southwestern region of Rukwa, the maternity ward staff of approximately 30 nurses and three doctors attend between 400 and 700 women giving birth each month (see photos below). On average, that means between 13 and 23 births per each 24-hour period. However, in actuality, during my fieldwork I found that averages did not hold; sometimes there were only a few women on the ward and, at other times, a flood of women whose babies could not wait to see life on the outside. Due to ongoing transportation and access challenges, poor infrastructure in the region, and some women's preference to avoid the expense of the large hospital, not all woman started out directly seeking care at Mawingu Hospital when their contractions began. Other women, primarily those living close by, would report straight to Mawingu, bypassing facilities lower down the referral chain in hopes of finding better, more comprehensive care at the regional hospital. Many women who had no complications successfully gave birth in more basic facilities, needing only minimal assistance from a nurse or medical attendant. Other women might hope to give birth in such a facility, often closer to home, or they might—through choice or necessity—be at home, even as this option is rapidly disappearing, as Megan described in the previous section.

However, when a woman starts to show signs of a complication during her pregnancy or while giving birth, she rapidly tests the limits of the expertise of those assisting her, whether at home or in a basic health facility. During labor and birth in low-resource countries like Tanzania—where many structurally vulnerable women are malnourished and burdened with high work and disease loads—complications that would not be problematic for a healthy

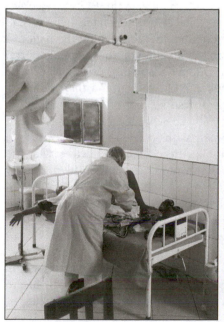 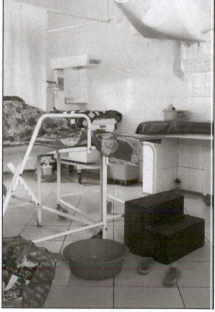

Nurse assisting a woman to give birth in Mawingu Hospital [left]; view of a labor and delivery room. Photos by Adrienne Strong

woman can precipitously spiral into life-threatening emergencies with little or no warning. If a woman is fortunate and able to access transportation, she might be able to receive more advanced emergency care at a place such as Mawingu Regional Hospital. But, despite the best hopes and efforts of policy makers, public health practitioners, and clinicians, a woman's arrival at a hospital did not, in 2014 and 2015 (and still does not), guarantee timely, respectful care, or her survival in the face of an emergency.

In this section, I use one woman's story combined with interview data from nurse-midwives to provide a window into many of the challenges of providing maternal health care in the Tanzanian hospital setting. As Megan showed, many Tanzanian women experience poor care, neglect, disrespect, and discrimination in their biomedical health facilities. These negative experiences work to deter women from seeking care early or from trying to overcome the structural barriers between them and their biomedical facilities. At the same time, women are increasingly giving birth in health facilities because of public health and advocacy campaigns, as well as the fines and penalties that Megan described. Here, I dive below the surface of low-quality care to explore what causes it and the tense interactions between biomedical health care workers and the women they serve.

Methods

I have been traveling to and conducting research in Tanzania for the last 10 years. For this project, I spent a total of 23 months in the Rukwa region of Tanzania conducting fieldwork at the regional referral hospital, which I call Mawingu, and in 11 randomly selected communities throughout the region. I conducted over 1,600 hours of participant-observation on the regional referral hospital's maternity ward, assisting nurses and doctors in routine tasks. I also attended meetings, fetched supplies, talked with women and their relatives, took samples to the hospital laboratory for testing, and, after apprenticeship-style instruction in 2013 from a nurse-midwife who is a nationally certified trainer, I even sometimes attended women as they gave birth. I also learned neonatal resuscitation and other techniques from hospital doctors who are also certified trainers. I formally interviewed more than half of the maternity ward's staff members and had countless informal interviews with all of the rest over tea or while engaged in ward tasks. In addition, I administered a "Conditions for Work Effectiveness Questionnaire" (Laschinger 2012) to all nurses on the ward. All the nurses I interviewed are nurse-midwives, either RNs or ENs (enrolled nurses) with midwifery training. Thus, I use the terms "nurse" and "nurse-midwife" interchangeably. I also interviewed hospital, district, and regional health administrators about maternal mortality and health, health sector procedures, and current challenges. In the randomly selected villages, my research assistant, Rebeca Matiku, and I conducted focus groups of 10–15 participants. We spoke with men, women, community leaders, and health care workers about their experiences with maternal health in their community.

Tumaini's Story

I was on the night shift one evening more than a year after I first started conducting fieldwork at Mawingu. The ward was relatively quiet. One or two women were in labor but showed no signs of giving birth imminently. There were only three nurses present—Nurse Linda, Nurse Lucy, and Nurse Rukia. I was talking with Nurse Lucy on the postnatal section of the ward as she passed through, administering antibiotics and pain medication to women who had recently had cesarean sections. We had settled in so I could interview her, when we were interrupted by a woman at the window, trying to talk to us through the closed pane.

Nurse Lucy tried to explain to her that she should talk to the labor nurses in the other room and explained where to go, but shortly thereafter, the woman circled back to us again, clearly not understanding what Nurse Lucy told her. I went out to help her find her way. She told me her *mgonjwa* (patient) was outside the doors of the ward, still on a motorcycle. I went to look at the woman, Tumaini, on the motorcycle outside the ward doors. A man, a relative, was sitting on the motorcycle still, unable to move because he had tied the barely conscious woman to his body at the waist and legs so she would not fall off during their ride. Tumaini responded to her name and attempted to answer but was too weak to move. I helped Nurse Linda and Nurse Rukia, the labor room nurses, bring Tumaini into the labor and delivery room with the ward wheelchair. It turned out, the male relative told me, to be a case of retained placenta; Tumaini had lost a lot of blood after delivering her baby around 8 P.M. at home in the village. He also told me they had tried to go to the dispensary nearest to their home. The only provider present did not have the keys and so did not have access to the facility and its equipment. Eventually, after trying to help and being unable to, the dispensary provider had told Tumaini's relatives to get her to the hospital as quickly as possible. Because it was late at night, they brought her on the motorcycle, the only form of transportation available, even as she was nearly unconsciousness due to blood loss.

The nurses on the maternity ward expressed their wish that she had passed by the Out-Patient Department because the night doctor there could have immediately done an evacuation, a procedure to remove the remaining parts of the placenta from her uterus, which would have stopped her bleeding. Instead, now that Tumaini had already arrived at the maternity ward, the nurses had to take care of her. I helped Nurse Linda ease Tumaini off the motorcycle into a wheelchair and then helped lift her into a bed. Nurse Rukia started gathering supplies to start an intravenous line. Tumaini's male relative said they had forgotten a lot of the supplies because of being in a hurry to leave. Under normal circumstances, health care workers expect women to bring many items when they arrive at the health facility, even at this, the largest hospital in the region. Nurse Linda went to the office in search of the scarce IV fluids she would need to help stabilize Tumaini. After some minutes, Nurse Rukia had started an intravenous line and we had drawn the patient's blood for analysis (so she could receive a transfusion), which I took over to the lab so the nurses would not have to leave their new patient. The lab doors were locked and the metal gate closed so I rang the bell. When Juma eventually emerged from inside the mostly dark lab, he said he was not sure if there was blood available but would bring us an answer and the results from the blood type, cross-matching, and hemoglobin level tests. I also tried to talk to the woman's male relative about donating blood, but he refused. First, he said his blood was not good, and then that he had just donated blood last month at a nearby, smaller private hospital. He said he was sure there would be blood, and I told him I didn't know; a lot of people lately had needed blood. I asked, "What if there's no blood and she needs it tonight?" He said more of Tumaini's relatives would be available tomorrow, but for tonight, God would help her.

Nearly two hours after Tumaini's arrival, I went back through the labor room to see how she was getting on. She had gotten a unit of blood and was covered in a thick hospital blanket. Nurse Rukia said Tumaini was responsive and talking. They were waiting for the operating theater team to arrive from their homes so they could remove the retained placental fragments from Tumaini's uterus. Before going to the lab, I had asked if they had taken her blood pressure and Nurse Rukia said no. She and Nurse Linda discussed how all the blood pressure cuffs do not work and said, besides, there was no stethoscope available, which is required to take blood pressure. In the end, they did not take any of Tumaini's vital signs. After checking on Tumaini, Nurse Rukia, and Nurse Linda in the labor room, I left for the night.

Tumaini's story is repeated over and over in places like Mawingu, but not all women are as fortunate. At other points in my fieldwork, women began bleeding and were unable to get a blood transfusion quickly enough because of the lack of matching donor blood or an unknown cause of bleeding. Other times, women or their babies did not survive because a shortage of nurses and doctors caused delays in lifesaving procedures. Or a shortage of supplies and medications delayed treatment, allowing sepsis, dangerously high blood pressure, or loss of blood to result in shock, multiple organ failure, and eventually, death. In other cases, as might have happened with Tumaini, a lack of functioning equipment could prevent a nurse or doctor from discovering a woman's underlying health problem at an early stage, before it became critical. Even the time of day (or night) at which a woman arrived on the maternity ward could influence her chance of survival. It was much more difficult to perform emergency surgery when all the doctors, nurses, and operating theater staff had to be called in from their beds at home.

Repeated Efforts and Little Change

The absolute number of women who died at Mawingu due to problems associated with their pregnancies was about 35 out of 6,100 births attended per calendar year, for an approximate maternal mortality ratio of 573/ 100,000.[6] This extremely high rate had remained the same for several years, despite an increase in staff members and other hospital improvements. What, then, contributes to these consistently high rates of maternal deaths? In the anthropological literature on childbirth and reproductive health, the focus most often is on women's experiences rather than on those of the health care workers involved. To begin to answer the question of why maternal death rates have not significantly changed at this hospital, I needed to move away from talking with women and to ask the nurses and doctors what they saw as the biggest challenges in their workplace. Their experiences attending women at Mawingu Regional Hospital reveal the wider context of women's treatment in this and similar health care facilities, highlighting significant barriers to furthering the improvement of maternity services.

Nurses and doctors in Tanzania (and much of sub-Saharan Africa, as well as other low-income countries globally) work within the confines of a health care system that is severely limited in professional or personal support, pay, access to promotions and continuing education, praise or encouragement, safe physical infrastructure, personal protective equipment, and material and human resources. At the same time, these systems expect these professionals to consistently provide timely, high-quality, lifesaving care with compassion, high ethical standards, and sometimes, personal sacrifice. When we explore only women's perspectives and only privilege their explanations of the care they received, it is easy to view health care workers as perpetrators of violence, discrimination, or neglect. When placed within the context of a broader exploration of their work environment and the structures of the country's health care system as a whole, we begin to see that health care workers' experiences and narratives of the same events women describe take on a different light, full of qualifications, improvisation, justifications, deviations, and even failures *necessitated by* the systems in which they work (see also Mselle et al. 2013; Penfold et al. 2013). It is only both sets of experiences and interpretations that can move us toward a better understanding of how to improve care for pregnant women in these settings.

Global goals for improving maternal and child health structure health care delivery and health sector strategies, particularly in countries beholden to international donors or loans. When others hold the purse strings, the state places a primacy on results and data to prove that the country has reduced deaths or met other indicators, because donors often require proof of progress toward achieving these goals as a requisite for further aid (Davis et al. 2012; Merry 2011). Maternal mortality is one of the indicators that can be a litmus test for a health sector more generally (Wendland 2016:62). Maternal death takes on this role because so many health system inputs are needed to prevent a woman's death from pregnancy complications—medications (which require a functioning supply chain); trained personnel (an analogue for the

---

[6] For comparison, the maternal mortality ratio is 26.4/100,000 in the US and 9.2/100,000 in the UK (Kassebaum et al. 2016).

country's education system); a referral system that helps a woman reach a higher level of care (communication technologies, electricity perhaps); transportation (passable roads, accessibility of vehicles and gasoline); and health facilities with operating theaters and doctors, blood for transfusions, the availability of anesthesia and of people who know how to administer it, laboratory facilities, imaging or other diagnostic capabilities (ultrasound, x-ray for certain complications, electricity for these machines). While some policy initiatives work to address many of the necessities listed here, others focus on improving the knowledge of health care providers or improving the "quality of care" through training or oversight and monitoring visits.

However, what has been missing from the discourse around improving maternal health has been attention to two crucial components: (1) the structural vulnerability of the women at highest risk; and (2) the needs of those meant to be implementing policies, techniques, or training: the nurses and doctors themselves. To address the structural vulnerabilities of the poor in any country would require improving the conditions of their lifeworlds—that is, ensuring adequate water, food, shelter, and education for all. Since this massive task seems too daunting for agencies involved in maternal child health, they focus instead on solving specific problems they feel they can actually do something about, such as moving women into facilities to give birth or offering seminars aimed at upgrading providers' clinical skills. Yet, given that such complex larger issues are *almost never* addressed by global or national health and development policy makers, the focus stays on the individuals: the women and their care providers, and not on the structurally dysfunctional systems within which they must live and practice. With this in mind, we now turn to the needs of the caregivers themselves.

In the Rukwa region where Mawingu Regional Hospital is located, the health administrators and managers made a valiant effort to support their employees, but the maternity ward—the proverbial black sheep of the hospital system—was always full of complications and exceptions, always consuming more supplies and financial resources than any other department. The financial strain was due, in part, to a Tanzanian government policy that dictates free care for pregnant women; they are exempt from hospital user fees. The maternity ward was, by far, the busiest one but brought in almost no money. Of the money the hospital collected in fees each day, the cost of regular maternity ward services amounted to three times the cash collected. These costs meant the hospital was nearly always operating at a loss, due almost exclusively to the burden of the care and material resources needed for pregnant women. The hospital was also dependent on the allocation of funds from the central government, which were delayed several times for the 2014–2015 fiscal year due to poor tax collection and other delays at the central government level (B. Mwasaga, personal communication November 2016; for more on this issue see Strong 2017). With these difficulties and constraints in mind, I return to the story of Tumaini.

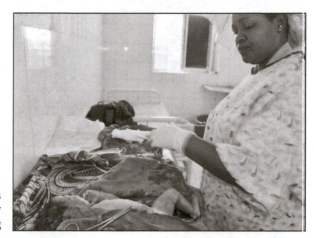

Nurse-midwife with a
newborn. Photo by
Adrienne Strong

Hospital Organization and Access to Supplies

Tumaini had arrived several hours into the night shift. Whereas the day shift (7 A.M. to 2:30 P.M.) usually had seven or eight nurses present, plus at least two or three doctors, the night shift was usually only minimally staffed. That shift lasted nearly 12 hours and, though followed by a sleeping day, had the power to ruin the nurses' personal or household schedules for considerable periods of time. Night shifts also resulted in sleep deprivation if the practitioners were unable to sleep during their sleeping days. Also, during the night shift, none of the maternity ward physicians were present at the hospital, which had no on-call room or similar place for the doctors to rest. Usually there was only one doctor, across the hospital grounds, in the Out-Patient Department and often he was not a full MD but an AMO—assistant medical officer—who had less training and, almost certainly, less experience with the complicated emergencies pregnant women could experience. To reach the maternity ward MD on call, if the nurses required his help, an entire chain of events and communication was necessary, resulting in delays of various lengths, sometimes hours.

On the night she arrived, Tumaini was lucky that the ward was relatively well stocked, though Nurse Linda had to go in search of normal saline because the ward was low on intravenous fluids. Also, Tumaini was fortunate that blood was available for a transfusion. The blood supply at the hospital depended on several factors, including the availability of donors, which often fluctuated throughout the calendar year. Many Tanzanians do not like to donate blood for fear of finding out their HIV status; others are ineligible due to having malaria, syphilis, or low blood-iron levels. These donor-related influences, combined with poor infrastructure in Tanzania, can make it difficult to collect, screen, and preserve blood, further reducing what is available during an emergency like Tumaini's. In cases where blood is not available,

Supply trolleys after a busy shift on the maternity ward. Photo by Adrienne Strong

the nurses are often left without any further ability to help their patients. This combination of human and material resource shortages is not unique to Mawingu Regional Hospital but is often a fact of life in many lower-income, lower-resource settings globally (Penfold et al. 2013).

Nurses, Supplies, and Blame

For the nurses on the maternity ward, the lack of supplies and money added stress to the already complicated task of providing care to pregnant women and their babies. Nurse Rachel once told me,

> For now, the current work environment has become difficult. And now equipment. Now you are told there are no medicines. We arrive at work, you will find me, I'm on the maternity ward there in the labor room, you find that the mother you're helping there, even to start a drip [IV]— there's nothing. You find the labor ward has dextrose, D5%,[7] now there you encounter a mother there who has eclampsia [a convulsive state], PPH [postpartum hemorrhage]. How do you help her? Truthfully, this environment is very difficult. . . . Many times the women here, they have problems. There are no supplies. It's necessary for them [the mothers] to buy a thing but they don't have any money. . . . The mother, you just look at her. I stay there with her, alright, [but] it is only God that helps a person to give birth or not. The baby has come out, s/he hasn't cried. Really, honestly the environment is hard.

Rachel is expressing here not only a frustration with the lack of supplies on the maternity ward but also a sense of powerlessness or helplessness when she is unable to help a woman who has developed a problem, such as when the baby is born but does not immediately cry. It is not that Rachel does not have the nursing skills or knowledge to help her patients but that her work environment does not allow her to use those skills, due to severe shortages of supplies. Many other nurses echoed Rachel's thoughts.

---

[7] Dextrose 5% is used to treat maternal exhaustion, dehydration and low blood sugar, but is not used to support women with fluid loss or to help support blood pressure, and therefore would not be useful if a woman was suffering from eclampsia or postpartum hemorrhage PPH.

As Megan noted, women like Tumaini were often poor subsistence farmers; it was difficult if not impossible for them or their relatives to access the cash necessary to buy medications or other supplies (e.g., gloves or urinary catheters) at private pharmacies. In an emergency, if a woman needed medicine or other supplies not available at the hospital, her family would try their best to obtain them. Yet their lack of resources could result in long delays, thereby threatening the mother's life, and/or the baby's. In these situations, the nurses were helpless. Nurses like Rachel were most often responsible for telling a patient or her family members that they needed to purchase medications or supplies. Sometimes family members would misinterpret this information as a sign of corruption, thinking the nurse was hiding supplies in order to extort money from patients. In other cases, family members blamed nurses for not providing high-quality care, even if the environment in which the nurses worked precluded best practices due to the scarcity lurking around every corner. Nurse Halima described it this way:

> You find someone comes, she needs to be cared for, you fail to care for her like is necessary. And many people from here [Rukwa] they don't have any [economic] means. To say, maybe, go, buy something, bring it for your patient, maybe, for example, you say Ringers Lactate [IV fluid]—right now there isn't any, if you tell [the relatives] to go find Ringers, they will be distraught; they don't have any money, and the baby there will continue to get tired. So, this environment is difficult. But, at the end of the day, the [relatives] . . . can't [comprehend] that there are no supplies, they will blame you like, "You, nurse, what have you done?" Or [say] that you have caused something. But to look if the environment in which you work is difficult—they can't see.

And Nurse Peninah added,

> I think it's really the fault of the hospital—from the beginning there—if in the past they were training those [patients] that "you, if you go to the big hospital, it's necessary that there are these and these and these and these necessary items or you will have to pay," they would prepare early, but right now it has come suddenly that things have run out and they got used to if you go to the hospital everything is free, and now they have been told "go buy this." She will see you, you are telling her to buy it and think that you are eating [the money].

"Eating money" is a Swahili expression that, in Tanzania, connotes corruption or bribery. Through advocacy and education campaigns, community members now know that health care for pregnant women is always supposed to be free in any government health facility and that all items necessary for their care should be available in the hospital (or any other health facility). In 2015, when Peninah told me this, the reality no longer matched the rhetoric (if it ever did); thus, the lack of supplies in both Mawingu and other lower-level facilities often disappointed women and their relatives. The mismatch between expectations and reality created conflict between pregnant women and their relatives and their health care providers, especially the nurses. Occasionally, such a conflict might reach the hospital's top administrators, and nurses faced harsh reprimands. The nurses lacked their superiors' support, rarely received any praise, and were the front line in conflicts with patients or relatives, all adding to the stress of trying to care for women. Most of the nurses with whom I spoke suggested that improving the availability of supplies at the hospital would be the number one way to improve the work environment and, by extension, patient care.

Workplace Stress Resulting in Abusive Care

The stress of working in a hospital that had few of the needed supplies and unsupportive administrators sometimes led the nurses to take out their frustrations on patients. Martha, one of the maternity ward's previous "nurses in charge" (similar to a nurse manager), gave an example of how a lack of care from the hospital administrators for nurses working on the wards could impact morale and patient–nurse interactions:

> Another thing is the harassment that the nurse has gotten coming from the administration; maybe a [nurse] had a problem and she went there [to the administration] and she encountered bad language and she goes and transfers that to her patient. . . . I mean, the labor ward, you can't compare it to the surgical ward because there [on the surgical ward] there isn't any chaos such that a mother is kicking you, spraying you with poop, and whatnot.

Martha's graphic description of the chaos and dirtiness of the maternity ward also serves to illustrate the challenges of working there. Not only did the nurse-midwives have to deal with a shortage of supplies, but they were almost always exposed to potentially infectious bodily fluids. Nurses encountered the unpredictability of women in labor who responded differently (and sometimes even violently) to the pain of contractions, for which there was never any pain medication available. The administrators deal with their own professional frustrations by yelling at their subordinates, the ward nurses. The ward nurse transmits these frustrations to the one person below her in the status hierarchy—the laboring woman. When an already frustrated nurse encounters a "noncompliant" woman in labor, for instance, she might yell at and hit the woman. Moreover, women, including nurses themselves, highly value giving birth silently as a sign of strength, and births in the hospital are no exception. Nurses would congratulate women who labored silently and did not make noise while pushing, reprimanding or hitting those women who engaged in what the nurses thought of as unnecessary histrionics while in labor.

Ultimately, despite these conditions, most women had no choice other than Mawingu Hospital. And even if women did have money to pay for other services, it was unlikely that another facility had an environment that was significantly different than Mawingu's. As giving birth at home with relatives or a local midwife (TBA) becomes a less and less viable option, women have less and less choice about whether they want to give birth in a place like

A mother and her newborn at Mawingu Hospital. Photo by Adrienne Strong

Mawingu Hospital. Though the ward may offer women the best chances of survival in case of an emergency, giving birth there also brings a high likelihood of abuse, delays in care, or even neglect due to the overburdened nurses and doctors and scarce material resources.

Conclusion: Structurally Violent for All

Tumaini's case of postpartum hemorrhage might be categorized as a "near-miss event," because she easily could have died but did not. She was able to access transportation (the motorcycle) and reach the regional hospital despite delays in her home community. Tumaini also reached the ward when it was not busy and when there were sufficient supplies for her care. As Megan has shown, women like Tumaini are often victims of structural vulnerabilities or "structural violence" (Farmer et al. 2006). That women in rural areas in low-income countries are subject to structural violence is clear: their socioeconomic status, lack of formal education, and gender serve to disadvantage most over the course of their lives. In the context of childbirth, a lifetime of poor nutrition, hard labor, little decision-making autonomy, and little schooling work in consort to put women at risk for life-threatening pre- and postnatal emergencies (Danforth et al. 2009; Gabrysch and Campbell 2009; Mrisho et al. 2007; Pembe et al. 2008).

I have highlighted here the ways in which health care workers are also victims of structural violence, yet in a different way from pregnant women. I have shown how Tanzanian political-economic organization results in resource scarcity in the hospital, which subsequently limits the care nurse-midwives can provide. These same forces result in delayed pay and, through lack of personal protective equipment, expose health care workers to the risk of contracting an infectious disease from women and vice versa. Professional and personal frustrations grow freely in this difficult workplace environment and can lead nurses to engage in abusive interactions with some laboring women or to neglect others.

Perhaps most detrimental for the prospect of future improvement is the hopelessness and powerlessness that can set in after a nurse-midwife has worked in this environment for many years. Again and again, her efforts to improve the care she provides will be met with failure due to systemic constraints beyond her control, yet she will be repeatedly asked to meet with women and their families to deliver the bad news that they must seek supplies elsewhere or wait long hours for services. In these interactions, not only does the nurse expose herself to blame, but she might even expose herself to physical harm at the hands of distraught relatives, or legal repercussions after accusations of wrongdoing. Due to the nature of nursing work, tied as it is to historical notions of selfless and feminine caring, nurses are universally expected to care for patients with compassion and forbearance regardless of their work environment or lack of professional or emotional support. In places such as Mawingu Regional Hospital, in which the structural and work environments disallow this type of caring in so many instances, both nurse-midwives and their patients are frequently dissatisfied. Paying attention to the lived realities of working on maternity wards in low-resource environments will help us to identify ways to improve care for pregnant women by supporting those engaging in this work. Staff can be trained and encouraged to provide skilled and compassionate care, but without the necessary resources, the system they work in can ensure their failure to do so. Donors and government agencies must work to ensure a viable infrastructure for pregnancy and birth care in all low-resource countries.

Registering Births and Becoming Modern Parents in Dar Es Salaam

Summer Wood

As we have learned so far in this chapter, giving birth in Tanzania, either at home or in a health facility, presents laboring mothers and families with many challenges. On top of these, the family confronts an additional hurdle: registering the new baby's birth and receiving the child's birth certificate. While this process is taken for granted in most wealthy and middle-income countries, for the majority of Tanzanian parents, obtaining birth certificates for their children is a source of anxiety. In Tanzania and many other low-resource countries, the majority of children's births are not registered. UNICEF estimates that worldwide, the births of nearly one in four children under five years old today have never been registered, with the highest proportions of unregistered children residing in low-income countries in sub-Saharan Africa and South Asia (UNICEF 2017).

The Importance of Birth Registration

Birth registration is of crucial importance for children, families, health workers, and governments alike. First and foremost, birth registration is a basic human right established by the International Covenant on Civil and Political Rights in 1966 and reaffirmed in the UN Convention of the Rights of the Child in 1989. Birth certificates provide a legal identity document and proof of a person's age. Birth certificates can also be invaluable tools in enforcing human rights laws preventing child marriage, child labor, trafficking, and other human rights violations, and to protect women's rights to custody of their children in the event of divorce or widowhood (Dow 1998). In countries like Tanzania, a birth certificate is also required to access many educational and economic opportunities, such as attending a private school, taking the national university entrance exam, joining the military, working in many formal sector jobs, opening a bank account, and inheriting property. Thus, people without a birth certificate can face exclusion from many avenues to economic mobility during their lifetimes. Improving birth registration services is also beneficial to the governments of lower-income countries. Birth registration records kept by health facilities and local government offices provide a crucial source of vital statistical data that allow countries to track and measure their efforts to improve maternal and child health outcomes and to plan health systems services and financing (UNICEF 2013; Setel et al. 2007).

Although birth registration has long been something of an "orphan issue" in public health and international development circles, in the past decade there has been renewed interest in the issue of birth registration among experts in several fields, including global health, human rights, and development economics. A landmark study in *The Lancet* in 2007 referred to the persistently low rates of birth registration in poor countries as "the single most critical failure of development over the past 30 years" (AbouZahr et al. 2007:8). UN agencies, nongovernmental organizations, and researchers in fields such as epidemiology, human rights, and child development have used birth registration as an indicator to measure the progress countries are making toward improving children's rights, maternal and child health, health system data quality, and access to justice. Most recently, the UN's Sustainable Development Goals adopted birth registration as an official indicator of progress on the issue of "access to justice" (United Nations 2016). Birth registration data are used to track issues such as the proportion of babies born in a health facility, the number of people in a country who have access to a legal identity document, and the number of girls who are married before their 18th birthday, to cite a few examples.

Birth registration is also an ethnographically rich aspect of bringing a new child into the world, encompassing a diverse array of issues of interest to anthropologists, including cultural values and knowledge systems associated with birth, kinship and family structures, health systems and the political economy of health, and biological and legal citizenship. However, very few ethnographic studies of childbirth have asked parents in low-income countries about their experiences with or views of birth registration (cf. Jewkes and Wood 1998; Seo 2016).

Tanzania has historically had one of the lowest rates of birth registration in the world: until recently only 16% of children's births were officially registered (UNICEF 2013). Between 2010 and 2015, rates of birth registration for children under five began to increase, and the most recent data show that 26% of Tanzanian children under age five are now at least partially registered.[8] Rates of birth registration vary widely within Tanzania, from a low of 4% in the most rural and remote areas, to a high of 92% on the densely populated island of Zanzibar (TDHS-MIS 2016). However, despite these impressive recent gains, the rate of birth registration still lags behind that of other countries in sub-Saharan Africa.

Methods: How to Study Birth Registration

As I explored the issue of birth registration in Tanzania from 2010 to 2016, I realized that the complexity of this seemingly simple technical problem—how to make sure that babies' births are properly registered and that parents receive paper birth certificates—was what made it so interesting to study, and so challenging for countries like Tanzania to address.

I conducted extensive Swahili-language interviews with 154 heads of household (defined as parents, grandparents, and other primary caretakers of children under age 18) in three predominately low-income neighborhoods in the city of Dar es Salaam. Located on the Indian Ocean coast, Dar es Salaam is a large and dynamic city of well over four million people and is Tanzania's *de facto* capital. My household-based ethnographic research centered around listening to detailed birth narratives that addressed such issues as place of delivery (home or hospital) and birth experiences for each child in the family. I then asked parents and guardians about their experiences of trying to register children, whether newborn infants, older children, or even young adults. I also asked families about their overall health, their experiences with receiving health and education services for children, whether they considered birth registration to be a human right, and what improvements they would like to see in the current registration system. Additionally, I observed birth registration activities taking place at three municipal government offices where birth registration services in Dar es Salaam are provided, and I interviewed government representatives involved in planning and delivering birth registration services nationwide.

Small but Insurmountable: Barriers to Birth Registration

Following families through the birth registration process drew my attention to a series of barriers that seem small to policy makers but are often insurmountable for ordinary families. Economic barriers to birth registration include steep user fees at hospitals and clinics; punitive late registration fees;

---

[8] The term "partially registered" refers to children who have the *tangazo* birth announcement but do not have a paper birth certificate, meaning that the family has started but not completed the birth registration process, for one of the many reasons detailed in this chapter.

payment of bribes or "extra fees" to obtain the birth certificate; and costs for travel and lost work time necessary to make multiple, day-long visits to queue up at government offices in search of birth certificates. Social and cultural barriers include poverty and social marginalization, lack of accurate informa- tion about the registration process, low literacy skills, lack of social capital needed to navigate the complex birth registration process,[9] and social sham- ing of single mothers. Structural barriers include an overburdened and severely underfunded public health system, government offices that can often feel intimidating and unresponsive, lack of correct and user-friendly informa- tion about how birth registration works, and the complicated and confusing multistep registration process.

The birth registration process in Tanzania requires two separate docu- ments. First is the *tangazo,* or birth announcement, which should be issued to the parents before the newborn baby leaves the health facility. In practice, the nurses and midwives in many delivery wards are too overworked and under- staffed to ensure that every baby is discharged with their birth announcement form, and sometimes the paper form itself is out of stock. Parents are expected to take the birth announcement form to a local government office and exchange it for an official birth certificate, or *cheti cha kuzaliwa,* within 90 days of the baby's birth. For babies born at home[10] the process is even more complicated, requiring multiple visits to local government offices to obtain both the *tangazo,* and then the *cheti cha kuzaliwa.*

The official policy is that children should be registered for free within 90 days of their birth. However, I found that fewer than 10% of my interviewees were actually able to register children for free. Those who did receive free reg- istration were almost all middle-class parents with sufficient education to confidently and correctly navigate the system during the 90-day free registra- tion window, but not those low-income parents who had the greatest eco- nomic need for free registration. As mentioned previously, the birth of a new baby is already an expensive life event, and the costs of the *vifaa* (birth sup- plies) that women must bring to the health facility where they give birth mean that generally little money is left over after the baby is born to pay the fees for a birth certificate (Spangler 2011). As one mother, Latifa, explained to me:

> When you go to give birth, if you do not bring all the *vifaa* that are
> required, the nurse might shout at you and you can feel very embarrassed
> that you are not prepared. If the nurse gets annoyed with you, she will

9   See footnote 4 for the definition of social capital. Social capital is often needed to navigate the complex birth registration process in Tanzania. For example, many low-income parents described to me their lack of confidence in interacting with government office workers, not feeling that they had the "right" to make demands of the staff due to their own perceived lack of social status/capital. Some families found that bringing along an older relative, such as a grandmother, or a relative or friend who could read and write well, helped them to bridge this social status gap and better advocate for themselves.

10 Approximately 50% of births in Tanzania occurred at home in 2010, falling to 37% of births at home in 2015, according to the most recent Tanzania Demographic and Health Survey (TDHS-MIS 2016).

not take the time after the baby is born to give the *tangazo* so that you can register. That is why my baby is not registered. . . . I can barely afford those services that are supposed to be free. Free birth registration? In terms of health, nothing is really free.

The complexity of the birth registration process introduces multiple opportunities for things to go awry through misinformation, mistakes, lost documents, and inevitable delays. This is especially true for low-income parents, who have many other demands on their time. Even when parents were motivated to register their children, it could take months or even years of persistent follow-up visits to various offices to obtain a birth certificate. During the time of this research, late registration fees began to accrue at three months of age, and continued to mount as the child ages, rising to as high as $20 US to register a child above age 10. Out of frustration, some parents may opt to pay unofficial "extra fees" in order to have their paperwork processed more quickly. These parents reasoned that paying "something extra" to a clerk up front in order to leave with a birth certificate in hand that day was a better bet than taking additional days off work to queue up and try to push the birth registration paperwork through the system using official channels. However, this was an option only available to those families with any income to spare. Although the official late fees are intended to encourage parents to register on time, in practice these fees may exceed the weekly or even monthly income of poor families, thus transforming birth registration, for many Tanzanians, from a basic right to an unattainable luxury.

Not "A Very Small Thing": The Importance of Studying Birth Registration

Given the lack of social scientific research on birth registration, I was not quite sure what I would discover as I knocked on doors and spent time in homes talking to families about this issue and how it impacted them and their children. Would people be interested in talking to me about a seemingly mundane bureaucratic issue, given all the other challenges they faced? When I began the research, one rather stern local government official informed me that birth registration was "a very small thing" that was "only women's business" and therefore totally unimportant. However, I found that ordinary people were, in fact, quite interested in birth registration. Certainly, for low-income families it was a much lower priority than basic needs such as food and water, shelter, school fees, health fees, and malaria medicine. But I found a high awareness of and support for birth registration, across lines of income, education, and religion.

Overall, close to 50% of the children in families I interviewed were at least partially registered, which is consistent with the overall higher rates of birth registration in Dar es Salaam because it is an urban area (TDHS-MIS 2016). In many families, there was a mix of children who were partially registered, fully registered, or unregistered, depending on factors such as whether an older child needed a birth certificate to attend school. The two factors most strongly associated with whether children were registered were: (1) whether at least one parent was registered, and (2) family income level.

While previous studies have argued that lack of knowledge or awareness about the importance of birth registration is often the primary barrier in developing countries like Tanzania (UNICEF 2013; Amo-Adjei and Annim 2015; Adi et al. 2015), I found that knowledge of the importance of birth registration was consistently high, even among parents and grandparents with the lowest levels of income and formal education. Almost everyone with whom I spoke knew what a birth certificate was and could name at least one reason that registering children was beneficial. Parents and grandparents were especially interested in the idea that having a birth certificate could help children to access better educational and economic opportunities in the future.

Amina and Serena: Neighbors but Worlds Apart

The challenges of acquiring birth registration are perhaps best illustrated by sharing perspectives from two new mothers living very different lives in the same central neighborhood of Dar es Salaam. Amina was the mother of three small children; she worked as a roadside food vendor near a major bus depot. Like many lower-income Tanzanian women, Amina helped to provide for her family by engaging in daily subsistence labor referred to as "small small business." I talked to her as she fried rounds of puffy chapatti bread over a small charcoal stove in preparation for her lunch-hour rush, charcoal smoke stinging her eyes as she worked over the fire. Although she had given birth less than a month earlier, Amina was already back at work. She had left the hospital where she gave birth without the *tangazo* document because she couldn't afford to stay any longer.

None of her children were registered, in large part because she could not afford to take a day off of work to queue at a government office to try to find out how to register her children. Her inability to read and write well also made her feel shy about trying to fill out paperwork. For Amina, the cost-benefit equation was stark: if she did not make and sell bread every day, her family would not eat that night. However, Amina told me she would very much have liked to get birth certificates for everyone in her family: "It makes many things in life easier if you have a birth certificate; it helps with many things such as education." Amina had a very practical suggestion to help the many Tanzanian mothers in her situation: "The government should set up special centers in neighborhoods where people can go and register. People like us, the poor, we are working every day just to feed our children; we cannot go and queue all day at a government office." For low-income families, the possible benefits of birth registration in future years seemed uncertain and distant, whereas the loss of income was an immediate problem.

A few minutes' walk away from Amina's small roadside food stall, I visited a young teacher and new mother, Serena, who lived in a tidy house behind a high, locked metal fence. The tile floors of her home were cool and spotless, and the walls of her living room were decorated with photos of her and her husband graduating from university. Serena was on maternity leave from the Christian private secondary school where she taught and her husband was an information technology (IT) consultant.

For many middle-class mothers like Serena, birth certificates have become something of a status symbol. Younger mothers with postsecondary education seemed to place a heavy emphasis on registering their children as early as possible so they could enroll them in private Pre-K "baby classes" and in private kindergartens. Serena was one such mother, and although her daughter was only three months old, she was already signed up for a "baby class" to promote early childhood development. Serena explained to me the importance of birth registration: "I registered my daughter within one month, because it will help her when she goes to school. It is not needed for public school, but you have to have it in order to attend the best private schools, and that is important if you want your child to get a good education. As a good parent, it should be your *first priority* to register your child." Serena had given birth in a private hospital and reported no problems with receiving her daughter's *tangazo*, which she accessed for free within 90 days as per the official government policy. However, she knew that her registration experience was made far easier by her social class and level of education. Serena was sympathetic to other mothers' experiences and observed that for most of the poorer families in her neighborhood, registering children was a very difficult process.

Conclusion: Visions for a New and Improved System

In urban areas such as Dar es Salaam, birth registration is increasingly becoming a signifier of social class and "modern" parenthood. Middle-class parents have the social and economic capital to ensure that their children are registered on time, and they view birth certificates as necessary to accessing quality education and other future opportunities. Paradoxically, middle-class parents who can afford to pay registration fees are able to register their children for free, while low-income families end up paying more for their children's birth certificate due to late fees and difficulties navigating the bureaucracy.

Tanzania has made steady progress in increasing rates of birth registration in recent years, as part of overall efforts to improve maternal and child health outcomes. This is a very welcome development, and registration rates for children under five are rapidly increasing. It remains to be seen whether the push to increase rates of birth registration could also have the side effect of placing additional strains on the already underresourced health system, especially maternal and child health services.

However, when I asked parents how they would like to see the current system improved, the vast majority still placed their trust in the health system to lead the push for better birth registration. I will end with a vision for a new and improved system, shared with me by Nadine, a hairdresser and mother of two children under age five. She said:

> When every baby is born, it is weighed by the nurse, and the weight is written down. Why can't birth registration be just like that? It should be done automatically, and right away after every baby is born. The government tells us it is important to have a birth certificate, so why don't they just send it home from the hospital along with the baby? Mama, baby, and birth certificate all together. We mothers would be very happy to see this change in the future. Then we would know that our children are registered, and they are known to the government as true Tanzanians.

Birth in Tanzania at the Crossroads of Choice and Policy

Our three sections explore the experiences of rural women giving birth with community midwives (*wakunga wa jadi*) and nurse-midwives working in hospitals, as well as rural and urban women's experiences registering their children's births. Several common threads run throughout the chapter, leading to concrete recommendations:

1. **The global importance of health indicators,** including percentage of women giving birth in health facilities, number of home births, maternal mortality ratio, and percentage of children with birth certificates, have become objects of fixation and take on power because the global community values them so highly as meaningful markers of more general progress or development required for funding and support from outside. Fixating on the numbers, however, conceals the complexity of the ways in which both women and their health care providers are struggling to improve their health, the health of their children, and the health of their patients in the face of inequity, scarcity, and structural violence. Numbers and development-driven maternal health policies have frequently become blind to the needs of those on the ground.

2. **The pervasive power of political-economic structures** is clear throughout. These structures act to allow some women and families to succeed, and others to fail. The same political-economic structures also function to reduce nurses' ability to care for pregnant mothers, to the point of abusing the women for whom they should be caring. Structural violence works on each of the levels we have discussed here, even though the actors in each case vary widely.

3. **The themes of choice and navigating complex bureaucracies** surface in each of the three parts. Fines for homebirths have essentially made biomedical health facilities the *only* acceptable and government-sanctioned place for giving birth, regardless of a woman's desires and emotional and sociocultural needs and of the lack of supplies and poor

quality of care in hospitals. Diminishing choices for women mean they have little recourse if they would prefer to give birth in a more nurturing environment, avoiding the disrespect and abuse they are apt to suffer in the hospital. Many nurses and doctors working in health facilities are aware that women have no alternatives (if they wish to avoid the new fines), particularly in remote areas of the country that lack a robust private practice system. "Customer service" is often minimal, yet women continue to return to hospitals and dispensaries that offer poor care because they have no other choice. Poor care becomes normalized as more and more women experience it, hear their female friends and relatives talk about it, and soon come to know little else. For policy makers, addressing the normalization of inattentive, even abusive care in institutions often takes a backseat to the more pressing concerns of saving the lives of women and babies with immediately needed emergency interventions. What these policy makers miss in focusing on short-term emergency care is the importance of addressing the normalization of bad care and abuse and replacing it with quality care, facilitated by adequate supplies in hospitals and a more supportive work environment. This other focus is a necessity for achieving long-term improvements in maternal and neonatal mortality.

4. **Women want to give birth in their communities. Dispensaries can be effective in saving lives and improving quality of care**, but they need to be adequately staffed and supported through resources from the central government. Most women prefer to take advantage of high-quality care close to their homes and, indeed, will be able to have healthy pregnancies and births in these locations if their health care providers receive the support they need. Homebirths can be made safe with skilled attendance and effective emergency transport available (see de Jonge et al. 2009, 2015; Cheyney et al. 2014; and Chapter 1). As Tanzania continues to improve both the quality of transportation infrastructure and provider availability, low-risk women without complications should not be fined for seeking support from their local *wakunga wa jadi*, whom they know and trust. We encourage Tanzania, and other low-resource countries, to consider innovative ways of enabling biomedical health care providers to visit women in their homes to ensure that each has access to skilled care during pregnancy, delivery, and the postpartum.

At the time of this writing (June 2018), there is no popular, widely used indicator to measure abuse or neglect in health facilities in lower-income countries. Global, national, and local policies and labyrinthine bureaucracies prevent women and their families from making free choices about place of birth or even about obtaining a birth certificate. Nurse-midwives working in hospitals have limited choices regarding how they wish to care for patients and what skills they would like to use due to scarce resources in their workplace and their constant states of stress and overwork. In all instances, these extremely limited ranges of choice for both practitioners and parents have detrimental consequences. As Megan wrote, though the government and organizations such as WHO envision access to health care services before, during, and after pregnancy as free choices that women can make, this chapter demonstrates *choiceless choice* in each of its three parts.

Despite the numerous challenges we have highlighted throughout this chapter, there are notable signs of success in Tanzania and other sub-Saharan African countries in the fight to reduce maternal deaths and improve maternal and neonatal health. We conclude with a few examples of recent innovative attempts in Tanzania to continue on a path of improvement and equal access for all women.

Innovations for Positive Change

In recent years, the Tanzanian government has been working steadily to improve access to birth registration. In 2013, the government partnered with UNICEF, the Tanzanian telecommunication company Tigo, and the nongovernmental organization VSO International to pilot test an innovative, mobile phone-based system for birth registration. Hospital staff in the Mbeya region of Tanzania used mobile phones to send birth registration data via SMS to the national birth registration database, and then issued new mothers birth certificates for their babies before they left the hospital, just as the mothers in Summer's study requested. Within six months, this pilot program had registered more than 150,000 children. The pilot was so successful that it has now been expanded to additional regions (UNICEF 2014).

A second project involving smartphone technology was launched in 2016 as a partnership between the Tanzanian and Canadian governments and UNICEF. In the two southern regions of Iringa and Njombe, parents can now register their children at most health facilities and local government offices, and through a new Android smartphone application, staff at the registration points can transmit data directly to a central data dashboard. Requiring only "one step, one visit" and making the birth certificate free of charge, this innovation has proven much more convenient for parents. The pilot program registered over 220,000 children under age five in its first month of operation alone, expanding access to birth registration to more than 700 locations compared with just 11 previously. This level of demand suggests what Summer's research showed: that families are eager to register their children if given the chance (Bedasa 2016). Both programs represent a hopeful step forward for Tanzania, responding to parents' concerns and offering innovative and practical solutions to increase birth registration.

As more and more people in countries such as Tanzania have access to smartphones and more reliable data networks, public health practitioners and policy makers seek ways to utilize this technology to improve health. In partnership with major funders, such as PEPFAR, the US Agency for International Development (USAID), and the Swiss Re Foundation, one of Tanzania's largest telecommunications companies, Vodafone, has, through its charitable foundation, partnered with several health organizations to implement a program called "Mobilising Maternal Health." The program aims to educate women about health during pregnancy through direct text messages, empower community health workers, refer women to treatment for the debilitating birth injury of obstetric fistula, and provide free transportation for woman and newborns when they are experiencing an emergency (Vodafone Foundation 2017). The organization's website says that more than 1,800 women and newborns have arrived at health facilities due to their "Uber Ambulance" program. Other numbers indicate that in less than one year, and operating in only two districts, the program transported more than 3,500 women in emergencies (Petronzio 2017).

The system works through local health care providers who connect the pregnant women needing transportation during an emergency to a local network of verified taxi drivers who then receive payment for their services via Vodafone's mobile money system (Petronzio 2017). While still in its early days and operating only in a limited number of areas in Tanzania's Lake Zone in the Northwest, the program's organizers believe these ambulance taxis are decreasing the time it takes women to reach a health facility that can provide emergency services, thereby addressing one of the biggest contributors to maternal death—poor government infrastructure[11] and lack of transportation (Petronzio 2017). While the Vodafone Foundation is currently paying the taxi drivers who work through the Uber Ambulance mobile phone service, organizers hope to make the system financially self-supporting.

Both of the above examples show that positive change can occur by utilizing innovative programs that take advantage of new technologies and changing landscapes of connectivity. Such technologies can help to circumvent government failures or lack of resources even as policy makers and states continue to work to improve health sector management and the availability of health services. Taken in turn, in conversation, and in synchrony, the voices of women, health care workers, policy makers, and states are generating new opportunities for improving health systems and, ultimately, the health of pregnant women and newborns. More babies are now receiving birth certificates, and more women are reaching facilities in a timely manner. Yet *what happens in those facilities* remains the most pressing problem these women and their caregivers face and must be addressed by providing much-needed funding to ensure the availability of "free care" and the necessary supplies these women arrive hoping and needing to receive.

For those women still wishing to give birth at home with their well-known and respected *wakunga wa jadi*, rather than fining them, their government should be supportive of their choices. The risks of developing complications or dying during pregnancy and giving birth are not uniformly determined by

---

[11] The program allows women to circumvent the government's health infrastructure, which does not have facilities close enough to enough women and has very few ambulances.

biology but are structured by access to resources, including nutrition and health care before the childbearing years and throughout the woman's life. As previously noted, many births for low-risk women can safely take place at home, and that choice can become a safer one as the availability of emergency transportation increases. For as long as Tanzanian hospitals are themselves unsafe, the more reasonable and viable the choice for homebirth remains.

THOUGHT QUESTIONS

1. Many of the challenges facing maternal health care in Tanzania are interrelated. Come up with at least three of these and discuss where you would start to address them and why.

2. What might the Tanzanian government and local communities do to try to deter women from giving birth at home? In what ways is the goal of reducing home-births problematic in the first place?

3. If you were a health administrator in a hospital in a low-resource country, what might you try to implement to improve conditions for your staff? Come up with three ideas that do not involve spending any money from your limited budget.

4. Based on Summer's description of birth registration processes, and the mobile phone registration programs, what other solutions would you design to ensure that families can obtain birth certificates?

RECOMMENDED FILMS

Dead Mums Don't Cry examines the problem of maternal mortality and efforts to reduce these deaths in Central Africa. The documentary follows one obstetrician in a hospital in Chad. Slightly dated now but still a great resource for learning about maternal health in sub-Saharan Africa. Available on YouTube: https://www.youtube.com/watch?v=OMt8Ubp6w2Q

A Walk to Beautiful is a documentary about obstetric fistula, a childbirth complication that almost exclusively affects women in sub-Saharan Africa and south Asia, and is related to access to health care services and infrastructure.

No Woman No Cry is a documentary by fashion icon Christy Turlington Burns that she produced after she experienced life-threatening complications during her first birth. The documentary covers the stories of women and their health care providers in four countries, including Tanzania, Bangladesh, Guatemala, and the United States in their fight to prevent pregnancy-related mortality.

Birth: The Midwives' Fight for Life in Africa is a half-hour-long documentary produced by the organization AMREF following four women engaged in improving health for pregnant women in Senegal. The documentary provides a view into health facilities, homes, and training for midwives. Available on YouTube: https://www.youtube.com/watch?v=mWfKP2DUoKY

Nyamakuta, The One Who Receives: An African Midwife is the story of a local midwife (traditional birth attendant). It is available through most libraries.

4

Comparing Childbirth in Brazil and Japan

Social Hierarchies, Cultural Values, and the Meaning of Place

K. Eliza Williamson and Etsuko Matsuoka

Our chapter, based on ethnographic research in Japan and Brazil, illustrates how the *places* of birth—and the social, political, and economic contexts they reflect and reproduce—shape birth practices and mirror broader cultural values and social realities in both countries. Of course, like cultures, birth models are not stagnant. They are always in flux and facing insistent challenges, even if they have core features that remain more or less constant. Here we pay special attention to *how birth care is changing* in both countries, but particularly in Brazil, where the dominant paradigm for birth care is undergoing significant changes. Brazil's movement to "humanize" childbirth, as we will show, draws part of its inspiration from the Japanese model of maternity care. Although rates of interventions such as cesarean section are on the rise in Japan—a topic we address below—the comparatively low-intervention Japanese birth practices serve as an inspiration for those seeking to reformulate birth in Brazil. We therefore also highlight collaborations between Brazil and Japan that have contributed significantly to an ongoing paradigm shift in Brazilian obstetrics. In our "Discussion and Conclusion" section, we highlight how birth in both countries reflects important features of each society, and especially how location influences how childbirth is viewed and practiced, affecting relationships between the social actors involved, sources of authoritative knowledge, and balances of power.

The transition from home to hospital has never been complete, in part because where birth takes place is never just about "progress" or the relative safety of the location; it is also a complex mixture of historically and culturally specific knowledge practices, ideological power struggles, and economic circumstances (Jordan 1993; Davis-Floyd 2003, 2018a, b; Rothman 2016). When Japan and its allies lost WWII in 1945, 98% of Japanese women were having babies at home. The subsequent reform initiated by US occupation forces, which included a group of American nurse-midwives, set a standard of institutional birth. By the end of the 1960s, most Japanese births were taking place in hospitals.

Brazil's long and uneven transition (from the 1930s to the 1970s) from home to hospital was hastened by interrelated concerns around hygiene and social progress at the turn of the 20th century. Yet this transition was slow because of the relative scarcity of hospitals and clinics, and because of women's resistance to giving birth outside the home. At first, hospitals and "maternity houses" had a reputation for being generally reserved for indigent women and complicated cases where the mother would likely die (Amaral 2008; Mott 2002; Otovo 2016). As birth in health institutions has become the norm in both Brazil and Japan, birth activists have had to fight both the medical establishment and the state for the right to give birth elsewhere (Matsuoka 2014).

Place of birth matters, not only in terms of differing outcomes, but also in terms of women's experiences. As Jordan (1993) has noted, who is authorized to accompany a woman in labor, which laboring and birthing positions are offered as possibilities, what artifacts are used, and how birth is conceptualized—all of these vary according to the place of birth and its cultural and historical contexts. Even where hospitals are widely accepted as the "normal" place to have babies, many women's preferences diverge from this norm.

Stratified Birth in Brazil: Place, Race, Class, and Technomedical Hegemony

K. Eliza Williamson

Brazil is a country of immense diversity in which there have always been multiple, coexisting ways of knowing about and doing childbirth. From Amerindian Indigenous peoples in remote Amazonian villages to cosmopolitan professionals of Italian and Japanese ancestry in São Paulo, from Afro-descendant traditional midwives in the arid northeastern interior to white obstetricians in the coastal capitals, knowledge and practices surrounding childbirth are multiple, situated, and constantly contested.[1] Despite this diversity, however, the dominant mode of bringing children into the world hews closely to what Davis-Floyd (2001; 2018a, b) calls the "technocratic model of birth": doctor-centered and heavy on medical technologies and interventions. Particularly since the latter half of the 20th century, the vast majority of women give birth in hospitals and, increasingly, by cesarean section (CS).

---

[1] For more on the rich variety of "traditional" midwifery practices in Brazil, see for example Carvalho, Chacham, and Viana (1998) and Fleischer (2007).

The rate of CS delivery in Brazil is currently a staggering 55% (Leal et al. 2012). While moving childbirth from home to hospital has reduced deaths from postpartum hemorrhage and obstructed labor, public health experts argue that the excessive use of medical technologies and interventions has actually ended up contributing to poor maternal and neonatal outcomes (Victora et al. 2011). Premature births have hit an all-time high, in part because of a rise in the number of babies surgically removed from the uterus before they have fully finished developing (Leal et al. 2016). This scenario constitutes what Simone Diniz calls Brazil's "perinatal paradox," akin to the obstetric paradox described in Chapter 1 of this volume: despite the hospitalization of birth and the increasing availability of obstetric technologies, maternal and infant health indicators have been slow to improve (Diniz 2009). Recent developments, however, show that the paradigm is slowly shifting.

Nevertheless, mothers continue to die from childbirth complications at rates disproportional to the country's economic development—68.2/100,000 live births (Szwarcwald et al. 2014). And while public health interventions successfully brought down infant mortality rates in recent decades, neonatal mortality remains high at 11.1 deaths per 1,000 live births (Lansky et al. 2014). Childbirth is deeply inflected with the social inequalities that characterize contemporary Brazil, and adverse health outcomes are unevenly distributed: the poor and working-class, Black, Brown, and Indigenous people, and those in the North and Northeast regions are all more likely to suffer the consequences of inadequate health care (Coimbra et al. 2013; IPEA 2017; Rasella, Aquino, and Barreto 2013). Black and Indigenous women are disproportionately represented in the numbers for maternal mortality and morbidity (Dalsgaard 2004; Martins 2006; Szwarcwald et al. 2016).

The two-tiered structure of health care in Brazil reflects these pervasive inequities: on the one hand, there is a vast and complex, but chronically underresourced, public health system (the *Sistema Único de Saúde*, or SUS) that provides services free of charge to all citizens and is funded primarily through taxes; on the other hand, there is a disjointed conglomeration of private hospitals and clinics paid for out-of-pocket or through "health plans" (*planos de saúde*).[2] Roughly three-quarters of the population use the SUS exclusively, while the remaining quarter has access to some form of private health care. While almost all Brazilians utilize the SUS at one time or another—for yearly vaccinations, for example—those with financial means usually opt for private services when it comes to medical care, including

---

[2] Health plans in Brazil are akin to health insurance in the United States. Paying a monthly fee, clients gain access to specific services, hospitals, and professionals. The amount of coverage varies widely with the price of the plan. Some of the most affordable cover prenatal care, but not childbirth, and many have a period of *carência* (like US health insurance plans' deductibles) in which certain services are not covered until the client has made a certain number of monthly payments. Women whom Eliza has interviewed who reported having health plans—or who looked into purchasing them—for pregnancy and birth coverage told her that many of the most affordable plans had a *carência* period of exactly 10 months. That is to say, they are purposely designed *not* to cover birth unless women were already subscribers before becoming pregnant.

childbirth. It tends to be the case, therefore, that SUS maternity services attend primarily women who are poor or in the low- to middle-income brackets (Paim et al. 2011). As we will see below, this class differentiation has important impacts on which women have which kinds of births and where.[3]

Birth in Bahia

Here I present two birth stories of women in Salvador, the coastal capital of the state of Bahia. Salvador is home to the largest Afro-descendent population outside of the African continent, and yet Black Bahians make up a disproportionate slice of the poor and working classes (Collins 2015; Perry 2013; Smith 2016). The average monthly income of Black and Brown people (*pretos* and *pardos*) in the city is nearly three times lower than that of Whites (*brancos*) (IBGE n.d.)—just one of the many indicators that Brazil's racialized social hierarchy continues to heavily condition the life chances of its citizens.

My dissertation research, conducted between 2012 and 2017, focused on the implementation of federal health policy geared toward improving maternal and infant health care in the SUS. Here I draw primarily on interviews conducted with women and health care professionals, as well as participant observation carried out in two maternity care services in Salvador—one maternity hospital and one birth center.

Bahian Birth Story: Ana Paula. Ana Paula, 32 years old, had just become a mother for the second time when we sat down in the unfinished living room of her home in Simões Filho, a small satellite city about an hour's bus ride from the center of Salvador. Ana Paula, who identifies as parda, gave birth to her daughter Camila in Salvador's first and only (to date) Normal Birth Center—an experience she describes as "unforgettable."[4] It contrasted starkly with the birth of her son, Gabriel, 13 years earlier in a municipal general hospital, which she described as "aggressive." The scene when she arrived in labor was like that of many public hospitals in Salvador and the rest of the country: "It was just one birth after the other":

> When I got there, they did the vaginal exam [*exame de toque*], and I was three centimeters dilated. The doctor admitted me, saying, "Ah, she'll stay here because she'll have her baby later." I arrived at 9:00 in the morning. . . . At 5:00 P.M. I started to feel very weak pains. . . . He was born at 9:10 P.M. The pain really began to get strong when I entered the delivery room. . . . Since he was high up [in the uterus] and wouldn't

---

[3] For literature on homebirth in Brazil, see Davis-Floyd and Georges (2018); Menezes, Portella, and Bispo (2012); Schut (2014).

[4] Normal Birth Centers (Centros de Parto Normal) are maternity care units designed exclusively for uncomplicated, vaginal deliveries. In NBCs, women remain in one room throughout labor, delivery, and 24 hours postpartum, with their babies and at least one labor companion of their choosing. Nurse-midwives (*enfermeiras obstetras*) are central in NBC labor care; obstetricians are optional. Current regulations require NBCs to be built inside or next to hospitals. Freestanding NBCs existing before the 2015 legislation, such as the one in Salvador, can continue to function and receive government funding, but no more will be built.

come down, [the doctor] had to get up on the bed to push [on my belly] with her arm. . . . It hurt a lot. (Interview with Ana Paula, April 7, 2016)

At the municipal hospital, Ana Paula was subjected to several practices still common despite concerted efforts to reduce or eradicate them. She was admitted in very early labor and hooked up to an oxytocin drip to bring on stronger contractions.[5] She was then left lying in a hospital bed until her cervix dilated fully. Later, just when her contractions were at their strongest, the doctor performed the Kristeller maneuver—also called fundal pressure, where the clinician pushes down on the fundus or the top of the uterus with the strength of their bodyweight to help press the baby through the vaginal canal. This method is now widely discouraged in obstetric practice, as no quality evidence of its benefits exists, and it carries significant risk (Hofmeyr et al. 2017; Ministry of Health of Brazil 2017; World Health Organization 1996).[6]

For her second birth, Ana Paula said that from the first moment she visited the Normal Birth Center (NBC), she knew she wanted to have her baby there. The staff gave her a sense of "peace, [and] that marvelous care [atendimento] they have there . . . I didn't see a better place to have my daughter. . . . And I kept praying, asking God for everything to go well so I could have her there. And, thank God, it did!" Since the birth center's admission protocol is strict, she had to make sure all her medical exams and prenatal appointments were up-to-date. She did a preliminary consultation with one of the center's nurse-midwives, in which these exams and prenatal records were evaluated to see if she fit the "profile." Because NBCs are not equipped to perform cesareans and can provide only limited emergency support to mothers and babies with acute complications, Ana Paula's medical records had to demonstrate that her pregnancy was "normal risk" (risco habitual). She was ready to jump through these hoops; she had always preferred normal birth, she told me, because it was "really more natural."

The first contrast to her previous birth experience was that she was not admitted in early labor. When she and her partner Denilson showed up at the birth center shortly after her mucus plug came out, the nurse-midwife who examined her told them to go home and relax, to let her labor progress more before she came back. She followed these instructions and returned a few hours later, her contractions intensifying. Also very unlike her first birth, at the NBC Ana Paula had the company of family members (Denilson and her sister-in-law) and a volunteer doula throughout labor, delivery, and 24 hours postpartum—a luxury practically unheard of in Bahian public health services until just a few years ago, and still rare. The emotional support they provided, she says, made all the difference. Ana Paula gave birth in a special bed that allowed her to push her daughter out in an upright position. After little

[5] At 3 cm, Ana Paula would have been in what is known as the "latent phase" of labor, a phase that can last many hours or even days. Normal, uncomplicated pregnancies do not need to be monitored in a hospital during this phase. "Active labor" is defined as beginning at 6 cm dilation.
[6] The evidence-based way to encourage the baby to move down is for the mother to be upright and mobile during labor and pushing (see, for example, Gupta, Hofmeyr, and Shehmar 2012).

Camila was born, the obstetrician placed her immediately in Ana Paula's arms, the vernix still clinging to the baby's smooth skin.[7] All the pain she had felt just moments before disappeared (*sumiu*), and for the next several moments Ana Paula felt as if she were in a dream. "All I wanted to do was look at her, just look and look and look." It was an emotional scene; her sister-in-law "cried a ton" (*chorou horrores*).

Ana Paula's first birth reflects what vaginal delivery is like for most Brazilian women—full of medical interventions not based on solid scientific evidence, in an assembly-line atmosphere where she felt abandoned (*largada*). Her second birth, in the Normal Birth Center, represents what only a small minority of Brazilian women experience in childbirth, and the paradigm toward which recent maternal and infant health care policy in Brazil aims: minimal intervention, continuous labor support, and low technology. It is precisely in between these two paradigms—technocratic and humanistic— that Brazilian birth care currently sits (Davis-Floyd 2018a; Davis-Floyd and Georges 2018).

Bahian Birth Story: Aline.   On the other end of the economic spectrum, we have Aline, a middle-class birth activist who lives in a gated housing complex in one of Salvador's satellite cities. On the day of our interview, after she picked me up in her small SUV, we sat and talked in the beautifully tended garden of the subdivision's leisure area. Aline became a birth activist after she had her first child several years ago. When she told her obstetrician that she wanted a normal (vaginal) birth, his response was that, for him, it wasn't "worth it":

> The first obstetrician told me, "Look, it's like this: before, I earned 3,000 *reais* [about $1,000 USD] to do a normal birth, and [I had] to be available either 15 days before or 15 days after [the expected due date]. It was worth it. Today, your health plan pays me 600 *reais* [$200]. And 600 *reais*, for me, isn't worth it for me to not go to conferences, to stop everything, to stop traveling with my family. . . . If you have a false labor alarm, your health plan pays me 70 or 80 *reais* [$23–$27] to come here and do a consultation with you. It doesn't pay my toll and my gas. So I can't be available for that [normal birth] anymore." (Interview with Aline, August 24, 2016)

Like Aline, many middle-class women I spoke with hear from their private-practice obstetricians that normal birth simply doesn't pay enough. Doctors like Aline's often blame health plans that offer insufficient reimbursement for their work. For many, it is simply "not worth it," financially speaking, to make oneself available for spontaneous labor onset and vaginal delivery. This argument then becomes justification for doing only cesarean births, which is how a large number of private-practice obstetricians in Salvador work.

---

[7] Vernix (*vernix caseosa*) is a white, filmy substance that covers newborns' skin when they are born. Evidence-based pediatrics recommends leaving this protective covering for several hours after the birth (rather than giving the infant a bath right away), as it has several important benefits for the skin (Visscher et al. 2005).

Planned cesareans are scheduled ahead of time and take about an hour from start to finish. Normal labor and delivery are much less predictable, so that obstetricians must be on call during a period of about a month surrounding the estimated due date.

Clinical justifications—real or invented—are also used to convince women that their babies must be delivered surgically. Several of my interlocutors, including Aline, mentioned that their obstetricians told them their babies would be too large to deliver vaginally:

> The pregnancy went along, and he did ultrasounds in his office. And in one ultrasound he said the baby was too big. . . . And then came a day when he said again the baby was too big—"and you still want a normal birth?!" I said, "Yes, I do!" And he turned to me and said, "You don't have pity on your genitalia." And he turned to my husband and said, "She doesn't have pity on your marriage."

Not only did Aline's obstetrician suggest, repeatedly, that her baby was simply too large to be born vaginally, he also brandished the widely perpetuated myth that normal delivery permanently stretches out the vagina and diminishes men's pleasure in heterosexual intercourse. His logic was both flawed and misogynist. But at the time, Aline told me, she had little access to alternative information. She even thought her doctor's comment was quite normal. The obstetrician scheduled her delivery at just over 39 weeks gestation.

As it turned out, Aline went into labor a day before her CS was scheduled. She stayed at home for several hours, waiting for her contractions to increase in intensity and frequency before calling her doctor. When she did, he was serendipitously on his way to the hospital to attend to some other business. He told her to meet him there.

> And then I got to the hospital, with clear labor contractions. Maybe it wasn't active labor, but it was latent labor. And he came and said that he wanted to send me in for a cesarean section. And I said to him, "But couldn't we try [normal birth]?" And he responded as if I were crazy for trying to have a normal birth with an almost 4.5-kilo baby.

During the surgical procedure, Aline felt "invisible." Her doctor did not look at or address her or her partner, who was in the room filming. Instead he joked around and told stories about other colleagues to the other clinical staff present:

> What impresses me is that it wasn't just us, you know? It was being filmed. [It was as if, for the doctor] nothing existed. Really, we did not exist. . . . I think if he had been able to minimally perceive that there was a camera on, even if he didn't have consideration [for us], he would at least shut his mouth and not talk about his colleagues. But no! The invisibility was so great that, in fact, he wasn't even aware of it.

Aline's experience led her to fight for other women in similar circumstances, and she is now a dedicated birth activist and photographer. When she became pregnant a second time, she actively sought a home birth and succeeded in delivering a nearly 5-kilo baby at home, in a warm tub, surrounded by her family (small terrier included), with a holistic obstetrician as her birth attendant and a doula by her side.[8]

Brazil's Cesarean Dilemma: The Public, the Private, and the In-Between

While the overall approach to childbirth in Brazil is predominantly technocratic and "interventionist" (*intervencionista*), the specific features of interventionist logic are decidedly different in public versus private health care. This fact only drives home the point that when it comes to childbirth, *place matters*—both physical place (hospital, birth center, home) and one's "place" in the socioeconomic hierarchy. The CS rates reflect Brazil's social inequalities and are quite differently distributed among the two health care sectors. Whereas cesarean sections make up 45.5% of births in the SUS, they make up almost 88% in private medicine (Leal et al. 2012).

Since CS births are so strongly associated with paid private health care, CS itself has come to be seen as a marker of class status. Some scholars, such as Dominique Béhague (2002), even point out that poor women receiving obstetric care in the public sector use various strategies—the famous Brazilian *jeitinho* ("little way," referring to any number of creative ways to bypass official procedures—see, for example, DaMatta 1984)—to obtain cesareans even when not clinically indicated. For Béhague, poor women demand CS because they see that their wealthier counterparts are able to "choose" surgical delivery in private hospitals, whereas they have no such choice in public maternity institutions. Their use of such strategies to get CS, then, represents a form of resistance to this injustice. Overall, Brazilian women face what Cecilia McCallum calls a "double jeopardy." They are caught between public obstetric care—which often means inhumane treatment and many routine and often aggressive interventions, including episiotomy[9]—and private obstetric care, where they are almost guaranteed a CS delivery (McCallum 2016). In other words, they can expect to get either "the cut above" or "the cut below" (Diniz and Chacham 2004).

The question of why exactly Brazil's CS rate is so high has been the subject of much public and scholarly debate. Some, including medical professionals, say women themselves want surgical deliveries. Women are afraid of pain in labor, they say, and worried that vaginal delivery will "ruin" their genitalia (Faúndes and Cecatti 1991; Faúndes et al. 2004; see also Edmonds 2010). Further research has repeatedly countered this assertion that women

---

[8] See Davis-Floyd and Georges (2018) for descriptions of Brazil's holistic OBs, many of whom do or did attend homebirths until they were prohibited from doing so.

[9] Episiotomy is a surgical cut made in the perineal tissue at the vaginal opening (between the vagina and the anus) in order to aid in difficult deliveries. Once routinely performed on most women, episiotomy is now recommended only in a minority of cases—5%–10% (Mayo Clinic 2015).

want CS, showing that, in fact, the majority of women begin their pregnan-cies wanting normal birth but change their minds as their due dates approach, often convinced by their own doctors to opt for surgical delivery (Domingues et al. 2014; Hopkins 2000; Potter et al. 2008). It is certainly true that many Brazilian women *do* want cesarean sections (Portela 2018). It is also clear, however, that the actual CS rate far outweighs women's reported preferences for the procedure. Importantly, *where* a woman gives birth heavily conditions *how* she will give birth.

Labor and birth in public hospitals, whether it ends in vaginal or cesar-ean delivery, is rife with interventions. Typically, women are restricted to their beds and instructed to lie down flat and receive intravenous drips of syn-thetic oxytocin to speed up labor. They undergo frequent vaginal examina-tions, the harmful and risky Kristeller maneuver, and episiotomies. Only 5% of women give birth without any of these interventions (Leal et al. 2012). On the other hand, practices backed by scientific evidence and considered benefi-cial often go un- or underused, such as the support of a companion through-out labor and delivery and upright movement to facilitate labor progress (Leal et al. 2014). Added to this is the verbal and sometimes physical abuse women often endure at the hands of the hospital staff charged with caring for them (Aguiar and d'Oliveira 2011), creating a scenario in which "painless" CS is an enticing alternative (Barros et al. 1991; Barbosa et al. 2003). In fact, this tendency is so prevalent in both public and private hospitals that the birth activist movement has begun using the slogan, "Enough with violent birth to sell cesarean!" (*Chega de parto violento para vender cesárea!*) (*A Pública* 2013).

In the private health care sector, there are generally two ways pregnancy and birth care might go, depending on one's health plan coverage and ability to pay out-of-pocket for services. More affordable health plans tend to cover prenatal and birth care in a small number of clinics and hospitals. Women with these plans generally see one obstetrician throughout prenatal care, then go to the private hospital where labor and delivery care is provided by the medical team on shift. Those with access to the more expensive health plans or the resources to pay providers directly often have the same obstetrician for prenatal care and birth. In these cases, women and their obstetricians typi-cally schedule a birth date that matches up more or less with the estimated due date. On the day of the surgery, doctors meet their patients at the desig-nated hospital, where the woman is given an epidural and prepared for CS. About 70% of women who give birth in private hospitals do not go into spon-taneous labor at all (*A Pública* 2013).

While public and private health care sometimes seem worlds apart, they also share much, including health care professionals, for example. Many of the same doctors and nurses who work shifts in public maternity hospitals also attend in private hospitals or clinics (McCallum 2005), and as I discov-ered, public health services are sometimes used as a kind of extension of phy-sicians' private clinics. One of my interlocutors, Lorena, explained to me that she chose her prenatal doctor specifically because he worked both in the private prenatal clinic near her home and also at the nearby public maternity hospital. Her health plan covered prenatal care, but not the delivery, so she knew she would have to give birth in the public sector. Her first son had been born by CS a few years earlier, and Lorena was "scared to death" of vaginal delivery, so she strategically cultivated a personal relationship with her obstetrician in order to get a surgical birth. She knew that without establishing this connection, she would potentially be subjected to the vaginal delivery she so feared. She was successful: her prenatal doctor "scheduled" her cesarean during one of his shifts at the public hospital, writing in her patient chart that her baby was too big to be born vaginally, which wasn't true.

Lorena's story illustrates the interconnection between public and private health care in Brazil, as well as the ways in which both patients and providers must "game the system" in order to get or provide the care they see as most desirable. Women know that where they give birth matters, and they know that CS is much easier to come by in private hospitals—or, in Lorena's case, in public hospitals used as extensions of private practice. Lorena's fear of vaginal

Obstetric unit in a public hospital in Salvador. The door on the left leads to the "normal" delivery room; the one on the right leads to the operating room. On the far left, the door to the room where women are induced (whether for live birth or miscarriage), and where women with "high-risk" pregnancies wait to be called in for c-section. Not pictured: the labor room (featuring *cavalinhos* and adjustable beds to support vertical positions), where women must dilate fully in order to be transferred to the delivery room. Photo by K. Eliza Williamson delivery must be understood within the context of widespread disinformation and alarmism around childbirth in Brazil. Next, therefore, I examine how the prevailing discourse of risk contributes to the prevalence of surgical delivery.

"Birth Is a Box of Surprises": Risks and Interventions

As I interviewed obstetricians, nurse-midwives, and mothers in Salvador, I began to notice one particular phrase repeated over and over again: "Birth is a box of surprises" (*o parto é uma caixa de surpresas*), meaning that one never quite knows what will happen. Everything might be going smoothly when complications suddenly arise and the birth becomes an emergency situation. My conversations and observations in maternity care services have made clear that, however else my Brazilian interlocutors may understand child-birth, they most certainly also define it as a situation of risk and danger.

In clinical parlance, there are two qualifiers for pregnancy and birth: *risco habitual* (low risk; literally, "usual risk") and *alto risco* (high risk). "No-risk" birth as a category simply does not exist. The way obstetric care is organized reflects this overarching definition. Prenatal care is designed not so much to prepare women for labor and delivery as it is to closely monitor any altera-tions in the pregnancy that might indicate danger for a woman or her child and, consequently, the need for a CS. Public hospital labor and delivery is a continuation of this risk-based care. Women arrive at the emergency unit, are triaged and classified according to their risk factors, and then are monitored throughout labor for signs of complications.

During a tour of one hospital early in my fieldwork, an administrator explained that the anesthesiologist on that day's shift had quit abruptly, which required the whole obstetric unit to shut down. When I asked whether the hospital couldn't admit only women with "usual risk" pregnancies for vaginal delivery, she looked at me as if I were missing something completely obvious. Smiling, she told me that *all* admissions to the labor and delivery unit required the presence of an anesthesiologist because they could turn into emergency CS.

Most professionals at the maternity hospital were highly skeptical of the local birth center and its low-intervention model of care. Whenever the topic came up, the practitioner—whether doctor, nurse, or nursing auxiliary—would say, almost as if on cue, that the only way a birth center should be able to function would be right next to or inside a maternity hospital. Anything could happen at any moment, they would tell me, requiring urgent action. The problem with the birth center, most said, was that it did not have the "struc-ture" (*estrutura*) to perform cesarean sections if needed. Although the birth center staff tended to have a more nuanced view of childbirth, some—particu-larly the more inexperienced doctors—shared this risk discourse. One young obstetrician, who had been working at the birth center for only a short time, uttered the word "risk" over 40 times in the span of a two-hour interview.

Other scholars have noted similar phenomena. Dias and Deslandes (2004) found that doctors and medical residents tended to minimize the risks of cesarean, expressing much more reticence about vaginal delivery because of the "danger" associated with it. Chacham (2012) also found that obstetricians tended to describe normal birth as unpredictable and risky, while they generally described cesarean sections as safer and less stressful for the doctor: whereas in normal birth "one never knows," with CS "everyone knows what to do."

Many women and their family members shared this view. Over the course of my fieldwork, numerous women told stories of friends, relatives, and acquaintances who had had "difficult" births. These stories are often shared in the context of conversations about the merits of normal birth versus cesarean section. Most say they prefer normal delivery, but they understand that "not all women can give birth normally" and will need a CS. I have also heard, especially in waiting areas in public hospitals, many family members expressing frustration that the doctors try to "force" normal birth when "it should be a cesarean section."

In fact, most of the complaints I heard from women and their accompanying family members were about doctors waiting too long for normal labor to progress. One mother of a woman who had recently given birth by CS told me that her daughter was "in pain for three days" before they finally sent her for surgery. "They don't want to do cesarean sections because it gives them work to do," the woman told me. "If she gives birth again I'm going to get some money to pay [for private health care]! We're not coming back here, God forgive me. Two cesarean sections went ahead of her! The baby was all purple when it came out." Her tone grew increasingly indignant as she continued: "This maternity hospital is shit [*merda*]; it's horrible. People talk badly about here, and it's all true. . . . They made [my daughter] squat down backwards on a chair to make the baby come down. They put her on a thing called a *cavalinho* [little horse]. These doctors make up so many things! [*É muita coisa que esses médicos aqui inventam!*]" she scoffed. Pointing to her daughter's bruised arm, she told me that the IV drip ran out during the night and no one came to replace it.

This mother insisted that her daughter had received inadequate care, not because she was subjected to unnecessary interventions, but because she was not subjected to the "right" interventions soon enough. The practices the woman refers to, such as having the woman squat down and rock herself on the *cavalinho*, are evidence-based measures promoted by current health policy (Ministry of Health of Brazil 2017; World Health Organization 1996). They are nonpharmacologic ways of relieving pain and helping labor to progress. But to this new grandmother, they were "inventions" of the doctors that did little for her daughter and her daughter's baby besides prolonging a difficult labor and potentially compromising the newborn's health. Her complaints were punctuated with a keen sense of injustice; because her daughter gave birth in a public hospital, she did not get the care she needed and deserved— which would have included a CS much sooner than it was finally provided.

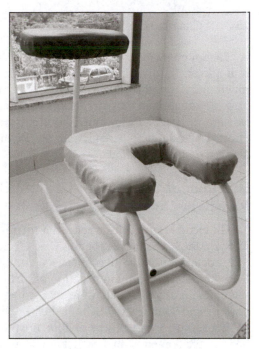

The *cavalinho* (little horse) has become an essential piece of equipment for promoting upright, physiologic birth in Brazil. The lower part of the *cavalinho* is shaped like a birthing stool, where women can sit and push as their labor companion supports them from behind. If she turns around, she can support herself on the upper part with her forearms while she rocks back and forth in a movement that helps to ease contraction pain. Photo by K. Eliza Williamson

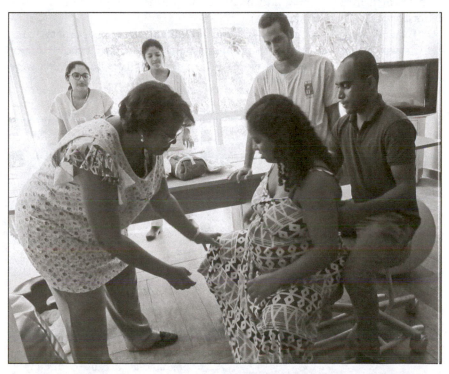

At the Normal Birth Center's weekly *roda de gestantes* (pregnant women's circle), a volunteer doula teaches a participant and her husband how to use the *cavalinho* (little horse) for delivery as NBC staff, nurse-midwifery residents, and other soon-to-be parents look on. Photo by K. Eliza Williamson

The high incidence of CS in Brazil, driven by many factors, may represent a kind of quick-fix response to deeper, structural problems that require much more sustained attention and resources. In the next section, I discuss how the situation in Salvador points to much broader inadequacies of obstetric care in Brazil. I then briefly outline some key activist and government efforts to tackle these perennial issues. Birth in Brazil is in crisis, but there is also a paradigm shift underway.

Brazilian Birth in Crisis: Chaotic Care Networks, Shifting Paradigms, and Birth Activism

In October of 2015, I attended a forum on the "Crisis in Obstetric Care in Salvador," which brought together elected officials, hospital administrators, doctors, nurses, doulas, mothers, and other members of the general public to discuss the alarming situation of birth care in the city. Salvador's seven public maternity hospitals were in a constant state of disarray, bombarded with patient volumes too high for their facilities and personnel. Women were having to go to up to three or four hospitals in labor looking for an open bed—a phenomenon in Brazil known as *peregrinação* (literally "peregrination," which means a long and meandering journey) (Lansky et al. 2014; Ministry of Health of Brazil 2004).

Exacerbating the situation was the lamentable state of prenatal care, which was leaving simple health problems untreated to later become major complications, and the fact that women from all over the state of Bahia were

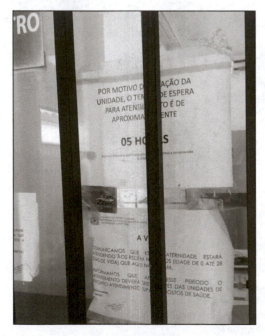

A sign posted at the metal barred reception window at a public maternity hospital in Salvador announces: "Because of this unit's overcrowding, wait time for attendance is approximately 5 HOURS." Photo by K. Eliza Williamson

seeking care in the capital due to sparse and unreliable hospital facilities in the interior. Added to this was chronic understaffing of public health services. Even private hospitals were beginning to see their units fill to capacity. At the forum, women who had given birth in Salvador spoke out adamantly against the disrespectful treatment they experienced, the difficulty in accessing the services they needed, and, for those who gave birth in private hospitals, the pressure they received from their obstetricians to schedule CS deliveries regardless of real clinical indication.

In Bahia, local efforts to reorganize the network of care have made some impact, but the situation has not improved significantly. The most recent statistics show that the Brazilian government's latest efforts to improve birth care did not succeed in budging the maternal mortality rate. Women and health care professionals alike feel the tremendous weight of these persistent inadequacies. In the public maternity hospital in my study, overcrowding became such a serious issue that women in early labor or close to their due dates were staking out spaces in the emergency waiting area for over 24 hours, hoping to secure a bed in the labor and delivery unit, which was nearly always full beyond capacity. The hallway of that unit was perpetually lined with gurneys that served as temporary holding spaces for postpartum patients and women pre- and post-miscarriage. Even with the addition of these unofficial "beds," the line of women waiting outside was consistently enormous and their wait times often staggering. With the recent passing of nationwide austerity measures—including a freeze on public spending in health care and education for the next two decades—this situation is likely to worsen across Brazil.

In addition to the perils of inadequate health care infrastructure, obstetric violence is prevalent throughout the country. Verbal, emotional, and even physical abuse are all but routine in Brazilian maternity hospitals. The most common include verbal humiliation from hospital staff, unnecessary invasion of bodily autonomy by medical personnel and students, lack of informed consent for procedures, abandonment, and isolation from family (d'Oliveira, Diniz, and Schraiber 2002; Diniz and d'Oliveira 1998; Diniz et al. 2015, 2016; Fundação Perseu Abramo 2013; Gomes, Nations, and Luz 2008; McCallum and dos Reis 2005; Parto do Princípio 2012). Black and Indigenous women, poor women, and women with little formal education are among those most vulnerable to abuse and neglect in health care. For instance, a commonly held moralistic belief that poor, dark-skinned women are promiscuous and reproduce "irrationally" (Zordo 2012) contributes to the ubiquitous pejorative phrases directed at women in labor: "You liked it when you made the baby, now deal with the pain!" and the dismissive "Don't make such a fuss; you'll be back here next year" are two of the most cited (Aguiar and d'Oliveira 2011). Obstetric violence, wherever it occurs, can lead to both immediate physical harm and to lasting psychological effects (Bowser and Hill 2010; World Health Organization 2014).

Birth, the Salvador forum participants agreed, was in crisis—assailed by a troubled health care system, social inequities and institutionalized violence, and conjoined political and economic crises that promise only to worsen the situation. However, the news is not all bad. The work of dedicated birth activists all over the country, some of whom have risen to important positions in the Ministry of Health in recent years, has brought a heightened awareness of the perils of Brazil's current model of obstetric care, as well as concerted efforts to build a better system.

The past three decades have seen numerous efforts from both government and civil society to shift the paradigm of obstetric care, with a rapid acceleration since the late 2000s (Maia 2010). Advocates for better birth have organized to form "the movement for the humanization of birth" (*movimento pela humanização do parto e nascimento*), making Brazil a vanguard of birth activism in Latin America (Carneiro 2015). The humanization movement is made up of a diverse array of social actors—mothers, fathers, health care professionals (obstetricians, nurse-midwives, traditional midwives, psychologists, physical therapists, practitioners of alternative medicine), doulas, lawyers, and international speakers (including Robbie Davis-Floyd, co-editor of this volume, who has given many talks at conferences all over Brazil)—who all envision and strive for a more humane culture of childbirth for Brazil and for the world.

"Humanization" is an umbrella term that encompasses a variety of approaches to childbirth, tied together by an overall emphasis on centering women's autonomy in their birth choices, valorizing the natural and physiological over the technological, and promoting respectful birth care (Carneiro 2015; Diniz 2005; Georges and Davis-Floyd 2018; Maia 2010; Rattner 2010; Tornquist 2004). Several important nongovernmental organizations have taken the lead in efforts to humanize birth in Brazil.[10] Additionally, the Sofia Feldman Hospital in Belo Horizonte has long stood as a beacon of humanized perinatal care in the SUS, and its staff has helped train health care professionals across Brazil in their respectful and effective model of care (Davis-Floyd and Georges 2018).

The current decade in particular has seen a proliferation of civil society mobilizations for better birth care and against obstetric violence (*violência obstétrica*). Humanization advocates have led marches in all of Brazil's capital cities to protest legislative restrictions on homebirth, call attention to the abuse of cesarean section, and revindicate women's right to choose where, how, and with whom they deliver their children. The Observatory of Obstetric Violence in Brazil (OVO-Brasil), for example, was launched in late 2016 to monitor obstetric health services in the public health system and foment broad-based dialogue about violence in these institutions. In early 2017, a local chapter of

---

[10] One of the oldest and most prominent is ReHuNa, the Network for the Humanization of Birth (*Rede pela Humanização do Parto e Nascimento*), which was founded in the early 1990s by a group of dissident health care professionals who sought to end violent and outdated practices in obstetric and neonatal care. Other important organizations include Parto do Princípio, Grupo Curumin, CAIS do Parto, the Support Group for Active Maternity (GAMA), Amigas do Parto, and Artemis.

Kangaroo care in the postnatal dorm, which is universally provided at Sofia Feldman, even for babies in the NICU when possible. Photo by Robbie Davis-Floyd

the Order of Lawyers of Brazil (OAB) in the Bahian city of Vitória da Con-quista worked with a local birth activist group to publish an informational pamphlet on obstetric violence directed at women and health care profession-als.[11] After one stunning example of disrespect for women's autonomy, in which a southern Brazilian woman named Adelir was taken from her home by police and forced to have a CS, activists organized a day of nationwide marches under the hashtag #WeAreAllAdelir: National Action against Obstet-ric Violence (*#SomosTodasAdelir: Ato Nacional contra a Violência Obstétrica*).[12]

Birth activists have also made significant headway in the legislative realm. Most recently, Federal Deputy Jean Wyllys introduced a bill in 2014 that would guarantee women the right to humanized birth care. The state of São Paulo signed a similar bill into law in 2015, and in early 2017, the state of Santa Catarina passed a law banning obstetric violence (Diário Catarinense 2017). The city of Salvador's "Right Maternity Hospital Law" (*Lei Materni-dade Certa*) was passed in 2010 (Leis Municipais 2012). To date, there are nearly 60 state and municipal laws on the books in Brazil regarding human-ization of birth or obstetric violence, and many of these are the products of organized doulas' efforts (Daphne Rattner, personal communication).

While legal protections are symbolically powerful, they have little impact unless they are enforced. Birth activists know that even legislation going back over a decade—such as the 2005 federal law allowing women one labor com-panion of their choice throughout perinatal care—routinely goes unenforced and is disregarded in practice.

Pressure from grassroots groups and NGOs has both led to and been fed by government initiatives. Indeed, one of the major achievements of the birth activist movement in Brazil has been to put humanization squarely on the

---

[11] For more information see: Observatório de Violência Obstétrica—Brasil, http://www.observatoriovobrasil.com.br; *Violência Obstétrica: conhecer para enfrentar* (Vitória da Conquista, Bahia, Brazil, OAB Vitória da Conquista, 2017),
[12] https://somostodxsadelir.wordpress.com

public policy agenda. One of the results is *Rede Cegonha* (Stork Network), an initiative launched by former President Dilma Rousseff to promote evidence-based birth care in the SUS. Other efforts focus on reducing cesarean sections in private hospitals. In 2016 and 2017, Brazil published its first-ever national guidelines for vaginal birth and CS, which emphasize mothers' and babies' physical and emotional well-being, prioritize midwife-led care in normal-risk delivery, and promote appropriate use of a range of interventions including CS (CONITEC 2016; Ministry of Health of Brazil 2017).

The results of all these efforts have been mixed. On the one hand, it seems they are making a dent in the CS rate: a pilot program aimed at private health care reported a reduction in CS by 20% on average in participating hospitals (Cruz 2015),[13] and in 2015 Brazil's overall CS rate remained steady from the year before—the first time in five years that it did not increase (Portal da Saúde 2017). On the other hand, since Rede Cegonha's inauguration in 2011, Brazil's maternal mortality numbers seem not to have decreased (Secretaria de Vigilância em Saúde n.d.), which raises doubts as to how effective the program's strategies actually are.

A woman from Brazil's Landless Workers Movement reads "myths and facts" about cesarean section at the National Health Conference in 2015. The sign, part of a traveling exhibition entitled *Sentidos do Nascer* (Senses of Birth), is designed to promote discussion around Brazil's interventionist birth care paradigm and encourage the public to see physiological birth as normal and desirable. The Senses of Birth exhibition is one of many efforts underway to shift the paradigm of birth in Brazil. Photo by K. Eliza Williamson

---

[13] See also: Agência Nacional de Saúde Suplementar (ANS), "Projeto Parto Adequado," http:// www.ans.gov.br/gestao-em-saude/projeto-parto-adequado. ANS's mission is to "promote the defense of the public interest in supplementary health care, regulate sector operators—including their relations with providers and consumers—and contribute to the development of health actions in the country."

It remains to be seen whether these efforts can break through the formi-dable barriers still in place. But Brazilian birth activism is here to stay, and advocates continue to make important strides toward more evidence-based obstetric care. One source of change has been international cooperation between Brazil and Japan, as we describe at the end of this chapter. In order to understand why and how this collaboration came about, we will first take a look at birth care in contemporary Japan.

Unstratified Birth in Japan: The Midwifery Paradox and the Influence of Place

Etsuko Matsuoka

Whereas birth in Brazil is heavily centralized in hospitals and stratified by race and social class, birth in Japan is characterized by decentralization and primarily facility-based hierarchies of care. In 2016, 54.3% of babies were born in hospitals; 45.0% were born in small-scale, community-based clinics owned by obstetricians, and another 0.8% were born at home or in freestand-ing birth centers (midwife-owned "maternity homes") (Vital Statistics Figure 2016). While Brazilian tertiary care hospitals may see up to 10,000 births per year, it is rare for Japanese hospitals to see more than 3,000 (Hospital Intelli-gence Agency 2015); on average, only around 515 babies are born in any given hospital each year, and clinics see about 350.

Economic stratification in birth care is also not nearly as evident in Japan as it is in Brazil, in large part because care providers receive the flat amount of 420,000 yen (about $3800 USD) per birth, irrespective of the mode of delivery, from the government-funded Japan Health Insurance Association. A woman only pays the difference out-of-pocket when the institution charges more than what the government pays, but she receives the difference back when it charges less, as birth fees differ between institutions and geographical regions. Prenatal checkups are covered by coupons worth around 100,000 yen per woman (the amount differs in each municipal government), which covers most of her prenatal care. While class differences do exist in Japan, the national health insurance system guarantees that they are not, as they are in Brazil, a primary determinant of availability and type of health care.

Midwives are a central feature of Japanese maternity care, and they work in all types of facilities.[14] Over the past two decades, more midwives have moved from hospitals to clinics; in 1996 only 10% of midwives worked in

---

[14] Before WWII midwives in Japan were called *samba*—literally "birth old woman" (no relation to Brazilian samba!). In 1948, a new law was established in which the word *josanpu* was used, meaning "help-birth-woman." In 2002, *josanpu* was changed to *josanshi*, meaning "help-birth-teacher"—a gender-neutral form that was adopted in concordance with the Gender Equality Law established in 1999. Nevertheless, current Japanese law does not allow male midwives. The suffix *shi* is used in such professional occupations as *ishi* (doctor): *yakuzaishi* (pharmacist), *kangoshi* (nurse), and *kyoshi* (teacher).

clinics, in 2015, 26.5% did. Why were midwives more likely to work in hospitals in the past? The answer has to do with relationships between midwives and obstetricians in clinics—a theme we will explore later.

Although almost all births in Japan are attended by midwives, the statistics collected from birth certificates tell a different story. Because the obstetrician's name is usually written on the birth certificate as the attending professional, even when a midwife has caught the baby, the official numbers show that doctors attend 95% of births and midwives 5% (Vital Statistics Figure 2016). Since doctors are considered responsible for all births that take place in hospitals and clinics, midwives are routinely erased from the record.[15]

The decrease in the number of obstetricians and gynecologists working in Japan, a trend that continued from 1994 to 2006, has resulted in the closing of many obstetric wards, especially in small towns, and women who were unable to book a place to give birth began being referred to as "birth refugees." Not unlike the *peregrinação* that Brazilian women often have to undertake, this phenomenon is all the more disturbing given that Japan is a high-resource country. This obstetrician shortage in Japan was the catalyst for the government initiative to create a system of "in-hospital maternity homes" (or "in-hospital birth centers") in 2008 (Ministry of Health, Labor and Welfare 2009). In these facilities, midwives look after women with low-risk pregnancies from about the middle of gestation to the postpartum period, acting with relative autonomy. In-hospital services are meant to combine the benefits of the continuous midwifery care provided in freestanding maternity homes with the readily available emergency backup of hospitals.

Another dramatic contrast to Brazil is Japan's very low maternal mortality rate (MMR): as of 2016, the MMR was 3.4/100,000 live births along with 3.6/1,000 perinatal mortality (Vital Statistics Figure 2016). The Japanese CS rate is increasing, but still remains lower than most countries. In 2014 it was 24.8% for hospitals and 13.6% for private clinics, for a national average of 19.7%.

Birth in Small-Scale Private Clinics: Japanese Values in Action

This section draws on ethnographic data collected in 2016. I (Etsuko) interviewed 20 midwives, 10 obstetricians, and four women who had recently given birth (three in clinics and one in a hospital); I interviewed each mother once during pregnancy and once after delivery. I also engaged in participant-observation at two prenatal visits, as well as at one woman's birth from entry to hospital to end of delivery. I toured three hospitals, seven clinics, and 10 independent maternity homes in order to write this section. Additionally, I have conducted fieldwork for over 30 years in Japan as well as in other parts

[15] Japanese birth certificates allow a space for only one person's name to be written as the birth attendant, but a mother-child notebook, prepared in early pregnancy and carried all through to the postpartum period by a woman, allows the names of two people to be written. In this notebook, the name of the midwife who delivered the baby appears together with the name of a doctor.

of Asia and Europe by being present at birthing scenes to observe the relationships among actors involved in births. I begin this section with a birth
story that illustrates what birth is often like in Japan's small-scale private clinics where nearly half of the country's births take place.

Keiko's Birth Story.   Keiko, age 33, lives in a small city near Kyoto in a
cozy apartment she shares with her husband. There I had a chance to listen
to her birth experiences three months after she gave birth to her first child, a
baby boy. Keiko booked her birth at a clinic based on its proximity to her
home and its good reputation—most births there are conducted by midwives
with little intervention from obstetricians. Prenatal checkups are normally
provided 14 times during pregnancy by the obstetrician-owner of the clinic, a
man in his 50s. At each visit, Keiko's obstetrician performed an ultrasound
and a vaginal examination, using a special chair for the latter that fully
reclined Keiko's upper body while elevating and parting her legs to facilitate
the doctor's access to her vagina. Keiko didn't see him, though; a screening
curtain comes down between her torso and legs, blocking the view of her
body below the waist, which Keiko preferred.

The repeated vaginal examinations were annoying and painful, but
Keiko enjoyed seeing the 3D/4D ultrasound pictures of her fetus. Other pregnant women felt the same. The medical checkup is always done by the doctor, but advice such as appropriate nutrition, caution against weight gain, and
so forth, are given by midwives, who always address the pregnant woman in
a friendly manner.

At 40 weeks and two days gestation, Keiko's water broke and labor
started suddenly. It was 1:20 A.M. when Keiko arrived at the clinic with her
husband. She was already trembling with pain from her contractions. After

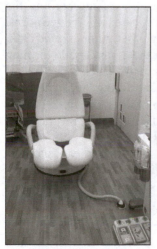 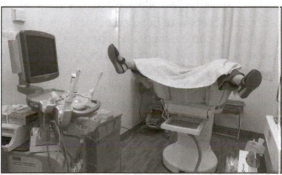

The prenatal exam chair, with Etsuko posing in it
wearing pants. This chair is a symbolic representation
of physician-centeredness, making the woman's bottom half part of the obstetrician's territory—an object
with no face or emotion. Nevertheless, this setup is
welcomed by most women in Japan, who prefer not to see the face of the obstetrician
while examining to avoid embarrassment. Photos by a hospital midwife

preparing her in a labor room, the midwife left, saying in a happy tone, "If you need me, call me," while she shut the curtain. She visited periodically to check on her, saying "Let's wait some more," and showing her husband how to massage Keiko to alleviate her pain. Keiko's pain peaked between 3:00 and 4:00 A.M., at which point the midwife told her: "Let's go to another room and try pushing." After she had pushed four or five times, the midwife asked: "Do you want to have a cut? If you have it a little bit, your baby will come soon." This suggestion presented a dilemma for Keiko: her birth plan clearly stated that she didn't want an episiotomy, but the midwife was suggesting it anyway. (This indicates that women's prior decisions are not always given priority in these supposedly "women-centered" birth clinics.) After several minutes of confusion and discussion with her husband, she agreed to the cut. The night-shift obstetrician appeared suddenly to perform the episiotomy.

At 4:53 A.M., after just one more push, Keiko's baby boy was born. The midwife reassured her, saying, "Don't worry, the doctor will suture you neatly." But for Keiko, that was not what mattered. She started to regret that she had agreed to an episiotomy. She told me that she would have acted differently if the midwife had encouraged her to go on: "If you are told there is a shortcut to heaven, can you resist it at a time of extreme pain?" she asked me rhetorically, adding, "It's not fair for a midwife to invite a cut when a woman is so vulnerable—I would not have said yes if the midwife had said the baby would come in 10 to 15 minutes." The doctor performed the episiotomy, sutured her, and disappeared. Yet, on the birth certificate, it is his name that appears, instead of the name of the midwife who had attended her throughout her labor process. Keiko's postpartum stay of five nights and six days in the clinic was very comfortable. She wanted to stay there much longer—meals were good, the facility was reasonably luxurious, and the whole atmosphere was celebratory. The clinic midwives were helpful in teaching her and the other mothers how to breastfeed, bathe, and generally care for their newborns.

Keiko's clinic experience, comparable with my other ethnographic data, reveals several core characteristics of births in Japanese small-scale birthing clinics: (1) an emphasis on service as a business strategy, which is very pleasing to women; (2) less attention to women's choices during labor and birth than should ideally be provided; (3) the navigation of often delicate relationships between midwives and doctors; (4) the habitual manipulation of certain components of births by obstetricians; and (5) the friendly and compassionate care almost universally provided by midwives, who do not leave mothers alone to labor (unless they wish to be left alone with their partners) but provide a great deal of hands-on and emotional labor support when needed.

Popularity of Clinics.   The fact that small-scale clinic births like Keiko's account for almost half of all Japanese births, despite the government's centralization policy, suggests that these clinics are responding to the needs and values of Japanese women. A clinic is a family-run business, often known by common family surnames such as "Tanaka clinic" or "Sato clinic"; they tend to be handed down from father to son. Clinics are popular because of their proximity, as everywhere, women prefer to birth in or near their communities. Moreover, the clinics offer a less "assembly-line" experience, more individualized care, and comfortable accommodations. Each clinic has its own website, which includes a welcoming message from the obstetrician-owner and lists staff members, including midwives and cooks, pictures of rooms for delivery and postpartum stays, fees for checkups and delivery, meals for postpartum women, as well as descriptions of the kinds of care the clinic provides. The website of Keiko's clinic includes the following content: "This clinic was born near Lake Biwa in November 1994 as a maternity resort. [We aspire] to become like [a] first-class hotel. We share the heart of the first-class hotel in serving customers so that they have a comfortable stay in our clinic."[16]

That birth clinics' focus on good service to women as guests is not surprising if we understand that such clinics are part of the service industry in Japan. For instance, women often have at least 14 3D/4D ultrasounds, even in low-risk pregnancies; this high number is justified by saying that "women enjoy seeing their fetuses." Two out of the four women I interviewed said that their primary reason for choosing a particular clinic included this service, in which the ultrasound images of the fetus become accessible online via a password or saved on a USB stick. The possible adverse effects of frequent ultrasounds are rarely brought up (Beech and Robinson 1994; Suzui 2016).[17]

In Japan, women generally expect to be appreciated and rewarded for the achievement of childbirth, and clinics are eager to meet that demand. For them, birth is at the very least a product of nine months' toil and a painful labor and delivery. Women want to be rewarded by being pampered and enjoying an atmosphere of luxury in hotel-like services with high-quality food, comfortable rooms, and massages for relaxation, all in a celebratory atmosphere. The level of comfort of the postpartum stay, which usually lasts four to six days for a normal delivery, is an important factor women consider when choosing a place of birth. In other words, clinics respond to women's expectations for reward and a sense of achievement by providing extra services, all of which may be seen as part of their business strategy, yet are also quite lovely for the parents enjoying these services.

As we saw with Keiko's unwanted episiotomy, the fact that clinics attend so closely to the quality of the postpartum stay does not mean that they provide truly woman-centered care during labor and delivery. The relationship between midwives and obstetricians in clinics is very delicate, even tense at

---

[16] The web page of this clinic is http://www.sato-clinic.com/message.php (summarized a message of the owner obstetrician)

[17] 4D ultrasound images especially can be harmful to the fetus in the first half of pregnancy due to their higher power output (https://www.babycentre.co.uk/a1014487/are-ultrasound-scans-safe). The evidence on the effects of repeated ultrasounds during pregnancy is contradictory and unclear; a cautionary approach would recommend as few ultrasounds as necessary during pregnancy, and none simply for the pleasure and interest of the parents. For a thorough analysis of possible adverse ultrasound effects, see https://chriskresser.com/natural-childbirth-iib-ultrasound-not-as-safe-as-commonly-thought/.

times—an uneasy space of simultaneous collaboration and tension. In many clinics midwives do everything—they are present from the onset of labor to the expulsion of the placenta and the cutting of the umbilical cord—but they usually call the doctor just in time for him to witness the birth or to perform an episiotomy. This timing is remarkably subtle, as it must occur within a narrow window that can be difficult to predict; the obstetrician must not be called in too early in order to avoid wasting his valuable time (considered more valuable than the midwives'), yet early enough to perform an episiotomy or say "congratulations" to the woman after witnessing her birth.

Similar to American nurse-midwives discussed elsewhere (Davis-Floyd 2018c, e), Japanese midwives often employ subtle tactics to allow women more time to push. One midwife said, "I always try to call the doctor late in order to avoid unnecessary intervention." Another said, "I feel that doctors trample underfoot the peaceful environment I have maintained when he comes in at the last moment. Up until then, we try to give as much calm and normality as possible, but then he comes in and violates it."

How is it possible for a midwife to call in a doctor just in time to do his final work? How is a midwife to know when it is just the right moment for an obstetrician, who may be some distance away, to come in? This precise tim-

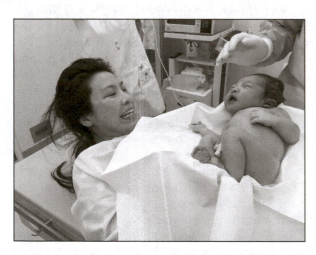

A clinic birth. Photo by Kohei Hirose

---

[18] An incident in 2003 changed the trends of employment in clinics. After a maternal death, it was found that the person who had performed internal examinations on this woman was not a midwife but a nurse. Up until then many clinics had hired nurses or even auxiliary nurses, who were less expensive and more compliant, and whom doctors trained in everything, including internal examinations. In Japan, nurses, who need one more year of education to become nurse-midwives, are not allowed by law to conduct internal examinations or to receive babies on their own but only under supervision of a doctor. After this incident, internal examinations by a nurse were proscribed by the government. Since then, some clinics have moved toward more utilization of midwives, while others abandoned birth in favor of gynecology and infertility treatment.

ing becomes possible only when a midwife controls the process of a woman's birth according to each specific circumstance. She either slows or hastens a woman's birth process to match up with the arrival of an obstetrician—a process of manipulation of normal birth physiology that may take a toll on the laboring woman. In a famous vignette in *Birth in Four Cultures*, Brigitte Jordan (1993:165) described a similar circumstance, in which a woman kept begging to be allowed to push but was repeatedly denied by the nurses present until a doctor arrived, performed a vaginal exam without even speaking to her, and finally gave permission. In Japan, the balance in time of calling is influenced by multiple factors, and doctors and midwives must "read" each other to judge the right time.

Thus, the relationship between midwives and obstetricians in private clinics is a delicate balance between conflicting values represented in dichotomies such as collaboration versus confrontation, subordination versus autonomy, and harmony versus maneuvering/manipulation. There is no one static picture of the relationship between the two professions: it manifests in different ways in different places. Midwives in Japan have a high level of autonomy because they are in a position to deliver most of the babies themselves. Yet Japanese midwives are also in a subordinate position because their work is made invisible in the official birth certificate. The hierarchical/collaborative relationship of the two professions manifests more clearly in clinics than in hospitals, because in clinics midwives are directly hired by the obstetrician-owner, who decides whether to keep them in his clinic or not. In fact, in many clinics, to avoid midwifery autonomy, the obstetrician-owner hires a nurse rather than a midwife to look after a woman prior to the time of delivery, while he shows up at the last moment to conduct the delivery.[18] A clinic is like a manor house with one dominant landlord; thus, many midwives feel that the clinic is not the place for them and find work in hospitals that, although equally hierarchical, can accommodate plural and diverse relationships. In hospitals, there are many doctors with differing attitudes toward midwives and birth, and clinical decisions are usually made not by one person but as a team. Also, some midwives want to experience attending many different types of women and so choose to work in hospitals with higher numbers of births.

There is wide variation in the way birth is managed in each clinic; some clinics advertise natural and woman-friendly birth (as Keiko's clinic did), while others advertise "painless delivery" via epidurals—intended to provide a gentler image than normal birth with labor pain. Epidural use in Japan was found to be 6.1% (*Japan Medical Journal* 2017)—an astoundingly low figure relative to the US, where, for example, over 60% of laboring women receive epidurals. This extremely low use of epidurals in Japan reflects cultural notions of the normality of birth in which labor pain is seen in a positive light, as *metamorphic*, necessary to produce the baby and transform the woman into a mother (Matsuoka and Hinokuma 2009). A well-known Japanese adage says, "The child that makes one's belly hurt is lovable"; this adage "echoes the cultural value attached to perseverance in Japanese society, and the acknowledgment of pregnancy and birth as physically and emotionally intensive but virtuous maternal labor" (Ivry n.d.). And again, it is important to emphasize that Japanese midwives do not leave women to endure pain alone; they employ a variety of methods, such as massage, touch, comforting words, and other techniques to ease pain, and see these measures as important part of their midwifery work.

Yet, even in those clinics presenting an image of providing "natural birth," in reality, an obstetrician may intervene in various ways. If he wishes to start labor by the woman's due date or thinks finishing birth quickly is better than waiting, he may employ small interventions such as sweeping or stretching the cervix digitally to induce the release of hormonal precursors to labor (Keiko underwent this procedure several times in the late stages of her pregnancy), artificially rupturing the bag of waters, forcibly dilating the cervix with his fingers during contractions (extremely painful for the mother), and performing an episiotomy. It is as if he sees birth as a product of his own work rather than that of the woman. The fact that obstetric care in clinics varies widely suggests that a large part of the care provided derives from the obstetrician's personal preference and routine practices.

In addition to standardized obstetric routines, which Davis-Floyd (2018a) has analyzed as rituals that display the core values of a culture, some practitioners add in additional, individualized rituals that enact their own core values. An 85-year-old clinic obstetrician I interviewed in 2016 used to carry a woman after birth to a bed by holding her body in his two arms, just like a newly-wed husband carries his wife into their new house. He had performed this carrying ritual with each woman after birth as a (highly patriarchal) service up until he handed over his business to his son. The perception of the obstetrician that such a practice can be a present and a prize to women illustrates a wide gap between obstetricians' understandings and those of women. Ritualized patriarchal behavior is inherent in medical practice in Japanese clinics. Ritual, medicine, patriarchy, and marketing strategies are tightly intermingled to the extent that boundaries between them are almost impossible to delineate.

Ie Ideology as an Underlying Value in Japan

Patriarchal ideas permeating Japanese clinics can be understood as examples of *ie*—an ideology that still affects all Japanese in many aspects of their lives. *Ie* (which literally means house, home, or family) represents a quasi-kinship with a patriarchal head and family members tied to him through real or symbolic blood relationship (Sugimoto 2014:164). *Ie* led by a patriarchal head equipped with absolute power over its members is a metaphor applied in many organizations in Japanese society, ranging from small-scale business corporations to community organizations, and in the prewar period to the Japanese nation itself, which was interpreted as one big family, with the emperor as the father and the people as his children. This *ie* metaphor is still very powerful and helpful in understanding the relationship between people and society in Japan, functioning as an often invisible, but highly effective, way of maintaining patriarchal order (Sugimoto 2014:170). *Ie* ideology is a vehicle for patriarchal ideas and a model of relationships that simultaneously give us both comfort (as it means coziness and belonging) and oppression (as it means exclusion of those who do not belong to a family and subjugation for women and younger men).

Clinics, which are often transferred to a son, run like a family business, titled with the family name and led by a male obstetrician, followed by female midwives and pregnant women, are apt examples of the powerful *ie* ideology that still persists in Japan. Indeed, very often a reason given by women to choose a clinic rather than a big hospital is that it is more family-like, besides being close to their homes. Women often do not consciously recognize clinics as being dominated by patriarchal values, but the perception that they are family-like places headed by reliable male obstetricians turns easily into the other side of patriarchy that manifests absolute power over women. In sum, patriarchy and medicine go hand in hand in Japanese clinics and cumulatively construct the power of obstetricians. If we accept the idea that births reflect the core values of the society in which they take place (Davis-Floyd 2003 [1992], 2018b), then we can see that births in clinics reflect Japanese *ie* ideology with both its positive and negative aspects. As clinics are a disguised modern form of patriarchy, it is understandable that they attract a considerable number of women and give them a sense of safety and comfort, as most Japanese are socialized into patriarchal practices in many spheres of life. They often find a certain level of comfort in such practices in the same way that US women, socialized into valuing high technology in birth as in life, often find the EFM tracings during labor comforting and reassuring that all is well with their babies—in spite of the fact that being belted to the machine limits their ability to move around to facilitate physiologic birth.

A Place In-Between: The In-Hospital Maternity Home/ Birth Center

In-hospital birth centers, implemented by the Japanese government to address the country's shortage of obstetricians, constitute a kind of middle ground between standard hospital maternity wards and freestanding maternity clinics. These spaces, newly renovated for midwifery practice, are, like birthing clinics, made to suit women's comfort, featuring tatami (matted) floors, a bathtub, dim lights, and so forth. Such a warm, homelike environment, coupled with compassionate midwifery care, is meant to encourage normal delivery and better birth outcomes. In these in-hospital birth centers where a midwifery model prevails, midwives expect to practice autonomously. Their physical infrastructure is akin to those of Alongside Midwifery Units in the UK, but their management and organization are heavily influenced by Japanese values. Yet in-hospital birth centers, supposedly spaces of

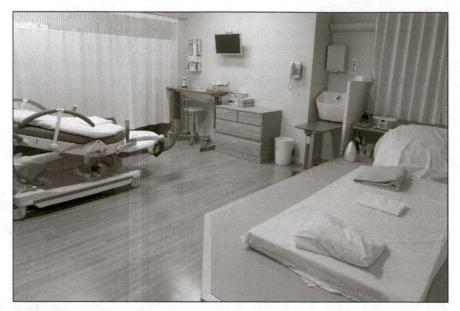

A room of an in-hospital maternity home in Nara Medical University Hospital in which a woman can choose to deliver either in a birth chair on the left or tatami floor mat on the right. Photo by Etsuko Matsuoka

autonomous midwifery practice, are affected by their location within hospitals and by the particular combinations of midwifery care and obstetric backup, which may or may not lead to empowerment for midwives and satisfaction for women. In the following section, I discuss how various forces come into play in these institutional spaces and how these forces affect birth.

Midwifery Care under the Hospital Umbrella

The existence and stability of in-hospital birth centers depends on decisions made by the head of the obstetric department and hospital directors. The same midwife in charge of both the obstetric units and the in-hospital birth center of a private tertiary care hospital in central Japan described to me that her hospital came to have a birth center because the number of births per year (around 700) was increasing. The family who owned the hospital heard about a case in which staff had refused a patient transfer from a community clinic: "They said if doctors were too busy, why not utilize midwives?" There was no option to refuse this "order from the top," yet this head midwife was rather doubtful of the benefits of the in-hospital birth center, as she noted that they were not all that different from maternity ward births, in that the midwives attend the labors while the doctors still come in for the deliveries:

> It is good to pursue natural birth as much as possible while ensuring safety by medicine. Women come here assuming they are safe in a big

university hospital like this. So refusing any medical intervention is unrealistic. We do our jobs within a boundary approved by obstetricians. Otherwise the hospital will not support us and we cannot maintain this midwifery system. After all, this is a space within a hospital. We need to maintain good relations with doctors.

Indeed, the model of care in the in-hospital birth center is similar to that in the obstetric unit: women are hooked up to fetal monitors, get intravenous drips, and deliver their babies on a bed. Practically the only difference is that the birth center midwives encourage women to lie on their side during delivery, instead of on their back—the most common Japanese delivery position. The head midwife I spoke with also emphasized that these birth centers can exist only with the approval of hospital management, so any change higher up could lead to their elimination, which has occurred in birth centers elsewhere in Japan. This precarious position highlights the paradoxes of the in-hospital birth center. First, because it occupies space within the hospital, midwives have less independence in care as compared to a freestanding maternity home. Second, the existing hierarchy in the hospital crosses over to the birth center, situating midwives and in-hospital birth centers lower in the hierarchy than obstetricians and obstetric wards.

This geographical ambiguity has a dual effect: on the one hand, life-saving support becomes easier to access in the event of obstetric emergencies; on the other hand, midwives tend to prioritize avoiding confrontation with hospital management over achieving autonomous practice. It's an extension of the "obstetric paradox": maintaining good relations with physicians in order to guarantee the birth center's continued existence often requires applying similar amounts of technomedical intervention in birth to those in the regular maternity wards. This sort of intervention, in turn, dilutes the midwifery model of care. Midwives attempt to find a middle ground between noninterventive care and the amount of interventions obstetricians find suitable. Compromise between humanistic and technocratic models of childbirth seems to be necessary in in-hospital maternity homes. One head midwife told me, however, that there are some positive differences from the obstetric ward:

> In terms of quality of births, what we provide in this midwifery practice is different from the one in the obstetric ward. Here we can develop trust with a woman from the early stages of pregnancy, which makes a big difference in the progress of birth. We provide two midwives to one woman all through. By staying with a woman, we have realized that a woman's tension affects the progress of birth and some signs can be detected just by staying with a woman continuously.

"Space" is an important factor for analysis when discussing the impact of the hospital on the birth process and on midwifery as profession. Two different paradigms—the midwifery and the obstetric—come into play in the in-hospital maternity home. As it becomes increasingly difficult for midwives to operate independent maternity homes in communities, working in in-hospital mater-

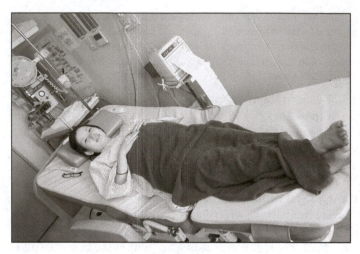

Laboring with a fetal monitoring machine in a clinic labor-delivery room. Photo by Tomoo Kayama

nity homes is a realistic option for those who want to work autonomously. A comparison of outcomes shows much lower rates of medical intervention and higher rates of normal births in midwifery practices than in obstetric units in Japan (Yamana 2016). Thus, the question arises, do in-hospital maternity homes empower autonomous midwifery practice or do they attenuate midwives' power by being housed in hospital obstetric units? This is a complex question, as the answer can vary. When compared with midwives working shifts in the obstetric ward, having a midwifery space where they can provide continuous care is empowering for midwives and women. But when compared to midwives working in freestanding maternity homes, even in-hospital maternity homes may be seen as a diminished form of midwifery practice.

Ethnographic research shows that the level of autonomy midwives can achieve relative to medical forces is not static but in flux depending on their skills and experience levels. The professional boundary between midwives and obstetricians is not fixed, but constantly renegotiated. How much midwives can do autonomously and how far medicine intervenes is determined not only by the power (im)balance but also by midwives' actual skills and self-confidence. If the skills of midwives (clinical and interpersonal) increase to the point where they earn enough trust from obstetricians, their midwifery model knowledge system may become the authoritative one, at least within their own spaces. However, Japanese cultural values that emphasize *ie* and harmonious relationships constrain midwives' behavior, and many feel pressure to conform to the expectations of their superiors.

Maternity Homes and Freebirth: Perpetual yet Important Practices in Japan

Maternity Homes in Crisis.   Japan has a spectrum of maternity care options, from highly technocratic hospital obstetric units to homebirth. High-intervention models of care tend to imply less midwife autonomy, whereas low-intervention models offer increased autonomy for midwives. Despite the technomedicalization of childbirth, Japan has a long-standing tradition of maternity homes run by independent midwives. These small, freestanding homes (where the midwife and her family actually live) have long been reservoirs of normal birth in which the full range of midwifery skills can be brought to bear and thereby preserved for future generations (Matsuoka and Hinokuma 2009). Although these maternity homes now accommodate only a small fraction of Japanese births, I describe them here because the competence and experience of Japanese independent midwives were fully utilized in the efforts to humanize birth in Brazil.

Before 1960 (the year during which the homebirth rate decreased to 50%), Japanese midwives' practice was largely still truly autonomous, as they attended almost all births in women's homes and in the freestanding maternity homes. Sadly, today, these maternity homes are on the verge of extinction. Over the past four decades, births in these services decreased considerably, so that as of 2016, maternity homes only saw 0.6% of Japanese births.

The decline in maternity home births is due to many factors. One of the most significant was the 2007 amendment of the Medical Care Law, which stipulated that freestanding maternity homes that handle deliveries must have *both* a backup obstetrician and a backup medical institution.[19] Because many obstetricians refused to act as backups, this law forced many maternity homes to stop attending births. This lack of physician cooperation suggests that doctors see maternity homes not only as potentially unsafe, despite their excellent statistics (Matsuoka 1995), but also as potential rivals; Japan's low birth rate has created genuine competition among obstetric care providers. And, although the law obligates every maternity home to obtain a backup obstetrician, obstetricians are not obligated to serve as backups.

This legislation must be seen in the international context of the ongoing battle in many countries by the medical establishment to drive midwives out of homebirths—the sites of their autonomous practice—and into clinics or hospitals—the sites of doctors' control. Technically there is no need for independent midwives to have a backup obstetrician; in an emergency, the midwife would simply transfer the mother to a nearby tertiary hospital or other medical institution. Why do obstetricians, while refusing to become backups for independent midwives, wish to maintain this required backup system? This system allows doctors to maintain control over independent midwives

---

[19] Midwives working in maternity homes comprised 4.6% of the total number of 38,486 midwives in 2015. Running a maternity home does not necessarily mean delivering babies nowadays; some independent midwives may provide only such services as breastfeeding support, sex education for teens, etc. For those who still attend births, besides other services there are two types, "with-bed maternity home" and "no-bed maternity homes," the latter of which whose midwife owners only attend homebirths. The requirement to have a backup contract with an obstetrician applied only to "with-bed maternity homes" in 2007. However, this requirement was extended to apply to "no-bed maternity homes" as well after October 2017, which raised the hurdle even higher for maternity homes.

by supervising them. Distrust and fear of independent midwives seems to run deep in many obstetricians in many countries, including Brazil and Japan, where they feel more secure when midwives work under their scrutiny (Witz 1992). In this way, the backup system can be seen as another form of patriarchal control in the name of clinical safety. Two major consequences of this backup system, consolidated by the 2007 amendment, are the diminishing number of maternity homes and a concomitant reduction in women's opportunities to deliver in the place and manner of their choice.

The independent midwives of the few remaining maternity homes usually expect women to deliver in a position they like; they may hang on a rope, kneel down while leaning forward on something, or be on all fours, side-lying, or semi-sitting. Japanese midwives almost always try to protect the perineum by applying pressure to it as the baby emerges (a procedure not scientifically shown to help, but that gives midwives the feeling that they are helping), which leads women to take a lying position at the very end when the baby's head comes out. This range of positions encouraged in maternity homes is an important asset to be handed on to others, as these diverse positions are not even tried or tolerated in hospital obstetric wards. The very low percentage (0.6%) of births in freestanding maternity homes does not reflect the actual demand for these services. Instead, this low figure is the result of the forced closure of maternity homes and the ensuing diminishment of women's choice of birth place due to obstetricians' control of birth care in Japan.

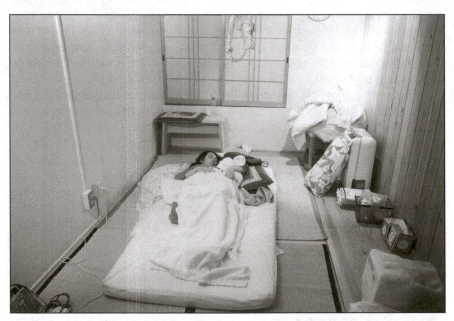

A new mother and her baby sleep on a tatami matted floor in a freestanding maternity home, a very peaceful night. A rope, after being used for the mother to pull down on to help her push, is now placed high above in the room. Photo by Teppei Matsuoka

Freebirth or Private Birth.   As in Brazil and many other countries, a very small minority of Japanese women opt to deliver outside of hospitals or clinics. Those who want a natural delivery, but are unable to deliver in maternity homes (due, for example, to a previous cesarean section or advanced maternal age)[20] are left with few choices. Some may therefore contemplate the possibility of "freebirth" or unassisted birth, referred to by those who practice it as "private birth" in Japan (Ichikawa 2017a, b)—a practice estimated to comprise only 0.02–0.03% of all Japanese childbirths. As with unassisted birth in the US (Shanley 1994), Japanese women's desires to deliver autonomously may stem from previous unpleasant medical experiences, self-confidence in their ability to give birth, and/or the wish for total privacy. Ichikawa's work suggests that some would not have chosen to deliver unassisted had there been more maternity homes or independent midwives who could respect and assist in physiologic delivery. The fact that more than 80% of the 30 women whom Ichikawa interviewed had indeed undergone antenatal checkups suggests that the majority of them are willing to seek medical support when necessary. In fact, they utilized antenatal checkups to evaluate their pregnancies in an effort to detect any risks in advance before making decisions to deliver privately. Although the choice to deliver unassisted may look deviant and misguided from the eyes of the medical and midwifery establishments, the reasons behind private births highlight some important criticisms pertaining to medicalized births common in both high- and middle-income countries.

JICA and *Projeto Luz*: An Important Cross-Cultural Collaboration

Japan and Brazil are, in many respects, worlds apart. Yet, these two countries have collaborated repeatedly around maternal and infant health care. Through transnational exchange programs via the Japan International Cooperation Agency (JICA), collaborations have been designed to facilitate knowledge exchanges between Japanese midwives and Brazilian birth care providers. These JICA cooperation efforts have made important contributions to the shift toward humanized birth in Brazil.

In the late 1990s, for example, JICA worked with Brazil's federal government and the state government of Ceará to found the Maternal and Child Health Improvement Project, better known as *Projeto Luz* (Project Light). From 1996 to 2001, this initiative focused on improving perinatal outcomes by bridging the distance, both literal and figurative, between traditional midwives and the public health system. Participants in the *Projeto Luz* training

---

[20] Advanced maternal age is defined as 35 years or older. A woman needs to satisfy the guidelines for low-risk pregnancy to book a maternity home, but also to live less than one hour's distance from it. Those rules set for "safety" further limit the number of those who actually can deliver in a maternity home.

sessions learned skills from Japanese independent midwives who ran their own maternity homes, and they were also encouraged to reclaim traditional Brazilian midwifery practices that the hospitalization of birth had pushed aside. For example, one former Brazilian traditional midwife, who was now a nursing auxiliary, said she was encouraged to re-adopt her practice of speaking gently to panicked women in labor—a practice she had given up when she went to work in a hospital (Mohri 2001:53).

In 2002, JICA began working with Brazil's Ministry of Health to train 50 Brazilian nurse-midwives in Japan over a period of five consecutive years, prioritizing those who worked in Brazil's public health system or taught at public universities. The Brazilian midwives spent one month visiting Japanese maternity care facilities. They observed births in three different maternity homes as well as in one general hospital. Participants in this exchange program have gone on to help institute significant changes in local maternity care services where they work. Their work in turn has helped speed the progress of efforts to transform Brazilian birth care.

One such nurse-midwife, Graziela, is currently the nursing coordinator at the Normal Birth Center in Salvador described by Eliza in the first half of this chapter. In 2007, Graziela was among those selected to travel to Japan to observe the work of Japanese midwives and learn Japanese midwifery techniques. There Graziela was struck by the professional midwives' autonomy, which is very rare in Brazil. "They did prenatal [care], they admitted women, they discharged women," she told Eliza (personal interview; March 23, 2016)—all things severely circumscribed for Brazilian nurse-midwives at the time.[21] She was also inspired by the level of "family integration" in Japanese obstetric care. Fathers, and often other family members, were present at all the births she observed; their participation was treated as normal and expected. In one birth Graziela witnessed, the woman was accompanied by her husband, her parents and sister, and the couple's oldest daughter. In another, she recalled that the woman's young sons fanned their mother when she was hot, gave her kisses, and brought her food. "These were things that made quite an impact on me," she said.

There were also significant differences in routine practices. In the births Graziela observed, Japanese midwives did not perform nearly as many vaginal exams to measure cervical dilation as did her Brazilian colleagues. Nor did they give women synthetic oxytocin to speed up labor, or perform the harmful Kristeller maneuver. "They allow respect for the moment, natural progression," she told Eliza, "They have the patience to wait." Whereas Graziela had "learned that you had to do Kristeller" and that the woman had to

---

[21] For years, Brazilian professional midwives only attended around 8% of births in Brazil. There are two types: the *enfermeira obstetra* (a university-trained nurse-midwife) and the *obstetriz* (a university-trained direct-entry midwife; these do not undergo nursing training and thus tend to have more autonomous attitudes). Cumulatively, they now attend just over 16% of Brazilian births—a sign of hope for the growth of their profession and of better care for mothers and babies (Gama et al. 2016).

"push like she's trying to defecate" while lying flat on her back, the Japanese mothers she saw in the independent maternity homes often gave birth in vertical positions or on all fours—something Graziela had never seen, and at first, seemed "crazy" to her.

Even in situations where Graziela was sure there would be heavy intervention, such as one instance where a baby was born not breathing, the Japanese midwives remained calm. Watching the scene unfold, Graziela joked that she and her Brazilian colleague "almost threw ourselves from the tenth floor from so much desperation" while their Japanese counterparts continued unruffled, put the baby on the mother's shoulder, and simply waited for the baby to let out its first cry, which he soon did. They were "very calm," she told Eliza, "Very confident. . . . They aren't afraid of what they're doing."

But, as she told Eliza, even though Graziela came back inspired from the JICA exchange, it took her a full year to even try to make any changes in the public maternity hospital where she worked. As soon as she returned, a colleague told her that a bill that would severely limit the scope of practice for nurse-midwives was quickly moving through the federal legislature. If passed, this bill would have practically ended nurse-midwives' legal ability to attend births—a serious setback for all efforts to demedicalize obstetric care.[22] This news, combined with her own colleagues' resistance to the ideas she was bringing back from Japan, deflated Graziela's hopes for making changes in hospital birth care. "I suffered a lot," she said, "It was very hard."

Graziela did eventually implement a project she is proud of—a breastfeeding support program that uses techniques she learned from Japanese midwives—though without almost any institutional assistance. An even greater accomplishment came several years later when she and a small group of health professionals from other hospitals inaugurated Salvador's very first (and only) Normal Birth Center. It was through her JICA contacts, in fact, that she got in touch with the folks who were planning the NBC. Under Graziela's and her colleagues' careful guidance, the center has become a reference for humanized birth in Bahia and a beacon for birth activists across Brazil.

Japanese midwives and their Brazilian collaborators have played a crucial role in the paradigm shift that is underway in Brazilian birth care, their exchanges greatly contributing to the ongoing changes that are now gaining ground in Brazil.

---

[22] The *Ato Médico* (Medical Act) bill proposed onerous restrictions on all nursing staff, nurse-midwives included. Nursing professional organizations and birth care advocates have fought it, and successfully lobbied for important modifications. It was eventually signed into law in 2013, with several key changes: the signed legislation does not contain any specific language about childbirth, instead stipulating that doctors are to work in mutual collaboration with other health care professionals in the care of patients (Congresso em Foco 2013).

Discussion: Outcomes, Stratification, Core Values, and Cultural Views of the Body

Japan's cesarean section rate is one of the lowest in the world (19%), whereas Brazil's is one of the highest (55%). Japan's maternal (3.4/100,000) and perinatal (3.6/1,000) mortality rates are very low, contrasted with 68.2/100,000 MMR and 11.1/1,000 neonatal mortality in Brazil. Another significant point of divergence between the two countries concerns the social stratification of birth care. In Brazil, class status—intimately entwined with skin color and income level—largely determines where and how birth takes place. In contrast, Japan's system of progressive taxation and guaranteed social benefits results in greater socioeconomic parity in health care. Since the Japanese government provides a uniform stipend to all pregnant women for prenatal and birth care, individual and family economic conditions are less influential factors in the kind of care women receive. The repercussions of social inequality also determine which mothers and babies will live and which may die, as is seen in their respective maternal and perinatal mortality statistics: Japan's are well within internationally agreed upon targets, while Brazil's are almost double the Millennium Development target goal.

Obstetric violence is another phenomenon deeply interwoven with social inequality and racial prejudice. In Brazil, obstetric violence has become a major organizing theme for feminist and birth activists responding to rampant disrespect and abuse in Brazilian maternity care services. In contrast, the term "obstetric violence" is practically nonexistent in Japan, in part, Etsuko suggests, because clinics and hospitals must cater to women's needs and desires in order to ensure adequate patient numbers. Japanese women's wide range of choices is practically unheard of in Brazil, except for a very small portion of the population (d'Orsi et al. 2014; Leal et al. 2014) who may find humanistic or holistic practitioners to attend them (see Davis-Floyd and Georges 2018).

There are also significant differences with respect to how the body and birth are conceptualized in each country. The tendency in Japan is to view the body as something natural and ecological (Ivry 2010), not to be physically tampered with or altered. Nutrition is a central focus of prenatal care in Japan, in part because of the cultural understanding that the woman is growing and nurturing the baby during pregnancy. In Japanese reproductive planning, condoms are much preferred to hormonal contraceptives, which are widely regarded as bodily invasions that disturb natural functioning and equilibrium. In Brazil, in contrast, bodily intervention is in many ways the norm. Brazilians tend to view the body as essentially fallible and malleable—open to, and often requiring, medical intervention in order to remain healthy and beautiful. The abundance of plastic surgery in Brazil attests to this understanding, as does the widespread use of hormonal contraceptives to eliminate periods, enhance muscle tone, and improve sex drive (Edmonds 2010; Sanabria 2015).

Given this culture of bodily intervention, it is unsurprising that CS and other medical manipulations have become ubiquitous in Brazilian maternity care.

For most Japanese women, vaginal delivery without analgesia is normal, preferable, and culturally valued as metamorphic, leading to an epidural rate of 6.1% of births in 2016—a dramatic contrast to Brazil's 31.5% vaginal birth epidural rate (Leal et al. 2014). So strong is the Japanese notion that birth should be vaginal that cesarean section can represent "failure" for women who undergo one. This sense of failure is rare in Brazil, where despite the fact that most women say they would prefer vaginal delivery, cesareans are normative.

The Significance of Space and Place

Anthropologists have long pointed out that childbirth is cultural, with practices and beliefs varying greatly from place to place. In this chapter, we have compared contemporary childbirth practices in two strikingly dissimilar countries, Brazil and Japan. Setting the two side by side allows us to see how different birth can be in these distinct cultures and also highlights persistent similarities. Overall, we note that birth practices in both Japan and Brazil are driven by social, cultural, and economic factors far more than by scientific evidence. The prevalence or paucity of surgical delivery is most certainly influenced by the very different views of the body and birth in these countries.

We also see that the culture-specific Japanese notion of *ie*, which paradoxically indexes both patriarchal power and the sense of comfort, belonging, and dependence it can bring, helps to construct Japanese obstetrical care, while Brazilian women must use *jeitinho*—a concept specific to Brazil—to get the births they want. It is not enough, however, to say that culture influences childbirth. It is also essential to consider the structural power dynamics at work in birth practices. Our analysis underscores the *impact of unequal social structures on how childbirth is done, whose voice counts, and which women have access to which kinds of birth care*. Race, class, gender inequities, and profit-driven medicine combine to make contemporary childbirth scenarios what they are. To Brigitte Jordan's assertion that birth is everywhere culturally marked and shaped, it is essential to add that birth is also shaped by the global structural forces of modernization, centralization, institutionalization, capitalism, globalization, and technomedicalization.

We have also sought to highlight positive changes, particularly in Brazil. Cross-cultural collaboration with Japanese midwives has been integral to attempts to transform Brazilian birth care. Both *Projeto Luz* and the nurse-midwife exchange program helped to enable Brazilian humanistic birth care to take root. We are now seeing the fruits of this and many other activist efforts to change childbirth in government initiatives like Rede Cegonha, as well as the rapid growth of grassroots birth activist movements throughout Brazil.

As we have shown here, birth is also heavily influenced by where it takes place. Home, hospital, birth center, obstetric clinic, private or public institution—all of these spaces imply different amounts of autonomy for women and midwives. Comparing birth in Brazil and Japan, and among its various settings, we see both troubling trends and reasons for optimism. Cross-cultural cooperation keeps the flame of the midwifery model of care burning, and dedicated activists and health care professionals in both countries continue to fight for women's choices. Humanistic, midwife-led care, we hope, will take up ever more space in ever more places in the always changing world of childbirth.

THOUGHT QUESTIONS

1. How do social inequalities affect childbirth differently in Brazil and Japan?

2. If you were to create a public policy for childbirth, what would it be and how would you implement it? What kinds of backlash would you expect, and how would you deal with that backlash?

3. Do you think dominant birth practices in your own country express core cultural values? How so? Give examples.

4. If you or a loved one were pregnant, where would you like the birth to take place— Japan or Brazil? Hospital, birth center, maternity home, or perhaps none of these? Why? What factors would affect your choice?

RECOMMENDED FILMS/VIDEOS

O Renascimento do Parto (*Birth Reborn*) 1 (Eduardo Chauvet 2013)–available on YouTube: (https://www.youtube.com/playlist?list=PLY-hZtX_CwE2_gUty9eDobebBH925Ttm0)
Produced by Érica de Paula and Eduardo Chauvet, 2013, this film was shown in movie theaters all over Brazil for five months and was viewed by over 30,000 people. It played a major role in moving forward the humanization of birth movement in Brazil. Robbie Davis-Floyd is one of the "talking heads" in this film, as are some of the holistic obstetricians she and Nia Georges (2018) have studied. It was this film that helped to generate the backlash from CREMERJ (mentioned above) that led to regulations prohibiting all OBs from attending homebirths. (http://tumeloyissakhar.blogspot.com/2015/10/watch-birth-reborn-online-2013-full.html).

O Renascimento do Parto 2 (Eduardo Chauvet) https://benfeitoria.com/orp2
This film, first shown in 2018, features an in-depth discussion of obstetric violence in Brazil, the Sofia Feldman Hospital's model maternity care program, birth centers in the UK, mixed public-private birth care in the Netherlands, and the World Health Organization's guidelines and recommendations. *Birth Reborn 2* shows the reality of births in this country and present humanized models, in Brazil and in the international arena. The intention is to call the attention of civil society, of public authority, of doctors, and of the judicial branch, and show that the change is urgent and possible. (https://benfeitoria.com/orp2). While this film did not have the same massive impact as its predecessor, it was shown in theaters all over the country and did serve as an important step in the humanization of birth process.

Violência obstétrica—a voz das brasileiras (*Obstetric Violence—Brazilian Women's Voices*) (Bianca Zorzam, Ligia Moreiras Sena, Ana Carolina Franzon, Kalu Brum, Armando Rapchan; 2012)—available on YouTube https://www.youtube.com/watch?v=eg0uvonF25M
Brazilian women tell their stories of obstetric violence on camera. Their narratives were filmed in their homes using low-tech equipment, including webcams and cellular phones, and then edited to compose this 51-minute documentary. The women share experiences of unwanted interventions like episiotomy, cesarean section, and the Kristeller maneuver, and the physical and emotional consequences that lasted long after their births. These women hope that by bringing their stories to light, other women might prepare themselves to confront the medical establishment, and perhaps avoid similar experiences.

Birthing in Peace (Peggy Oolsthorn, Image Media Services, 1993).
This 32-minute film documents the successful fusion of traditional and biomedical obstetrical systems achieved by Brazilian obstetrician Dr. Galba Araujo, who organized the building of maternity clinics throughout northeastern Brazil, staffing them with local midwives who were given biomedical training but were strongly encouraged to continue with their traditional style of birth: the mother labors while walking or resting in hammocks and gives birth upright on a birthing stool with little or no insertion of hands into the vagina; after birth, the baby stays with the mother. Such practices kept infection and mortality low, and were incorporated by Dr. Galba as far as possible into hospital practice in Fortaleza, Ceará, where he was director of obstetrics. (Yet after he died, younger obstetricians reverted back to their traditional technocratic ways.) http://www.worldcat.org/title/birthing-in-peace/oclc/872675120&referer=brief_results

Hanami—o florescer da vida (*Hanami—the Flowering of Life*) (Nathália Souza, 2010)—available with English subtitles on Vimeo (https://vimeo.com/32779480)
"This moving film reveals practices linked to a mode of experiencing conscious maternity, active birth and what these represent in the formation of more conscious human beings" (http://dochanami.blogspot.com.br; Eliza's translation).

Parir é natural (*Giving Birth Is Natural*) (Fiocruz, 2015, 26 minutes)—available from https://portal.fiocruz.br/pt-br/content/video-parir-e-natural
"The documentary presents testimonies from women who lived the experience of childbirth and the positioning of health care professionals specializing in birth with the aim of augmenting the debate about the banalization of cesarean section and all of its consequences" (https://portal.fiocruz.br/pt-br/content/video-parir-e-natural; Eliza's translation).

Nascer no Brasil (*Birth in Brazil*) two-part series (Fiocruz, 2014, 37 minutes total)—available from https://portal.fiocruz.br/pt-br/content/video-nascer-no-brasil
Produced by Fiocruz's Sérgio Arouca National School of Public Health—the institution responsible for the "Birth in Brazil" study mentioned in this chapter, this documentary features women's stories about their births. The first part discusses the theme of interventions in vaginal delivery, obstetric violence, and recommended best practices. The second part tackles the overuse of cesarean sections in Brazil, the risks it engenders, and common myths about surgical delivery.

Parto no Brasil (*Childbirth in Brazil*) (Melânia Amorim, 2009, ~30 minutes total in 4 parts, with English subtitles)—available on YouTube: https://www.youtube.com/watch?v=T_c9FwVlVw4;   https://www.youtube.com/watch?v=AVPLkiemt1c;

https://www.youtube.com/watch?v=iX3OKeJSFzY; https://www.youtube.com/watch?v=wK9iKYckmCA

The *Parto no Brasil* series details a project to institute humanized birth in a large public maternity hospital in Campina Grande, Paraíba, Brazil. Videos of women's births, followed by discussion by Dr. Melânia Amorim, weave throughout the documentary. Dr. Amorim—obstetrician, birth activist, and project coordinator—shares her wealth of knowledge and elaborates on the evidence-based practices of her team, which often go against the grain of technocratic obstetric practice in Brazil.

Freedom for Birth: The Mothers' Revolution, Toni Harman, Producer/Director. https://vimeo.com/ondemand/freedomforbirth

Genpin (2010, directed by Naomi Kawase) http://www.genpin.net/english.html

Childbirth & Living in the Era after the Great East Japan Earthquake (written and directed by Sakae Kikuchi, produced by Gendai Shokan) https://www.sakaekikuchi.com

5

Divergent Meanings and Practices of Childbirth in Greece and New Zealand

Eugenia Georges and Rea Daellenbach

Although both Greece and New Zealand (NZ) are high-resource countries in which feminists have been very influential in shaping cultural conceptions of women and their social treatment and roles, their birthing systems could hardly be more different. These differences, as always, reflect strongly contrasting cultural beliefs about the nature of birth and appropriate ways to manage it. While the technocratic model of birth, as described by Davis-Floyd (2018a) is highly visible in both, in Greece it is almost completely hegemonic, while in NZ a much more holistic, midwifery model of care often prevails. In Greece, the majority of women seek an obstetrician to provide their maternity care, and 60–70% have their babies delivered by cesarean section (CS). In NZ, 94% of women choose a midwife to provide their care, and midwives are present at 100% of births—even when women are scheduled for a CS. About 25% of NZ babies are born by CS, and of those born vaginally, almost half are born without the use of any technocratic medical interventions.

Despite these sharp contrasts, the perinatal and maternal mortality rates are similar in both countries. The perinatal mortality rate (PNMR) in NZ was 4.2/1,000 in 2015, and the maternal mortality rate (MMR) over the 10 years from 2006 to 2015 was 5.56/100,000 (Perinatal and Maternal Mortality Review Committee 2017). In Greece, the PNMR is 5.42/1,000, and the MMR was 4.6/100,000 in 2016. These rates reflect the generally good health and nutrition of the Greek population and the fact that almost no children are born to very young or unmarried women (ELSTAT 2017). The fertility rate in NZ is around two children per woman compared to 1.3 children per woman in Greece (OECD 2017). In other words, in terms of physical outcomes, both models work to produce healthy mothers and babies. And in both countries, women's conceptions about birth are deeply embodied and enacted in their birth choices. The main differences lie in the ideologies of the birth practitioners and women in each place, as well as in their effects on the treatment of women during pregnancy, labor, birth, and the postpartum period.

Following a brief overview of birth models in each country, we map the historical contexts for the current cultural constructions of childbirth in Greece and New Zealand. We trace how these have been produced through ongoing conflicts and negotiations between women and the State, as well as the ways in which childbirth ideologies have been caught up in the geopolitical nation-building endeavors in each country. We discuss how birth is symbolic of core values and how the meanings of salient concepts common to both settings, such as "choice" and "modernization," differ markedly between the two. We then look at the structures of maternity services in each country, focusing on how these structures affect women's expectations and experiences of maternity care. Women in Greece and New Zealand similarly place high value on and seek continuity of caregivers, even though they utilize divergent means to achieve this continuity and have very different ultimate goals in what they want. We next focus on the meanings women attach to childbirth that shape their aspirations and how they interpret their embodied experiences of birth. The final section explores some emergent possibilities within each maternity system that have the potential to challenge the technocratic control of childbirth knowledges and practices.

The information and analyses provided in this chapter stem from long-term fieldwork conducted by its anthropologist authors Eugenia (Nia) Georges and Rea Daellenbach. Nia has been conducting research on midwifery, obstetrics, and birth in Greece for over 20 years. Her most recent research focuses on the transformations in maternity care that have resulted from the arrival of large numbers of refugees into Greece. Rea has been conducting research with women and midwives in New Zealand since the mid-1990s. More recently, Rea has been involved in large research projects with women about their choices for and experiences of childbirth. Her research for her doctoral thesis was with activists in the homebirth movement in New Zealand; that work also involved extensive historical study.

Childbirth in Greece: Technocratic Knowledge as Authoritative

Unlike New Zealand, where midwives are the main providers of maternity care, birth in Greece is dominated by obstetricians and their technocratic model of authoritative knowledge. Discourses of choice and rights in childbirth that characterize New Zealand are largely absent in Greece, and activists advocating for reform and alternatives to the dominant model are few, scattered, and largely unorganized. Up to the present, no formal oppositional or alternative movements have emerged in Greece to seriously challenge the hegemony of obstetricians and the rigid protocols of hospital-based birth. The Greek feminist movement, which peaked in the 1980s and 1990s, was instrumental in effecting profound cultural, social, and legal changes (Papagaroufali 1990). However, much of the movement's energies coalesced around the urgent task of revoking Greece's repressively patriarchal family law (the now defunct "Family Code") that had effectively defined adult women as minors and enshrined their subordination to men in the judicial process. Issues in women's reproductive health, while also of concern, were not at the top of the feminist agenda.

Due at least in part to this absence of opposition, the provision of maternity care throughout Greece is remarkably uniform. Whether Greek women give birth in a posh private clinic or a no-frills public hospital (statistics on the percentages of births in these settings are unavailable), they experience very similar sets of technocratic protocols and procedures. When I (Nia) began my research in Athens and on the island of Rhodes some 20 years ago, pregnancy and birth were already thoroughly medicalized. Since then, the use of technological interventions has steadily intensified, even as media reports of evidence-based critiques of conventional obstetrical practices have proliferated. Greece's cesarean rate, for example, which stood at around 25% in 1990, had reached 60–70% by 2017 in the public hospitals and is believed to be higher still in the private sector, prompting the UN Convention of the Elimination of Discrimination Against Women (CEDAW 2013) to proclaim it "the highest in the world."

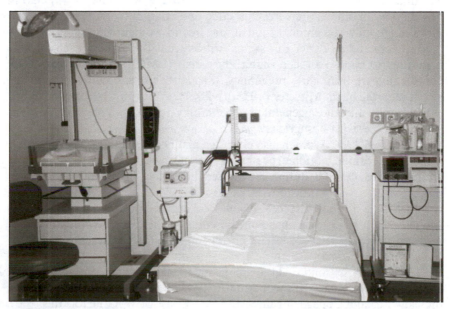

Technology is central to every Greek woman's maternity care. Photo by Nia Georges

Vaginal births, despite being popularly called "natural births," are also routinely subjected to an intensive array of technomedical procedures. Episiotomies are nearly universal, and women continue to give birth almost exclusively lying flat on their backs in the lithotomy position. The use of electronic fetal monitors and IV pitocin drips is routine and universal, effectively immobilizing the laboring woman. Most have their contractions induced and augmented by stripping the membranes (amniotomy) and administering labor-enhancing drugs and/or prostaglandins by the 39th week before their calculated due date. Few reach 40 or 41 weeks. Until recently, epidural analgesia was generally unavailable.

Today, in 2018, private hospitals may offer epidurals, but pharmacologic pain relief is typically unavailable in public hospitals due to a chronic shortage of anesthesiologists. Most doctors enter one of just seven specializations, and anesthesia has not been a popular choice. Until relatively recently, few anesthesiologists had acquired the training to administer epidurals. Although nearly all of the interventions described here intensify the pain of labor and birth, sometimes considerably, women who give birth in the public hospitals generally can only get pain relief by undergoing a cesarean section, which is commonly performed under general anesthesia.

Childbirth in New Zealand: The Primacy of Choice

In dramatic contrast to Greece, in New Zealand, the maternity system is based on autonomous midwifery practice and continuity of care. Maternity services are fully government funded and free to women who are New Zealand citizens and residents. In a system introduced 20 years ago, each woman is entitled to choose a "lead maternity carer" (LMC) who will provide or coordinate care from early pregnancy, through labor and delivery, until six weeks after the birth (Ministry of Health 2007). While an LMC can be either a community midwife, a general practice family doctor with obstetric training (GP), or a specialist obstetrician, *almost all women (93.6%) choose a community midwife as their LMC.* Women also choose a planned place to give birth, which can be in a hospital, at home, or in a birth center with midwifery care only. If complications develop during a planned home or birth center labor, the mother will be swiftly transferred to a hospital.

In stark contrast to Greece, in New Zealand, each wave of feminist activism over the past 130 years has put midwifery or the care of women in childbirth on its political agenda. The current maternity care system, based on midwifery-led, woman-centered care, came out of demands of feminists in the 1980s. Activists contested the increasing medicalization of childbirth and the devaluation of women's work and in 1989 joined with midwives to form the New Zealand College of Midwives (NZCOM). By working together, they were able to bring about legislative changes that reinstated the right of midwives to practice without medical supervision and introduced "direct-entry"[1] midwifery education as separate from nursing education, to prevent mid-wives from first being socialized into the subordination of nursing—socializing them instead into an attitude of autonomy. However, over the past 20 years, the government payments made to community (LMC) midwives have not kept pace with inflation or the increases in incomes for other professions, leaving many midwives struggling financially. In the past couple of years, a new generation of feminists has emerged who have taken up the midwifery gender pay equity cause and demanded government action to address it.

Women's views and experiences of birth in New Zealand are much more diverse than in Greece. According to the Ministry of Health report on maternity, one-third of NZ women have a "normal birth," defined as a "spontaneous vaginal birth (including spontaneous vertex and spontaneous breech)" without induction or augmentation of labor, epidural pain relief, or an episiotomy (Ministry of Health 2017:39). By comparison, in the US, only about 5% of women giving birth in hospitals have this kind of physiologic, noninterventionist birth. The 25% CS rate is about average for a high-income industrialized country (Ministry of Health 2017) yet is much higher than the World Health Organization's recommended rate of 15% (World Health Organization 2015). Despite their joint focus on normal physiologic birth, midwives' and women's decision-making is influenced by the wider societal and professional expectations that risks should be controlled and that technocratic interventions can achieve this control. Thus, most women in New Zealand choose to give birth in hospitals, where there is access to specialist services, "just in case" these are needed. About 10% of women give birth in a midwifery-led birth center and 4% birth at home (Ministry of Health 2017). These rates, which are much higher than the combined US community birth rate of 1.36% (which itself is higher than that of Greece), indicate a dynamic interplay between the technocratic and the midwifery (humanistic, holistic) models of childbirth that influence women's choices and midwifery practice. Many women who book a hospital birth expect to have a normal, natural birth and look to their midwife both to facilitate this kind of birth and to carefully monitor the progress of labor for any signs of abnormality.

Contrasting Cultural Models of Birth

Greece: Rapid Change from Traditional to Modern

Until the late 1960s, most births in Greece took place at home assisted by a "practical" midwife. This older cultural model shared many features described by Brigitte Jordan for the Yucatan Maya in 1970s Mexico. Before birth moved to the hospital, every Greek village and urban neighborhood had

---

[1] "Direct-entry" describes an educational model whereby students enter midwifery training directly—that is, without first becoming a nurse. Direct-entry midwifery is also discussed in Chapter 6 on the United States and the Netherlands, this volume.

a local midwife, most of whom learned their skills from their own mothers or other kinswomen. As I (Nia) was told by one long-retired village midwife, "only God and women" can bring life into the world: midwifery was regarded as a spiritual calling, as well as a heavy moral responsibility. Greek traditional midwives were not only experts in childbirth, they were also important ritual specialists who helped mother and infant navigate what was perceived as the dangerously liminal (ritually mediated spaces/times "betwixt and between"[2] two states of being) periods of birth and the postpartum. Their expert knowledge was grounded in humoral understandings of health similar to those found in many other nonmedicalized contexts around the world (Oberhelman 2016). The humoral model of the body that had informed understandings of health, illness, pregnancy, and birth since ancient times was premised on maintaining balance between opposing qualities— most importantly, between those symbolic and physical substances and forces that were categorized as "hot" and "cold." Women's bodies in particular were regarded as porous and fluid, and wombs were believed to "open" and "close" in response to hot and cold substances, respectively. During pregnancy and birth, care was taken through diet, dress, physical heat, and other means to maintain or restore the beneficial openness of a woman's body in order to ensure a good outcome. Many Greek midwives' techniques (for example, having women pull on a rope, inducing gagging to strengthen contractions during labor, and birthing in upright positions) were also used by Maya midwives in the Yucatan (Jordan 1993).

By the 1970s, this centuries-old cultural model of birth was practically extinct. Once World War II and the lengthy civil war that followed were over, Greece began the process of rebuilding its devastated institutions. Greek national recovery took off in the context of the Cold War, a time when the United States was determined to contain the influence of the Soviet Union and to prevent the "dominos" of southeastern Europe from falling under communist influence. Greece was regarded as a frontline of Soviet containment, and to help rebuild the nation, massive amounts of nonmilitary aid poured in from the US. As a result, by the early 1960s, the Greek economy had one of the highest growth rates in the world (Kalyvas 2015:105), and US "soft power" had come to exert a strong cultural influence on the institutions being rebuilt as Greece recovered from war.

Medicine was no exception. Before the war, the locus of "authoritative" biomedical knowledge had been Western Europe as Greeks looked to Germany and France in particular (where midwives attended, and still attend, the majority of births) for models of the most advanced and modern medical practice and training. After the war, the authority and prestige of these European models were replaced by US-style biomedicine. Talented Greek medical students preferred specialized residency training in the United States. The imprint of US influence on the development of Greek obstetrics was decisive

---

[2] The use of the terms "betwixt and between" to describe liminal ritual spaces and/or times comes from British cultural anthropologist Victor Turner (1967).

and remains so. For example, "normal births" in Greek obstetrics are not distinguished from those that are "high risk." As in the US, but unlike nearly every other country in Europe, all births are generally understood to be pathological or potentially pathological events that should properly take place under the surveillance of physicians.

Thus, within the span of a decade or two, birth had moved from home to hospital, and a US-influenced technocratic model of birth became dominant and culturally authoritative. Even women living in the most remote rural areas now traveled to the closest town or city for a hospital birth. As practical midwives began to age, their daughters showed little interest in learning their mothers' craft. Instead, they attended school and eventually left their villages to pursue education, employment, and other opportunities in the cities. By the 1970s, the last practical midwives had stopped attending births; even if a woman wanted a local midwife, that option had disappeared—and few women would have even considered it anyway.

Greece's "economic miracle" in the postwar years resulted in greater access to formal education, including university education, and unprecedented social mobility as young people moved from rural to middle-class urban lives. These rapid transformations were accompanied by a shift in understandings of the body and health. As literacy and levels of education increased, knowledge associated with modern science and medicine came to be understood as standard, while traditional knowledge of all kinds became identified with "backward" practices or "irrational superstitions" (Stewart 1991). Thus devalued, these knowledges eventually ceased to be transmitted and were replaced by a modernist narrative that optimistically linked biomedicine and its technologies to notions of progress, improvement in the standard of living, and increased control over health and the quality of life. Biological and anatomical understandings of the body and health, and the implicit metaphor of the body-as-machine that women acquired in the classroom, were supplemented and reinforced by information acquired outside the classroom as well. For example, nearly all of the women I interviewed had read one or more pregnancy guides, consulted the internet, watched videos, and attended childbirth classes to educate themselves further about the biomedical facts of pregnancy and birth. Reinforced by almost uniformly positive media coverage, reproductive technologies of all sorts, from prenatal tests to the battery of interventions routine in technocratic childbirth, came to be seen by doctors and women alike as essential to the management of the broad array of manufactured risks (radiation, pesticides, pollution, etc.) associated with modern life and to ensuring a positive outcome.

Similar experiences with the medicalization of pregnancy and birth can be found in many societies, particularly those in which the processes of modernization and social change are relatively recent and have taken place in a context of *symbolic domination*—in which meanings of "modernity" and "the modern" have evolved in continual reference to definitions already devised by more powerful outsiders (Faubion 1991:14; Bourdieu 2010 [1984]). In such contexts, forging a modern national identity has entailed a process of constant comparison with those few nations that modernized early ("the West") and came to exert cultural hegemony over the rest (Jusdanis 1991). In Greece, such persistent and usually invidious comparisons have also been shaped by the distinctive features of its history and politics. Specifically, the perceived gap between the achievements of classical Greece, long idealized by powerful Western states and their elites, and the less impressive realities of contemporary Greek life, have periodically led powerful outsiders, as well as Greeks themselves, to question their location along the continuum of modernity (Papagaroufali and Georges 1993). Thus, for Greeks, consuming the latest technologies and expert knowledge serves to counter the stigma of being considered "backward" or "less developed." For women in particular, such consumption also provides vehicles for enacting and crafting desirable identities as modern pregnant subjects. This historic dynamic has helped promote the often-enthusiastic adoption and intensification of medicalized maternity care in Greece.

New Zealand: Rapid Change from Technocratic to Humanistic/Holistic

Unlike Greece, New Zealand is a relatively young nation and its founding aspirations and conflicts still exert a significant influence today. The intensive migration of British settlers to New Zealand began in the 1840s after Māori (the Indigenous people of these islands) tribal leaders from all over the country signed a treaty with the British Crown in 1840. European colonization had devastating consequences for Māori. Exposure to new diseases to which Māori had not yet acquired natural immunity, numerous wars with White settlers, and illegal land confiscations led to the massive loss of lives, reducing the Māori population by an estimated two-thirds (Durie 1998).

For the British Crown, the treaty opened the door to a more organized and controlled approach to European settlement than had happened elsewhere in the world. Explicitly seeking to attract respectable young couples and skilled workers, the aim was to create "a new and better society" (Kedgley 1996:2) based on an agricultural economy. However, for many settlers struggling to adapt European farming practices to a new environment and living in small, isolated communities, life was very hard. While they came with Victorian inhibitions in relation to sexuality and pregnancy, they also found a new fortitude and resourcefulness enabling them to develop a practical orientation to birth as a straightforward normal event in a woman's life (Clarke 2012; Kedgley 1996).

The New Zealand government's role in childbirth began in 1904 with legislation that established a register of midwives.[3] The first state-funded

---

[3] Registration is similar to licensure, as the standards and right to practice are set out through government legislation. This is distinct from "certification," which is administered by nongovernmental professional organizations.

maternity hospitals were also established in major towns for working-class, married women where midwives could also be trained. The Midwives Registration Act of 1904 was introduced three years after nurses had also achieved registration. Both were instituted in response to lobbying by key activists within the women's movement who wanted better standards for health care for families and more career opportunities for women. The Midwives Act was also supported by advocates for more governmental responsibility in addressing high rates of maternal and infant mortality in the White population, in order to build the economic and military strength of this fledgling nation (Donley 1986). The act prohibited unregistered midwives from attending births without a doctor's supervision. As also happened in the UK from the 1930s through the 1950s, "practical midwives," who came from the communities where they worked and usually had children themselves, were replaced by professionally qualified midwives who were generally young, single, and middle-class, or at least trained in middle-class values (as shown for the UK in the popular television series *Call the Midwife*). Nurses have never been able to practice as midwives in New Zealand unless they have a midwifery qualification and are on the register of midwives.

Traditionally, Māori women gave birth just outside their villages, sometimes in a specially constructed hut called a *whare kohanga* (a nest house). Women were supported in childbirth by members of their *whānau*[4] (extended family), including, sometimes, husbands and fathers (Mikaere 2000). In addition to providing practical assistance, birth attendants utilized ritual practices to support the woman and maintain the spiritual integrity of childbirth (Simmonds 2018). The Māori language had no specific equivalent word for "midwife," as *whānau* members supported each other in childbirth. A Māori word that explains this role is *kaiwhakawhānau*—those who "facilitate the creation and development of *whānau*" (Kenney 2011:126). Within Māori communities, there were also *tohunga*, experts with specialized knowledge of rituals and traditional medicine who would be called to births that were particularly important to the community or in cases with difficulties in labor or postpartum (Clarke 2012). The Tohunga Suppression Act of 1907, which was passed three years after the Midwives Act, prohibited *tohunga* from practicing, resulting in the loss of much of the deeper cultural and spiritual Māori knowledge connected to childbirth (Kenney 2011; Simmonds 2018).

In 1938, again with pronatalist intentions, the introduction of the nationalized public health system included free maternity services for all NZ women; this system still exists today. It entitled all women—Māori included—to maternity care provided by a GP of their choice and free hospital care. Unlike qualified midwives, GPs were permitted to prescribe various forms of pharmacological pain relief and use forceps to deliver babies. The

---

[4] Traditionally, *whānau* would include elders, some of their children and spouses, and grandchildren, who generally lived together. The current usage of the term is more flexible and contextual and can include people who are bound by close ties but not necessarily genetically related (Walker, 2011).

new arrangements reduced the role of midwives to looking after women during labor, calling the doctor when birth was imminent and caring for postpartum women in hospitals.

At this same time, the hospital birth rate for Māori women was less than 20%. Most Māori women lived in rural communities and gave birth with their *whānau*, who would call in a rural district nurse/midwife to attend when needed. As part of an explicit assimilation policy, Māori women were now being directed to have their babies in maternity facilities. As Mikaere (2000:385) notes, this sudden change meant that Māori women were "forced into a completely passive role as patients; they were also denied the fundamentally important role of assisting other women within their *whānau* with their births."[5]

The rise of obstetric influence in childbirth occurred in New Zealand at about the same time as in Greece. In the 1960s, obstetricians gained influential positions within the NZ Health Department and on regional hospital boards. They argued that all births should take place in centralized hospitals under obstetric supervision and restricted the role of GPs to normal births, requiring them to transfer women with complications to an obstetric team (Donley 1986). They advocated that obstetric nursing should replace midwifery—an initiative that was supported by the national nursing organization. By the end of the 1970s, direct-entry midwifery programs were discontinued and midwifery education became available only for registered nurses through an advanced diploma.

Women and midwives in New Zealand and Greece responded differently to the rising obstetric influence in their respective nations. Greek women embraced it as a positive aspect of modernization, while many women in New Zealand resented the loss of their local community birth centers and the special relationships they had with family GPs. They also disliked the depersonalization of the modern obstetric hospitals and the routine use of interventions to actively manage labor and birth. Feminists in New Zealand framed this depersonalization as part of a wider patriarchal medical agenda to control women's bodies and reproductive rights (Bunkle 1988; Daellenbach 1999). They deployed a different type of "modernization" defined by feminist aspirations for women's autonomy and empowerment. They explicitly drew on the "emancipatory spirit" (Grigg and Tracy 2013) of pioneer women to add legitimacy to their rights-based claims and to construct women's autonomy in birth as part of the next battle in the ongoing fight for women against male domination.

Some White, middle-class NZ women began considering giving birth at home as a way to regain control in childbirth. Homebirths continued to be

---

[5] This scenario of removing birth from the care of traditional practitioners and from native land has been repeated many times, from Australia to Canada. See Daviss (1997) and Epoo et al. (forthcoming) for descriptions of how the Canadian Inuit of the Nunavik region have reclaimed birth by bringing it back into the communities via the construction of maternity centers and the professional training of Indigenous midwives.

funded through the 1938 Social Security Act and thus were still part of the state maternity services. But remuneration for midwives was very low, and few GPs agreed to provide care for women planning homebirths. Groups formed around the country to promote and support homebirth families and midwives. Influenced by the nascent US homebirth movement of the 1970s, some NZ midwives took on homebirth practice because of their disillusion-ment with hospital births. Similar to what Cheyney (2008) characterizes as the "systems-challenging praxis" ("praxis" means practice embedded in a meaningful ideological and methodological system) of homebirth in the United States, NZ homebirth midwives and families together had to cre-atively work out what was "normal" when labor and birth were not actively managed according to obstetric protocols. From the recognition of their shared marginalization and interdependence, women and midwives forged a new kind of professional relationship, based on mutual trust and a commit-ment to negotiated and informed shared decision-making.

As well as developing new cultural practices around birth and new, strong relationships between women and midwives, homebirth consumer and mid-wife activists became increasingly political over the decade of the 1980s. In 1989, a group of midwives and women formed the New Zealand College of Midwives (NZCOM), a professional organization to represent and advocate for midwives. A year later, the law was changed to enable midwives to attend births without medical supervision. They also gained rights to prescribe med-icines, to book women into hospitals and attend them there in labor and birth, and to refer women and/or babies to specialists when needed. Helen Clark, the Minister of Health, introduced the legislation to address "the injustice . . . [of] the loss of autonomy for midwives" as well the "monopoly of registered medical practitioners" (Clark 1990:2–3). At the same time, bachelor's degree--level direct-entry midwifery programs were established, and now two-thirds of the midwives who are practicing in New Zealand have come through these programs (Midwifery Council of New Zealand 2017).

The new ways of conceiving and negotiating the relationships between women/families and midwives that had developed within the homebirth com-munity became incorporated into the professional framework of NZCOM, meaning that *the midwife's primary accountability is to women* and is described by the term "partnership" (Guilliland and Pairman 1995). The onus is on the midwife to "create a functional partnership" (Midwifery Council of New Zea-land 2007:1), which she does by establishing a relationship with her clients and providing the information they need to make informed decisions.

The framework of partnership between mothers and midwives is closely intertwined with another concept: *cultural safety* (Nursing Council of New Zealand, 1996). While health practitioners worldwide recognize that discrimi-natory practices have harmful consequences for the health of marginalized groups, cultural safety has been developed in New Zealand in a specific way that was pioneered by Māori nurse, midwife, and educator Irihapeti Ramsden (2002). She argued that the health service is, in itself, a culture shaped by the dominant Western culture and thus particularly alienating and disempowering to those most in need—socially marginalized individuals and groups. Cultural safety begins with all health practitioners recognizing their own professional and personal culture and critically reflecting on their *ethnocentrism* in order to avoid disregarding or disrespecting the cultural identity and beliefs of those to whom they provide care. Ramsden emphasized that those receiving health care should determine whether this care is culturally safe for them. Also, she argued for a broad definition of cultural diversity that included differences based on "socio-economic status, age, gender, sexual orientation, ethnic origin, migrant/refugee status, religious belief or disability" (Ramsden 2002:114). While midwifery partnership focuses on negotiated decision-making and shared responsibility, cultural safety requires a deeper analysis of power imbalances and an active respect for women's rights to cultural self-determination in childbirth (Midwifery Council of New Zealand 2012).

The Formal and Informal Political Economy of Maternity in Greece

Maternity care in Greece is provided exclusively by obstetricians and direct-entry midwives. Nurse-midwifery does not exist as a profession. Greek midwives are all highly educated professionals who undergo a rigorous four-year program of university training and upon completion are certified as direct-entry midwives (*maia*). (The defunct traditional midwives were called *mammi*, now considered a derogatory term if applied to a professional midwife.) In the decades following World War II, professional midwives provided maternity care to rural areas throughout the country, often in fulfillment of the compulsory rural service that was part of their training and certification. By the 1970s, several trends combined to effectively end this brief stint of independent practice for midwives. Postwar migration to the nation's largest cities, particularly of young people, helped depopulate the countryside, diminishing the need and opportunities for rural service. At the same time, the supply of obstetricians began to expand as the Greek economy experienced unprecedented growth and many new universities, including new medical faculties, were founded throughout the nation. Doctors have long enjoyed high status and prestige in Greek society, and so the new medical schools attracted (and continue to attract) large numbers of students, despite a serious oversupply of physicians in many specialties. Since 1990, for example, the number of medical school graduates has more than doubled, with the number of obstetrician-gynecologists (OBs) increasing by 34% (Mossialos et al. 2005). As the national birth rate plummeted to historic lows during this same period, the supply of obstetricians soon outstripped demand for their services. By 2000, Greece's ratio of obstetricians to inhabitants was roughly double that found in the other countries of the EU. Inevitably, given the significant oversupply, many obstetricians found it difficult to secure full-time work.

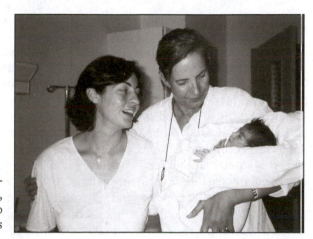

A new mother, her new-born held by the midwife, in a hospital room. Photo by Nia Georges

This situation has resulted in strong competition among doctors for pregnant clients and also in the almost complete elimination of midwives as independent providers of maternity care. Today, almost all Greek midwives work in hospitals or as part of an obstetrician's private practice. For example, in Athens, a city of three million people, only a handful of midwives work autonomously and assist homebirths. Midwives *do* still participate in birth but almost always as auxiliaries to a particular doctor—a dependent status clearly indexed by the fact that pregnant women and their families may refer to them as "the doctor's midwife." A distinctive characteristic of Greek midwives is the degree to which they share the prevailing favorable attitudes toward technological interventions across the course of pregnancy and birth (Pechlivani and Adam 1999). While a more holistic approach characterizes the few midwives who work autonomously, the great majority share the technocratic approach that dominates maternity care more generally in Greece. Yet despite their rigorous scientific training and strong allegiance to the dominant technocratic model, midwives' responsibilities are essentially limited to teaching childbirth classes, providing doula-like support during labor and delivery in the hospital setting, and promoting breastfeeding among new mothers. It is likely that Greek midwives' strong commitment to reversing the older trend toward bottle-feeding has helped promote today's relatively high level of breastfeeding in the first months after birth. Still, many feel that the kind of work they are restricted to does not make use of their extensive training and professional knowledge (Lauren et al. 2001).

Doulas are exceedingly rare in Greece.[6] Very recently, a handful of women in Athens and Thessaloniki (Greece's two largest cities) have trained to become

---

[6] North American researchers borrowed the word "doula" from the Greek in the 1970s and its use has since spread widely. However, childbirth activists in Greece take exception to the term, which is derived from the Ancient Greek for "slave" or "servant," and thus has derogatory connotations in the modern language. For this reason, many prefer to use the term *"voithos mitrotitas,"* which translates literally as "motherhood assistant."

professional doulas, most after experiencing their own homebirths. This development has sometimes provoked hostility from midwives, who have long provided similarly supportive functions for birthing women. In Greece's current context of economic hardship and high unemployment, the relationship between doulas and midwives is fraught with antagonism and competition.

Unlike New Zealand, in Greece, the provision of health services in the public sector is subtly and sometimes profoundly affected by the existence of an informal, shadow economy of care. In the formal realm, health care in Greece is comprised of a mix of the private sector and the public, universal access National Health Service (ESY), established in 1983. The two sectors are popularly regarded as differing in terms of quality and comfort, and many Greek women prefer the comparatively more luxurious private clinics to public hospitals. Still, some ESY hospitals, including the ones where I conducted my research, enjoy reputations for good doctors and modern technology that attract a broad range of women, many of whom could afford private care. ESY doctors are salaried employees of the state, and most are not permitted by law to see patients privately.

In practice, however, patients and their families manage to finesse the impersonal, bureaucratic public sector to achieve the kind of personalized care they value and desire through the widespread practice of giving gifts. Forging reciprocal relationships through gift giving is intended to ensure that they will receive continuous care from the doctor of their choice, shorter waiting times for prenatal appointments, and doula-like support from the midwife when it comes time for them to give birth. Typically, gifts consist of cash, generally in the range of a few to several hundred euro to doctors (and much less to midwives and staff), with the amount varying mostly according to the financial capacity of the family. Cash is often complemented by such nonmonetary gifts as flower arrangements, boxes of pastries, chocolates, and the like.

Patients also regard gifting as a way to express their gratitude, empathy, and support for their doctors, who work hard but, as everyone acknowledges, receive relatively low salaries. "You give it because you *want* to," people might insist when I asked them about the practice. It is therefore important to distinguish gift giving from the institution of the *fakelaki*, or "little envelope," which is an extra fee that doctors may occasionally demand in advance to expedite a procedure, usually a surgery (Colombotos and Fakiolas 1993:140). Although it is difficult to estimate how much money doctors make in the informal economy, one study calculated that cash gifts to doctors amounted to approximately 2.5 times their annual ESY salaries (Nikolopoulos 2010). Ultimately, gifts of cash offer an incentive for public sector doctors to maintain an exclusive relationship with their patients. This widespread practice of giving gifts to National Health Service doctors has often been publicly denounced as another example of the corruption endemic to Greek bureaucracies. However, from the patients' perspective, it can also be seen as a way to forge relationships of reciprocity and trust with their providers and to achieve the continuity of care and degree of responsiveness they actively desire.

Typically, when women learn they are pregnant, they consult their family, friends and the internet for the name of a good doctor, and may shop around across private and public sectors until finding one they feel they can trust and "bond with." Francesca,[7] a 25-year-old hairdresser who had just given birth to her first child, explained that she had found her doctor after careful deliberation, ultimately picking him because of his responsiveness and his willingness to "help her" in terms similar to those expressed by many other women:

> My doctor helped me a lot. I could ask him about anything. He gave me support. That's why women say, "You've got to be bonded, *dhemeni*, with your doctor. . . ." Me, I go to my doctor with my eyes closed [*me ta matia klista*], with complete confidence. He's very good—he helped me a lot.

Francesca's confidence in her doctor did not, however, reflect blind and unreflective trust in doctors in general. Women and their partners often criticized the medical profession as a whole, and many readily pointed to the greed and self-interest of other obstetricians as reasons for the high cesarean rate. Like many women, Francesca, who gave birth by cesarean, believed that some doctors performed the operation largely for their own convenience: "That's why you see that most of the babies in the public hospital are 'Saturday-born'" (*savatogenimena*), she explained, referring to the fact that ESY doctors' day off is Sunday (as confirmed by Mossialos et al.'s survey of births in three Athenian hospitals, 2005:290). But also like most women, she did not impute these sentiments to her *own* doctor, with whom she and her husband had cultivated a trusting relationship.

For their part, doctors strive to foster trust and closeness as a way to gain and retain patients in a highly competitive environment, even if they might also complain about the inconvenience and overwork that results from the extra time and effort such closeness entails. One highly respected ESY obstetrician who had practiced in both the United States and Greece compared his experiences in the two countries:

> My patients want an exclusive relationship with me [and thus, as he went on to explain, would not accept a group practice as his US patients did]. They are very tied to me, very dependent, even compulsive [*psichanangastikes*]: they can call me 30 times, at my office or on my cell phone, at any hour, midnight even. I am like their confessor. I know things even their husband doesn't know. . . . That's the kind of relationship a Greek woman has with her doctor. It's very tiring, unbelievably tiring. I'm tied down, whereas in the US I had more free time. But if a doctor doesn't do these things for them, they don't stay, they will go elsewhere.

However overworked ESY doctors are, and however "compulsive" they might consider their patients' demands, they still want to attract and keep pregnant women, whom they treat as their individual, quasi-private patients, for the often substantial extra income they provide. The informal gifting

---

[7] All names of respondents are pseudonyms.

economy has thus promoted the semiprivatization of the ESY hospitals and effectively blurred the boundaries between the private and public sectors. As a result, except for the relatively more luxurious facilities and the availability of epidurals in the private clinics, the protocols, CS rates, and birth outcomes are essentially identical between the two sectors. The intensity of the doctor–patient relationship fostered by financial incentives has also reinforced the exclusion of midwives from childbirth and restricted opportunities for residents to acquire extensive hands-on experience, as the obstetrician must attend the birth in order to get his "gift."

The Social Contract for
Maternity Care in New Zealand

As in Greece, maternity care in New Zealand is primarily provided by midwives and obstetricians, with a few GPs with obstetric training also offering maternity services. The midwifery educational requirements in New Zealand meet the same European Union (EU) standards as the midwifery programs in Greece. But, unlike Greek midwives, graduate midwives in New Zealand are able to work across the scope of midwifery practice throughout pregnancy, labor, and up to six weeks postpartum, as *continuity of care and of carer are cornerstones of the NZ maternity care model*. "Community midwife" is a relatively new term for LMC midwives, all of whom can attend women at home, in birth centers, and in hospitals. Like Greek OBs, community LMC midwives are on call 24/7, as they commit to being present at the births of the clients they take on. The midwifery education programs prepare midwives to work both as *community* and as *core* midwives. Core midwives work on shifts in birth centers or hospitals, in prenatal clinics, postnatal wards, and labor and birthing rooms, in collaboration with community midwives. For example, if a community midwife brings a laboring mother to a birth center, the core midwife on shift will be there to greet the woman and her support people and locate necessary supplies; the two midwives may attend the birth together while the community (LMC) midwife remains the primary caregiver. When a woman requires hospital-based obstetric specialist care, depending on the circumstances, the community midwife may transfer care to the core midwives.

It would be a mistake to assume that core midwives working shifts in birth centers or hospitals lack the ability to practice autonomously as community midwives do, as many midwives move back and forth between these roles—community and core—as their life circumstances change. For example, rather than always being on call, for some midwives, working on shift as a core midwife may be more compatible with raising small children. But when those children are older, the former core midwife might wish to return to—or to begin—community practice. For others, continuing to practice as a community midwife but maintaining only a small caseload of two or three births per month might offer more flexibility to combine with motherhood.

LMCs/community midwives are remunerated through a contract that was negotiated between the Ministry of Health, NZCOM, and the New Zealand Medical Association in 1996, referred to as the Primary Maternity Services contract. Rather than being paid for the care actually provided, the LMC community midwife, GP, or obstetrician is paid per client and thus receives the same fees, irrespective of the amount of care a given woman requires (Ministry of Health 2007). LMCs are responsible for assessing, planning, and coordinating all the maternity care a woman and her baby need from early pregnancy until six weeks after the birth. Their responsibilities include appropriate referral to other health practitioners (Ministry of Health 2012) and ensuring that another LMC is available if they are, for example, at another birth.

When the LMC contract specifying that one practitioner would take primary responsibility for managing a woman's care was first established, GPs were still the majority of maternity caregivers, with midwives as a distinct minority. One might ask, then, why the GPs, who were already in a position of power, accepted the idea of the LMC, which ultimately led to the near-universal use of midwives as LMCs? In their history of NZCOM, Guilliland and Pairman suggest that the "only probable explanation is that in advocating this model, doctors expected women to choose *them* as the primary carer 'in charge' of their case, rather than midwives whom they presumably saw as their 'secondary assistants'" (2010:309). Obstetricians only serve as LMCs for the 6% or so of women who choose them and for those referred to them by midwives, leaving all the normal, low-risk births to the midwives. *In a stunning reversal of the norm in most other countries, NZ OBs confine themselves to what they are actually trained for: the care of high-risk pregnancies and the performance of surgeries.* Many work both in public hospitals and private practices.

Community/LMC midwives, who are fully integrated into the health care system, practice autonomously and are considered to be self-employed. They usually work in small, independent, community-based group practices of between two and eight midwives and thus are able to give each other professional and personal support, as well as make arrangements with each other for time off-call. In a study on birthplace choices[8] in which I (Rea) was involved, Pip (a pseudonym) explained:

> I had my backup midwife, because my midwife was away. . . . She came
> at midnight when my contractions were on top of each other and then as
> soon as she arrived my labor disappeared so it didn't kind of build up
> again until like 5 the next morning and then we transferred to [the birth

---

[8] The Evaluating Maternity Units study (EMU) using mixed methods, conducted in Christchurch, included: a prospective cohort study (see Grigg et al. 2017) on birth outcomes for well women according to planned place of birth; a survey (571 respondents) to collect information about women's decision-making and birth experiences, and focus groups (eight groups, 37 participants) to provide the opportunity for more in-depth discussion. I (Rea) organized the focus groups along with Celia Grigg and Mary Kensington and the quotes used here come from these group interviews. These have also been reported on in Grigg et al 2014, 2015.

center]. Then I got in the pool and it disappeared again. And I was hours. She got really exhausted . . . and so she then got [another midwife] in the practice to come as well . . . and she was a breath of fresh air in the room, because we were all exhausted. And she just took a look at the situation and went "You're fine," just "It's cool," which was just fantastic, I don't know, to have that double backup. I wrote a very long birth note, thanking all the midwives.

The maternity services contract enables community midwives to exercise a great deal of control over how they manage their practice. For example, they can make their own decisions on how many women/births they will book per month. The average caseload for LMC community midwives is between 40 and 50 women per year (Midwifery Council of New Zealand 2017:24).

As in Greece, there are a very few doulas in New Zealand, and most of them have begun offering doula services only in the past few years. Some have become certified through US programs, but they do not have a professional association in New Zealand. Some midwives are happy to support women's choice for doula care. Other midwives, and many women, expect that the provision of continuous physical and emotional care in labor and facilitating the involvement of partners and other support people are part of the community midwife's responsibilities. The midwifery profession is concerned that health authorities could view doulas as a cost-saving substitute to midwifery care, and thus NZ midwives do not support any expansion of doula services (New Zealand College of Midwives 2009).

Our practice is looking for 1-2 qualified Midwives to join us. We work in partnerships and offer full continuity of care to women and families within Christchurch and surrounding areas of your choice.

New graduates or upcoming graduates very welcome.

We offer the following:
Alternate weekends off
Alternating Xmas/New Year holidays
Other holidays as you arrange
Reliable back up
Regular practice meetings
Supportive practice midwives
Caseload to start practicing

If you are interested in finding more about how we work we would love to hear from you so please contact us on any of the following numbers:

Excerpt from an advertisement for a midwife to join a group practice posted on a notice board for midwives. Photo by Rea Daellenbach

Women in both New Zealand and Greece place a great deal of value on the promise of individualized care from a key maternity provider whom they have chosen, whether this is an obstetrician, as in Greece, or a midwife, as in New Zealand. New Zealand women generally appreciate this flexible mater- nity system, as many are aware that it is not available in most other countries. Roz explained, "The system here is fabulous . . . that continuity. . . . It just makes so much sense to have one person with your notes and follows it through, and afterwards, and knows you." In both countries, many women are seeking a relationship based on trust and an emotional bond. However, while Greek women want an obstetrician they can trust to take charge and make the clinical decisions about their care, for New Zealand women, a shared philosophy and shared decision-making are more important. Dee explained: "I think you want a midwife that's in line with your beliefs. When you're giving birth, you're vulnerable and you're not thinking. You want someone who can be there for you, so you need a midwife who understands what you want and is willing to advocate for you."

To find the right midwife, New Zealand women use methods similar to those that Greek women use to find obstetricians: recommendations from family, friends, and other health professionals or through the internet (NZCOM has a "find your midwife" website). Women will often talk with quite a few midwives before they decide. In contrast with Greece, where there is an oversupply of obstetricians, there are rural areas in New Zealand where there are intermittent shortages of midwives and consequently fewer to choose among. Shortages of Māori midwives have also been identified by Māori *whānau* (Kenney 2011); 25% of women who give birth are Māori (Min- istry of Health 2017), while only 9.4% of practicing midwives are Māori (Midwifery Council of New Zealand 2017).

For many women, finding the "right" midwife is an important but also troubling task. As Pat states: "It's not that all midwives are good in NZ. It's making sure you get a good one." Many women in Greece distrust obstetri- cians in general, suggesting that their decision-making is often motivated by financial self-interest or expediency. In New Zealand, some women who tend to believe more in OBs may distrust midwives' competence. In part, this sort of anxiety has been fueled by regular media attention on midwifery and childbirth in New Zealand over the past two decades. Rather than celebrating NZ's excellent maternity care system, news reporters, always searching for the sensational, seek out firsthand narratives about tragic childbirth experi- ences, with the women constituted both as victims of poor midwifery practice and as authoritative voices about the quality of their midwifery care. These news stories can be quite divisive as women take different positions in terms of defending or criticizing midwifery. However, as midwives *are* the maternity workforce in New Zealand, many women resolve these tensions by endeavor- ing to choose their own midwife carefully. As Min explained:

> I think it's a personal fit for an individual. You hear, "Oh you shouldn't
> go to that midwife or you shouldn't go to this midwife because they've

done this or they've done that." And there's always going to be inci-
dences. They are not going to be able to keep everybody happy all of the
time. And I just think that they get quite a hard time. But I also think that
it is our choice to be able to just say, "You're not suitable for me."

As in Greece, trust is cultivated in the individual interpersonal relationships
women develop with the health practitioner they have chosen themselves.

The Normalization of Cesareans in Greece: Doctors and Women's Expectations of Birth

Greece's high cesarean rate is popularly attributed to doctors' desire for
financial gain and for convenience and control over their schedules, on the
one hand, and to women's fears of childbirth and their own desires for convenience and control on the other. Unfortunately, studies that attempt to disen-
tangle the complex conjuncture of factors that have led to today's Greek CS
rate of nearly 65% are almost nonexistent. In this section, I (Nia) focus on the
birth narratives of women as a lens through which to explore the dynamic
complexity of their attitudes and perceptions toward the dominant technocratic model of birth in general and toward cesareans in particular. Although
the majority of the women I spoke with expressed a preference for vaginal
birth, most (60%) ended up with a cesarean anyway once they entered the
hospital. Women held a range of perceptions about the operation, but two
themes were particularly salient and recurred across their narratives, whether
they had given birth vaginally or by cesarean. First and foremost was the
widely held perception that cesareans reduced risk of harm to the infant, and
thus were the safest and most prudent way to ensure the health of what, after
all, might be the only child a couple will have (or at most, one of two). Cesareans were also regarded by doctors and women alike as the safest option for
older women (a supposition not supported by the evidence). Since the average age of my sample in 2010 was 35 (tracking the national trend toward
delaying marriage and the formation of families), many women said that the
operation had been justified because of their age. The perceived safety of CS
enabled women and their families to consider it a viable option for avoiding
the pain of childbirth and safeguarding the woman's own health and bodily
integrity—a fascinating contrast to a country like Japan and to the members
of the humanization of birth/alternative birth movements in many countries,
where women often consider CS a violation of their bodily integrity.

In Greece as elsewhere, reproductive technologies such as genetic testing, prenatal diagnosis, fetal ultrasound imaging, and, as I will argue, cesareans, are increasingly understood as means by which doctors can assist
women to reduce risk and take responsibility for the medical futures of their
children (Rose 2007:9). By the time pregnant Greek women enter the hospital, they typically have gathered information about birth by reading one or

more pregnancy guides, watching videos, searching the internet, and taking childbirth courses from a midwife. They will have also spoken with their friends and families about what to expect and garnered an array of opinions and advice from other women. Their education continues across their monthly prenatal consultations, which offer them (and often their husbands or partners as well) repeated opportunities to view the fetus on the ultrasound screen and converse with their doctor about its health and development, and in the later months of their pregnancy, about the probable mode of delivery. Together, these sources of information have worked to shape women's perceptions of the advantages and disadvantages of vaginal and cesarean birth.

Although when asked, most women expressed a preference for vaginal birth, their narratives typically revealed a mix of positive and negative perceptions of both vaginal and cesarean options. The most commonly mentioned undesirable aspects of the cesarean that women wished to avoid included postoperative pain, longer recoveries, and anesthesia—notably, all fears for themselves and their own well-being. However, these concerns were often outweighed by the aura of reduced risk for the baby that perceptually accrued to the cesarean. Doctors, along with women and their families, often used the word *taleporia*, which means hardship or suffering, to describe the process of labor. Labor was a *taleporia* for women, to be sure. But they believed that labor posed the greatest hazards for the baby, who had to navigate the birth canal, and it was commonly felt that the risk of injury or other harm to the fetus' health only increased as labor dragged on and the infant was squeezed and stressed. The misshapen head or discoloration of babies born vaginally was often mentioned as evidence of this stress (despite the fact that these are normal and vanish within a few hour or days). For example, Magdaleni, 34, told me that she initially wanted a vaginal birth, but when her doctor recommended a cesarean because the fetus was too big for her small pelvis, "I accepted gladly." She had been present at her sister's vaginal birth "from beginning to end," and witnessing her sister's fear and insecurity had left her "with a very bad feeling. It was a difficult birth and I saw the fear in her face. She didn't express it, of course, but I saw that she didn't feel fully safe. I didn't want that." Comparing her own infant "that came out immediately, with a peaceful expression, pink and fresh and didn't suffer at all" with her sister's, who was born "dark and bruised," reinforced Magdaleni's satisfaction that her cesarean had been better: "That's what I wanted and I was satisfied. I don't regret it."

The perception that cesareans are generally safer was also surprisingly common among those closest to the birthing woman, and their personal accounts of difficult vaginal births often helped reinforce a positive inclination toward the operation. Nikoleta's mother told her daughter that she was relieved when the doctor suggested a cesarean. She herself had experienced a difficult delivery with forceps some 25 years before:

> My mother had torn down below and was in pain and couldn't sit for a month . . . she said to me, "Better not to have a vaginal birth!" And my

brother's head, for the next two months after he was born, was injured, traumatized, like this . . . [using her two hands to indicate the extent of the swelling]. A cesarean is better, my mother said, because "the baby will come out unharmed, just fine, so don't give it another thought."

During my interview with Georgia, who had just given birth by cesarean, her husband, Niko, a computer programmer, joined in our conversation and had this to say about the operation:

I believe that women who prefer vaginal birth haven't realized that the cesarean is an advancement of medicine that we have now [*mia ekseliksi tis ghiatrikis pou ekhoume tora*]. They believe that it's better to give birth vaginally; they don't accept the medical developments that are now part of our lives.

Georgia, who expressed satisfaction that her cesarean had been necessary to ensure a good outcome, agreed with her husband's views but, significantly, went on to cite additional advantages of the operation:

There are some women who don't want to give birth vaginally because of the pain . . . I believe that the way of birth is a woman's choice. If she believes that she can't stand the pain, and she doesn't want it, she says to the doctor, "I don't want to." It's her choice, because she's the one who will give birth, the husband doesn't give birth.

As this exchange between Georgia and Niko hints, women and their families have come to attribute positive dimensions to cesarean sections on multiple, often overlapping fronts. Reflecting at least in part the intersection of a liberal discourse of "choice" with the maternal moral responsibility for their children's health, the cesarean can be interpreted as just one more among the many modern reproductive technologies that prudent women must consider to ensure an optimal outcome (Rose 2007).

Over the course of the last two decades, a clear shift has occurred in the way the way the pain of childbirth is perceived. When I began my research in the early 1990s, it was not uncommon to hear women express disappointment and regret after giving birth by cesarean, primarily because it robbed them of experiencing the pain that, in their words, "completed" their transformation as mothers (a belief still common among many Japanese mothers; Williamson and Matsuoka, this volume, Chapter 4). As several anthropologists have pointed out, a poetics of pain (*ponos*), and in particular, the pain of childbirth, has long figured as an important cultural resource in the fashioning and performance of maternal identities in Greece (Dubisch 1991; Caraveli 1986; Paxson 2004).

Yet by 2010, women no longer attributed this transformative quality to the pain of childbirth; some even laughed or otherwise scoffed at the notion. In the preceding decades, feminist and liberal discourses and legislation promoting gender equality exerted a strong influence on women's expectations of birth. Informed by a new ethics of choice, well-being, and self-care that "prioritiz[es] their own mental and physical health" (Paxson 2004:35), Greek women have overridden, and in some cases, explicitly rejected, the older poetics of self-abnegation and maternal suffering as essential to the project of motherhood. In short, they have come to expect technomedical benefits to extend not just to their infants but to their own care during labor and birth as well. From such discussions, the outlines of a popular and pragmatic calculus of "best practices" can be discerned.

Although vaginal birth in Greece is popularly referred to as "natural birth" (*physiologikos toketos*), given the intensity of medical interventions involved, it is in fact more properly described as an "operative delivery." Thus, when women considered the options of cesarean versus "natural" birth, they were essentially comparing two sets of technomedical procedures and interventions—in effect, two modes of operative delivery. Within this framework, the cesarean had accrued value because, compared to the invasive and often painful procedures that inevitably accompanied a vaginal birth, CS was seen as protecting valued aspects of a woman's bodily health and function. In this calculus, stories of other women's experiences with episiotomies appeared to have been particu-larly influential in shaping perceptions about mode of birth. For example, Rena, who at 32 had just given birth by cesarean to her first child, explained that her preference for the operation had been influenced by her best friend's account of her episiotomy: "She hurt when she went to the bathroom for months afterward and had to be restitched." Similarly, Irini, 34, referred to her mother-in-law's experience: "She told me that the doctors tore her up and that she couldn't sit down without hurting for a long time." Ritsa, a 27-year-old accountant who had just given birth to her daughter by cesarean, added, "I have friends [who delivered vaginally] who still can't make love with their hus-bands because of [complications from] the episiotomy, and another friend who, after all these years, still remembers the doctor sewing her up; she can't forget it." Thus, Ritsa appreciated the operation for the protection it offered from the risk of iatrogenic damage (both corporeal and psychological) that could result from the episiotomy. Ultimately, the women I interviewed knew that they would be surgically cut, either "above" or "below" (as in Brazil; Diniz and Chacham 2004; see also Williamson and Matsuoka, this volume, Chapter 4).

They were also well aware that they would experience pain, as they put it, either "during" or "after" the birth. They considered the trade-offs to each medicalized way of giving birth, which they pragmatically evaluated in light of their own experiences and the embodied experiences of others in their net-works of female kin and friends. With the cesarean, the pain was expected to be temporary, lasting a few days or so after the operation. The side effects of the episiotomy, in contrast, could be long-term and could negatively affect their marriages, as well as the healthy routine functioning of their bodies. In sum, the cesarean has gained *relative* value within the intensely technocratic regime of Greek maternity care, chosen with pragmatic logic. (My focus here has been on women's perceptions of the accrued value of cesareans; for information on doctors' perceptions of that value and their motives for performing them at very high rates in Brazil, see Williamson and Matsuoka, this volume, Chapter 4.)

The Normalization of Vaginal Birth in New Zealand

The number of discourses and practices for women in New Zealand to draw on in creating their understandings and desires for birth are much greater and more diverse than for women in Greece, where, as Nia points out above, the choice is between two kinds of operative deliveries—"the cut above" of the cesarean or "the cut below" of an episiotomy that will be accompanied by many other interventions in the process of vaginal birth. New Zealand women's accounts of their decision-making and experiences suggest that the technocratic model of childbirth counts but is not the only authoritative knowledge that they consider in their decision-making about birth. In this section, I (Rea) explore how women and midwives negotiate some of the diverse approaches to childbirth that are available in New Zealand.

As we have seen in Greece, the technocratic obstetric paradigm is dominant, with little challenge from alternative approaches to childbirth. In New Zealand, obstetric knowledge sits, sometimes uneasily, alongside other paradigms and ways of understanding and working with childbirth. Midwifery, in New Zealand and globally, is based on the tenets that childbirth is a normal life experience and that most women can birth naturally with the support of their families and skilled midwives in conducive environments. Indeed, the Midwifery Scope of Practice in New Zealand includes the requirement that the "midwife understands, promotes and facilitates the physiological processes of pregnancy and childbirth" (Midwifery Council of New Zealand 2010). The midwifery (humanistic/holistic) model of birth is further supported by the Ministry of Health. Unlike in Greece, in New Zealand, "recognis[ing] that pregnancy and childbirth are a normal life-stage for most women" (Ministry of Health 2007:1033) is a key objective of government-funded maternity services, and annual maternity reports are published to act as a lever to reduce intervention rates.

Based on authentic epidemiological research, the NZ *Report on Maternity 2015* outlines that: "Spontaneous vaginal birth is known to provide multiple benefits for the woman and her baby. These benefits are evident at time of birth and have long-term effects for society as a whole" (Ministry of Health 2017:32). Some of these benefits include: facilitating bonding and attachment, healthy colonization of microbiota, reduced risk of respiratory problems for the baby, higher rates of exclusive breastfeeding for longer duration, and "an easier transition to motherhood with easier physical recovery following birth" (Ministry of Health 2017:32). In these words, the authoritative status of the midwifery model of birth is made clear; in this humanistic and holistic midwifery model, physiological, emotional, psychological, and social effects all interconnect, and individual benefits to mother and baby are under-stood to intersect with the health and sustainability of the population.[9]

New Zealand maternity service providers are aware of the many risks associated with cesareans and are concerned that the current CS rate of 25% is higher than necessary. These risks include (1) infections that can occur at the incision site, in the uterus, and in other pelvic organs such as the bladder; (2) hemorrhage or increased blood loss, which can lead to anemia or a blood transfusion (one to six women per 100 require a blood transfusion); (3) possible injury to organs such as the bowel or bladder (two per 100); (4) the possibility of scar tissue forming inside the pelvic region causing blockage and pain; such adhesions can also lead to future pregnancy complications such as placenta previa (when the placenta implants over the cervix or opening of the uterus, preventing vaginal birth and causing significant bleeding—a life-threatening situation for both mother and baby) or placental abruption (when the placenta prematurely detaches from the uterine wall); (5) extended recovery time that can range from weeks to months (one in 14 women report incisional pain six months or more after surgery); (6) risk of additional surgeries, including hysterectomy, bladder repair, or another cesarean; and (7) a higher maternal mortality rate—three times higher than with a vaginal birth.

Risks and complications for the baby of a CS include premature birth if the CS is scheduled too early; possible breathing and respiratory problems stemming from not receiving the lung stimulation of passing through the vaginal canal; low APGAR scores at birth, which can be the result of anesthesia; and fetal distress before the delivery or lack of the natural stimulation during delivery provided by vaginal birth. Babies born by cesarean are 50% more likely to have lower APGAR scores than those born vaginally. And very rarely, the baby may be nicked or cut during the incision (on average, one or two babies per 100). (See http://americanpregnancy.org/labor-and-birth/cesarean-risks/ and Caughey et al. 2014.)

Again, 15% of women in New Zealand give birth either at home or in a birth center (far more than the 1.36% who do so in the US) while the rest go to

---

[9] Editor's note from Robbie: Toward the end of a two-week speaking tour of New Zealand in 2011, I was relaxing in a hot springs spa with my companion and guide Larissa, a recently graduated midwife, when we began conversing with three people from Iran—a mother and father and their daughter, who was engaged to marry a New Zealander. Her only concern about moving to NZ was giving birth there—her mother had had three children by CS in Iran, and the daughter was terrified of vaginal birth, exclaiming with horror, "Here they make you do it naturally—you don't have a choice!" Of course Larissa and I explained to her that in New Zealand women have the *full spectrum of choices,* from midwife-attended births in homes and birth centers all the way to scheduled cesareans with obstetricians in hospitals; she was greatly relieved! To me, her belief that "Here they force you to give birth naturally" was a clear indication of the success NZ midwives have had in convincing the public that childbirth is a normal, natural process requiring little, if any, intervention most of the time—which, in fact, it is, especially when women are well-nourished and well-treated throughout the process of parturition.

hospitals (Ministry of Health 2017). Women's choices for home- and birth center birth are ideological—they tend to trust their bodies and the birth process, want a natural birth, and seek to avoid unnecessary medical interventions. Pip stated: "I wanted to keep my birth as natural as possible; I didn't want it to be medicalized." Ann explained, "I wanted a natural birth, I didn't want drugs, I wanted to do it all myself. I heard that if you had drugs you increase the risk of having a cesar [cesarean] and I just didn't want a cesar at all."

NZ women who want to have their babies in hospitals tend to view childbirth as potentially hazardous, as the "riskiest thing women do" (Fay). Mia describes, "I would have in the back of my mind if something happened, I'd never forgive myself for not having been in the right place when I had that choice." Comparable to Greek women's choices for CS, Mia's feelings are linked to a moral imperative to do what is best for the baby and avoid the potential for "mother guilt." While, as we have seen, NZ women are much less likely than Greek women to frame cesarean as routinely safer for babies, many are still influenced by the technocratic view of childbirth, having more confidence in the capacity of technology and medical specialists to ensure the safety of childbirth than in themselves or the birth process (Grigg et al. 2014).

Choosing a hospital birth does not necessarily entail lack of desire for a natural birth. Ana, who had two hospitals births, noted that while some of her friends desired an epidural, she considers that not having one provides a better experience:

> I was healthy, I was quite fit and stuff but because my labor was so long and slow I had an epidural, even though I didn't really want one. But then, of course, with your subsequent pregnancies you think, "Oh well, I had an epidural the first time—I might need another one." I still can't believe that four years later that I gave birth with absolutely nothing. Amazing!

Just over 25% of women who give birth vaginally in New Zealand use epidural analgesia in labor (Ministry of Health 2017) (as compared to over 60% in the US, around 77% in France, and only around 6% in Japan); epidurals can only be administered by an anesthesiologist in a hospital with obstetric backup.

Ready access to medical intervention, just in case it is needed, is seen by some women as supporting them to birth naturally by mitigating their fear. Yet, women recognize that natural birth in a hospital is only possible because their own midwife can serve as their advocate and intermediary. Bre said, "What I was most adamant about was having a natural, active birth. So there was a lot of discussion [with my midwife] about how we could still do that in the hospital . . . and that is what we ended up with." Bev recounts that "because I knew I had a midwife who I knew would fight my corner, I think that gave me the confidence to go into a place where someone might try and take over, because I knew that she was always listening to me."

Community (LMC) midwives employ a range of strategies to protect the birthing space in the hospital setting. Midwives who participated in a study by Davis and Walker (2010) talked about preparing women during pregnancy through information sharing, positioning women as the decision-makers, and building their confidence in their own ability to birth. In the hospital, mid-wives try to maintain the privacy of the birthing room and create a "woman-centered" space in which the woman feels safe and can remain active. Many New Zealand hospitals have birthing pools or showers and other physiology-enhancing props such as birth balls and mats. However, Davis and Walker also found that midwives were acutely aware that within the hospital, "The obstetrician too often assumes that obstetric knowledge is the only and most important component of decision making, and that the childbearing woman and midwife will acquiesce to their management plan" (2010:606), thus reflecting the hierarchy inherent in the technocratic paradigm of health care generally. As is so often shown, research from New Zealand has found that healthy women who choose to have their babies in a hospital are more likely to be subjected to unnecessary interventions than those in a birth center or at home (Davis et al. 2011; Dixon, et al. 2014; Grigg et al. 2017). A study by Miller and Skinner (2012) found that the same midwives were more likely to use interventions with women who planned hospital births than with women who planned to birth at home, illustrating *the power of place and space* to influence the treatment of birth—a theme that runs through all of the ethnographic chapters in this volume.

A birthing room in a birth center with a pool, ball, and other equipment to support active labor. The message on the wall affirms, "Believe in Yourself and Magic Will Happen." Photo by Lorna Davies

Women who plan to give birth in a birth center, but have to transfer to a hospital when complications arise, look to their midwife to be their advocate in their consultations with medical specialists. In her birth story, Princess explains:

> At home, before I went into labor, my waters broke and there was meconium that wasn't supposed to be there, so I rang my midwife and she said, "You need to go straight to [the hospital]." . . . [The obstetric registrar] looked at my birth plan and went, "Hmm, probably none of that is going to happen because of the meconium." They said, "Oh you're on the emergency C-section list and you'll get induced if it doesn't start moving quickly." . . . And then actually it went really well, and she [the baby] was completely fine and there were no problems, and they didn't induce, but I kind of had the feeling that my midwives—my backup midwife, and then my midwife came in later, because I was there all day—I kind of had the feeling that they were sort of protecting me from it all getting pushed through, which was really lovely. I was really happy because I mostly only saw my own midwives and it was fine. But I did have a sense that it could have gone differently [had the midwives not been there].

Kay had a similar birth story but with a different outcome:

> My waters had broken at home. . . . I knew what that meant. So I kind of stalled calling [my midwife] and I kind of didn't overdescribe the situation and she gave me a day and then she came and had a look and said "That's meconium, I'm sorry." . . . [At the hospital] the registrar said I was going to have to have [a cesarean] straight away and I thought, "Okay give me a chance, can I have a chance?" . . . We gave it a go for 11 hours. Then I still didn't have the baby. . . . My midwife, in the end, she tried, and she was an advocate and after the birth [by cesarean] she made sure the baby was on me, she said, "Looks like the baby is healthy, don't go measure it, unless there's an immediate problem, stick the baby on her right now"—to try and make it okay, to try and make some good.

Kay's midwife enabled Kay and her baby to have immediate skin-to-skin contact after the baby was delivered by a CS, which eases the baby's transition to extra-uterine life and supports bonding, the initiation of breastfeeding, and the transfer of beneficial bacteria from the mother's body to the baby.

These accounts illustrate how women and midwives in New Zealand negotiate between competing knowledge systems to make decisions about maternity care. While midwives have full responsibility in normal birth, obstetricians exert considerable control over the interface in determining which complications midwives need to identify and when they should refer women and babies to specialist care. This obstetric control means that midwives work with risk assessment continuously in the background and need to manage the tension between predicting risk and protecting the normality of birth while being committed to supporting women's informed decision-making.

In their accounts of their childbirth experiences, women from both Greece and New Zealand emphasize their agency in decision-making, even when the "decision" is to follow professional advice. Greek women employ a pragmatic logic to their rationalizations of the advantages of cesarean births and locate these within a narrative of technological progress. New Zealand women also display a pragmatic approach to evaluating their options, but locate them rather in their awareness of their great range of choice both for birth and in bodily discourse. As in the US, there is diversity in the ways NZ women conceptualize the childbearing body; sometimes they use differing views concurrently. These include the technocratic metaphor of "body as machine" and the humanistic understanding of "body as organism" (Davis-Floyd 2001, 2018a). The view of the body as an organism fits well with the emerging ecological model of science and with a more agricultural ethos of "tending to" and "working with" the natural body rather than trying to control it. In contrast to Greek women, NZ women are more likely to deem that bodily integrity is preserved in a birth without technological intervention, seeing the CS as a much greater threat to bodily integrity than normal birth. Yet, NZ women are not faced with the binary choice of either the cut above or the cut below; as in the US, the episiotomy rate is low (about 14%), and most episiotomies are only performed on the 9.3% of women who have forceps or vacuum deliveries.

Emergent Possibilities: Toward a Holistic Paradigm of Birth in New Zealand

According to Karen Guilliland, CEO of NZCOM, "In 2013, an independent study commissioned by the New Zealand Ministry of Health found that New Zealand showed similar or better birth outcomes across a wide range of measures compared with Australia, Ireland, United Kingdom, the Netherlands, Canada and the USA (Malatest International 2013). In 2014, our normal (spontaneous vaginal birth with little or no intervention) birth rate was 66%" (compared to 5% in the US and close to 0% in Greece) (Guilliland 2018:3). Karen further explains:

> The "New Zealand Report on Maternity 2015," published in 2017, demonstrates that New Zealand has more spontaneous vaginal births, fewer inductions of labor, fewer instrumental births, fewer cesarean sections, more intact perineums, fewer episiotomies and similar levels of third and fourth-degree tears, compared to other similar countries (Ministry of Health 2017). The exclusive breastfeeding rates at discharge are some of the highest in the world (82%) as are the number of hospitals that are Baby-Friendly Hospital Initiative (BFHI)-approved . . . 96% of our babies are born in BFHI-accredited facilities with 4% born at home (Ministry of Health 2015b). In 2015, almost 94% of NZ babies were breastfeeding at 2 weeks of age, 70.1% exclusively, 9.1% fully breastfeeding, 14.6% partial and 7% were artificial feeding.
>
> Almost 96% of families were referred by their LMC to a family physician and 98% to a child health service provider on discharge from mater-

Midwives and supporters getting ready to march to Parliament to lobby for midwives' pay equity on International Day of the Midwife, May 2018.
Photo by Rea Daellenbach

nity care, ensuring that ongoing health services are well integrated for women and babies (Ministry of Health 2017). . . . Perinatal mortality rates have fallen significantly since our model was instituted; maternal mortality is extremely rare.

Over 95% of women express satisfaction with their midwifery care and it's "partnership with women" foundation. . . . We find that midwives working in partnership with the woman as the central decision maker brings deep satisfaction for midwives. Many keep working happily for decades as a result.

Guilliland (2018:9) goes on to describe how the pay equity issue mentioned in the introduction to this chapter has been successfully resolved:

Journalists, media women, women's groups and individual mothers walked the streets with midwives. They bombarded social media and the Minister, demanding that the government recognize and fix the longstanding lack of funding and support infrastructures for the midwifery profession. The Government listened, and we now have a timeline for implementing a new funding and contracting model by 2020, based on the co-designed model agreed upon in 2017.

Clearly, the NZ model works; it works for women, and it works for midwives, for OBs, and for the nation. This framework seeks to integrate the humanistic and the holistic paradigms of health care provision (Davis-Floyd 2018a; Chapter 1, this volume). So we might ask, are there possibilities for even more holistic approaches to childbirth in New Zealand?

There is still deep spirituality embedded in the traditions of the Māori. In the 1980s and 1990s, Māori leaders challenged the government on the significantly poorer health outcomes for Māori compared to non-Māori in New Zealand. They framed this challenge as a failure by the government to safeguard Māori health, thus breaching its obligations under the Treaty of Waitangi (Durie 1998). The treaty principles of "partnership, participation and protection" mean that health services need to acknowledge and respect *tikanga* (cultural practices) and *mātauranga* (Māori knowledge) (Kenney 2011). In the mid-1980s, a Māori health collective began working on reclaiming practices related to the placenta after birth, and Māori began asking to keep the placenta to bury it. The word for placenta in Māori is *whenua*, which also means land, and in returning the *whenua* to the *whenua*, the ancestral or other special connections of the baby to a place are affirmed and honored. *Tikanga* around the burial of the *whenua* is specific to each *whānau*. Often a container (*ipu whenua*) is made during the woman's pregnancy out of clay, wood, a gourd, or woven flax, and there are different traditions about where it is to be buried and by whom. Initially, Māori mothers had to rely on the support of sympathetic midwives to enable them to take the *whenua* home if they gave birth in a maternity facility. However, with Māori reclaiming placenta burial as a right—rather than a privilege—it has become standard practice to ask all women what their preferences are (see for example Ministry of Health 2018). Placenta burial has also become popular with non-Māori, in a signifying practice that imbues the birth process with a deeper symbolism than just viewing the placenta as medical waste. In some New Zealand areas, city councils have set aside land and provided trees for families to bury their placentas.

Another aspect of hospital childbirth practices that Māori have challenged is how many people a woman can bring along to the birth, reaffirming the integral role of *whānau* as birth attendants. More recently these principles have been codified by *Nga Maia o Aotearoa*—a national collective of Māori midwives and *whānau*—in a set of principles or rights called the *Turanga Kaupapa*. This document has been formally adopted both by NZCOM and by the Midwifery Council of New Zealand, as part of the competencies midwives have to meet for registration (Midwifery Council of New Zealand 2007, 2012). The Turanga Kaupapa outlines a holistic approach to childbirth that affirms the special role of the woman as *Te Whare Tangata*. This term refers to the womb; it literally translates as "the house of the people" and describes women as bearers of genealogy—connecting the past to the future and the people to the land (Mikaere 2000; Simmonds 2018). The Turanga Kaupapa also promotes a set of rights in childbirth, including the woman's right to involve her *whānau* in her birth, as well as to use traditional practices such as *karakia* (prayer/chanting), *oriori* (songs of *whakapapa*/ancestry and past deeds), *mirimiri* (massage), and other healing rituals to support the birth process. The focus is on preserving the woman's dignity (*mana*) and bringing together the spiritual, mental, physical, and community dimensions of well-being, irrespective of the place or the mode of birth. Childbirth is redefined as an event of great social and psychological significance. This holistic redefinition has the potential to disrupt the dichotomy between "technologically managed birth" and "natural birth" by configuring new ways of using interventions when needed, while simultaneously respecting women's cultural needs and enhancing cultural safety.

Emergent Possibilities: Immigrants and Midwives in the Greek Public Hospitals

Unlike New Zealand, in Greece, the technocratic model of the body and its metaphors remain dominant and almost completely unchallenged. The normalization of cesareans, and the fact that vaginal births after cesareans (VBACs) are rarely allowed, has intensified this dominance by limiting the opportunities for medical residents and midwifery students to observe and participate in vaginal births. An alternative, humanistic or holistic view of the body can be found among a handful of highly educated women, some diaspora Greeks who've returned to live in Greece, as well as a few celebrities. Tapping into the tiny network of independent (and often beleaguered) midwives who practice in the big cities, they manage to achieve the holistic homebirths they desire. Still, their numbers are exceedingly small and their influence registers only faintly. In the margins of the public hospitals, however, the social and demographic changes that have recently transformed Greece have also had a more influential impact on the provision of maternity care. In particular, they have generated new spaces and opportunities for midwifery practice within the hospital.

Over the past three decades, transnational migration has transformed Greece from a relatively homogeneous society into one that is ethnically diverse and multicultural. After the collapse of the Soviet Union in 1991, unprecedented numbers of people began to migrate across Greek borders from neighboring postsocialist countries of the Balkans and Eastern Europe, and increasingly from Africa and Asia as well. By 2011, over 1.2 million immigrants were living in Greece. Today, immigrants comprise over 10% of the total population of 11 million—one of the highest proportions in the European Union. Most recently, large numbers of refugees have arrived on Greece's shores fleeing war and dislocation in Syria, Afghanistan, and elsewhere. Given their large numbers, relative youth, and higher birth rates, immigrants have played an important role in increasing the national population and keeping Greece's very low birth rate from falling lower still (Cheliotis 2017).

Immigrants, who can seldom afford the cost of private clinics, overwhelmingly tend to give birth in the public hospitals. Spatially, maternity wards are divided into three tiers, called "Alpha," "Beta," and "Gamma." Ethnic Greek women typically pay an extra fee to stay in a private suite or semiprivate room in the more desirable Alpha and Beta wards, while immigrant and other poor women are concentrated in the more basic Gamma ward, where there may be up to eight beds to a room. Because immigrants do not have the economic means—and perhaps also the intimate cultural knowledge—to participate in the informal economy of gifting, they provide no incentive and hold no attraction for the obstetricians, who focus almost exclusively on their ethnic Greek clientele. As a result, midwives have been left to fill in as the primary birth attendants for immigrant women. One striking consequence of this division of labor is that the cesarean rate for immigrants is less than half that of ethnic Greek women: about 25% versus 65% (Mossialos et al. 2005).

Further reinforcing this division of professional labor and care may be the perception among doctors that immigrants have different, and by implication, inferior, needs than Greek citizens (Lawrence 2007). In the popular imagination, immigrants may be stigmatized as backward, "Balkan," and culturally "lagging behind" Greeks by a couple of generations, and so may be perceived as not needing the same level of modern goods and services as ethnic Greek citizens. By this same logic, it is possible that doctors deem cesareans, with their positive associations with technological progress and modernity, as technologies more suitable for Greek citizens than for immigrants. Similarly, it is also possible that doctors implicitly regard midwifery, with its low-tech, "less-than-modern" connotations, as a more appropriate model of care for immigrants and poor "others."[10] From these perspectives, the presumably second-class model of care provided by midwives may be seen as a better fit for immigrants and other poor women. Whatever the reasons, the outcome is that their births are typically vaginal. Ironically, immigrant women, who are subject to multiple forms of discrimination, stigmatization, and even violence outside the hospital, tend to be less susceptible to what birth activists and other critics have identified as the "obstetrical violence" of unnecessary cesareans. Maternity care in Greece thus offers an example of how *stratified reproduction*—a term coined by Ginsburg and Rapp (1995) to bring to light the multiple ways in which reproduction and reproductive practices are hierarchically and often invidiously structured across social and cultural boundaries—can also on rare occasions confer protection to vulnerable others.

Midwives are also responsible for providing training and supervising the hands-on experience of midwifery students and many OB residents as well. Typically, students and residents are present only as observers during the births of ethnic Greek women, which are almost exclusively under the control of the obstetrician. Midwives have seized the opportunity presented by immigrant women to practice their otherwise devalued midwifery knowledge and skills and to extend and transmit them. As a result of this intersection of professional interests, immigrants have opened up a space within the public hospital that encompasses the devalued and stigmatized knowledge and bodies—in this instance, of both the immigrants (and other poor women) and the midwives—that are regarded as undesirable and out of place within the central and dominant spaces and practices of the hospital. While Greek midwifery care cannot be characterized as holistic or even strongly humanistic, it does expand the opportunities to experience, observe, and teach vaginal birth. Of course, this degree of freedom from the purview of obstetrical power is precar-

---

[10] An inverse relationship between economic deprivation and cesareans was also found in England by Barley et al. (2004:1399, quoted in Mander 2007:79). Like working class Britons, immigrants and the poor in Greece may also be implicitly stereotyped as "too proletarian for cesarean."

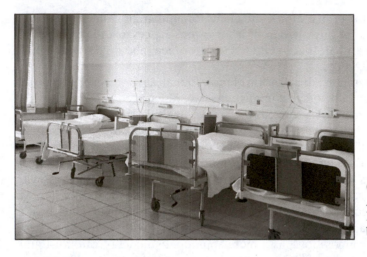

Gamma ward in Athens Public Hospital. Photo by Nia Georges

ious, contingent and restricted to the shadow spaces of immigrant maternity care—in distinct contrast to New Zealand, where midwives have achieved professional autonomy and practice in all settings. At the same time as the presence of large numbers of immigrant women permits the use and reproduction of midwifery knowledge and skills, it also reproduces the broader conditions of subordination to doctors and thus offers no sustainable possibility of overcoming or even blunting the subordination of the midwifery profession. Still, at least for the present, this parallel space remains open and productive.

Conclusion: Major Differences and a Few Commonalities

Midwifery in New Zealand—based on autonomy, continuity of care, and partnership with women—is ideally placed to provide maternity care that extends far beyond options dictated by the biomedical and technocratic approaches to birth. Can the initiatives by Indigenous social movements to reclaim the birthing space create even more holistic knowledge to secure a more sustainable future for childbirth and families? Or will technocratic obstetrics continue to define the acceptable parameters of risk?

At present, New Zealand is widely considered to have one of the best maternity care systems in the world. This system extends beyond partnership at the individual level to the organizational level: non-midwife consumers sit on the National Committee of the New Zealand College of Midwives, assist in choosing which applicants should be accepted to the midwifery college programs, and even help choose the course content, which generally includes courses in social science and gender to ensure that budding midwives will have a strong feminist orientation. Meanwhile, Greece continues to devalue its midwives, assigning them to subordinate roles and to determinedly proceed down the road of performing ever more cesareans and technological interventions in birth, in a conceptual consensus between mothers and doctors that CS is best for both mother and baby—despite its many proven risks. Since one of the worst risks of CS is the dangers that ensue from having multiple cesareans, and most Greek families have only one or two children, this risk factor is rarely considered an issue. A focus on normality, women's choices, and midwifery care prevails in New Zealand, while a focus on pathology, doctors' choices, and obstetric care prevails in Greece.

Yet there are also interesting commonalities. In both, women's mental conceptions about birth are deeply embodied and enacted in their birth choices. In both, *the place and space of birth matter.* In New Zealand, even with midwives as LMCs, hospital births can be both humanistic and at least moderately technocratic, whereas home and birth center births are entirely humanistic and holistic. In Greece, the Gamma wards for the immigrant poor offer much more humanistic spaces where midwives can practice their model of care and exercise and transmit their expertise. Both countries have strong feminist movements (though they have taken different directions regarding childbirth) and a strong value on continuity of caregiver and the importance of developing trusting relationships with that caregiver. Moreover, in some ways, their differently stratified systems of reproduction might actually be protective of normal birth (as in the Greek Gamma wards and via the influence of the NZ Māori) and facilitative of the kinds of cultural innovation that can arise in both the margins and the mainstreams of midwifery care.

THOUGHT QUESTIONS

1. What are the primary differences between the Greek and New Zealand systems of maternity care?
2. Which country would you personally prefer to give birth in?
3. Why has midwifery in New Zealand been so successful in achieving autonomy, while Greek midwives are so subordinated?
4. What are the differences among the Alpha, Beta, and Gamma maternity wards in Greece?
5. Why are space and place such strong determinants of how labor and birth will proceed?

RECOMMENDED FILMS ON BIRTH IN NEW ZEALAND (THERE ARE NO FILMS AVAILABLE ON BIRTH IN GREECE)

Hayley M. 2016. *Midwife Nicky with Hannah.* Published 4 May 2016 for www.miwife.org.nz YouTube: https://youtu.be/MdTQzj4eB-g
Hayley M. 2016. *Midwife Juliet with Rachel.* Published 4 May 2016 for www.midwife.org.nz YouTube: https://youtu.be/GyYu0544pXY

These two short promotional videos were produced for the New Zealand College of Midwives to celebrate the International Day of the Midwife, May 5, 2016. They illustrate the partnership relationship that midwives and women can develop over the course of the pregnancy, birth and the first few weeks after the baby is born.

Emmett, Cassie. 2016. *The Birth of Maggie.* www.capturinglife.co.nz. Vimeo: https://vimeo.com/191917340

Emmett, Cassie. 2016. *Nina's Birth.* www.capturinglife.co.nz. Vimeo: https://vimeo.com/187279875

These two videos were created by birth photographer Cassie Emmett. They capture the commonly held New Zealand view of the ideal birth: a birth without obstetric interventions, with the woman supported by loved ones and the midwife assisting as needed. *The Birth of Maggie* takes place in a birth center and Maggie is born in water. *Nina's Birth* takes place in a hospital—a vaginal birth after a previous cesarean (VBAC). The midwife undertakes closer monitoring of the fetal heart rate in this birth, but it also occurs without any other interventions. In both videos, nitrous oxide and oxygen gas inhalation pain relief are used. The same midwives attended at both the births.

Te Karere. TVNZ 2014. *Huawere: Heather Muriwai empowers expectant mums to reclaim childbirth practices.* Published Jan 1, 2014 YouTube https://www.youtube.com/watch?v=zjsJGPnv7dM

This video describes a Māori childbirth education initiative that was produced for a Māori language current affairs television program. The focus of the classes is on preparing for the birth through making a flax string (*muka*) that will be used to tie the umbilical cord (*pito*) and a clay pot to collect the placenta (*ipu whenua*). The discussions that ensue around the making of this birth kit are important in passing on knowledge about childbirth. Subtitles are available for this video and can be enabled using the CC icon at the bottom left hand side of the YouTube video player.

6

Giving Birth in the United States and the Netherlands

Midwifery Care as Integrated Option or Contested Privilege?

Melissa Cheyney, Bahareh Goodarzi, Therese Wiegers,
Robbie Davis-Floyd, and Saraswathi Vedam

In 1978, Brigitte Jordan began the first edition of her now-classic *Birth in Four Cultures* with the following observation:

> Our knowledge about the management of pregnancy, labor, delivery and the postpartum period is, by and large, the knowledge of one particular birthing system: Western and especially American, obstetrics. In the United States, birth . . . falls into the medical domain. The definition of birth as a medical event, in turn, has served to focus research on the physiological and often pathological aspects of childbearing. As a consequence, we have paid little attention to the social interactional and socioecological aspects of birth, which for members of a social species are of fundamental importance in orchestrating the biological event. . . . There are indications, then, that for a more comprehensive view of childbirth, we will need to go beyond purely biomedical research and give equal priority to . . . biosocial studies of birthing. (1993[1978]:xv)

Jordan went on to develop a compelling argument for the use of a biosocial framework for the cross-cultural comparison of childbirth practices, noting that there is no known society for which birth is constructed as merely a physiologic or clinical function. On the contrary, in all places and times, pregnancy and birth are culturally marked and elaborated, as the preceding chapters in this volume so clearly show. In addition, because birth is often considered a time of vulnerability and mystery, societies shape both the ideology and performance of childbirth as a means of managing existential uncertainty within their own cultural contexts. "It is not surprising, therefore, that—whatever the details of a given birthing system—its practitioners will tend to see it as the best way, the right way, indeed *the* way to bring a child into the world" (Jordan 1993:4). That every culture tends to hold that *its way is the right way* is a form of "cultural blindfolding." We rarely perceive "the world out there" as it is; rather we perceive it through the lens, filter, or category system of our own culture, our own experience.

Keenly aware of the influence of culture on our perceptions of "reality," Jordan argued that cross-cultural analyses are essential—for "normal" is not the same everywhere, rather, it is simply what we are used to. In the arena of birth, cross-cultural comparisons provide information we can use to construct a deeper understanding of the multiplicity of ways in which the processes of childbirth are historically, socially, and physiologically shaped—a depth of understanding that Jordan (1993[1978]) argued can never be available from the inside point of view of any singular system alone.

In this chapter we examine contemporary conceptualizations of childbirth in the Netherlands and the United States.[1] Our aim is to reveal how historically constituted ideologies powerfully shape the ways that childbirth is performed in two distinct cultural settings. We begin by examining notions about pregnancy and birth that shape not only the understanding of but also the doing of birth. We contextualize our comparisons historically, drawing attention to the fact that history is not simply about the past; in both the Netherlands and the United States, historical antecedents powerfully shape how birth is performed today. Next, in keeping with Jordan's call to heed the biosocial nature of childbirth, we examine the effects of the Dutch and US conceptualizations of childbirth on measurable health outcomes for babies and their mothers, who must navigate maternity care systems in these respective contexts. Finally, using Davis-Floyd's theoretical constructs of the technocratic, humanistic, and holistic models of birth (Davis-Floyd 2001a, 2018a; Chapter 1, this volume), we conclude with reflections on how these models work on the ground in the United States and the Netherlands. This grounding of theoretical constructs within our specific ethnographic contexts allows us to reveal new culture-specific and comparative complexities as we describe the systems of maternity care in our respective countries.

The focus of this chapter is on midwifery and social constructions of childbirth in the US and in the Netherlands. This is due in large part to our respective positionalities. Our varied expertise converges around the study of midwives and the practice of midwifery within the larger fields of epidemiology and the anthropology of childbirth. Therese Wiegers is a psychologist, epidemiologist, and maternity care researcher with more than more 25 years of experience. She defended her PhD thesis: *Home or Hospital Birth. A Prospective Study of Midwifery Care in the Netherlands* in 1997 at the University of Leiden. She is currently working as senior researcher at Nivel, the Netherlands insti-

---

[1] The US and the Netherlands were two of the four cultures Jordan analyzed in her original *Birth in Four Cultures.*

tute for health services research. Bahareh Goodarzi qualified as a midwife in the Netherlands in 2007 and practiced as a community midwife until 2012. From 2012 to 2015, she worked as a policy advisor at the Royal Dutch College of Midwives while teaching at the Midwifery Academy in Amsterdam. Currently, she combines teaching with doctoral research at Amsterdam UMC, Vrije Universiteit Amsterdam, Midwifery Science, AVAGM–Amsterdam Public Health research institute. She has a master's degree in health management.

Melissa Cheyney (Missy) is a midwife and clinical medical anthropologist whose research has focused on midwifery and the culture and safety of homebirth in the United States. Over the past decade, Missy has served as director of the Division of Research for the Midwives Alliance of North America (MANA) where she led the development of a national data registry that can be used to study undisturbed, physiologic birth in community settings. Missy is also lead investigator at the Reproductive Health Laboratory at Oregon State University, where she oversees more than a dozen ethnographic and mixed methods (qualitative and quantitative) research projects aimed at finding culturally respectful ways to reduce preventable maternal and infant death and suffering in the United States and globally. Saraswathi Vedam is lead investigator of the Birth Place Lab at the University of British Columbia. She has been a midwife, educator, and researcher for over 35 years. Saraswathi has been active in setting international policy on place of birth and interprofessional collaboration. She has convened three national Home Birth Summits that catalyzed transdisciplinary imagination in the US to address equity and access to high-quality care among marginalized communities. And while Robbie Davis-Floyd has studied numerous topics over her career, she is best known for her pioneering work on the anthropologies of childbirth, midwifery, and obstetrics.

Disparate Maternity Care Systems: Provider Types, Midwifery Education, and Maternal Choice

The Netherlands

In the Netherlands, maternal and newborn care is provided by community midwives (midwives who work in homes, out-patient clinics, and birth centers), clinical midwives[2] (midwives who attend births in the hospital), obstetricians,[3] and general practitioners[4] (GPs), as well as maternity care assistants and pediatricians (NZa 2012). Dutch midwives complete a four-

---

[2] In 2015 the Netherlands counted 3,150 practicing midwives, of whom 919 (29.9%) worked as clinical midwives in hospitals (NIVEL 2016).

[3] All obstetricians in the Netherlands are called "gynecologists," although not all gynecologists practice obstetrics. For the purposes of consistency, we refer to these specialists as obstetricians, although they would be called gynecologists in the Netherlands.

year, direct-entry, theoretical and practical education[5] and specialize in the management of healthy pregnancies, birth, and newborn care, while attending to the biopsychocultural context of the individuals and communities served. They are licensed to practice at the bachelor's degree–level. Following four years in general biomedical science and two years of general clinical rotations, obstetricians complete a six-year specialization program focused on the management of complex pregnancies and women's health issues, which includes gynecology and surgical training. GPs complete a three-year specialization program following medical school. In 2002, maternity care was dropped from the GP curriculum. For GPs who wanted to provide birth care, an additional, short specialization in midwifery was available until 2016, when this program was discontinued due to lack of participation. Postpartum maternity care assistants receive three-year, mid-level vocational training as health care assistants (described in more detail below).

In the Netherlands, as long as there are no complications that would benefit from specialist care by an obstetrician, community midwives (and some GPs) are responsible for caring for women during pregnancy, labor, childbirth, and the postpartum period. Women experiencing healthy pregnancies receive "standard" maternity care, including 11–12 prenatal visits with community midwives, lasting between 10 and 20 minutes, and an average of two ultrasounds (Wiegers et al. 2013). Women choose their place of birth: on the labor ward in a hospital, in a birth center, or at home assisted by their own community midwife (see the photos below). When complications or requests for pharmacological pain relief arise, an obstetrician assumes responsibility for the person's care. When a woman asks for an epidural, for example, her care is transferred to "secondary care" because an epidural is considered a medical intervention that can only be performed under the supervision of a physician. In practice, as long as no complications arise following an epidural, such a woman would still get some of her care from a midwife in the hospital. A pediatrician is present when neonatal complications are expected following the birth.

Standard care immediately after childbirth includes five or six visits at home from a community midwife during the first 10 to 12 days postpartum. During the first seven to eight days following birth, a maternity care assistant also provides in-home care to the new family for three to eight hours per day. The maternity care assistant's most important tasks during this time are to: (1) identify postpartum complications in the mother and/or baby as early as possible; (2) provide information and instruction regarding newborn care and hygiene; and (3) support breastfeeding. Standard maternity care is concluded with a visit with the midwife or obstetrician at six weeks postpartum (Wiegers et al. 2014).

---

[4] A relatively small number of GPs practice midwifery, and this number is on the decline. The estimated number of births attended by GPs dropped from 5% in 2002 to 0.5% in 2008 (NIVEL 2013).

[5] "Direct-entry" midwives do not become nurses first but go directly into a midwifery educational program.

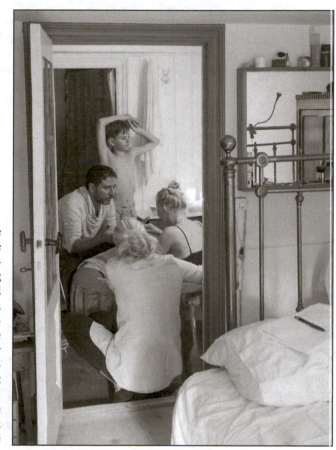

Homebirth in the Netherlands. The woman in the photograph is giving birth to her third child, assisted by a community midwife. Both the father of the baby and her other children are present during the birth. Photo by Pauline van Berkel, Lukk Geboortefotografie

Hospital birth in the Netherlands. The woman in the photograph is in labor with her second child. Her partner is present to support her. She has another contraction as she stands to leave the bathroom and uses the sink for support. Photo by Pauline van Berkel, Lukk Geboortefotografie

The United States

The United States is unique in having three types of credentialed, professional midwives: the Certified Nurse Midwife (CNM), the Certified Midwife (CM), and the Certified Professional Midwife (CPM) (Cheyney et al. 2015a; Vedam et al. 2018; Davis-Floyd 2018e). Although largely distinct, these credentials share key similarities. For example, all credentialed midwives in the US are distinguished from "lay," "traditional," or "plain" midwives who practice without having demonstrated formal education and national certification requirements. Uncredentialed midwives (a distinct minority) attend only homebirths; some prefer the complete autonomy of staying "outside the system" where they are not bound by its rules and regulations, and others remain uncredentialed because there is no pathway to licensure or certification in their state. Such midwives are completely unregulated in most states. In contrast, all professional, credentialed midwives in the US are educated and practice according to national standards for accreditation and certification;[6] all specialize in the management of healthy pregnancies, birth, and newborn care, within the biopsychocultural context of the individuals and communities they serve.

Obstetricians in the US complete two years of education in general biomedical sciences and two years of general clinical rotations, followed by a four to five year residency focused on the management of complex pregnancies, gynecology, and surgical skills. Family physicians (GPs) who choose to include maternity in their scope of practice complete a three-year specialization program following medical school, which includes a part-time emphasis on maternal and newborn management and care.

Few US obstetricians or family practitioners are exposed to skills and knowledge to support normal physiologic birth, and few are exposed to midwifery practice or taught by midwives during their basic education, while such mentorship has long been normative in the Netherlands for obstetricians. The obstetric profession in the US is a surgical specialty. Like their Dutch counterparts, US obstetricians as a whole rarely attend totally unmedicated, spontaneous, physiologic, vaginal births. This approach to education contributes to a cultural norm for obstetricians, where surgical intervention and rapid access to cesarean section, rather than supports for normal birth processes, are thought to increase safety. This way of thinking can produce the conundrum we call the "obstetric paradox" (Cheyney and Davis-Floyd, this volume, Chapter 1) wherein clinicians intervene in birth, see outcomes worse than expected, and in response, intervene *more* in birth in an attempt to improve safety, thus escalating medicalization. In a technocratic society, the potential solution of less intervention and more supports for normal processes might simply never be recognized or explored.

The vast majority of healthy, low-risk women in the United States (90%), receive maternity care from obstetricians in group practices. Obstetricians,

---

[6] The CPM, CNM, and CM credentials are all accredited by the National Commission for Certifying Agencies, which is the accrediting arm of the US Institute of Credentialing Excellence.

family physicians, and CNM/CMs who are based in publicly funded clinics or multidisciplinary practices typically offer 10 to 15 prenatal visits that last on average 15–20 minutes (*Prenatal Care Fact Sheet* 2017). Community midwives (CPMs and some CNMs/CMs in private practice) see clients according to a similar visitation schedule but spend closer to one hour per visit (Cheyney et al. 2015a). The content of care for all providers in the US includes physical assessment and diagnostics, but midwives spend proportionately more time on assessing and addressing biopsychosocial concerns (Cheyney 2011; Cheyney et al. 2014a). Pregnant women in the United States generally have limited choice regarding place of birth, and access to different models of care is dependent upon the degree of integration of midwives in their state (Vedam et al. 2018). In US hospitals, as in the Netherlands, assistance at birth is generally provided by labor and delivery nurses. Neonatal Intensive Care Unit (NICU) nurses and, in some cases, a pediatrician may also be present when neonatal complications are anticipated.

Scopes of Midwifery Practices Compared

The US has no equivalent to the Dutch maternity care assistants who provide in-home care for new families following birth. The standard of care following childbirth in US hospitals includes one six-week postpartum visit after discharge. If complications or breastfeeding challenges arise in the interim, new mothers may contact a pediatrician or their primary provider for an office visit or try to gain access to lactation consultation. Despite their demonstrated benefits, postpartum home visiting programs for women who have given birth in the hospital are relatively uncommon in the United States (Cheng et al. 2006). The only exception is the care provided by community midwives, who routinely provide frequent in-home postpartum visits. However, since community midwives care for less than 2% of the population of childbearing families, the public health benefits of intensive postpartum care are not realized nationally. Following recent high-profile publications describing cases of inadequate postpartum care leading to increased morbidity and mortality (see the Lost Mothers series at: https://www.propublica.org/series/lost-mothers), the American College of Obstetricians and Gynecologists (ACOG) has issued guidance recommending a change in the schedule and content of postpartum care in the US (McKinney et al. 2018).

Conversely, in the Netherlands, maternity care assistants observe the health of mother and infant and report to the midwife if necessary. They provide information and instruction about care and hygiene, assist the mother with breastfeeding, and help with any other issues she may have; they may also do some cooking and housework to allow the parents to spend more time with the baby and the mother to rest and recuperate. In 2016, the copayment for these services was €4.20 (about $4.50 USD) per hour. In the United States, community midwives visit their clients five to six times at home during the first six weeks postpartum, and more often if needed (Cheyney et al. 2015a).

Thus, care for this small minority of US women is similar to the standard of postpartum care to which all Dutch women have access. For the other 98% of the US childbearing population, only those with the ability to pay between $20 and $40 per hour for postpartum doula services are able to access the level of in-home postpartum and breastfeeding support that is normative in the Netherlands. In practice, doulas (professional prenatal, labor, and/or postpartum support companions) support about 3% of women who can afford to pay out-of-pocket for their services (Declerq et al. 2007). More commonly, US women patch together assistance from friends, family members, hired help, local support groups when available, and online resources to create their own care networks following birth. As a result, US women's experiences of postpartum support vary significantly from almost none to a level of in-home care from midwives and doulas that rivals common practice in the Netherlands. This variation in access to postpartum care likely contributes to lower than optimal rates of breastfeeding and high rates of postpartum depression among some populations in the United States (Schmied 2011; Xie 2009).

The midwife's position in the Dutch maternity care system is unique because, unlike in some other high resource countries, the Dutch midwife is responsible for risk assessment and for deciding when referral to a higher level of care is necessary. In fact, for uncomplicated pregnancies and births (Ministerie van Volksgezondheid en Sport 1993) midwives are seen as the

In-home postpartum visit in the US. Community midwives visit multiple times in the first few weeks following birth to help support breastfeeding and to make sure the baby is growing well. Photograph by Matt Bunten

experts in the management of most normal, healthy pregnancies, and the payment system reserves the physicians' jurisdiction for medically compli-cated pregnancies. Like the GP in general health care, the midwife is the gate-keeper to specialist obstetric care, which is covered by health insurance only after a midwife (or GP) referral. Furthermore, Dutch midwives attend and supervise with autonomous authority of judgment a large proportion of preg-nancies and births, including homebirths, although their share is decreasing. Within the boundaries of their profession, Dutch midwives are legal equiva-lents to their obstetrician peers; they interact as colleagues, collaborating on cases as needed. Midwives are respected members of the obstetric team, not seen as employees or assistants who must be supervised and report to obste-tricians (Aitink, Goodarzi, and Marijn 2014).

Unlike in the Netherlands, the status of midwifery as a profession in the United States varies by credential, as well as by region of practice. While all 50 states license and regulate CNMs, CPMs (who attend births at home and in birth centers, and not in hospitals) are only licensed and regulated in 36 US states. CMs are licensed solely in New York, New Jersey, Missouri, and Rhode Island and are authorized by permit to practice in Delaware (Vedam et al. 2018). Although CNMs are well integrated into hospital systems in many states, only a small percentage (between 4% and 6.4%; Vedam et al. 2018) are able to provide community birth services. A large body of research documents an array of interprofessional experiences for CNMs that range from high levels of professional autonomy with mutually respectful collabo-ration with physician colleagues to oppressive and hierarchical relationships where CNMs struggle to be seen, heard, and treated as independent, highly qualified members of the obstetric team (Downe et al. 2010; King et al. 2012; Waldman et al. 2012; May 2017).

In the states where CPMs are not licensed and regulated, they practice completely outside the system and are dependent on the willingness of indi-vidual, sympathetic physicians to provide consultation and collaboration when necessary (Cheyney 2011). Many community midwives in unregulated (and even some in regulated) states describe finding collaborative working relationships with physicians or hospital-based midwives as challenging, if not impossible (Cheyney, Everson, and Burcher 2014). While all credentialed midwives in the US self-identify as managing assessment and referral to a higher level of care as needed, this continuum of care is not a broadly accepted standard for interprofessional care across settings in the United States. In fact, the inverse is more common; midwifery care in the commu-nity—which is far more cost-effective—is often not covered by insurance, while specialist obstetric care is. In addition, some states require physician oversight and "gatekeeping" for women to access community midwives.

Community Birth Practice and Midwifery Integration

During my (Missy's) early fieldwork as a reproductive anthropologist and an apprenticing student midwife in the Midwestern United States, I worked with a high-volume practice of homebirth midwives who attended around 150 births per year. The first 30 or 40 births I observed or assisted at during my training were so straightforward that we hardly had time to come in and get set up before the baby was born. I reflected in my field notes:

> These babies come so fast and are born so gently and sweetly that we often hardly have time to get both gloves on! Sometimes I wonder at all the emergency equipment we bring to each birth and then never use. Are all of these healthy women supposed to try to make it to the hospital? It is hard to imagine after attending them how a $4000-$5000 hospital birth managed by a surgeon would be anything but an enormous waste of valuable health care dollars and expertise. (Cheyney March 17, 2001)

While I have certainly gone on to attend dozens of births where that emergency equipment was absolutely needed, it remains difficult to comprehend, given my own experiences as an anthropologist and a midwife, how the US debate over place of birth can still be dominated by the question of *whether* any woman should be "allowed" to give birth outside of the hospital and not by more nuanced questions like: What place of birth is most likely to lead to optimal maternal and newborn health, given specific pregnancy characteristics and regionally available birthing options? Or, how can clinicians most effectively collaborate across birth settings and provider types to achieve the best possible outcomes for women and babies? I am excited to see that some systematic work on the potential cost savings of community birth is underway. As Anderson and colleagues (forthcoming) have recently argued:

> We find that an expansion in the accessibility of out-of-hospital births is warranted. In the United States, the savings [of increasing homebirths to just 10% of the birthing population] could amount to $10 billion per year. So whether the primary goal is safety, social justice, or cost savings, *public policies that support community births simply make sense.*

In practice, there are multiple state- and national-level barriers that often prevent, or at least make very challenging, autonomous (or any other kind of) practice for community midwives; access and choice of birth place are severely limited for the vast majority of US women, and especially for women of color. However, despite the barriers to practice and compensation that must be overcome by midwives and the families they serve, home and birth center births are on the rise in the United States. After a steady decline between 1990 and 2004, community births increased by 72%, from 0.87% of US births in 2004 to 1.5% in 2014 (MacDorman and Declerq 2016).

The US trend of increasing rates of home and birth center births has amplified the need for collaboration between obstetricians and community midwives. Between 11% and 15% of women who go into labor intending to give birth at home or in a birth center transfer to a hospital as a result of complications that arise in labor or in the immediate postpartum period (Cheyney, Everson, and Burcher 2014; Olsen and Clausen 2012; Out-of-Hos-

Homebirth in the United States. In this photograph, Missy has just assisted one of her graduate students in giving birth to her second baby. The assisting midwife is another graduate student who works with Missy. The little girl in the picture was also born at home with Missy in attendance. Photo by Alicia Juniku

pital Births in Oregon 2012; Snowden et al. 2015). Essential interprofessional interactions that occur during transfers from home to hospital bring the dominant obstetric knowledge system into contact with the contested and marginalized knowledge system of community midwifery (Cheyney, Everson, and Burcher 2014). In some regions of the United States, this contact has helped to create locally integrated systems with high degrees of autonomy for midwives and interprofessional collaboration. In others, contact has functioned to entrench differences, exacerbating what anthropologists call "the US home/hospital divide" (De Vries et al. 2001). From homebirth as normative to homebirth as felony,[7] from midwives as respected primary maternity care providers to community midwives as a contested subclass, how did two such distinct systems of maternity care—those of the Netherlands and of the US—come into being?

---

[7] In several states in the US, it is a felony for a CPM to attend a homebirth. Because her certification is not recognized by the state, she may be charged with practicing medicine without a license.

Locating Midwives in the Netherlands and the United States: Unique Historical Trajectories

Dutch Midwifery History

Unlike in many other European countries, Dutch midwifery has been formally recognized as an independent profession since the 1600s. Prior to the 19th century, local councils regulated the practice of medicine, and a diversity of other clinical practices, including midwifery, flourished. Early midwives were educated through local guilds, training under the supervision of experienced midwives. After successfully completing their preparation, certified midwives were allowed to practice within their municipal areas, carrying authentication documents that attested to their qualifications; local councils punished the practice of uncertified midwifery (Klinkert 1980; van Lieburg & Marland 1989). Up through the early 1900s, almost 98% of women in the Netherlands gave birth at home (van Daalen 1988).

During the 20th century, the rate of physician-attended hospital births gradually increased, as a growing number of women began requesting them (Centrale Raad voor de Volksgezondheid 1972; Werkgroep Geneeskundige Hoofdinspectie 1969). By 1932, the number of homebirths had declined to about 92% (Drenth 1998). Some midwives adjusted to this change by leaving their position in autonomous, primary care to work within clinics under physicians' supervision. At these clinics, midwives collaborated with nurses to provide maternity care—an alliance that resulted in the "nurse-midwife" designation that we know today in the UK and in the US. However, in the Netherlands, midwifery was never fully hospitalized or directly connected to nursing as a profession, in part because direct-entry midwifery education was established prior to this trend toward the merging of midwifery and nursing. As such, Dutch midwives' educational trajectories remained separate from nurses' training, allowing midwives to maintain their autonomy and philosophy of practice as a distinct profession (Lieburg and Marland 1989; Schultz 2013).

In writing about the uniqueness of the Dutch maternity care system (and especially the autonomy of midwives), Raymond De Vries and colleagues (2009; De Vries 2004) have argued that the persistence of homebirth and independent midwifery in the Netherlands results from a unique set of rules, regulations, educational programs, and arrangements between professionals that emerged from a specific historical past and that was continuously renegotiated over decades. Midwifery in the Netherlands is thus "not just another quaint feature of the lowlands, akin to wooden shoes, destined to disappear from everyday practice. It is a way of birth that is closely tied to both cultural and structural features of Dutch society, a way of birth that can serve as a vanguard for midwives elsewhere" (De Vries et al 2009:49).

According to historical sources, the impetus for Dutch midwives' unique historical trajectory compared with other countries seems to have at least two dimensions. First, the emergence of clinics/hospitals in the Netherlands was limited relative to other places in Europe. As a result, the majority of Dutch midwives and rural GPs continued to practice as primary maternity care providers outside of hospitals and clinics. Second, but no less important, the Dutch in general, including many obstetricians, hold to the belief that pregnancy, labor, and the postpartum period are primarily physiologic events that do not necessarily require medical management—a view supported by Dutch legislators (Goodarzi et al. 2018; Schultz 2013).

In 1818, Dutch legislators introduced the "Regulation of Medical Professions" Act (Staatsblad van het Koninkrijk der Nederlanden 1818) designed to structure and control the practice of medicine at the national level. It stated that both obstetricians and general practitioners were allowed to practice across the full scope of *midwifery*. The same law restricted midwives' jurisdiction to the practice of attending community births that "were natural processes or could be delivered manually, so that the midwife may never use any instruments for this purpose" (Beekman 1836:197). These historical developments furthered the institutionalization of midwifery as a distinct profession and functioned to preserve it as it is known today in the Netherlands (Klinkert 1980; van Lieburg and Marland 1989).

The midwife's scope of practice as described in the 1818 Act was reconfirmed in the Medical Act of 1865 (Staatsblad van het Koninkrijk der Nederlanden 1986) and then again by the Ministerie van Volksgezondheid en Sport in 1993. Over the last century, midwives' tasks and responsibilities have been specified and expanded. Suturing, episiotomy, and use of ultrasound are a few examples of the many skills that were added to the midwife's competencies during this time period. The latest amendment by administrative decree to the Healthcare Professionals Act took place in 2014, making it possible for midwives to: (1) prescribe and administer nitrous oxide (an effective means of pain relief during labor that is completely woman-controlled); (2) prescribe contraceptives; and (3) insert intra-uterine devices (Ministerie van Volksgezondheid en Sport 2014).

The 1941 Sick Fund Decree (*Verordeningenblad voor het bezette Nederlandse gebied* 1941) also played an important role in the history of the midwifery profession in the Netherlands. The Sick Fund Decree provided for compulsory health insurance for low- and middle-income people and reimbursed all maternity care costs. However, for uncomplicated pregnancies and births, the costs were *only* compensated if the birth had taken place under the care of a midwife at home, as attendance by a doctor in a hospital was seen as medically unnecessary, and thus wasteful, in such cases. Women with healthy pregnancies and births, who simply wished to give birth in the hospital even though there were no medical indications for it, had to pay an extra fee. In this way, the Sick Fund Decree further confirmed midwives' expertise in normal, healthy, physiologic birth and limited the physicians' jurisdiction to medically complicated pregnancies (Abraham-van der Mark 1996).

In the years that followed the Sick Fund Decree, insurance expenses increased, due in part to more women choosing hospital births. Aiming to regulate expenses, in 1957 insurance companies started using a list of medical conditions for which hospital care was advised. The list was also used by midwives to decide when referral was indicated. This list was published in a textbook by Holmer and colleagues (1956) for the education of obstetricians and midwives (Amelink and Buitendijk 2010). In 1973, Professor Kloosterman, a renowned Dutch obstetrician and gynecologist, revised Holmer's textbook, including the list of medical conditions that required hospital admission; this list became known as the *"Kloosterman lijst"* (Kloosterman 1973).

Kloosterman's list of medical indications has been revised three times since: in 1987 (Werkgroep Bijstelling Kloostermanlijst 1987), in 1999 (Ziekenfondsraad 1999) and in 2003 (Commissie Verloskunde 2003). The list has come to be known as the "Obstetric Indication List" or *Verloskundige Indicatie Lijst* (VIL). The VIL distinguishes four levels of care: primary care by the community midwife or GP (Level A); consultation between the midwife and the obstetrician (Level B); secondary care by the obstetrician (Level C); and labor at the hospital under supervision of the community midwife (Level D) (see Tables 1 and 2). The VIL has had an enormous impact on the organization of Dutch maternity care and the position of midwives within it (Goodarzi et al. 2018). Today the VIL fulfills a dual function. It is used as a tool to support collaboration between midwives and physicians, and as a cost-regulating instrument for health care insurance companies (Commissie Verloskunde 2003). At the time of this writing, the VIL is under revision again. Yet, this time the revision process has become complicated by debates between midwives and physicians fueled by contradictory perspectives on physiology, pathology, and risk.

I (Bahareh) remember attending the general meeting of the Dutch Association of Midwives (*Koninklijke Nederlandse Organisatie voor Verloskundigen, KNOV*) in June 2015,[8] during which the midwives had to decide about the

---

Table 1   Categories of care, level of care and care provider as described in the VIL (Commissie Verloskunde, 2003)

Level of care	Responsible care provider
A	A community midwife or GP is responsible, birth can take place at home or in hospital
B	Consultation between community midwife/GP and gynecologist The responsible care provider depends on outcome of the consultation
C	The gynecologist is responsible, birth must take place in hospital
D	The community midwife/GP is responsible, birth must take place in hospital

---

[8] Source: Notulen Algemene Ledenvergadering KNOV [Minutes general assembly KNOV] June 12, 2015.

Table 2   Some examples of risk conditions as described by the VIL (Commissie Verloskunde 2003, pp. 104, 106, 117)

Condition	Category of care	Comments
Preterm birth (≥ 33 weeks) in the previous pregnancy	A	
Preterm birth (< 33 weeks) in the previous pregnancy	C	In case of an uncomplicated pregnancy following the preterm birth, the next pregnancy can be attended by a community midwife/GF
Failure to progress in labor	B	
Hemorrhage postpartum (>1000 cc) in the previous pregnancy	D	Considering the chance of repetition, the birth must take place in the hospital, however may be under midwife care

VIL's revisions. During that very tense meeting, the draft revisions of a few medical indications—including gestational diabetes, fetal growth restriction, and large for gestational age—were on the agenda for authorization, meaning we were considering changing the requirements for how women with these conditions should be cared for. Revisions were discussed and proposed by a committee consisting of representatives from the professional associations for obstetricians, pediatricians, and midwives. The committee needed the consent of all three groups before finalizing them.

Although multidisciplinary collaboration is highly valued in the Netherlands, and the midwives had no intention of alienating the other professionals, they felt that the new proposals on consultation and referral would increase the chance of unnecessary medical interventions. For example, the proposed revised version of the medical indication of fetal growth restriction stated that the midwife *should always* consult the pediatrician in cases where the neonatal birth weight is beneath the 10th percentile on the birth weight chart. According to the midwives, the decision to draw the line for consultation—and thus pathology—at the 10th percentile was not evidence-based, but rather arbitrary. Furthermore, midwives have the expertise to assess each individual case and to determine whether consultation and referral are needed at *any* birth weight. In the midwives' opinion, in practice, this proposal could mean many unnecessary consultations that would likely lead to unnecessary medical interventions and their consequences. In the end, the midwives voted to reject all three revisions.

For me, this meeting crystallized just how different perspectives on physiology, pathology and the need for intervention can be. Different professional groups share a desire to have the best possible care outcomes, yet may disagree on how to achieve them. Mandating complicated and inflexible rules for how and when collaboration must occur across different providers with different perspectives can sometimes actually hinder optimal care (de Vrieze 2018). While I can certainly understand how different professions as products of their differing educations, expertise, and experiences will sometimes arrive at different views on physiology and pathology, I find it even more intriguing how different perspectives can occur *within* the same professional group (Goodarzi et al. 2018).

I remember working as a midwife in a practice that collaborated with two intermediate-level-care hospitals located just 20 km apart; yet some of their protocols and guidelines were very different, even contradictory. Both hospitals, for example, regarded a 42-week-pregnancy to be the upper limit of gestational length, and thus, the time when induction of labor should occur. When a client's 42-week mark was nearing, Hospital A would routinely recommend that women consider induction before the end of the 42nd week, whereas Hospital B would advise women to wait until the end of the 42nd week and would conduct an extra checkup in the meantime. This difference in policy had major consequences for women, as well as for collaborating midwives and obstetricians. Midwives would inform women about this difference so that they could choose which hospital they preferred, and many women asked us midwives for our recommendations. However, midwives' views also differed on whether it was best to induce before the end of the 42nd week or to wait until the end of the 42nd week to give women more time to go into spontaneous labor. In addition, sometimes the hospital of choice would be full, and women would have to go to the other one, which meant automatically having to abide by its protocols. This situation left me wondering about the relationship between women-centered care, professional opinions, and evidence-based practice: why was care organized around the hospitals' protocols? How was it possible that in a time so focused on "evidence-based practice," such contradictory protocols and variation among professional opinions could exist? That is when I realized that, because of its unpredictable nature, risk and its management can never be purely scientific, and attitudes are often affected by differential content of professional education, exposure, and practice experiences (Healy et al 2016; Daemers et al. 2017). Therefore, women-centered care—care that puts women at the center of decision-making and respects maternal autonomy—is essential.

US Midwifery History

The historical trajectory of professional midwifery in the United States, at least until the last few decades, much more closely parallels that of the United Kingdom than the Netherlands. In early colonial America, as in Britain and elsewhere at that time, childbirth was predominantly a social occasion controlled by women (Wertz and Wertz 1989; Cheyney 2011). Births were semi-public events attended by small groups of female relatives, neighbors, and a midwife who assisted the mother and baby. Historical sources are biased toward wealthy and middle-class women whose journals have survived, and so generalizations about the skills and practices of early US midwives are difficult to make. However, information on births throughout the 18th and 19th centuries suggests that difficult or obstructed births occurred in fewer than 5% of cases, and that midwives generally enjoyed excellent outcomes (Ulrich 1990). In the case of difficult births, a barber-surgeon or physician could be called; however, until the mid-18th century this action often constituted a death knell for the child and perhaps for the mother. Thankfully, such conclusions to a woman's labor were quite rare. Several recent demographic studies have significantly revised previous assumptions about maternal mortality in childbirth in the US, demonstrating that in the 17th and 18th centuries, the mother died in less than 1% of births (Epstein 2010; Hay 2002). Whether the risk of death in childbirth translated into pervasive fear and dread of the process is a matter of contention among historians. Many US birth historians (Crawford 1990; Porter and Porter 1988; Pollock 1990) emphasize the traumatic potential of birth, while others assert that because the usual outcome was positive, fear was likely not the predominant emotion associated with birth for most early US women (Hay 2002). In fact, they argue, most women diarists in 18th-century America describe childbirth rather matter-of-factly (Wertz and Wertz 1989).

Historians who focus on early US women's fear for their own well-being often overlook what may have been a very real source of anxiety—the risk of death or damage to the child. While precise historical infant mortality rates are difficult to ascertain, all available evidence suggests that they were significantly higher than maternal mortality rates (Hay 2002)—a pattern that is still the case today. Thus, fear for the life of the unborn fetus may have contributed to perceptions of risk in childbirth then as it does now in the United States, and this fear may have been an important factor in the gradual transition from female midwives to male surgeons or "man-midwives," as they were first called. "Man-midwives" began to displace female midwives in the birthing chambers of upper-class British women in the early 19th century, and this practice quickly spread to the United States. Indeed, changes in US birth practices were often the direct result of new technologies and trends that occurred first in Britain and were later replicated in the Colonies (Ehrenriech and English 2010; Hay 2002).

Historians point to two developments in particular—the invention and dissemination of forceps by the Chamberlen family between 1620 and 1730, and the publication of several new medical texts reflecting a view of the female body as a defective machine—as the "beginning of the end" for midwifery as an autonomous profession in the United States, and in many places in Europe (Martin 2001; Hay 2002; Davis-Floyd 2003[1992]; Cassidy 2007; Ehrenriech and English 2010). European midwives were systematically excluded from using forceps, and forbidden from enrolling in formalized schools for physicians. Graduates of these schools later came to be known as "obstetricians"—a word that comes from the Latin root *obstare*, which means "to stand opposite to" or "to obstruct." Community midwives in the United States today sometimes reflect on this linguistic detail, describing their colleagues' historical naming as prophetic. As US midwives continue to organize in their attempts to increase access to midwife-led, physiologic birth in community settings, narratives of obstruction, rather than of support or facilitation, still occur in some communities (Cheyney, Everson, and Burcher 2014; Craven 2010; Davis-Floyd 2018h), though many others report smooth and collegial interprofessional collaboration.[9]

The movement toward physician-attended birth was further solidified in Victorian era (1837–1901) America, as male gynecologists and obstetricians gained even greater control and acceptance in the birthplace. The sentimental focus on female delicacy that characterized the "cult of domesticity" during this period emphasized the notion that civilized and refined white women could not and should not tolerate the "degradation of childbirth" (Stone 2009; Wertz and Wertz 1989:114). Enter the notion of "childbirth without pain"—a feat that was first achieved through the use of chloroform in labor in 1847. During the 1920s, some upper-class White women actually traveled to Germany to have their babies under the influence of the new drug scopolamine, bringing quantities of it back to the United States and encouraging obstetricians to use it so women would not be forced to feel the pain of childbirth. Scopolamine did not actually take away the pain; rather it made women unable to remember their labor and birth experiences. Women under the influence of this drug often screamed, tried to scratch their caregivers, and writhed about uncontrollably. Thus, they were frequently tied to their hospital beds with arm restraints. The "scopolamine era" of birth in the US, which lasted from the 1920s until the early 1970s, is a black mark on the history of US childbirth. Many women had flashbacks of their drugged experiences; thousands wrote letters of protest to various magazines; and eventually scopolamine use was discontinued in favor of the epidural. Scopolamine was never as widely used in the Netherlands, where birth was viewed as a normal part of life and not something women had to be anesthetized to bear.

British colonial influence, combined with racism and enslavement, deeply shaped perceptions of childbirth and access to resources for Black, poor, and immigrant women in the US (Yoder and Hardy 2018). For example, the converse of the logic that "civilized women" were unable to cope with pain was that "uncivilized" Mexican American and African American women and lower-class White women did not suffer in childbirth to the extent that genteel White women did; the former were stereotyped as just "squatting in the field, picking up the baby, and going back to work." An unintended result of this racist logic was the preservation of midwifery traditions among communities of color in the United States. Significant regional childbirth attendants, including the Mexican American *parteras* of the Southwest and the Black "granny

---

[9] See: http://www.washingtonmidwives.org/documents/Smooth-Transitions-Hospital-Transport-QI-Project.pdf for one example of a state-wide program committed to seamless collaboration across referring and receiving providers.

midwives" of the African American South, practiced well into the mid-20th century, in contrast with Euro-American midwives, who were almost completely displaced by physicians by the end of the Victorian era. Many wealthy White women (in both the South and North) were still attended by the Black granny midwives who were considered appropriate for this now "unclean," uncivilized, distasteful role (Yoder and Hardy 2018).

In 1910, the Flexner report (Stahnisch and Verhoef 2012)—which described the need to centralize and standardized medical education—led to the closure of community- and apprenticeship-based educational routes and to an increase in institutionalized birth (Yoder and Hardy 2018). Soon, to respond to the recommendations of the Flexner report, and in order to guarantee more cases for medical students to practice on, wealthy and educated White women were paid (incentivized) to deliver in hospital. As wealthy White women turned increasingly toward male obstetricians, women of color, poor, and rural women continued to give birth with community midwives in their homes (Hay 2002; Fraser 2009).

The exception in the United States was the lying-in hospital built to serve populations of poor, urban, often-unmarried mothers and some women of color (Wertz and Wertz 1989). Training in these early hospitals furthered the tendency to focus on birth as pathological and dangerous. Importantly, even as the Black granny midwives were being blamed for poor hygiene and uneducated methods in community births, deaths and complications were high in these early lying-in hospitals due to the unsanitary conditions that existed prior to our understanding of germ theory. These hospitals, in both Europe and the US, were the primary breeding grounds for deadly childbirth (puerperal) fever—a postpartum infection transmitted to women via the unwashed hands of nurses and physicians. Practitioners trained in this environment understandably came to see each birth as a potential disaster and every woman as a potential victim. These beliefs—again, quite distinct from the Dutch notion of pregnancy and birth as a primarily healthy life event—form the historical foundation in the United States for the contemporary medical management of childbirth and the subsequent marginalization and underutilization of midwives.

A logical outgrowth of the perception of birth as risky was its comprehensive movement into the hospital (Hay 2002), which took place far more quickly in the US than it did in the Netherlands. In 1900, only 5% of US babies were born in the hospital. By 1935, 75% were born there, and by the early 1970s, 99% of births in the United States took place in the hospital. In contrast, 70% of Dutch births still occurred at home at this time. Yet US death rates did not decline as birth was hospitalized, as many assumed they should; instead, they rose. In the 1920s, as middle-class women began having hospital-born babies in increasing numbers, the maternal mortality rate increased slightly, rising from 60 deaths per 10,000 in 1915 to 63 deaths per 10,000 in 1932. In urban areas where hospital births were more common, the maternal mortality rate was 74/10,000—substantially higher than the overall national rate. In addition, between 1915 and 1929, infant deaths from birth injuries and from infections passed from baby to baby in the hospital nurseries increased by more than 40% (Goer 1999). During that period, mothers were rarely allowed to have their babies with them immediately following the birth; instead, newborns were cared for by nursery nurses until mother and baby went home.

Eventually, institutionalized birth was touted as a critical public health measure required to improve maternal and infant health, and Black granny midwives were systematically excluded from attending births within facilities (Yoder and Hardy 2018). The Sheppard-Towner Act (1921) required regulation of Black midwives and oversight of their practices by White male physicians. Black midwives were later systematically disenfranchised and excluded from community birth, as the medical system introduced increasingly technocratic models, devices, procedures, and medications to "modernize" birth using "scientific methods." Hence, as the narrative of "modern, technocratic birth" as better, cleaner, and safer spread, families of color were eventually denied access to culturally matched midwifery care in their own communities as their midwives were forced out of practice.[10]

Given the self-perpetuating and tautological nature of the move to hospitals and the consequent cultural perception of birth as dangerous, the underutilization of midwives in the United States is perhaps not particularly surprising. An emphasis on the need for medical intervention and physician management also makes sense within the contemporary for-profit maternity care system, as the use of technology to manage births, regardless of established need, generates higher profits than "low-tech, high-touch" (Naisbitt 1984)—and low cost—approaches that characterize community births in the United States (Cheyney et al. 2014b; Washington State 2007; Stapleton et al 2013; Anderson, Daviss, and Johnson forthcoming). Community midwives and the families who seek their care today are still struggling to carve out a small niche within this deeply entrenched, technocratic US hospital birth monopoly. Women who desire community birth in the US are pushing for access to high-quality maternity care in a system where any and all forms of maternity care are a costly privilege, and not a basic human right. Women and babies in the United States, as in the Netherlands, inherit maternity outcomes that are an outgrowth of these distinctive historical legacies. The "cultural safety" that clinicians and policy makers explicitly strive for in New Zealand (see Chapter 5) is in no way a reality for the vast majority of birthing people in the United States.

---

[10] See Joseph (forthcoming) for a description of a program that has successfully reintroduced culturally matched care and used midwifery care to eradicate maternity care disparities among women of color in Florida.

Barriers to Integrated Care and Their Impact on Outcomes in the Netherlands and the United States

Safety and Place of Birth Debates in the Netherlands

In 2008, Euro-Peristat, a large European network that conducts comparative research on health care outcomes of mothers and babies, published a report showing that the Netherlands had one of the highest perinatal mortality rates among the nations included (Euro-Peristat 2008). The country was shocked. Although numerous studies had shown that homebirth in the Netherlands is as safe as birth in a hospital (Damstra-Wijmenga 1984; Eskes et al. 1993; Wiegers et al. 1996), the ensuing debate centered on homebirth, midwifery care, risk selection, and (lack of) cooperation between midwives and physicians. The entire system of providing maternity care in the Netherlands was blamed, including the practice of homebirth. The debate that ensued fueled animosity between obstetricians and midwives and led to unsubstantiated accusations, resulting in an atmosphere of fear and distrust. Multiple explanations were proposed.

Policy makers and most researchers emphasized that homebirth was not to blame, though the popular press claimed otherwise. Later research showed that perinatal mortality was especially high in high-poverty areas among the Dutch as well as in immigrant communities, and that a large proportion of the perinatal mortality rate was caused by prematurity, but the media damage had already been done. Currently, more women than ever before are being referred by primary care midwives to secondary care during pregnancy and labor, stimulating questions and doubts among physicians about the current system of maternity care and the role of the midwife as gatekeeper within it. Currently, more than 70% of all Dutch women give birth with physicians or clinical midwives in secondary or tertiary care hospitals. The total referral rate (during pregnancy and labor) increased from 46% in 2000 to almost 57% in 2014.

Two publications, one in 2009 and one in 2010, with contradictory conclusions, further incensed the debate. In 2009, de Jonge and coauthors (2009) compared outcomes from 529,000 births and concluded that in a low-risk population *the intended place of birth was not related to perinatal outcome*. But in 2010, Evers and colleagues concluded that women starting labor under supervision of a midwife (low-risk) had an increased risk of perinatal mortality compared with women starting labor under supervision of a physician (high-risk). The de Jonge publication was cited extensively in scientific publications, while the Evers piece was quoted in the Dutch national media alongside condemnations of primary care midwifery. One newspaper even used the front-page headline: "Don't try this at home!" (Reerink 2010). The second Euro-Peristat report, published in 2013 with data from 2010 (Euro-Peristat 2013), showed some improvement, with the Dutch perinatal mortality rate closer to the mean for the countries and regions included; however, the second report did not receive as much press attention as the first. A singular message was touted nationally: perinatal mortality in the Netherlands is still too high, and the system would have to change. In 2014, de Jonge and colleagues (2015) merged three national datasets and expanded the analysis of perinatal outcomes up to 28 days post birth (n = 743,070). The conclusion was the same; the authors found *no significant differences in newborn health between home and hospital birth among low risk populations.*

Another relatively recent change in the Dutch maternity care system has been the establishment of birth centers. In the years around the turn of this century, a small "baby boom" (an unexpected increase in the number of babies born) occurred in the Netherlands, leading to a shortage of both primary and secondary maternity care providers (Wiegers et al. 2000). At the same time, in order to be able to provide around-the-clock care, smaller hospitals were closed or merged with larger hospitals, and maternity departments were combined into a smaller number of larger locations. As a result, homebirth was no longer possible in some regions because the closest obstetric department was considered too far away for safe transfers during emergencies. Because of the high workload, some midwifery practices were similarly no longer able to assist all of the women planning a birth at home, and some had to be sent to the hospital. However, Dutch hospitals were not keen to receive so many women without a medical indication. They needed the limited space and care providers to serve women with more medically complicated pregnancies. (Robbie vividly recalls visiting a Dutch hospital some years ago where the obstetricians with whom she spoke complained bitterly about the additional workload and the overcrowding stemming from the sudden new influx of women who could have birthed at home.)

To accommodate women without a medical indication being routed to the hospital, some units introduced a new maternity care department (often called a birth center) where autonomous community midwives could attend to more than one birth at a time or could cooperate with clinical (i.e., hospital-based) midwives and/or nurses to care for low-risk women. These birth centers were seen as an "in between" solution—not at home, but also not in the clinical environment of the hospital. While their objective was primarily to reduce the pressure of the suddenly high patient volumes on hospital maternity wards, one of the side effects may have been, at least in some regions, a further decline in the homebirth rate.

When the baby boom ended and the annual number of births declined, the birth centers were no longer needed and most closed after just a few years. However, after an advisory report in 2009, birth centers were revived, but with a slightly different goal. Rather than being seen as an alternative location for giving birth, birth centers were heralded as an opportunity to create a new model founded on provider cooperation. The expectation was that in a birth center located close to a clinical ward, cooperation between primary and secondary care could occur smoothly because professionals would be more familiar with each other. Ideally, a more integrated form of care would emerge (Wiegers et al. 2012).

Since 2010, a number of new birth sites have been established, most of them close to or inside a hospital, yet separate from the clinical ward. Some are freestanding with community midwives and maternity care assistants providing care for women with uncomplicated pregnancies. Some are run by a hospital, some by cooperation between hospitals and midwifery practices, and others by community midwives in combination with maternity care assistance organizations. They are referred to as "birth centers," "birthing suites," or "birth hotels," but a clear definition of what constitutes a birth center in the Netherlands was initially lacking.

In 2013, a large national study, called the Dutch Birth Centre Study (Hermus et al. 2015), set out to formulate a definition of "birth center" in the Dutch context. A clear definition was needed if optimal birth outcomes, client experiences, and costs and levels of integration of care in birth centers in the Netherlands were to be established. The researchers inventoried all birth locations that might be considered birth centers and concluded, based on their definition (Hermus et al 2017), that in 2013 there were 23 birth centers operating—from freestanding to "alongside" (on hospital grounds or in the hospital, but separate from the clinical ward) or on-site (a separate room inside the clinical ward). The Dutch Birth Centre Study examined characteristics of birth centers, level of integration of care, quality of care, the effects of birth center care on maternity care outcomes, the experiences of clients and care professionals, and costs relative to homebirth or hospital birth attended by a community midwife (Wiegers et al. 2012; Hermus et al. 2015; Hitzert et al. 2017).

In 2014, more than 60% of all births occurred after referral to obstetric care. Birth in a birth center or hospital out-patient department (that is: births, not at home, but without referral to obstetric care) decreased from 36% in 2000 to 29% in 2014, and the homebirth rate decreased from 24% in 2000 to 13% in 2014). Rising referral rates have been tied to several factors. The majority of referrals to secondary care during the first stage of labor among women who started labor in primary care at home and in birth centers were due to requests for pharmacological pain relief (27.7%), meconium stained liquid (24.0%), and failure to progress (18.2%) (Perined 2015). Since 2008, pharmacological pain relief (mostly meaning epidurals) has been available upon request, and the referral rate has risen with ease of access (Klomp 2015; *Stichting Perinatale Registratie Nederland 1999–2012* n.d.).

Many reasons have been given for the rise in epidural use among Dutch women. A recent study showed that epidural analgesia rates vary widely across the Netherlands at between 12% and 38% in first-time mothers and between 5% and 14% for women who have already had at least one birth (Seijmonsbergen-Schermers et al. 2018). In the US, epidural rates also vary but are commonly cited at between 38% and 61% of all births (Hansen et al.

2017). From our perspectives as midwives and researchers, it seems as though women are not choosing epidurals more often simply because they are more available; rather, it is a combination of factors. Many Dutch women have come to believe that they cannot manage labor without drugs, partly because that is the way mainstream media frame the situation. In movies and on TV, labor pain is often portrayed as something either scary or humorous, as opposed to an inherent and important part of the birth process and experience. Have you ever seen a depiction of the side effects of an epidural? Or one about a woman who regrets using pharmaceutical pain management? We have not. Yet these are the stories we tell one another and those women hear from each other. In this way, epidurals have become more normative in the Netherlands, as they have long been in the US, and giving birth without one has become marked as "abnormal" in the same self-reinforcing manner we have seen around place of birth. Moreover, due to their high caseloads, midwives have been forced to spend less time with patients, and being unable to provide continuous support has made matters worse.

In addition to the growing desire for pain medication, many new screening and diagnostic techniques have made it possible to quantify some kinds of risk, and this quantification may be playing a role in the rise in referrals in the Netherlands. Whereas in the past, place of birth and caregiver were heavily determined by the presence or absence of medical complications, today midwives, other care professionals, and women themselves increasingly make decisions based on perceived risk as influenced by expanded testing, media portrayals, and popular perception.

Together, these factors have increased uncertainty in choice of birthplace in the Netherlands. In practice, this ambiguity/complexity is borne out in several ways, but perhaps especially so in the changes within the VIL ("Obstetric Indication List" or *Verloskundige Indicatie Lijst*) over time. The VIL has become longer with every revision and the number of indications that move women from A to B and C categories of care has increased substantially. The medical indications for specialist care, for example, have quadrupled since the 1960s (Amelink and Buitendijk 2010)! Practice guidelines and protocols have also increased (Hollander and van Dillen 2017). Likely, these increases reflect the fact that Dutch society as a whole has become more "risk-adverse" over time. Women's choices to give birth in a hospital, along with midwives' decisions to refer more women to specialist care, are both increasingly based on the feeling that it is better to birth in hospital "just to be on the safe side"—despite the previously described evidence on the safety of homebirth.

In addition to the introduction of birth centers and changing cultural tolerances for risk and labor pain, the implementation of client-centered care has also introduced new and unintended barriers to integrated care. One particularly problematic conundrum arises: placing the client at the center of care and allowing her wishes and needs to guide the care delivered may sometimes put midwives at odds with the standards they are expected to follow. Midwives' mandate to follow their ever-increasing number of rules can functionally restrict the client's control over the care she receives. On the one hand, midwives aim to put women at the center of care and to honor their full autonomy, yet on the other, they are expected to strictly follow guidelines and protocols. In individual cases, it can become a challenge to find a care path that is best suited for a particular client that does not leave the midwife open to professional risk. This conundrum has been addressed by developing different care paths for women in different situations with unique needs and preferences (KNOV & NVOG 2015); the primary difficulty has been finding care paths that are simultaneously acceptable to women, midwives, *and* obstetricians. Some investigators have noted for various countries that women's autonomous choices are reduced because of the collusion and coordinated pressure that they perceive when midwives strive to be integrated into a health care system by collaborating with, or deferring to, physician consultants (Hall, Tomkinson, and Klein 2012; Healy et al. 216; Barclay et al. 2016).

Despite the increasing referrals by midwives to obstetricians, most women still go on to have healthy, uncomplicated births. Of all women who gave birth in secondary/tertiary care in 2014, 62% gave birth spontaneously, and the majority (59%) were attended by clinical midwives. As a result, the benefit of specialist care over primary care has been questioned, as has the undeniably shifting boundary between "normal" and "abnormal." Dutch midwives fear they are slowly moving toward a "risk paradox" as described by Scamell and Alaszewski (2012), wherein midwives claim to be committed to physiologic birth, yet they categorize an increasing number of births as abnormal or at high-risk for complications. The recent emphasis in the Dutch maternity care system on risk has forced midwives to focus on potential pathology instead of normal physiology, producing a greater overlap with medicalized obstetrics than historically has been the case.

Since the publication of the first Euro-Peristat articles, many changes have been made in Dutch maternity care with the goal of optimizing maternal and newborn health outcomes. However, wide-ranging debates between midwives and physicians continue (Bonsel et al. 2010; Evers et al. 2010). The current focus on "integrated care" should improve cooperation between midwives and doctors, as it provides for the option of discussing all midwifery clients in multidisciplinary consultations, giving obstetricians a say in the risk assessment and referral process. In the meantime, the homebirth rate continues to decline, posing a new threat to the current system: for midwifery students, it is becoming increasingly difficult to attend enough homebirths to finalize their education. To qualify as a midwife in the Netherlands, student midwives need to attend 60 births as the primary attendant, at least eight of which must be homebirths, and at least 30 of which must have started in primary care (Ministerie van Volksgezondheid en Sport 2014, *artikel* 3, lid 4b). Midwifery academies worry about training students as it becomes increasingly difficult to attend the required eight home births within the allowable study period. Exposure to community birth during education is linked to both favorable attitudes towards homebirth and willingness to practice in community settings (Vedam et al. 2014a, b). Many in the Netherlands fear for the future of physiologic, midwife-attended homebirth, for which the Dutch used to be (and still are in most researchers' minds) the leading international example because of the excellent outcomes associated with homebirths in their system.

The US Home/Hospital Divide

Barriers to integrated care in the United States share some similarities to those described for the Netherlands—a problematic focus on risk over normal physiology, methodologically flawed studies from low-quality data sets, ambiguous and shifting perceptions of normal versus abnormal features of pregnancy and birth, and interprofessional strife, to name a few. However, there are also some unique barriers to integration that stem from the fact that the US maternity system has never been integrated, let alone midwifery-led, for the vast majority of women with healthy pregnancies. Very few maternity care practices in the United States are, or ever have been, characterized by a professional division of labor whereby all physiologic birth care is led by midwives in community or hospital settings with more medically complicated labors referred to obstetric colleagues.

Karen's Story.   During a research project I (Missy) conducted with women who planned homebirths in the early 2000s, I heard a story that still haunts and inspires me today. Karen (a pseudonym) was having her first baby and had hired a very experienced practice of community midwives to attend her. Labor came on hard and strong around midnight a few days before her due date, but she had heard that first births could take a while, so she tried to let her midwives sleep. Around 5:30 A.M. her husband called the midwives, worried that he would be alone for the birth. The midwives arrived shortly after 6 A.M. to find Karen seven centimeters dilated and working hard. About 30 minutes later Karen was squatting during a strong contraction when her water broke. The midwives listened to the fetal heart tones (as is common practice following rupture of the amniotic sac) and were immediately concerned as the heart tones had dropped far below the physiologic baseline. They quickly had Karen get into a knees and chest position; one midwife called 911 while the other felt inside the mother's vagina, fearing that the umbilical cord had slipped down in front of the baby's head when the water broke. This condition is called a cord prolapse; it is a rare and true obstetric emergency because the pressure of the baby's head coming down into the birth canal can compress the cord and prevent oxygen flow to the fetus. Indeed, the midwife felt the cord stretched tightly across the top of the baby's head but was able to push it off to the side of the head to relieve some of the pressure. Heart tones returned to normal, and the midwives prepared for a hospital transfer with the mother in the knees-chest position, one midwife pressing up on the fetal head, and the other monitoring heart tones with a hand-held device called a Doppler.

The ambulance brought them to the hospital in this position and the midwives prepared the mother en route, explaining that she would stay in this position until the anesthesiologist put a mask over her face to put her to sleep with general anesthesia. At that point, they would flip her to her back and begin an emergency cesarean section. Upon arrival, the receiving physician declared that he could hear normal fetal heart tones projected from the Doppler and informed Karen that her midwives were mistaken, ignorant, and had no business doing births at home. They wheeled her to a normal labor and delivery room and insisted that she flip to her back so she could be attached the electronic fetal monitor; this would enable him to figure out "what was really going on." The mother and midwives tried to recount the events precipitating the transfer, but the obstetrician had the midwives escorted out of the room. The mother ultimately flipped to her back as directed (a regret she still lives with) and was reassured that the heart tones were normal, and that she was almost ready to start pushing. The midwives, who were in the hall, worried that the physician was actually monitoring the maternal heartbeat and not the baby's. After 30 minutes of pleading, they succeeded in convincing a sympathetic nurse to check the mother's pulse. Just under 60 minutes after arriving at the hospital, Karen received a much needed, but too late, cesarean, as the physician realized that indeed they had been monitoring the mother's heartbeat and that the baby *was* in distress. Karen's daughter was live-born, but never able to breathe on her own. She died three days later—a casualty of the US home-hospital divide. Karen went on to have a triumphant homebirth two years later, having "lost faith" in the medical establishment.

It has been argued that the home (community)/hospital divide has contributed to less than optimal birth outcomes (as with the story above) for both midwife- and obstetrician-led births in the United States. Most importantly, however, more researchers are beginning to look at the impact of systems integration (or lack thereof) on outcomes. Where systems are not well integrated, the solution is not to restrict women's right to choose where and with whom they birth, but to work together to increase collaboration and integration across birth settings (Cheyney, Burcher, and Vedam 2014; Vedam et al. 2014c; Vedam et al. 2018). Thus, it is clear that in the United States, community/midwifery and obstetric/hospital perspectives are often at odds (Roome et al. 2015) and that data (especially from small, often-conflicting studies) cannot always help to resolve differences. Many midwives, physicians, and childbearing families have been socialized into accepting this divide as normal, even unavoidable. While the Netherlands and other societies appear committed to devising ways to maximize integrated care, provider expertise, and the advantages of each setting (i.e., physiological birth for midwives, medical management for obstetricians, and an explicit focus on collaborative care), powerful interests in the United States see no place for community birth, and homebirth in particular (Grünebaum et al. 2015).

Furthermore, in the United States, interprofessional tensions and a reluctance to acknowledge the benefits of the care provided by the "other" are also exacerbated by different definitions of, and values associated with, the very concept of "safety." Safety constructs are culturally shaped and emerge from popularized versions of childbirth models. As Tilden and colleagues (2016) have argued, obstetrician-attended hospital birth is likely to be perceived as the safest way to give birth when childbirth is regarded as inherently pathological, and the ability to respond immediately to emergent complications are most highly valued. Alternatively, home or birth center may be valued as safest when childbirth is regarded as a physiologic process (ACNM, MANA, NACPM 2012) that can be disrupted or even harmed by routine obstetric intervention.

The choice of birth setting is highly contentious in the United States, and mothers-to-be commonly face extraordinary scrutiny for their decisions, as a visible pregnancy marks women's bodies as public spaces open to social critique, unsolicited advice, and judgment (Cheyney 2008). Despite these pressures, as previously mentioned, community/home births have steadily increased over the last decade (MacDorman and Declerq 2016). The rising demand for community births has encouraged some leaders within national midwifery and obstetric organizations to call for the explicit elimination of debates over place of birth[11] and the question of *whether* women should be "allowed" to choose a community birth (Cheyney et al. 2015b). The fact is that increasing numbers of women *are* choosing homebirths, and this trend is unlikely to reverse any time soon, given the unnecessarily high CS rates in hospitals (32% nationwide, with great variation among regions and individual hospitals) and a growing body of research indicating that community birth is safe for many women (Stapleton et al. 2013; Zeilinski et al. 2015). Instead of debating whether homebirth should be allowed, many are calling for a more thorough examination of the factors that make birth safer across all settings—home, birth center, and hospital (Cheyney et al. 2015b; Tilden et al. 2016).

The Dutch example is instructive here. Integrating midwife-led home and birth center care more formally into the US maternity care system is highly likely to improve outcomes for the growing numbers of families seeking community births. Similarly, increasing the availability of midwife-led undisturbed, physiologic birth in the hospital would decrease unnecessary interventions and associated iatrogenic maternal morbidity (harm or injury to the mother) for the vast majority of low-to-moderate risk US women who are currently choosing hospital birth (and are likely to continue to do so) (Tilden et al. 2016).

Advocates for bridging the community birth–hospital birth gap emphasize findings from recent studies that indicate that the vast majority of healthy women in the United States will give birth safely regardless of where they plan their birth (Cheyney et al. 2015b; Neilson 2015; Snowden et al. 2015; Tilden et al. 2016). Many recognize the American College of Obstetricians and Gynecologists' (ACOG's) 2017 statement, which still formally opposes homebirth, yet offers guidelines for its safe implementation and acknowledges a woman's right to choose it, as a step in the right direction (ACOG

---

[11] See http://www.homebirthsummit.org for the story of how these leaders came together to find ways to address our shared responsibility for making community birth as safe as it can be.

2017). This statement seems to reflect a concerted and growing effort on both sides to reduce polarization over birth setting and provider type. This beneficial cooperation, which Jordan called "mutual accommodation," is urgently needed if the United States is to improve interprofessional collaboration and increase the safety of the maternity care system for all women.

Among birth activists in the United States, the Canadian, Dutch, New Zealand, and British systems in particular have been extolled as potential models for increasing maternal autonomy, choice in birth place and provider type, and relatedly, safety in childbirth—though there are still outspoken US obstetricians who adamantly believe that the solution to maternity care issues lies in the abolition of homebirth and its practitioners (Chervenak et al. 2013)—a highly misguided (and statistically impossible) belief because home and birth center birth together account for only about 1.5% of US births. Common features of more integrated systems include high-quality midwifery education, the formal incorporation of all midwives within the maternity care system, regulatory conditions that allow midwives to practice to their full scope, and clear, evidence-based guidelines for client selection (Tilden et al. 2016; Vedam et al. 2018). Normalization of community birth and expanded integration of midwifery care in the United States would very likely help to decrease political and cultural barriers separating hospital and community providers (Cheyney, Everson, and Burcher 2014; Vedam et al. 2014c).

Indeed, a recent study of midwifery integration in the US showed that states with midwife-friendly laws and regulations tended to have better maternal and infant health outcomes, including lower rates of premature births, cesarean deliveries, and newborn deaths (Vedam et al. 2018). These states also had higher rates of physiologic birth, breastfeeding, and vaginal birth after cesarean (VBAC). The research team created a midwifery integration score based on 50 criteria covering key factors that evaluate: access to midwives, scope of practice, availability of home and birth center birth, and acceptance of midwives by other health care providers in each state. Washington state had the highest integration score at 61 out of a possible 100, and at 17 North Carolina had the lowest. The authors were careful to note that statistical associations between midwifery integration and birth outcomes do not prove a causal effect; other factors, particularly race, are better predictors of outcomes, with African Americans experiencing a disproportionate share of negative birth outcomes. However, about 12% of variation in birth outcomes, and especially in neonatal death across the US, is statistically attributable solely to the roles midwives play in each state's health care system. Findings from this study suggest that *in states where families have greater access to midwifery care that is well integrated into the maternity system, mothers and babies tend to experience improved outcomes.* The converse was also demonstrated; *where integration of midwives is poorer, so are outcomes.* A large body of cross-cultural research has demonstrated similar relationships between midwifery care, systems integration, and improved maternity care outcomes (Homer et al. 2014). This study suggests that the same relationships hold true in the US; integration is a critical starting point.

However, there are added complexities in the United States relative to the Netherlands, owing to its size, political organization, and as the above study illustrates, wide variability by state. Whereas the Dutch have worked at the national level to modify and re-evaluate risk criteria over time, the United States is unique in that selection criteria for place of birth are decided at the individual state level. Thus, the criteria for risk screening range from no standards in some states to very broad regulatory standards in others. An additional barrier to integrated care in the United States may be a lack of national-level, evidence-based guidelines for allocation of cases to planned birth site by maternal or fetal condition (Tilden et al. 2016), as is present in the Netherlands.

In addition, among US midwives, there is significant variability in educational pathways and experience levels. This variability has contributed to a belief held by many physicians: that US midwives attending community births are poorly educated and underprepared for autonomous practice (DiVenere 2012), although there is no evidence for this assertion. Uniformly high standards or midwifery education may be another key to improving the status of home and birth center midwives in the United States, as would more consistent education and licensure by eliminating confusion and stigma around credentialing (Cheyney et al. 2015a). Currently, pregnant people in the United States are faced with determining which of the many licensed and unlicensed midwives are best equipped to meet their needs. For the last several years, US midwifery leaders have worked through US MERA (United States Midwifery Education Regulation and Association)[12] to align all domestic midwifery education and licensure criteria with International Confederation of Midwives (ICM) standards (US MERA Representatives 2014). Alignment among US midwives is widely seen as a critical step in the right direction.

Discussion: Childbirth Paradigms in Dutch and US Contexts

As described in Chapter 1, Davis-Floyd (2001a, 2018a) has defined three paradigms that she argues have heavily influenced childbirth globally, often superseding or overshadowing local notions and ideologies of birth. To recap here, the *technocratic paradigm* is characterized by mind/body separation, the "supervaluation" of technological childbirth management, reliance on a body-as-machine metaphor, and the patient as object (see also Soliday 2012). The *humanistic paradigm*, which arose in reaction to the excesses of technocratic birth, strives to make birth more relational, partnership-oriented, individually responsive, and compassionate. The *holistic paradigm* views the birthing body as an energy system, and both healing and the treatment of birth are thought to involve the mind-body-spirit of the whole person in the contexts of their larger social and physical environments. Davis-Floyd sees the humanistic paradigm

---

[12] See http://www.usmera.org for a description of this work.

as a sort of middle ground between the technocratic and holistic paradigms and, as such, the paradigm with the most potential "to open the technocratic system, from the inside, to the possibility of widespread reform" (2018a:14).

In the Netherlands, the humanistic paradigm in both its forms is preva-lent among all maternity care providers; pregnancy and childbirth are essen-tially seen as natural life events, and, as a consequence, the government and the majority of physicians support midwives as independent care providers. In 1989, the Dutch government explicitly reaffirmed homebirth as the pre-ferred choice for healthy women (Tweede Kamer 1988–1989), indicating a willingness to acknowledge childbirth as a normal part of the reproductive phase of the lifespan for most women in accordance with the tenets of both the humanistic and holistic paradigms. However, the technocratic paradigm is also present in Dutch maternity care among physicians and midwives, and as we have seen above, tensions do exist.

This gap between the technocratic and holistic paradigms in the Nether-lands is often overlooked by researchers and physiologic birth advocates in the United States, as there is a long-standing tendency among birth activists to idealize the Dutch system as fully holistic due to its historical high preva-lence of homebirths. Indeed, the divide between paradigms *is* somewhat bridged in the Dutch context by the facts that midwives are acknowledged as autonomous professionals and as the experts in physiologic birth, and that Dutch doctors do tend to see pregnancy and births as physiologic phenom-ena. Physicians in the Netherlands generally acknowledge that unnecessary medical interventions can cause more harm than good, rather than viewing pregnancies as pathologies waiting to happen, as many US obstetricians do (hence the low CS rate of 16% in the Netherlands as compared to 32% in the US). Among Dutch practitioners, mutual respect enables meaningful collabo-ration between midwives and physicians in ways that are missing in less inte-grated systems like those of the US, Brazil, Tanzania, Greece, and Mexico, as described in the other chapters in this volume.

Even so, paradigmatic debates are never far away in the Netherlands, and advocates of all three paradigms make themselves heard on occasion. Controver-sies are most apparent when research is published with less than ideal perinatal outcomes, or when the media sensationalizes a problematic birth. Whenever a poor outcome makes the news in the Netherlands, the entire maternity care sys-tem tends to be questioned, and particularly homebirth and an assumed holistic approach. Representatives of the technocratic paradigm argue that every birth is risky and should take place in a hospital (a minority also argues for physician oversight of all births), while representatives of the humanistic and holistic para-digms emphasize that pregnancy and birth are usually physiologic processes that should not be interfered with unless there is a clear medical indication.

As we reflect on such debates in both the Netherlands and the US from the point of view of birth paradigms, we are even more struck by the degree to which perceptions of what constitutes physiology versus pathology are socially and culturally constructed. Both physiology and pathology have wide spectrums of presentation; both are often highly individualized and difficult to fit into guidelines, definitions, and protocols. Yet that is precisely what practice guidelines and standards of care attempt to do: maternal and newborn care is reduced to quantifiable, standardized, measurable and static concepts that can exclude individual variations that under specific circumstances are actually perfectly healthy and normal. As Davis-Floyd (2018c, g) has argued, midwives are more likely to expand protocols to "normalize uniqueness," while obstetricians are more likely to narrow those same protocols to "standardize pathology." Protocols and guidelines (as opposed to individual needs) are not only the basis for cooperation among professional groups, but also influential shapers of the care women receive.

Furthermore, definitions of physiological versus pathological have become self-reinforcing over time. For example, as so few women give birth past 42 weeks in the Netherlands and past 41 weeks in the United States (due to protocols that require induction at these times), midwives, doctors, and woman have less and less exposure to gestations that exceed 41 or 42 weeks, which reinforces the narrow notion that longer gestations are always pathological, despite robust evidence to the contrary (Rydahl, Eriksen, and Juhl 2018). Furthermore, Dutch research shows that women without a homebirth example in their vicinity (sister, friend, neighbor, etc.) no longer perceive homebirth as normal, which is similarly self-reinforcing (Sluijs et al. 2015). Going forward, we are essentially stuck with the definitions of physiological and pathological that our protocols have allowed us to see, and not what is actually physiological or pathological from the standpoint of our evolved biology. This is one reason why anthropologists repeatedly assert that "normal is simply what you are used to."

We (midwives, anthropologists, clients, and other physiologic birth advocates) all find it quite concerning that we are losing our understanding of physiologic pregnancy and birth (even in the Netherlands). We are all committed to teaching, studying, and transmitting the knowledge about what constitutes normal, healthy physiology (see Oladapo et al. 2018). We also want to see guidelines expanded to include and support a wider range of normal. Some labors can safely take days, some cannot; some labors need some intervention, many others do not; *care must be individualized, rather than standardized, to account for the characteristics of particular mother-baby/ies units.* This understanding drives us to look past numbers and protocols to the individual human beings in front of us. It also reinforces our commitment to cross-cultural research, for in seeing the many ways "normal" is socially constituted, perhaps we can re-examine our own constructs of physiology and pathology. Below Bahareh recounts the story of a birth that taught her the importance of seeing the individual, of normalizing uniqueness, and of recognizing just how blurry the lines between "normal" and "not normal" can be in practice.

Bahareh's Story.   On this particular night I (Bahareh) was not on duty but was on-call to provide backup for another practice. This is normal in the Netherlands—a way to guarantee midwifery care. At around 3 A.M., I received a call from my on-duty colleague telling me that two women were in labor at the same time. She was with one of them at home and could not leave. She had just come there from visiting the other woman, a first-time mother who was 38 weeks pregnant (whom we will call Mrs. Anderson), who was laboring in the hospital. During a vaginal examination, my colleague had felt 4 centimeters dilation and a hand; the baby's arm was the presenting part (the part coming first into the birth canal). This presented a challenge. My colleague explained that she had tried to refer Ms. Anderson to the obstetrician present, but he and his backup were stuck in the operating room (OR). Since the baby was doing fine for the time being, Mrs. Anderson would have to wait. My colleague had agreed that she would stay with Mrs. Anderson until the obstetricians were out of the OR, but since she now realized she had to stay with the woman laboring at home, she asked me to care for Mrs. Anderson.

When I arrived, the obstetricians were still in the OR, managing a difficult case of postpartum hemorrhage. Mrs. Anderson was lying in bed breathing through regular and strong contractions. She was attached to the electronic fetal monitor (EFM). The tracings on the computer screen showed the baby was in good condition. I asked her how she was doing. She said the pain was bearable. Then, with fear in her voice, she asked me whether she was going to have to have a cesarean section. She explained to me that she was an emergency room doctor, and she knew all about cesarean sections and that it was the last thing she wanted. I felt sad for her, because it was indeed the way she was headed.

We talked for a bit, then she suddenly said she had to push. Push? The arm was presenting! She could not push! The baby would never fit! I did a vaginal exam to confirm full dilation and to feel the presenting part. I was curious, since I had never experienced the arm as the presenting part before. During the exam, I felt full dilation and a hand sticking out, halfway engaged in the cervix. The mother was pushing reflexively; there was no stopping that. Then she again started pleading with me to help her avoid a cesarean. This is when I made my decision to help her achieve a vaginal birth. What other options did we have? Her body was pushing anyway, and she wanted to try. The baby was doing fine, and the obstetricians were unavailable.

I started thinking: What would be the most favorable conditions that would enhance the chances of vaginal birth? A vertical birth position would widen the pelvic diameters and gravity would help, so I suggested a birthing stool, and in seconds she was sitting on the stool and continuing to push as if her life depended on it. I kept my eye on the EFM, and the baby kept doing fine. With every push, the arm came out further. First, I only saw fingertips, then whole fingers, then the whole hand and finally the arm. To be honest, it looked very strange: a tiny blue arm hanging out of a vagina, especially because the hand was moving: the baby's fingers would grab the labia during pauses between contractions and let go of the labia during pushing. I mentioned this to Mrs. Anderson and she asked me if she could see it. I got a mirror and she watched, laughing and smiling the whole time. I still don't know how she did it, but 50 minutes later, her baby was born. Just like that, vaginally, on the birthing chair. You might think I should have done some sort of hand maneuvers, but I didn't do anything—that was the amazing part. Once the arm and shoulders were out, the head followed smoothly. A beautiful pink baby girl, who weighed 2900 grams! Her arm was a deep blue, but all reflexes were normal and otherwise she was doing fine. This is when I learned that "risk" is both a relative and an individualized concept. Looking back, this birth would have been considered pathological by many (if not most) of my colleagues; however it was never pathological for Mrs. Anderson. Luckily, because of the circumstances, we all got the chance to experience a birth that, for me, reinforced my understanding of the wide range of normal physiology, as well as my positionality as a humanistic care provider.

Whereas we might then see the Dutch as having a *predominantly humanistic system* with relatively smooth, though not perfect, integration between holistic and technocratic practitioners, the United States may be more aptly characterized as a *largely technocratic system* heavily focused on the use of machines such as ultrasound and the electronic fetal monitor, with a humanistic gloss that varies regionally in the form, for example, of more hotel- or home-like labor and delivery rooms and policies that allow some number of family members and friends and perhaps a doula to participate in the birth. The US system is also characterized by active marginalization, even prosecution in some cases, of holistic providers, including holistic obstetricians. As in the Netherlands, the three paradigms do not track perfectly with provider type, though a higher percentage of obstetricians adhere to the technocratic paradigm than do midwives and vice-versa for the holistic paradigm.

In the United States, "choice" regarding provider type and place of birth for any one family is structured by inequalities in access to birthing options, cost, regulatory status, and the medical complexity of individual pregnancies. This structuring means that women with healthy pregnancies often have a hospital birth with an obstetrician in attendance, not because they adhere to a technocratic view of childbirth nor because they have a complication that requires specialized care, but simply because there are no or too few home or birth center midwives in their communities.

In addition, Missy has argued elsewhere (Cheyney 2011) that components of all three paradigms can be found within the midwifery model of care (Davis-Floyd 2018h), which is most commonly (and erroneously) equated with the holistic model of care in the United States. Interviews and participant-observation with US midwives suggest that the midwifery model of care is best understood as a continuum of diverse views and approaches to childbirth that overlap in key ways with all three of the paradigms explicated by Davis-Floyd. The continuum of paradigms operationalized during the provision of midwifery-model care is multidimensional, dynamic, and flexible, and varies according to several important factors, including the practitioner's experience level, the particular pregnancy characteristics and individual circumstances of particular clients/patients, barriers to collaborative practice, physician backup, state-level regulatory status, and even a midwife's own birth experiences. That is, midwives tailor their approach to the needs of individual clients and in response to systems-level barriers and supports.

Thus, a US midwife who identifies as holistic in approach may employ clinical practices and patterns of thought that are more characteristic of the technocratic paradigm, for example by recommending tests and focusing on risk assessment during prenatal visits for a client with gestational diabetes or a history of cesarean section. Certainly, the midwife's interactions with a collaborating physician may be marked by discussions of anticipated pathology and plans for the medical management of labor and birth in specific pregnancies. Throughout the provision of care, the midwife may continue to hold to the tenets of the holistic model of care in theory, but will borrow, out of perceived necessity, from technomedicine to help ensure a healthy mother and baby who have been treated throughout the process of care in accordance with the values of the humanistic paradigm. We ourselves have all observed many instances in which paradigms begin to blend into one another (for example, during an intrapartum transfer from a planned homebirth to the hospital), as all involved work together to create a dynamic amalgam of multiple approaches, with the goal of ensuring the best possible birth experience and outcome for a shared client/patient. The boundaries of paradigmatic distinction can feel very blurry during these encounters in both the United States and in the Netherlands, as practitioners work using *informed relativism* (Davis-Floyd 2018f), applying whatever tools or knowledge systems are most effective in a given circumstance. Application of theoretical birthing models to specific ethnographic contexts such as the Netherlands and United States thus reveals the many ways paradigms may defy simplistic classification, functioning in much more complex ways that move beyond healthy mothers utilizing holistic midwives and higher risk, medically complicated pregnancies being managed by technocratic obstetricians.

Those US and Dutch providers who do find ways to speak and collaborate across paradigmatic divides often find more theoretical commonality than anticipated. It is our sense that any practice-level differences that exist between providers often emerge more from the needs of unique patient or client bases and the institutional constraints associated with location of practice, than from any unbending ideological commitment to a particular paradigm. In this way the humanistic paradigm, insofar as it allows a "coming together" or "mandorla" (the almond shape created where two circles overlap) space for self-identified technocratic or holistic providers, does seem to function in our respective contexts as a critical middle ground that facilitates interprofessional communication and collaboration. That the humanistic approach holds the power to open the technocratic system to the possibility of widespread reform (Davis-Floyd 2018a:114) helps to explain why the Dutch system has never been nearly as fragmented as the US system; its providers have been able to unify around a (relatively) common humanistic value system. It may also help to explain much of the movement we have seen in the last decade in the United

States toward more collaborative professional relationships in some communities, as well as the rising rate of midwife-attended births more generally.

Conclusion: History, the Biosocial Nature of Birth, and Working across Paradigms

In this chapter, we examined conceptualizations of childbirth in the Netherlands and the United States, with the aim of comparing the ways in which historically constituted ideologies shape childbirth as performed and perceived in two distinct cultural settings. We began with a comparison of primary provider types, training systems, and the opportunities for maternal choice in each setting; these comparisons revealed significant differences in the approaches, birth territories, practitioner types, and hierarchies of power considered acceptable in each context. Next, we situated our respective systems historically, drawing attention to the ways in which the history of midwifery in the Netherlands is unique, not just in relation with the United States, but also in relation with other European nations. In both the Dutch and US contexts, historical antecedents powerfully shape how birth is viewed today—from the Netherlands' paradigm of childbirth as in most cases a healthy process best supported by midwives, to the US model of childbirth as a medical event best managed by surgical specialists within a hospital setting.

Next, in keeping with Jordan's call to heed the biosocial nature of childbirth, we provided an overview of measurable health outcomes in each context and also discussed the contested nature of the research that informs each country's safety debates. We also described the comparative barriers to integrated care experienced by the mothers and babies who must navigate such distinct maternity care systems. Finally, using Davis-Floyd's theoretical constructs—the technocratic, humanistic and holistic models of birth—we reflected on ways these models are implemented in the US and in the Netherlands. Application of theoretical birthing models to these specific ethnographic contexts reveals their complex and fluid nature, while highlighting the value of the humanistic paradigm (at least as it is performed in the Netherlands and in the US) as an essential middle ground that can facilitate interprofessional communication and collaboration across paradigmatic differences. It is our hope that this work may contribute to making childbirth emotionally meaningful and medically safe for all people (Jordan 1993).

Postscript

As we neared final edits on this chapter, we reflected on what we had learned through our collaboration. Each of us entered this process acutely aware of the strengths and weaknesses of our own systems. Yet, after reading each other's sections, we began to feel our perspectives shift in response to our growing cross-cultural knowledge. Bahareh and Therese found affirmation of a long-held belief that indeed, the Dutch still have one of the best maternity care systems in the world. As most maternity care providers in the Netherlands believe, we have the best of both worlds: the intimacy and privacy of community care and homebirth, with specialist help available when needed. This system is possible because, in general, obstetricians regard midwives as complementary, not subservient, and tend to see pregnancy and childbirth as normal physiologic phenomena. Therese and Bahareh reflect: Of course, we can do better—everyone can always do better. However, in striving for "better," it has been helpful to be reminded of all that is good in the Dutch system, especially in comparison with the United States.

For Missy, Saras, and Robbie, the process was more disheartening. From us there is a sense of sadness and frustration with how far there is yet to go. When will all pregnant people in the United States have access to a model of care aligned with their desires and individual pregnancy characteristics? When will high-quality and respectful maternity care be treated as a basic human right, rather than as a privilege for those who can pay for it? When will women of color and non-binary parents be provided with compassionate, culturally congruent, and easily accessed care that can reduce or even eradicate rampant disparities in mortality and prematurity rates? And when will new families be adequately supported as they transition into parenthood? Yet, there is also reason to feel proud and hopeful as we look at what has been accomplished by US midwives in the last several decades, despite very powerful opposition. Midwifery care is on the rise, and the coordinated efforts of midwifery researchers and consumer activists have dramatically improved hospital practice in many regions.

It is our hope that midwives' compassionate and evidence-based care will become increasingly accessible to all women globally during the childbearing year, as well as across the lifespan, and that the expertise of obstetricians will be increasingly focused only on those who truly need their care. In this way, we envision a world where all pregnant families and babies have what they need to survive, thrive, and transform (World Health Organization 2016).

QUESTIONS FOR THOUGHT AND DISCUSSION

1. How are the birthing cultures in the Netherlands and the United States products of their distinct histories? What were some of the pivotal historical events that have contributed to the unique situations and statuses for midwives in the United States and in the Netherlands?

2. Why do you think the United States still has such a low reliance on midwives as primary care providers (in both community and hospital settings)? Do you see a way forward? How might reproductive anthropologists play a role in speaking across the home-hospital divide?

3. What do you think of the changing perceptions of risk and their effects on where Dutch women choose to give birth as described by the authors? Can research be used to help inform these debates? If so, how? If not, why not?

4. The authors describe a particularly problematic paradox where placing the client at the center of care and allowing her wishes and needs to guide the care delivered may sometimes put midwives at odds with the standards they are expected to follow in their field. In this way, maternal autonomy and professional responsibility may sometimes collide. How do you think these types of situations should be handled?

5. What has a comparison of these two systems allowed you to see that you had not thought about before? Do you agree with Jordan's premise—that cross-cultural comparisons provide information we can use to construct a deeper understanding of the multiplicity of ways the processes of childbirth may be historically, socially and physiologically shaped? What can you now see that was perhaps not available from the inside point of view of your system alone?

6. Throughout this book the terms "low-risk," "normal," "physiologic or physiological," and "healthy" are used by various authors to try to describe uncomplicated pregnancies and births that do not require medical intervention to proceed safely. We also know that language matters because it can powerfully influence the way we think about things. How might each of these terms shape the ways researchers, consumers of maternity care, and clinicians think about birth? Are there possible, unintended negative consequences of their use that you can see? Which term or terms do you prefer and why?

RECOMMENDED VIDEOS AND FILMS

Why Not Home? The Surprising Birth Choices of Doctors and Nurses. Produced and directed by Jessica Moore, 2016. This film focuses on hospital birth providers who choose homebirth for their own births. See http://www.whynothome.com/

Pregnant in America. Produced by Steve Buonaugurio, 2008. This film tells the true story of Steve and Mandy Buonaugurio, an expectant couple, who decide to have their first child outside the modern US medical system. See http://www.imdb.com/title/tt1231290.

The Business of Being Born. Produced by Ricki Lake and Abby Epstein, 2008. This film follows several New York City couples who decide to give birth on their own terms. Through their stories, we see birth as a miracle and rite of passage, but also as big business. Ultimately, this film questions whether most births should be viewed as natural life processes, or whether every delivery ought to be treated as a potential medical emergency. See http://www.thebusinessofbeingborn.com/

Under Her Own Steam: A Dutch Home Birth. Produced by Saskia van Rees, Astrid Limburg, Beatrijs Smulders, 1988. This film shows each stage of the birth of child at home in the Netherlands. See https://birthinternational.com/product/under-her-own-steam-dvd/

Hoe bevalt Nederland. NPO 2. 2017. https://www.vpro.nl/programmas/dit-zijn-wij/afl5-hoe-bevalt-nederland.htmll

Babyboom. NRCV. 2013. https://www.npo.nl/Babyboom/POMS_S_NCRV_093280

Bevallingsverhalen. RTL8. 2011. https://www.uitzendinggemist.net/programmas/3439-Bevallingsverhalen.html

Ik word moeder. RTLXL. 2013. https://www.rtl.nl/gemist/ik-word-moeder/

7

Reflective Ethnographic Vignettes
Confronting Yourself in the Field

Ethnography is a complex process that often forces the anthropologist to confront the deepest aspects of herself via a sometimes extensive series of moral and ethical issues she may confront. When we see something being done that we think is wrong, should we name it and try to change it? Doing so might get us kicked out of the hospitals and other sites we have worked so hard to enter and become accepted in. As some of our stories illustrate, sometimes we can find subtle, more covert ways to advocate and help. At other times we can do absolutely nothing; confronting our own powerlessness is both humbling and frustrating.

Missy and Robbie decided to include this chapter in this volume to give students a feel for what it is like to conduct fieldwork—the sad, the challenging, the devastating, alongside the funny and exhilarating parts. We asked each chapter author to provide one or two stories, and chose two of Gitti's from *Birth in Four Cultures* to include. The stories here are both reflections on how some of the authors dealt with the events recounted and self-reflexive analyses of the meanings of their actions. They reveal the dilemmas anthropologists get into while conducting fieldwork and how they cope with them, for better or worse, and hopefully offer valuable lessons in cross-cultural contact as well. Several of these stories also reveal the blurriness of the lines between participation and observation—the two principle tenets of anthropological, ethnographic fieldwork, and the occasional total merging of the participant and observer roles, of the professional and the personal, of the analytic mind, the emotive heart, and corporeal body. These stories are for your reading enjoyment and for a glimpse into the joys and complexities of ethnographic work. May they inspire you as you hone your own ethnographic skills and confront the paradoxes and dilemmas you will inevitably face.

Rules and Rumors: A Stillbirth in a Village in Central Java

Etsuko Matsuoka

One early morning in 1995 in Central Java, Indonesia, in a village near Mt. Merapi where I was conducting fieldwork and living in the home of *bidan* (midwife) Warsini's house, I was awakened by the voice of a husband whose wife was having a problematic birth. I knew this because village people wouldn't call a *bidan* unless birth went wrong. They usually preferred to call *dukuns* (community or traditional midwives/"TBAs") whom the villagers experienced as friendlier and more responsive than *bidan* Warsini.

Warsini told the husband to wait until she had changed into her uniform—there was a rule that she had to wear it when acting in her professional capacity. Heading out on motorbikes, we stopped along the way to pick up another midwife—a *bidan di desa* (a village midwife whose education is one year shorter than a regular *bidan*), because according to the rules, the husband was supposed to call the *bidan di desa* in his area first before coming to Warsini. So now we had delayed our arrival by following two rules—Warsini's uniform change, and the rule to bring the other *bidan*.

When we entered the small house, a young woman lay on the elevated floor, her bottom half covered by a cloth. Right beside her an old *dukun* named Kismo sat quietly. When Warsini took away the cloth, we could see that the umbilical cord hung loose from the woman's vagina (a condition called cord prolapse), yet the baby was still inside. Knowing that the only solution now was to get the baby out as quickly as possible, the two *bidans* hastily sat on both sides of the woman and insisted that she push with all her might. All the while Warsini was scolding the woman for not calling her sooner and saying that the next time round, she should call a *bidan* directly, not a (lower-ranking) *dukun*.

Finally, the baby came out in complete silence and immobility. The two *bidans* ordered the neighbors present to bring buckets of hot and cold water, into which they alternately placed the baby. They also held the baby upside down, patting and hitting her repeatedly in the hope of bringing her to life. When these efforts were unsuccessful, Warsini put the baby on the floor and massaged her heart with her thumb—again to no avail. Warsini took the baby to another room and gave her more massages, finally stopping while muttering "too late," then wrapping the baby in white cloth. Kismo came to sit beside the baby and murmured, as if to disclaim responsibility for this death, "The previous baby I delivered was healthy with no problems." The *bidans* asked neighbors to quickly change the mother's clothes or she would catch a cold, to put a pillow under her feet to elevate them, and to give her a warm coffee. Then they packed up their equipment and left. Later I heard the baby was buried by noon that day.

A few days later I went to *dukun* Kismo to ask why she called the *bidan* in the first place. When was she aware of an emerging abnormality? Did she think she had called the *bidan* early enough so the baby could be saved? Kismo responded that she was called to this woman's birth around 11 P.M. that night. When she saw that the umbilical cord was about to come out, which she knew was a sign of danger, she told the woman's husband to call *bidan* Warsini, because Kismo knew she couldn't handle such a birth, due to "lack of sufficient equipment" (a rationale traditional midwives in the area sometimes use when they feel they cannot deal with a given situation—and also a critique of the government's refusal to give them such equipment). She remembered it to be between 4 and 5 A.M. The husband, who didn't have a motorbike, had to go find one he could borrow and finally reached *bidan* Warsini around 5:30 A.M. "It was God's will that the baby died," Kismo said quietly.

If not with God, where do we place responsibility for this death in this remote village? *Dukuns* are often blamed for calling *bidans* too late. But it seems that there was no notion of urgency in anyone's mind (except the husband's and my own). Conforming to the rules she had been taught, *bidan* Warsini took time to change into a uniform and to pick up the other *bidan*. A prolapsed cord is compressed, thereby cutting off the baby's blood and oxygen supply, which can result in its death unless the baby is gotten out very quickly, either by the mother pushing hard, as the *bidans* asked her to do, or by the midwife putting the mother on her hands and knees (which takes the pressure off the cord) while the practitioner kneels behind her and pushes up on the baby's head so that the cord is not compressed between the head and the mother's pelvis. Keeping her hand inside the mother's vagina, the practitioner must hold up the baby's head until the baby is delivered by cesarean—a dramatic scenario to say the least, the success of which depends on how quickly the cesarean is performed. Yet, a cesarean was not an option in this case—there was no way to get to a hospital, as that would have required both more time and a car, neither of which they had. The only thing the midwives could have done was what they did do—get the mother to push with all her might—yet they arrived too late for this effort to succeed. Were "the rules" to blame?

In safe motherhood and development discourse, one often hears about the "three delays" that can lead to maternal or fetal mortality: (1) delay in making the decision to transport; (2) delay in obtaining transport; (3) delay in receiving appropriate care once at the facility. In this case, delay #3 is irrelevant as there was no way to get the mother there in time. Delay #2 is relevant in that it took the husband time to find a motorcycle to borrow to go ask for help—he needed local assistance, not transport for his wife. Delay #1 is also relevant—did *dukun* Kismo wait too long to ask for help? Did the delays created by the uniform change and picking up the other *bidan* play a role in the stillbirth? Most likely not, as the baby would have needed to be delivered within a few minutes of discovering the cord prolapse, and we do not know if the mother was fully dilated at that point. Death is common with prolapsed cords even when an operating room is just down the hall. It seems impossible to lay blame at any-one's feet, but one wonders—could things have turned out differently?

I do not know when Kismo discovered the prolapse. In a village birth, a laboring woman's bottom part is always covered; the *dukun* only uncovers it to take a look every now and then. Also, it was very dark inside the room. (I was scolded once when I turned on an electric light I had brought from Japan to help the *dukun* see well. She said a baby would be too embarrassed under the light.) So, it could be that Kismo sent for the *bidan* immediately after she realized the abnormality, but by then the cord could have been out for some time. Warsini later said that the *dukun* must have had the woman start push-ing too early, which might have caused the prolapse—an example of the gen-eral lack of respect that *bidans* have for the village *dukuns,* as well as a misunderstanding of the causality in cord prolapse.

The rules taught to *dukun* Kismo said that she had no authority to order a hospital transfer—only the professional *bidan* could do that. Recognizing the danger, *dukun* Kismo had followed this rule by asking the husband to send for the *bidan*, her superior in matters of birth attendance and the only resource she had. Because they had no telephones, the simple act of summoning the *bidan* took a great deal of time, leaving no time for a transfer that would have been impossible anyway. Everyone and no one was responsible, and a baby died.

Conversations in the Field

Lydia Dixon

It turns out that when people find out that you are a researcher studying childbirth in their community, their eyes often light up—they want to talk about their own birth experiences. During my fieldwork in Mexico, I was continuously surprised by people's openness and eagerness to share with me their opinions on how things went for them or their loved ones. Often these conversations did not take place within the formal confines of my field sites; indeed, it was during informal conversations with people around town—with taxi drivers, fruit vendors, hair stylists—that I would learn some of the most interesting details. These conversations would send me back to the midwifery schools or clinics where I was conducting observations to ask follow-up ques-tions of my interlocutors, to try to make sense of what I had learned.

Sometimes the stories people would tell me were straightforward in their critique of the hospital system. In 2012, I was getting my hair cut in San Miguel de Allende, which had a large, new general hospital and a smaller midwifery clinic and school called CASA (*Centro para los Adolescentes de San Miguel de Allende*). The stylist asked what I was doing in town and when I told her about my research, she began to tell me about her hospital birth. As soon as the baby was born, the doctor leaned over her and asked if she wanted him to insert an IUD (intrauterine device). She said no, that she might want to have more children in the coming years, but he pressed her and patronized

Lydia Dixon taking notes in the field at Mujeres Aliadas (Allied Women) midwifery school in Pátzcuaro, Michoacán, Mexico. Photo by Alison Bastien

her, finally wearing her down by telling her that she could "always get it taken out later." In the weeks that followed, she began to have horrible pelvic pain and a high fever. She went to see another doctor, who told her that the IUD had become embedded in the wall of her uterus. The IUD was removed and the female doctor urged the stylist to lodge a formal complaint. She told me that she still hadn't filed it, though; life had moved on and she was busy, but she would not forgive the doctor who coerced her into getting the IUD. After hearing this story, I began to ask more questions about the use of IUDs in the immediate postpartum period and learned that such coercion is routine in public hospitals.

Perhaps the most interesting stories people told me were those where people's opinions about their experiences differed significantly from my own interpretation of what happened to them. While chatting with a manicurist who was 38 weeks pregnant, she told me she was looking forward to having the baby at the new general hospital. Because I had by that point heard many critiques of that hospital, I was interested in her enthusiasm for it. What struck me about her response was how much her reasons sounded to me like reasons *not* to give birth in the general hospital. But, for her, they were positive elements. She told me, "Husbands cannot go in with you there, but that doesn't bother me. My friend told me that you can't bring someone with you because all the laboring women are in a big room together, naked from the waist down with their legs open—so I wouldn't want someone else's husband seeing me!" To me, this manner of laboring sounded inhumane and scary. But the manicurist went on to say that birthing alongside other women would be helpful for her—"because it will be like a competition" to get her baby out first. Again, the idea of labor being set up as a competition sounded inhumane to my ears, even as it clearly made sense to her.

"Is this your first pregnancy?" I asked her. "No, I have a four-year-old," she told me. "His labor was easy, not like some of those long labors you hear about." But when she went on to tell me about that birth, I was again confused by how her own feelings about her experience differed so drastically from my own. She said that in that pregnancy she had taken a lot of vitamin pills, and that the doctor told her the baby's head had grown too big as a result ("which is why," she told me as an aside, "I am not taking any prenatal vitamins this time around!"). The labor was quick, but when the head got stuck the doctor did an episiotomy. When this still didn't work, he "just about sat on top of my tummy to make the baby come out!" She laughed at the memory of this, but to me it was anything but funny.

Hearing such stories from people in the communities where I conducted fieldwork enriched my research by getting me to consider new angles and ask new questions. When I opened up to strangers about what I was doing there, they opened up to me and shared intimate details and personal reflections that ultimately helped me become a more compassionate and open-minded researcher.

Random Samples, Wrong Turns, and Goats

Adrienne Strong

For two months in 2015, I traveled to several different villages throughout the region in which I was working in southwestern Tanzania to talk with community members about the challenges they were facing related to maternal and reproductive health, and also more generally. I hoped that casting the net wide would produce further insight into the ways in which maternal health is connected to gender relations, community organization, labor and resources, as well as the more obvious access (or lack thereof) to health care services and providers. On previous village trips, I had always taken the local bus or hitched a ride with government officials or NGO employees going to the same places. However, in 2015, I bought a car to facilitate my village visits and to give me more freedom to choose communities to visit and to decide how long I stayed. Many of my Tanzanian friends urged me to consider getting a driver, someone who knew where all these villages were. I resisted, insisting on principle that I could drive myself. I got a small SUV with all-wheel drive and a relatively good ground clearance, frequently checked for flat tires, and hoped for the best on the region's bad roads, made worse every year by a long rainy season. I chose the villages to visit through a random sample taken from all the villages in each district that were home to a government health facility. This meant that I knew virtually nothing about where they were other than what the districts' hand-drawn maps roughly indicated.

For my very first trip, I selected a village that appeared nearby on the map. Though I had a smartphone, there were several barriers to using Google Maps. Chief among these was a deathly slow data connection (or none at all in many areas) and the fact that many villages were literally not on the map. Convinced I knew where the village was, and that I had seen the sign for it on the main asphalt road, I boldly set off, with my research assistant, in that direction, not bothering to ask directions until I had been driving long enough to begin questioning my (rather terrible) sense of direction. The first man I asked appeared to know which village we were talking about and vaguely motioned in a direction, indicating we should leave the asphalt road and cut across the green hills to our left. We would see the village "soon"; it "wasn't very far." I turned off the main road and we started bumping along in the dirt.

Eventually, a man on the road generously offered to show us the way because he was headed in that same direction. He added that he would need to take his goat, was that OK? Lacking other options for filling the position of navigator, I shrugged my shoulders and got out of the car to open the trunk for the goat and the man's other belongings. While mostly quiet, the goat would let out a bleat of protest every time we went over a particularly large bump in the road. Well before we had reached Songambele village, our destination, the man and his goat were replaced by four women headed to the antenatal clinic in yet another community further on. Eventually, after at least four hours of similar experiences, and asking all available bystanders for directions at any and every intersection, we pulled into Songambele. The village leaders gave us a warm reception, and we had many interesting conversations with the health care workers, the village chairman, and the village dispensary committee that afternoon. When it was time to return to the main town where my research assistant and I lived, one of the community members offered to give us directions if we could give him and another person a lift into that town. I gratefully agreed, not fancying another four hours wandering in the hills. How long did it take to get to town by the normal route? Approximately 30 minutes! That was the last time I ever embarked on a village visit without first asking for directions.

On Discovering Inner Strength

Mounia El Kotni

I often get severely carsick, an especially unpleasant situation on the steeply curved roads in the Highlands of Chiapas where I conducted much of my fieldwork. One day, I accompanied one of the midwives I conducted research with in San Cristóbal to a neighboring village to attend a homebirth. It was a one-hour drive, and the friendly driver knew I often got severely carsick, so he drove slowly. Labor started during the night, and on the next afternoon, the woman grew tired and asked to be transferred to the hospital. Suddenly I found myself in the back of an ambulance, on the winding and bumpy road to San Cristóbal, with a woman in labor, her husband, the midwife, and two other passengers also needing emergency care. Having, with great trepidation, jumped in last, I had to sit at the end of the bench closest to the door—the worst possible place for the carsick-prone like me! Because I was closest to the woman's feet (she was lying on her back with her legs bent up), the paramedic, who was in the front seat next to the driver, told me, "Every time she has a contraction, you tell her *not* to push, and check if anything is coming out." So, with every contraction, I had to bend over and check, while managing not to fall and not to get sick. All of us eventually made it safely to San Cristóbal, and the baby was born that night. *Ni modo!*[1] Participant-observation sometimes entails going above and beyond one's limits, and discovering new strengths.

The Closest I Ever Came to Catching a Baby

Robbie Davis-Floyd

One pleasantly sunny-yet-cool afternoon in 2009 found me and my friends Debra Pascali Bonaro (doula, doula trainer, and producer of *Orgasmic Birth*), Ricardo Jones, a holistic Brazilian obstetrician, and a student intern, Tricia Hadley, at the birth center of renowned Mexican *partera tradicional* Angelina Martinez Miranda, who has traveled to many countries to share her extensive midwifery expertise and continues to practice midwifery and teach in a midwifery school in Mexico. At that time, "Lina" lived in the small city of Temizco, about 45 minutes south of Cuernavaca, where she had managed a very full practice for over 20 years after taking over from her mother and grandmother, both midwives as well.

Angelina's excellent reputation was so widespread and her outcomes so good that she and her assistant, who was also her niece, were attending about 24 births a month when Debra, Ric, Tricia, and I arrived at Angelina's home. Her small birth center, located on the other side of the grass lawn from her home, had a "waiting room" in the form of a lovely outdoor patio filled with white plastic chairs with comfortable backs and armrests; it was full of women, some with small children by their sides. Two of the women were in labor, yet gave little sign of it; the rest were there for pre- and postnatal check-ups. It was a great place to film births, which Debra intended to do, as they were nearly always happening.

Soon Angelina appeared at the door to escort out a mother, father, and newborn, and to call in the two women in labor—Lorena and Liliana. Since Liliana was making the most fuss, we assumed her birth would come first. So Debra and Ric went with Liliana to one of Angelina's two birthing rooms. Lorena, whom Angelina had informed me (without doing a cervical check) was nearly at 10 cm, seemed almost preternaturally calm; later she informed me that she had indeed been in pain but did not wish to upset her four-year-

---

[1] *Ni modo,* an extremely common Mexican expression, can translate as "oh well," or "whatever!" implying that if we cannot do anything to change some aspects of our lives, then we should accept these as they are.

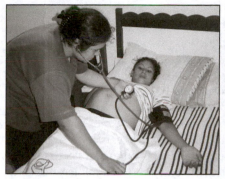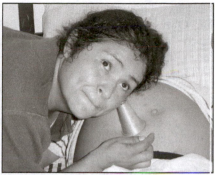

Angelina checking blood pressure—an allopathic skill she learned from her doctor-trained midwife mother [left], and using the Pinard [right] to monitor heart tones, as her traditionally trained grandmother and midwives everywhere have done for centuries. Photos by Robbie Davis-Floyd

old daughter, who had accompanied her in the waiting area but stayed outside, watched over by the other mothers, during the birth.

Not wanting to leave Lorena alone in labor, I stayed with her in the other room; she was still very calm. We danced together for a while to the samba music Angelina had on the CD player, until Lorena said she wanted to lie down. She slept between contractions, which had slowed to about 10 minutes apart—I recognized this slowdown as a normal end-of-labor labor plateau, where contractions can sometimes slow or stop for a while when birth is imminent to allow the uterus to readjust and reshape itself in preparation for pushing out the now-descended baby.

Each time a contraction came, Lorena would open her eyes, stare into mine, and grip my hand tightly. So, when Angelina's assistant/niece came into the room to suggest that I get Lorena up and moving again, I responded without thinking that she was in (what birth anthropologist Sheila Kitzinger called) "The Rest and Be Thankful" phase, and so we should just let her rest and be thankful. The assistant nodded and left. Lorena and I stayed in that space of peaceful rest (while I pondered upon the fact that I had just effectively and instinctively practiced midwifery without training or a license) for about half an hour, until suddenly Lorena opened her eyes wide in surprise at the strength of the contraction now gripping her body.

At that point, Angelina came to check Lorena and told me to get her up and dancing again, then left to go back to Liliana, who was by now shrieking. Lorena, still silent, wrapped her arms around me in a full-body hug, and I held her tight as we swayed to the rhythm of the samba music for around 10 minutes or so. Then for the very first time she started to say, "*Ya no puedo--ya no aguanto*" ("I can't do this—I can't stand it anymore"—something unmedicated laboring women often say when the end is very near). Her body gave a volcanic shudder. Although I could not see her vagina because of the gown she was wearing, I knew for certain that the baby's head was out—I could just *feel* it—and OMG, what am I supposed to do? At any second the baby could fall out on the hard tile floor. Yet her whole weight was on me—she would not loosen her hold—so if I knelt to catch the baby, she was clearly going to fall too.

Intuiting the situation, at that very second, Angelina, who by popular report has "eyes in the back of her head," sent Ric running into the room with his gloves already on. Listening to me yelling that the head was out, and realizing that Lorena was not going to let go of me, *he picked us both up* and carried us to the bed, laying Lorena on her back with her feet on the floor. I was trying desperately to get out of the way, but she still had a death grip on my neck. Ric was about to have to catch the baby between my legs too! But after a few seconds, she loosened her grip a bit, and I was able to step aside just in time for Ric to receive the baby and lift it up to her arms.

That was the closest to catching a baby I've ever come. I was thrilled and relieved for Lorena's sake when Ric came rushing to help, but to this day, I wonder what I would have done if he had not. Perhaps Lorena would have let go of me on her own and instinctively reached down to catch her baby. Perhaps I could have moved her hands to the nearby dresser and knelt down to catch it myself. I wish I knew!

Contrasting Perceptions: Reflections on Helping Out at the Health Dispensary

Megan Cogburn

It was just getting dark when a nurse came to my house to tell me that there was a mother at the health dispensary in active labor and around 7 cm dilated. Once inside the darkness of the labor room, I could hear faint moans coming from the laboring mother, who was naked on the examination bed, lying on her right side. Donning my headlamp, I saw that forceps, glass vials, sterile gloves, and syringes were laid out on the top of a white metal rollaway tray, covered with a colorful *khanga* (a special kind of cloth). The nurse was trying unsuccessfully to get a makeshift flashlight to work, so I held up my headlamp for her as she completed her preparations and then instructed the mother to move onto her back and spread her legs wide open, hitting the mother's inner thighs in a rousing, authoritative manner.

The mother was fully dilated and ready to push, but I could tell that the nurse did not like the strength of the contractions. As I continued to hold up the headlamp, she broke open a vial of synthetic oxytocin, prepared a needle and syringe, and injected the mother's thigh. Every time the mother let out cries of pain and fear, the nurse and the elder women waiting just outside the room would tell her to leave this noise behind her and not to cry—this is the will of God and God will help her. Clearly uncomfortable on her back, the mother held onto her legs by placing her hands around her ankles with the nurse's help. In urgent appeals the mother expressed her worries to the nurse—that she could not do it, that she was too tired, that she needed the nurse to help her, *"Nisaidie nesi."* The nurse comforted the mother by repeating that she was at her side, that she was helping her, but that the mother needed to breathe, *hema,* and push, *sukuma,* whenever a contraction came.

As the head began to crown, the mother continued to cry out in pain—*"Nesi, nisaidie, Mungu nisaidie!"* The nurse placed two gloved fingers inside the mother's vagina, wedged up against the perineum to help guide the head through. Watching from the foot of the bed, I held my light steady on the nurse's hands. Soon the head emerged, followed by the body, and the nurse uncoiled the umbilical cord wrapped around the baby's shoulder and arm. In a sigh of relief, the mother thanked God several times—*"Asante Mungu, Ninashukuru Mungu."* Her infant, a boy, started to cry.

The nurse set him aside at the foot of the bed and went about clamping the cord and cutting it with a sterile scalpel. I had barely spoken since my arrival and decided to break my silence by asking the nurse why she did not lay the infant on his mother. The nurse let out a slight chuckle and responded, in English, "Oh yes, Kan-Ga-Roo care," before plopping the bloodied infant down on his mother's bare chest and abdomen. The mother was exhausted and clearly uncomfortable with having to balance the infant on her body while her contractions continued to expel the placenta. She asked the nurse to remove him, fearing he would fall off, so the nurse wrapped the infant in a fresh *khanga* and moved him over to the top of the metal tray, hastily removing the other items first. Then she received the placenta, cleaned the mother from the waist down, and removed a plastic tarp and other dirty items from the exam table. The mother had a slight perineal tear, and the nurse advised her to be very good about keeping herself clean.

When the women outside brought in the mother's clothes, they had no pads with them, so the nurse inspected two pieces of *kitenge* to be used instead. Holding the cloth up to my headlight, she shook her head disapprovingly, harshly explaining that the mother would start to hurt in her stomach if she got an infection from her dirty clothes. I could not help sharing the nurse's frustrations. The pieces of cloth were very dirty and would have to be used to bandage the mother's bleeding vagina. The nurse scolded all the women, asking why they let their relative come to the clinic with such dirty things. Why did they not bring the necessary, clean items to the facility for birth?

As the women pleaded with the nurse to forgive them, I reminded myself about the dry season we were in that left the community with too little water for washing clothing and pieces of cloth for delivery. As the nurse helped the mother get her makeshift pad and underwear on, I picked up the infant, who had been crying on top of the tray, and placed him by his mother's side, where he again began to cry. With a gentle laugh, the nurse told the mother that the infant was her work now, and instructed her to offer him her breast. I followed the other women outside, listening to the joyful sounds of their collective relief replacing the tension of their previous encounter.

As I walked back to my house, I reflected on my own positionality, and the many ups and downs of birth at the health dispensary. I was surprised at the embarrassment I felt over the "Kan-Ga-Roo" care mix-up, feeling I had added to the mother's discomfort by trying to follow "scientifically correct" procedure at a time that didn't work for her. I was even more surprised at how, for a moment, I had sympathized with the nurse's harassment over the dirty items—sharing her point of view before remembering the larger context that made clean clothes impossible to achieve for the women she was scolding.

Taking a moment to reflect and write about these contrasting feelings and embodied moments of tension, awkwardness, and calm is essential to an anthropologist at the health dispensary—where she is always much more than a participant-observer, serving also as a witness to, and sometimes a helper for, birth.

Giving Birth to Ninkasi: A Whole New Level of Participant-Observation

Missy Cheyney

On May 4, 2009, I was exactly 38 weeks pregnant. A practicing home-birth midwife myself, I had one mother left who I thought would give birth before me, and she was due any day. As I relaxed on the couch, I had a sudden and strong intuition that someone was going to go into labor that night. I had my husband help load all of my birth equipment into the car so that I would not have to pack it up in the wee hours of the morning when I would surely be called.

I fell asleep on the couch reading a book and slept deeply until pain in my back woke me around 3 A.M. At 4:30, contractions came on like a freight train, hitting every two to three minutes, dropping me to my knees and breaking my water. I woke my husband Andy, who sat up, dazed. Another contraction, stronger than the last, came, and I was screaming: "Rub my back! My back! Oh god, my back. What the hell? The baby is posterior. I knew it! Damn it! You have to turn around, little baby."

In between contractions, I called my midwifery assistant and asked her if she could handle my prenatal visits that day. I instructed her to keep my labor a secret until I had given birth. I had felt so under the microscope during my pregnancy. Many well-meaning people made stress-inducing comments like: "Wow, wouldn't it be crazy if you ended up with a cesarean after all of your research?" Or, "What if you have to transport to the hospital?" "What if after all of your work on natural birth, you end up getting pain medications?" The hardest thing about my pregnancy was definitely the mental work of dealing with other people's commentaries. My midwives helped me to process the pressures and to set some of that baggage aside, but the sense of being onstage came back with the start of contractions—until the excruciating pain in my back removed all thoughts of anything else.

My midwives, Colleen and Carla, arrived around 8:30 in the morning and attempted to talk me down off the ledge about my baby's position. I knew too much, and I kept thinking, "As a first-time mom with a posterior baby, I am 34 times more likely to transfer to the hospital." They reminded me that it was not a problem unless it was a problem and that my labor seemed to be progressing well; I was already 5 cm dilated. That seemed like relatively quick progress given the baby's position. Maybe if I got to complete dilation before exhaustion set in, I could push the baby down far enough that she would rotate at the pelvic outlet. Clinically speaking, things went smoothly for the next few hours, though I was not performing labor the way I had hoped. No quiet, focused breathing through the contractions, no surrendering to the pain, no candles, soft music, or letting my body do it. I was screaming and swearing like a sailor: "My back! My back! Holy shit! My back! Rub my back!"

Colleen, Carla, and Andy took turns holding my hands, pressing on my back, and encouraging me to walk and change positions. I climbed the stairs, got in and out of the birthing tub, and complained as loudly as I possibly could, using the F-word as my birth mantra at the peak of every contraction. Through it all, I was distantly aware of getting to experience so many of the sensations I had witnessed in my clients: back labor, exhaustion, wondering if I could do it, hoping that the baby was OK. I asked the midwives to listen to the baby's heartbeat using headphones, for I knew that if I heard it myself, the sound of the fetal heartbeat would move me out of my birthing mother space and into midwife mode, assessing safety and evaluating fetal well-being. They honored my request, and just being able to trust my midwives, who were also among my closest friends, enabled me to get out of my midwife-brain and into laborland, where my body could do what it needed to do.

Around 3:00 in the afternoon, my cervix was completely dilated, and it was time to start pushing. The baby was high and still posterior, and I knew I had a lot of work to do to bring her down. I pushed for three hours in every position we could think of. The midwives were encouraging, but I could tell I was not making progress, and my uterus was starting to tire. Contractions were lighter and spacing out. I ate, drank, and took several herbal concoctions to help restore my energy and increase the strength of my contractions. At some point, it became clear that I would just have to gut out the pushing, relying primarily on my abdominal muscles. My confidence faltered, and I told Colleen that I didn't think I could do it. She said, "You've only been pushing for three hours, the baby sounds great, you're healthy and strong. You have a lot more in there. You have to dig down deep inside to find the strength you need to continue."

Things turned the corner over the next few hours as I pushed in a squat, leaning against the edge of the tub as Andy and Carla grasped arms and pushed against my hips as hard as they could, trying to open the pelvic outlet to give the baby space to rotate. "God damned, piece of shit hip squeeze! I can't believe I'm getting the hip squeeze! Please turn, baby. Please, get out of my back!" Legs cramping, trembling with fatigue, sun setting, I kept pushing.

At the five-hour mark, while squatting during a hip squeeze, a contraction started that was harder and longer than the ones my tired uterus had been churning out before, and at the peak of it, pushing with all I had, I felt the baby's head rotate and begin to descend in the birth canal. I let out a blood-curdling scream that brought Colleen up from the basement where she had been heating towels in the dryer. "Now we're going to have a baby!" she said. I pushed for another hour, finally making progress. I felt the baby start to crown, and I walked over to the birth stool. I looked down at Andy, whose eyes were glassy with tears as he sat waiting to catch our baby.

The craziness and intensity of the day melted away and it was just the three of us, suspended in time, an incredible cosmic moment that I imprinted forever. I reached down, pushing into my own hand, finally feeling her head and knowing I would be holding my baby soon. I felt her head emerge, and then her little body twisted slowly as her shoulders cleared the bones. She dropped into her daddy's waiting hands, and Andy sobbed as he caught her, looked her over, and passed her up into my arms. We held her together, kissing and nuzzling and laughing as she gradually came into her body after that difficult journey. She opened her eyes and stared intently at me. We watched her little body turn pink as she took her first breath—a warm rosiness starting first over her heart and then slowly spreading out across her body as she began to wiggle and coo and sputter, clearing her own airway. I can't imagine anything ever topping those first few moments with her. The relief and joy were definitely proportional to the pain and exertion that had consumed me just minutes before.

Colleen monitored my blood loss and helped the placenta to be born while Carla watched over our baby. Andy and I just stared in awe. At some point, we remembered that we didn't know the sex. For a while she was just a baby, and neither of us had thought to check. Andy looked and announced what I had felt all along—a baby girl! She weighed 7 lbs and 3 oz and was born at 8:52 P.M. after six hours of grueling pushing and 10 hours of back labor. The most amazing part is that she was born on May 5—International Day of the Midwife! We named her Ninkasi after the Sumerian goddess of beer. My husband is a middle school world history teacher and an amateur brewer. She has a little bit of each of us in her.

Colleen and Carla cleaned up, performed the newborn exam, fed us, and tucked us into bed for our first night together. Throughout the night, Andy and I kept waking up, staring at her, and talking about the birth. We were both elated. It's hard to put into words the joy and magic of my birth and our first few days and weeks together as a new family. It was surreal and intoxicating and without a doubt the most transformative, pushed-to-the-limit, triumphant, summiting-Mt. Everest experience of my life to date. The hard work and pain were so worth it, and Ninkasi's birth, more than anything else, renewed my commitment to homebirth as a political movement.

I felt proud of being a midwife and a bearer of such invaluable specialized knowledge. Low-tech, time-honored strategies for rectifying Ninkasi's

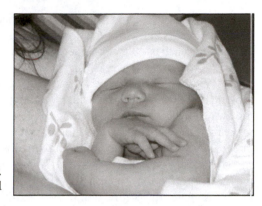

Beautiful Ninkasi Cheyney.
Photo by Andrew Meskil

position had worked for me, and I renewed my commitment to see other women begin their families the way I did—on top of the world! Through it all, I never stopped being an anthropologist—my own birth was fodder for my fieldwork, as it gave me a fresh perspective on why place of birth matters. I understand better than ever the women who choose to give birth at home, even in states where community midwives have not yet achieved licensure and regulation. These women are so committed to experiencing unmedicated birth on their own terms that they drive for hours to birth with midwives in other states, and the mothers who, feeling scarred and disempowered by their hospital births, are determined to do it differently the next time. Most of all, I felt gratitude to my little Ninkasi, who has taught me more than anyone else about midwifery models of care and why some of us make the counter-cultural choice to give birth at home.

The Hospital Birth that Wasn't: When Fieldwork and Practice Merge

Bahareh Goodarzi

She is eight weeks pregnant when she takes the seat in front of me, back straight and arms crossed, and announces firmly that she wants to give birth in the hospital. "No homebirth, at any cost." She wants this choice to be clear because she had heard about the Dutch "homebirth mafia"—midwives who are vehemently against hospital birth. As a Dutch midwife, of course I am aware of this stereotypic image, but I personally have no vendetta against hospital birth. I do see homebirth as a means to promote physiologic birth. Yet, I also believe it is essential that women can choose their place of birth based on objective information. I am proud to work in a country where this is made possible. I reassure the woman in front of me that I will support her in any setting she chooses. But she keeps looking at me suspiciously, as if thinking, "I'll believe that when I see it!"

Over the course of her pregnancy we meet several more times, and every time she stresses her wish for a hospital birth. Her pregnancy goes by the book. When she reaches 40 weeks, she tells me that she wants an induction if the baby is not born by 41 weeks. The next day her husband calls and urges me to come. Within 10 minutes I arrive at their house. Her husband opens the door looking frenzied. His wife is standing next to her bed fully dressed and breathing away during contractions, flushes on her cheeks and sweat on her forehead, insisting that she wants to go to the hospital. I explain to her that I would first like to conduct a vaginal examination and check the baby's condition. She says she is in a lot of pain and wants to go NOW. Before she can finish her sentence, the next contraction comes. She closes her eyes to concentrate and starts breathing. After the contraction, I try to explain to her again the importance of a checkup before we leave, but there is no convincing her. She wants to leave NOW. In the meantime, three more contractions have passed, each stronger than the last. By just watching a woman, a midwife can tell a lot about the phase of labor she is in, and I'm pretty sure that delivery is nigh.

Nevertheless, she starts walking to the stairs. Before she makes it to the first step another contraction comes. I see her belly making reflexive push movements. Okay, we are definitely in the last phase. I tell her what I see, and explain to her that I think she is too far along, and I would like to check her dilation. "We don't want the baby to be born in the car," I say. There is still no convincing her, she needs to go to the hospital. I look at her husband desperately, and he shrugs as if saying, "There's nothing I can do, just go with it." She takes two steps, and another contraction comes, during which her knees buckle, and she starts pushing. I am stressing that we won't make it to the hospital and that we need to get back to the bed. Meanwhile she has turned around and is on her hands and knees on the stairs: "I'm comfortable here." The contractions come quickly now and she is pushing along with them.

I instruct the husband to get me towels, the delivery kit, and my delivery bag. In the meantime, I once again explain that it would really be better to move to the bed. But she has retreated into her own world, fully concentrating on the contractions and pushing. When I ask her whether I can take her pants off, she doesn't oppose. Now I see part of the head already visible between her legs. I listen to the baby's heartbeat, and he is doing fine. Well of course he is fine; he isn't bothered about being born on the stairs.

So, there we are, the four of us. Me, standing halfway down the narrow stairs, one knee on the step below her and my back against the wall trying not to fall backwards, the contents of my delivery bag spread around me on the steps. I'm looking at the baby's head as the mother is now on all fours, facing her husband. He is sitting on top of the stairs, awkwardly bending down to wipe her head with a wet towel. She seems to have totally accepted this unusual situation and is doing great. Fifteen minutes later a healthy baby boy is born, on the stairs.

About two hours later, after everything was cleaned up, she was lying in bed, breastfeeding her baby with a sandwich in her hand. As I walked in, a

Bahareh showing an intact placenta
to the parents just after a birth.
Photo by the new father

satisfied smile appeared on her face. "I had a totally different image of homebirth, but now I would recommend it to everyone!" she exclaimed. Smiling
back, I asked her, "Please, whatever you say, do not recommend to anyone to
give birth on the stairs!" She laughed—a wonderful laugh of pure joy and
complete fulfillment.

Writer's Block

Bahareh Goodarzi

Writer's block: a phenomenon many researchers are familiar with. I
wasn't, however, until I reached the final phase of writing my Master's thesis. I
knew *what* I wanted to write, but I didn't know *how* to write it down so it would
be understandable for others. It had reached a point where I was so frustrated,
I was thinking of quitting. So, I discussed it with my supervisor, who advised
me to turn off my head. I was thinking too hard and that made me choke, she
said. The medicine was to undertake activities that predominantly involved my
body and would distract me from all the thoughts racing through my brain.
"Bake a cake," she said. "Go for a swim," she advised. "Take a long bath," she
proposed. "Then it will come to you, like a eureka moment."

So, essentially her advice was to relax. Relax? How could I relax with the
clock ticking? This was insane. But, I had no choice. I couldn't bake or swim,
so I started running. It felt great. I ran and ran, and 45 minutes later I arrived
back home, sweat dripping off my forehead. But I had not had a eureka
moment yet. I felt frustration starting to boil up in my stomach. This was
never going to work, I was sure of it.

Yet, as I stood in the shower, I closed my eyes and for the first time in a
long time I felt my shoulders relaxing. I noticed my thoughts had become a
slow stream instead of a wild river. And then, out of the blue, like someone
hit me with hammer, it came to me. It was just there. I knew what I had to

Bahareh teaching midwifery students at the Midwifery Academy in Amsterdam—the result of overcoming her writer's block and getting her degree. Photo by Ruud Pos

write. YES! I got my wife to come running with my laptop. And as she sat on the floor next to the shower, I dictated and she typed until my fingertips shriveled up from the water. The first complete version of my paper was finished that very night.

Ever since that day, whenever I'm blocked up, I'll undertake some sort of physical exercise and my wife will be waiting by the shower with my laptop when I get back. I write this story with special thanks to my supervisor, Prof. Dr. Antoinette de Bont, for helping me deal with my writers' block.

Are Babies "Delivered"?

Therese Wiegers

I am a researcher, not a midwife. I collect data, analyze them, and write papers or reports, but I don't do fieldwork like anthropologists do. So, I have no real fieldwork stories to share with you. But there is something else I want to draw your attention to, and that is the language we use in describing and discussing care regarding pregnancy and childbirth.

Early in my career as a researcher, I learned that in most scientific literature, maternity care was referred to as "obstetrics," to give birth was "to deliver" and that a birth was a "delivery." As I am not a native English speaker, I accepted that language as the rule and used it in my own papers. However, my PhD supervisor, Professor Marc Keirse, had different thoughts about that and occasionally would say: "Pizzas are delivered, not babies." I thought that was funny, because it put the word "deliver" in a totally different perspective. But I didn't change my writing, because I had to produce scientific papers and to use the proper scientific language.

But the issue stuck in my mind, and I started to wonder: Why is a birth called a delivery? Outside the context of maternity care, "to deliver" means "to bring"—for instance, a pizza indeed, or the mail, or flowers. The item that is delivered is brought to someone who did or did not expect it. But what does it mean exactly within the context of maternity care? Who is bringing what? And to whom? I didn't have an answer. There is another meaning of "deliver," as in the prayer: "Deliver us from evil," where it means "rescue." Would that be the origin of the use of the word "deliver" in maternity care? But who, then, is to be rescued? Is the baby to be rescued from its mother? Or is the mother to be rescued from her baby? This felt kind of cynical to me, especially as it puts the care provider in the role of rescuer. To frame every childbirth as a "delivery"—a rescue operation—implies that care providers are heroes, and that it is their achievement when mother and baby survive. This language does not acknowledge the labor of the woman. Yet, the process of giving birth is not called "laboring" for nothing: the woman is doing the work. I was still confused.

Only after I read Robbie's articles (Davis-Floyd 2001, 2018a) about the technocratic, humanistic, and holistic models of care did everything fall into place. The use of the words "deliver" and "delivery" are an integral part of the technocratic model of care, where the care providers take central stage because of their "superior" knowledge, and their patients are objects that need rescuing. Some care providers will say: "I have delivered so-and-so many babies," but that always makes me think: "And how often have you been pregnant?" The word "delivery" subverts the women giving birth. In the humanistic and holistic models of care, the words "deliver" and "delivery" have no place, except in the general meaning of delivering care. In those models, the mother gives birth and the attendants "catch" or "receive" the baby.

To end these thoughts on a light-hearted note, I can disclose to you that I know of one place where babies are actually delivered like gifts, at least according to local folktales. That is in the Netherlands, where babies are delivered by storks, as you can see in this picture.

The Dutch often announce the arrival of a newborn in this way. Photo by Mark Warwick

The Challenges of Focus-Group Interviews: Of Noisy Children and Triggered Emotions

Rea Daellenbach

In several research projects, I have used focus groups to collect women's views and stories of their experiences around reproduction. I like this method because it enables participants to exchange ideas, coconstruct meanings, and engage in their own analyses in relation to the research questions. Mothers who participate in these focus groups often bring their babies and small children to the interview site—often a community center near their homes. So my interview kit includes a toy box and healthy children's snacks.

Such group interviews develop their own rhythms. Women move in and out of the discussion as they simultaneously attend to the needs of their children and to each other. They breastfeed, get up and walk around to calm a baby, change nappies, or check on a toddler. When babies fuss or smile to capture attention, the conversation pauses or changes direction. Toddlers, fascinated by my recording device, often try to grab it. Such focus groups can be exhausting, and transcribing the interviews is often challenging, as women's words can be drowned out by children's noises. However, I also feel a real appreciation for that special mother-of-small-children efficiency that keeps the momentum of the interview going even when it verges on chaos. The children's presence brings the reality of childbirth as part of the continuum of mothering into the interview process; into the relationships created between me, the researcher, and the participants; and into the interactions among the participants. These interviews, then, become more a part of the flow of life and community and less of an abstracted space.

In talking to women about childbirth, there is the ever-present possibility that the conversation can bring up feelings of grief and trauma. So, I ensure that I have information to give to participants about how to make complaints and how to access mediation/patient advocacy and free counseling services. Sometimes I have discussed these options with participants. But once, I really did not manage well. Looking out the window as the participants left, I saw one of them standing on the sidewalk in obvious distress, maybe even sobbing, her back turned toward me, her baby in a portable car seat on the ground in front of her. I felt dismayed; I had not seen this coming. Exhausted from the long meeting, and having no clue as to how I could help, I nevertheless went outside, and then saw one of the other participants talking with her. The caring support of this other participant was almost palpable, and I could see that the distressed woman seemed to be standing taller. I thought, "She is doing this much better than I could have," so I simply watched for a moment and then went inside to finish packing up. All of us need an "emotions midwife" sometimes to help us process our feelings, and I was relieved that woman found hers, and I resolved to do better the next time around.

"Always to the Right":
The Lasting Power of Medical Tradition

K. Eliza Williamson

One evening I was chatting with a family doctor friend of mine in Salvador about my research on birth care in Brazil's public health system. I mentioned how difficult it seemed to be for many health care professionals to change their practices even when presented with solid evidence against those practices—such as the continued, routine use of episiotomy. My friend smiled knowingly and then shared a story from his obstetric rotation during residency. When he and his colleagues were taught how to perform an episiotomy, their professor told them that one must always cut into the perineum downward, at an angle—and always to the right of the person cutting. This "always to the right" sounded strange to him, but no one questioned the professor.

Then, when actually performing episiotomies, my friend and fellow residents began noticing how onerous cutting to the right was. Most of them were right-handed, so to cut downward toward the right they had to maneuver their hand, wrist, and forearm into uncomfortable positions. After a while of twisting themselves into knots, my friend finally asked his practicum director why the episiotomy had to be cut toward the right. "That's just the way it has to be done!" was the indignant reply. Unsatisfied with this response, my friend finally learned after much searching that his professor's teacher had been left-handed. Things suddenly became clear: this person had cut to the right because it was the easier side for him. His students simply followed suit. And by now whole classes of doctors had graduated believing that episiotomies must always be cut to the right.

As Brigitte Jordan is famous for saying, "the power of authoritative knowledge is not that it is correct, but that it *counts*." This story illustrates how powerful and authoritative medical "knowledge" is, correct or not, and how practices—right or wrong—become "tradition" and get reproduced and remain uncontested through generations. This story is also a good reminder to be attentive to *everything* during fieldwork, even the moments when you're not officially "doing" anything beyond just chatting with a friend over beers.

Finding My Voice: An Episiotomy Experience

Eugenia Georges

Like many of the other authors in this volume, I frequently faced the emotionally and morally challenging question that Robbie and Missy lay out in their introduction to this chapter: "When we see something hurtful being done, should we name it and try to change it?" Since almost every woman giving birth in Greece undergoes all sorts of interventions, the effectiveness and necessity of which have been repeatedly refuted by scientific research, this was a question I regularly faced as I conducted my research on birth in Greek public hospitals. My first field site was a public hospital in eastern Greece that served as the center of health care for the surrounding region. It was an old building, but it was airy, sunny, and clean, and the longtime Director of Obstetrics and Gynecology, who was deeply invested in his department, was always trying to make improvements to the facility. Fond of the United States, where he had been educated, he accepted me and supported my project, at first in his signature gruff style, but over time with increasing trust and even warmth. I was allowed, and often invited, to be present at a wide variety of procedures, some of which were not particularly relevant to my research but that I felt would be impolite, awkward, or even judgmental and off-putting on my part to refuse.

Of all the routine procedures I observed, however, the most physically and emotionally difficult for me to deal with was the episiotomy. Witnessing my very first birth, I discovered that episiotomies at this hospital were done without any anesthetic whatsoever—for the most part, the only anesthesia available in the hospital was general anesthesia for cesareans. As I watched Doctor A, who was the most popular and sought-after of all the obstetricians for his bedside manner, use a pair of scissors to cut into the woman strapped down to the delivery table they called the "boom," the room turned pea-green and started to sway beneath my feet; my vision blurred and then disappeared entirely. I had to leave the room to avoid making a scene. I was ashamed of what I regarded as my wimpy and unprofessional lack of control. With time I developed some strategies to deal with my deeply embodied responses to the episiotomy—mostly by looking away.

Of course, the doctor and the many other care providers present in the delivery room noticed my distress and, as often happens in fieldwork, this situation opened up what turned out to be a productive space for dialogue with my interlocutors about our different perspectives on episiotomy. Dr. A, with whom I got along well, unsurprisingly insisted on its medical necessity, and I did not challenge him at that point. But when he went on to explain that, in any case, because the perineum was stretched so tightly, the woman felt no pain as he cut and later sewed up her incision, I simply couldn't keep quiet and I began to debate the point with him, based on my observations of the birthing woman and my own embodied standpoint.

A few days after our conversation, I once again observed Dr. A in the delivery room. As he was about to perform the episiotomy, he picked up a syringeful of local anesthetic from the steel tray at his side, glanced over at me, and lifting the syringe slightly in the air, made a toasting gesture in my direction ("Cheers! This one's for you!") before injecting it into the woman's perineum. After that, Doctor A regularly used a local when I was present at a birth. There is humor and some absurdity in this anecdote, and I don't know if Dr. A continued the injections after I left the field. But I think this story also offers an example of how, as feminist medical anthropologists, our responses to the dilemmas and challenges of studying intensely medicalized births can and even ought to vary depending on our evaluations of the specific situation, the nature of our relationships with our interlocutors, and the locus of authority from which we decide to speak out, or not.

Confronting the Violence of Birth in a Mexican Hospital

Vania Smith-Oka

This fieldwork took place in 2011, during my first foray into a large public hospital in the city of Puebla, Mexico. One of the directors introduced me to some of the obstetric residents so they could show me around the sterile area of *Tococirugía*—labor and delivery. The births I witnessed that first day were very illustrative of the forms of obstetric violence present in many births in Mexico. I eventually discovered that they were normative for this hospital.

The first patient I saw was a teenager who was weeping as she tried to push while lying on a narrow gurney in a delivery room. A male resident had his fingers in her vagina, checking the position of the baby's head while yelling "Push!" at her. I immediately felt my eyes pricking with tears because of the lack of dignity the patient was subjected to—her legs were spread and her entire lower quarters were exposed. A second-year female resident walked in, put on a glove, and also did a vaginal exam. The patient tearfully kept on asking, "Now? Is [my baby] out?" Whoever heard her would laugh and shake their head as if to say, "Silly girl." The only times people spoke to her were to scold her, or to tell her how to breathe, to cooperate, to be a good girl.

I hovered at her head, trying to chat with her and calm her down. She said she was having a boy whom she wanted to name Antoine. Periodically someone would poke their fingers into her vagina, telling her to relax and open her legs. She would whimper. Invariably, the clinician would say, "Push, push hard, as much as you can bear." And she would strain and push but they would say she was not doing it correctly. She would look up after each large push and ask, "Is it over?" She gripped my hand and squeezed as she pushed. I kept trying to encourage her, smiling at her.

No less than six different people, some on more than one occasion, inserted their gloved fingers into her vagina to check her cervix and the baby's head. They kept saying, "She's fully dilated." A senior male resident came in. He stuck his fingers into the patient with little preamble, and when she whimpered, he sharply told her not to cry. He pulled his hand out abruptly and made a quick slashing motion with his hand over her belly. I knew immediately he meant a cesarean. I stood with the patient, trying to comfort her. The female senior attending obstetrician came in to determine whether a cesarean was necessary. I thought the patient would be horrified at this decision, but she just lay on the gurney, mute, as her belly was exposed and completely covered with iodine, readying it for the cesarean. She stopped talking much after that, lying dazed as she was cut into and her baby taken out.

Afterward, I heard some loud cries outside the delivery room so I walked out, curious. I saw a laboring woman in one of the curtained cubicles with her legs spread and the baby's head peeking out. Clinicians were shouting at her because she was pushing when they were telling her not to push—because all three delivery rooms were occupied and they were trying to figure out where to place her, wheeling her gurney into one room and then another. The patient begged for someone to massage her legs and was laughed at. I followed at a trot, wanting to comfort her. She was eventually rolled into a delivery room where another patient had just given birth vaginally. The room was quite crowded, and the gurney was pressed up against a wall. By some miracle, I managed to squeeze in and stand at her head. Only two other clinicians were by her. No one else fit. The attending yelled instructions from across the room to the young resident as she attended the very quick vaginal delivery. The resident lowered one of the gurney's railings to have better access. The patient gasped and said she would have nothing to hold on to. So, I quickly put her hand in mine, which she squeezed as she strained. The baby girl seemed to pop right out.

The resident attended to the afterbirth, but scolded the patient repeatedly for moving and fidgeting. The patient burst into tears and could not stop. I stroked her head, wishing I could talk to her and comfort her. She wept uncontrollably for a long time. No one seemed to even notice. I was still stroking her hand and softly congratulated her. She did not seem to really know I was there.

I suddenly felt so powerless and horrified at everything I had witnessed that I realized I had to get out of there, but I had to be polite to all the staff, telling them how great it had been. I felt like such a fraud for seeing these injustices and not doing anything. In my notes for that day I wrote, *"I feel like a traitor to my profession, gender, feelings, everything. So powerless."* I was nauseated. But I knew I needed to return the next day and all the subsequent ones to continue witnessing these births and to write these women's stories, trying to make some sense of these terrible, cruel, and completely unnecessary forms of obstetric violence.

Dilemmas and Interference

Brigitte Jordan

Whether birth takes place in a hospital or at home, whether it is produced as a technological achievement or as an intimate family affair, it carries with it special obligations and demands for the fieldworker. The relationship between the woman in the throes of labor and the fieldworker is a very special one, a privileged relationship built on trust and demanding of the fieldworker not only that she do no harm, but that she contribute, to the best of her ability, to the successful outcome of the enterprise. The often-painful conflicts generated by this kind of responsibility are illustrated in the two following stories.

Susan

The very first American hospital birth I observed was a powerful experience. It confronted me, in the most painful fashion, with a dilemma I have found myself facing many times since: whether, and when and how, to interfere in birthing practices that appear to me to be contrary to the best interests of mother and child. At the time, I was a graduate student and tremendously intimidated by the medical establishment. As a properly socialized member of American culture, I subscribed to the unexamined, taken-for-granted notion that in relation to all things obstetric, the medical profession was *the* authoritative source of knowledge.

Susan was an unmarried 15-year-old who had managed her labor admirably. Her boyfriend had deserted her but she very much wanted this baby, who would be her own to love and care for. She talked about the clothes she had made for the baby, and the little bathtub she had bought. The baby would sleep in her room so that she could hear any cries, and she would breastfeed her child. Susan's mother was there, too, but she appeared relieved when I was introduced by the nurse as somebody who was studying birth and would they mind . . . ? Of course they wouldn't. The mother went out to have a cigarette, call friends, take a nap—it was the middle of the night. The nurse left us pretty much alone, and in a short time Susan and I established a close relationship, exchanging stories about our very different lives and then, with increasing seriousness, monitoring her experience. The nurse came in from time to time to check Susan's progress, but she, like Susan's mother, seemed quite happy that I was occupying the interactional slot that she might have had to fill.

As time went on, Susan's contractions became somewhat painful, but she lasted them out with her deep, joyful conviction that this was going to bring her baby out, really, so she could see it, and touch it, and love it. She looked into my eyes during those contractions and, when they were over, told me she was glad I was there. I knew, without doubt, that my presence was good for her. The little cubicle was darkened; we could hear her mother snoring on the chair just outside of it, and we laughed.

Finally, she was completely dilated. The nurse rolled in a gurney and transferred her onto it with my help. The delivery room was filled with a bunch of people in white coats and green outfits. Bright lights. Gleaming metal. They transferred her to a narrow table, flat on her back, her legs grotesquely spread apart, her feet in stirrups. And then I noticed, to my horror, that they were tying down her hands with leather straps. I had flashes of medieval torture chambers—whips and iron instruments. I felt sick. I didn't remember that sort of thing from my own births. Had they done this to me too? I couldn't remember. I was trying to make sense out of their actions. Surely they wouldn't do this without good reasons. But what awful thing was going to happen to make this necessary? All of a sudden the situation had changed from the intimate, exciting atmosphere of the labor room, where we had worked together to help this wonderful baby be born—a straightforward proposition, easily understandable to us two neophytes—to a situation that was out of our hands, foreboding, and fraught with danger.

They told her to push. Susan, who had been so courageous during the long hours of labor, made an effort. Her body strained and fell back in discouragement. "My God, I can't push like this. How can I push like this?" she wailed. She was already transformed into an object strapped onto a table. They told her to push again. Her eyes were searching for me. I stepped close to her head, knowing that I was violating a nurse's territory. She looked at me imploringly. "Gitti, *please* untie my hands." I don't think I have very often in my life felt as miserable as then. I knew that I couldn't muster the courage to untie her hands, which was the only thing I could do to honor the unspoken contract between us. I held her hand, saying "I can't, Susan. It'll be all right."

Well, it wasn't all right. She gave up. Her contractions stopped. The green team stood, gloved, sterile hands in the air. Waiting. I felt an impotent rage. I thought I would get sick. Throw up right there. Burst into tears. Scream. . . . Susan was lying with closed eyes. Her body refused to work. The green team began to feel awkward in the silence. They tried some jokes. They wondered what I was doing there. They asked me how the Indians did it. They ended up artificially stimulating her labor and pulling the baby out with forceps. I wasn't able to face her after that. I went home and looked at my own children and swore my daughters would not have to go through that. Susan is still with me. I did a lot of thinking after that, and decided that there are certain situations where I have to act as a woman and a human being first and as a researcher second.

I do feel very strongly that most of the time my major responsibility lies in recording, as respectfully, objectively, and unobtrusively as possible, whatever it is that is going on, regardless of what my personal opinion or reaction might be. At the same time, however, the very act of admission to the intimate event of birth implies a special kind of trust and relationship. The role of the uninvolved objective *observer* thins out at times to the point that the involved *participant* becomes predominant, even takes over, in the process of "participant observation." As a consequence, I have "objective" records of births, where the effects of the anthropologists' presences were minimal, but I also have thoroughly "contaminated" records, like the videotape of Rosa's birth in Yucatan.

Rosa

During my Yucatan fieldwork, Rosa became a good friend. She helped my colleague Nancy Fuller and me with the many problems we strangers

faced, cooked meals for us, wove us hammocks, and facilitated our interactions with other women in the community. We had followed the course of her
career as a young woman, her engagement, her marriage, her hopes for a
child, finally her first pregnancy, and the tragic news of a stillbirth, which we
received by letter between field trips. There was some talk about her performance during labor, which led us to believe that she was blamed for the death
of the baby. She also told us that her husband had left the house in anger (or
was it sadness?) even before the birth of her placenta. We knew that she
grieved deeply over the death of her first child ("He was a perfect little boy")
and that she hoped from the depths of her heart that God would give her
another one so that she could redeem herself.

So it was with great joy that we received the news of her second pregnancy, and we timed our next fieldwork period so that it would coincide with
her expected due date. When we arrived, Rosa was happy to see us and suggested that we videotape the birth. We were only too glad to agree. After several years of attending births with paper, pencil, and tape recorder, we were
eager to get a visual record for detailed analysis. We knew by then that this
would be an important and unique film, since to our knowledge nobody had
ever filmed an Indigenous birth in Yucatan or anywhere else before.

Rosa's labor began late one afternoon. We set up our camera equipment
and started the first tape as soon as labor was established, intending to fully
document this birth from early labor through the postpartum hours. At first,
everything went well. The usual Yucatecan scene: Rosa lying in her hammock,
the midwife, her husband, and her sister-in-law sitting around, talking, joking,
assisting her as the contractions became more severe. It was a long night. Rosa
appeared to be in more and more pain. The camera was compiling a continuous record. I had the urge more than once to abandon my position behind the
camera and take my usual place next to Doña Juana, but the importance of
faithfully recording this event was uppermost in my mind. Every time Nancy
put on a new tape, I noted with satisfaction that we were that much closer to
finally producing that elusive recording of an Indigenous birth.

But Rosa's situation was becoming more and more precarious. She was
obviously in much pain, yet was determined to perform well during this
labor. She needed this child, not only to redeem herself but also to secure her
marriage and her position as a woman, the mother of children. I gritted my
teeth and pointed the camera. It was clear that the pain was becoming intol-
erable. Her grandmother and her husband exhorted her to push. A beseech-
ing look at me and a desperate, "*Quiti, ayudame*" ("help me"). I handed the
camera to Nancy. For a moment I thought I would just try to comfort Rosa,
and we could simply cut that piece of tape from the record and still end up
with an essentially "pure" recording of a Yucatecan birth. But only for a
moment. There was no return. The following tapes do not contain a record of
a "pure" Maya birth, but show a Maya woman in labor desperately holding
onto an anthropologist flung over her abdomen, the birth of an apparently
lifeless baby, Rosa's incredible quiet despair, the midwife's frantic efforts to

revive the baby, and finally the anthropologist blowing into the baby's mouth and nose and, after agonizing minutes, the baby's first rasping sound. I remember thinking "It has eluded us again; there goes our Yucatecan birth," and "I don't give a damn." I felt a tremendous sense of relief. My place very obviously was not behind the camera but with my friend Rosa. Rosa who was suffering. Rosa who needed me.

I should add here, parenthetically, two things: first, we did get a tape of an Indigenous birth a few days later, and second, Rosa gave us a gift the magnitude of which one can understand only if one appreciates the power of *vergüenza* (modesty, shame at exposure) in the thinking of Maya women: she offered to let us videotape her *baño de los tres dias*, the herbal bath that is given to the new mother three days after the baby's birth in order to assure an adequate milk supply.

"Holding Space": The Intimacy of the Ethnographic Interview

Adrienne Strong

I moved my finger off the iPad, where it had been resting on the last question on the screen. My posture changed a bit, relaxed, as I announced that my interview questions were finished. Nurse Aneth looked at the time and laughed, wondering where the last two and a half hours had gone. I asked her if I had left anything out, if I should have asked anything else to really understand the work the nurse-midwives on the maternity ward did. She said no, that I'd touched on just about everything, and added, "No one has ever asked me about my work like this." After nearly a year and a half conducting fieldwork here, I knew that the fast pace and strained environment of this regional hospital did not lend itself to focused listening. Many of the nurses repeatedly expressed that they felt the hospital's administrators did not care about, or listen to, the nurses on the wards. In my best form as an anthropologist, I think of myself as a space-holder[2] and professional listener. Aneth, and many of the other nurse-midwives to whom I listened, had gone for many years in their current positions with only a few opportunities to honestly express their views of their own work, the hospital, and the nursing profession as a whole in their country.

Particularly present in the beginning of my research, but persisting throughout, were the many questions from the nurse-midwives on the maternity ward: What was I going to *do* for them? Why should they take time to

---

[2] I use the term "holding space" to mean that we are willing to walk alongside another person in whatever journey they're on without judging them, making them feel inadequate, trying to fix them, or trying to impact the outcome. "When we hold space for other people, we open our hearts, offer unconditional support, and let go of judgement and control" (Heather Plett, March 11, 2015: https://heatherplett.com/2015/03/hold-space/)

talk to me? What, exactly, was I doing there anyway when I wasn't a doctor, or a nurse, or anything else comprehensible in their context? As anthropologists, we often ask a great deal of our research participants, our interlocutors, and the institutions that give us access. We need time and space, we ask countless, sometimes annoying, questions, and scribble endlessly in notebooks. I often struggled with feelings of wishing I could do more to assist in alleviating the difficult working conditions at Mawingu hospital. But, as one person, a foreigner, a student, I was absolutely unable to restructure the entire health care system in Tanzania and how it is financed, nor was that my job—though in the long run I did plan to use my research to inform policy makers and others and to try to influence policy in any positive way I could.

Yet, in the moment, the one small thing I could offer up was that space-holding—a safe, nonjudgmental opportunity for the nurses to tell their stories, voice their concerns, and vent their struggles and frustrations. Along with assurances of anonymity, confidentiality, and honesty about my limited abilities to compensate them for their time and the access they granted me, all I could really give them was my full attention. In that moment, when Aneth told me that no one had ever asked her such questions, or listened to her thoughts, I felt that maybe I was offering my interlocutors something, small though it was.

In the singular space of the ethnographic interview, occasionally something like magic can happen. A form of intimacy develops that is only broken when I press the "stop" button on the voice recorder. Many of the interviews took place in the nurses' homes. I conducted several more during the slow hours of the long night shift when dim bulbs or cell phone flashlights threw soft globes of light over sleeping mothers and babies and women in the throes of contractions. During the best interviews, I simply let the stories unfold, drawing out a detail or clarification here or there and stringing out, one by one, questions from my list. Always after such "magical" interviews, I felt profoundly grateful for the nurse's trust, for "letting me in." And I hoped that my simple act of holding space had been beneficial, perhaps even cathartic, for her as well. So, I am an anthropologist but, perhaps first and foremost, I am a steward of the stories these women gifted to me with such trust and grace.

Conclusion: Does Our Work Help the World?

These last few stories bring us full circle to the question with which we began this chapter: "When we see something being done that we think is wrong, should we name it and try to change it, despite what might be severe consequences for ourselves and perhaps others?" We are proud of the positive changes we have all been able to make, while remaining very aware that many anthropologists, like journalists, can do nothing beyond recording what they observe in efforts to make others aware of problems they might not know exist. Yet in our final story, Adrienne teaches us that the simple act of

listening can make magic happen by providing an outlet for self-expression—
and thus for greater self-esteem—for people whose voices are rarely, if ever,
heard. Many of our stories show that the anthropological interview, and the
helpful participation of anthropologists in even the simplest tasks at hand,
have their own intrinsic value.

We, your editors, along with thousands of other anthropologists, do
believe deeply in *applied anthropology*, in which anthropological findings are
put to work to create effective change, as well as in *anthropological activism*, in
which anthropologists put their analytical minds, compassionate hearts, and
sometimes their fierce feminist spirits into supporting local social movements
for change. We encourage all anthropologists to come out of the "ivory
tower" and seek to make our work useful at local, regional, national, and
international levels by listening to communities, standing alongside the people we work with, and throwing whatever expertise, power or resources we
have into supporting communities in their own rights to cultural self-determination. Otherwise, are we not just building academic careers on the backs of
research participants?

THOUGHT QUESTIONS

1. What do you think? Is it OK for anthropologists to intervene in the lives of the people they study? Are there times when they should not? How might you determine
   when to intervene and when to refrain?

2. What have you learned from the stories presented here that might help you with
   your own research?

3. Do you believe that the anthropological interview has intrinsic value? That just listening to someone and recording their words can be useful to them in itself?

8

Where We Have Been and Where We Are Headed

Robbie Davis-Floyd and Melissa Cheyney

The childbirth practices of a nation are the reflections of that nation's beliefs concerning the integrity and dignity of life and influence that nation for good or evil, and ultimately the world itself.
— *Grantly Dick-Read,* Childbirth Without Fear, *1942*

This book has focused on knowledge systems—ways of knowing about birth—via ethnographic examinations of cultural birth knowledges and management systems. From them we have learned about some vast dissimilarities in cultural conceptualizations and treatments of birth: we saw that, on a scale ranging from the most to the least technocratic, births in Greece, Brazil, Mexico, and the US are highly medicalized, while hospital birth in Tanzania is based on an older, more industrial assembly-line approach, and in Mexico, Tanzania, and elsewhere homebirth and traditional midwives are rapidly disappearing. In these nations, as Dick-Read notes above, obstetric violence has developed in tandem with deep structural, social, and racial or ethnic inequalities, and the 1-2 Punch and the obstetric paradox are pervasive. On the least technocratic side of the global scale—the more humanistic/holistic side—we find Japan, the Netherlands, and New Zealand. In these countries, conceptions of women's bodies, births, and babies, combined with the care of skilled midwives, work together to create a style of maternity care more in keeping with the evidence on how best to support both birth physiology and women's autonomy. Structural inequities do exist in these countries, but on a lesser scale. The ethnographic chapters in this volume not only illustrate the truth of Dick-Read's words, but also show that autonomous midwives working in partnership and collaboration with obstetricians, and not below them in a hierarchy, is critical to healthy mothers, babies, and families everywhere.

The ethnographic chapters in this volume also introduced key concepts that help us to understand birth practices in their respective countries. Chap-

233

ter 2 on Mexico showed us the importance of the *hidden curriculum* in both midwifery and obstetrics—the often-unconscious modeling of behavior considered appropriate during *teaching moments*. Chapter 3 explored *choiceless choice*—the narrowing of birth options in Tanzania due to the development push for facility birth, despite the fact that those facilities often provide little or no care, with rampant obstetric violence, disrespect, and abuse both of women and of overworked and undervalued practitioners.

Chapter 4, comparing birth in Brazil and Japan, and Chapter 5 on Greece and New Zealand showed us the enormous importance of *place of birth* as a major factor that determines how women will be treated and how their births will proceed. We find it remarkable that in all of these countries, the same practitioners will treat birth differently according to place, using fewer or no interventions in community settings and more interventions in the hospital. This cross-cultural commonality demonstrates the power of the *technological imperative*—if a technology is available, it must and will be used—and also the obstetric paradox, in which intervening with the intention to keep birth safe/controllable often causes harm. We also find it remarkable that psychological outcomes differ so dramatically according to how women are treated—respectfully or not—yet mortality outcomes for low-risk pregnancies can be extremely similar for both high- and low-intervention births, as in Greece and New Zealand. This similarity highlights the safety of community settings for uncomplicated births and the relative uselessness of technological intervention to "improve safety"—except in the minority of medically complex cases where they are truly needed.

We saw that most facility births are treated with the same "cascade of interventions," when most of them may not require any, or need only a few. And we saw how that cascade is too often accompanied by disrespect and abuse. The postbirth interviews with women described in our chapters powerfully show that in most cases, any lasting psychological trauma stems not from experiencing the pain of labor—which is quickly forgotten once babies are in their mothers' arms—but from mistreatment by facility practitioners.

The chapter comparing birth in Greece and New Zealand introduced the notion of *cultural safety*—the idea that birth practices must honor the woman's cultural beliefs and values to the greatest possible extent. The authors showed the importance of *marginal spaces*; the Gamma wards facilitate autonomous midwifery practice in Greece, and in New Zealand, truly autonomous midwifery practice has been essential to the development of what may well be the most effective and highest-quality maternity care system in the world. These authors also demonstrate the *symbolic domination of modernity* that became so prevalent in Greece after World War II, and indeed around the world, showing how Greek women's quest to be viewed as "modern" led them quickly into appreciation for cesarean delivery. They both literally and metaphorically embody modernity as their babies are birthed via this surgical procedure.

Chapter 6 shows that the Netherlands and the US are not as different as they once were, as the technocratic approach to birth seeps ever more deeply

into the (still) primarily humanistic system of the Netherlands, and technocratic US practices slowly give way to more humanistic approaches. Midwives in both countries are caught in a conundrum—how to foster and
preserve normal physiologic birth in increasingly risk-oriented societies. Yet,
the fully integrated Dutch system does in general still stand out as optimal,
while the fragmented and disorganized US system, despite some significant
recent improvements, still has a long way to go. This chapter also provides an
apt description of the blurriness of the three paradigms—the technocratic,
humanistic, and holistic—showing how aspects of each are effectively
merged in *midwifery models of care*, which are designed to provide neither too
much too soon (TMTS) nor too little too late (TLTL), but rather what we call
RARTRW—the right amount at the right time in the right way.

Cumulatively, these chapters demonstrate the wave of change currently
rushing through the world's maternity care systems, as activists in many countries and international agencies, governments, and NGOs work to improve
them. The US system has already changed dramatically—episiotomy rates
have gone from 70% to 14% in recent decades (Friedman et al. 2015), care has
become much more humanized, and the CS rate has held steady at around
32% for a decade now, instead of increasing as it has done in many other countries. US midwives cumulatively have reached attendance at 11% of births, as
opposed to the 2% they attended in 1980. The midwifery models of care they
seek to practice have contributed greatly to the humanization of US birth, as
have the efforts of the thousands of birth activists and of the obstetricians who
pay attention to emerging evidence showing the benefits of support for normal
physiologic birth and for culturally matched care. Brazil's midwives attend
around 14% of births, and the humanization of birth movement there has been
driven in part by those Brazilian midwives who went to Japan to learn its gentle birth model. Tanzania is making slow progress toward increasing birth registration, so central to a child's chances for success in any country.

Even as Mexico's traditional midwives are dying without replacement or
being intentionally phased out of practice, its *parteras profesionales*—who have
only existed for a few decades—are improving the nation's maternity care.[1]
New Zealand's midwives, massively supported by women marching in the
streets, have resolved their pay equity issues with the government and, thus,
can remain sustainable for the future. And even in Greece—the country with
the highest CS rate in the world—the handful of doulas and the women who
give birth at home are holding open a cultural space for positive change, as
are the few remaining independent midwives of Japan, whose knowledge
transmission to the Brazilian midwives via the JICA program made their
priceless skill set transnational and preservable. The scientific evidence supporting the facilitation of normal physiologic birth continues to accumulate,
activists and agencies continue to disseminate it, and more and more practitioners and consumers are paying heed. Thus, the winds of hope for the reso-

---

[1] For the story of their beginnings, see "*La Partera Profesional*: Articulating Identity and Cultural
Space for a New Kind of Midwife in Mexico" (Davis-Floyd 2001b).

lution of the obstetric paradox—for the ends to both TMTS and TLTL and their replacement with RARTRW—are blowing across the maternity care systems of the world.

Chapter 7 took us inside the fieldwork experiences of contemporary, practicing anthropologists to give us a feel for conducting ethnographic research and, for our authors who are also practitioners, for "holding the space" for women to give birth in their own time and in their own ways.

Collectively, these chapters have served to affirm Gitti's insight that "[birth] is everywhere culturally marked and shaped" (Jordan 1993:3) and that science is but one of many ways of knowing about birth—nor is it necessarily neutral, as science too is culturally marked and shaped. The ways in which various societies apply birthing knowledges—what they see, what they miss, what they value, what they ignore—can guide us toward approaches to birth that include *cultural safety* while not doing harm. As we have seen, some cultural systems are marked by obstetric violence and cause a great deal of harm. Others see birth as a normal, heathy process and seek to respect the autonomy and dignity of all childbearing people. How can we find approaches to maternity care that do not destroy viable local cultural systems, but work collaboratively to provide the best possible care to mothers, babies, and families using the (often scarce) resources available?

Making birth better globally will entail an end to all types of obstetric violence and violations of women's rights during parturition. Educating both practitioners and women everywhere about their rights and about how to facilitate normal birth physiology will make an important contribution toward this end. The winds of hope discussed in this volume have generated a veritable hurricane in the form of the new human-rights-based *International Childbirth Initiative (ICI): 12 Steps to Safe and Respectful MotherBaby-Family Maternity Care* (2018), which includes as its Step 12 the entire 10 Steps of the well-established *Baby-Friendly Hospital Initiative* (BFHI)—these BFHI 10 Steps focus on skin-to-skin contact and the mother and baby staying together after birth to facilitate both bonding and breastfeeding. The ICI as a whole provides a template for optimal, humanistic, evidence-based maternity care that keeps the childbearer at the center of care during labor, birth, and the postpartum period. Please see www.ICIchildbirth.org for more information about the ICI and its ongoing implementations in facilities around the world. Researchers will be needed for years to come to study the implementation process and to document any barriers to it in various facilities around the world. For those students looking for a research topic, here is an ideal one!

In conclusion, we ask, what does the future hold for birth? Will we continue on our present path, until all births are heavily technologized and more and more babies are born by cesarean? (The current global cesarean rate is around 18%—nearly one in five.) Or will the pendulum swing in the opposite direction—toward the ICI 12 Steps, for example? Will they and/or other similar initiatives be implemented worldwide, leading to birthing systems that more effectively use midwives and physicians in support of the normal physiology of birth? Will we see a flourishing of structures that allow all people the full spectrum of choice in birth setting, provider type, and access to cultural safety?

That *full spectrum of choice* is what we, your editors, ceaselessly advocate for: from home to birth center to hospital, from midwives to obstetricians, from entirely organic births to scheduled cesareans. All parents should have the right to fully informed choice and to compassionate, respectful treatment during parturition as well as throughout life. We ask you, our readers, to reflect back on the ethnographic chapters in this volume, to contemplate the many ways births may be culturally constructed, and to give some thought to where we will go next. These are issues that many of you, who have long lives ahead—possibly to 100 years or more—will have to navigate as we make choices that affect the future of our planet and all the creatures that live upon it.

THOUGHT QUESTIONS

1. What are some of the theoretical constructs presented in the chapters in this book, and how can they be useful to you in other areas?

2. What are the primary lessons you have gleaned about cultural differences and similarities in ways of managing and knowing about birth? How might they influence your own birth choices?

SUGGESTED CLASS ACTIVITIES

1. Go to www.ICIchildbirth.org and read the ICI 12 Steps. How do these overlap with themes that have been discussed in this book? How might the ICI impact birth outcomes in low-resource countries? In high-resource ones? What would have to happen for a facility or practice to be able to implement these 12 Steps? What barriers to implementation might arise?

2. Read the important commentary in Kennedy et al. (2018), "Asking Different Questions: A Call to Action for Research to Improve the Quality of Care for Every Woman, Every Child" (https://doi.org/10.1111/birt.12361): What is the central argument in this piece? How might this call to action shift the focus of maternity care research globally? What impact might this way of thinking have on global birth outcomes?

3. Skim the Annotated Bibliography available at https://goo.gl/heqkX7, paying special attention to the categories that Robbie has devised. How do these sections reflect the growth of the field of reproductive anthropology and the anthropology of childbirth more specifically? How might this resource inform your future work in this field? What other categories might you wish to add to this Bibliography?

RECOMMENDED FILM

These Are My Hours is a documentary about Emily Graham's physical, emotional, and psychological experience of labor, birth, and postpartum, during which she is supported by husband, her midwife, and her mother. Available at www.vimeo.com/ondemand/thesearemyhours

References

A Pública. 2013, March 25. "Violência no parto vende cesárea, diz pesquisadora." http:// apublica.org/2013/03/violencia-parto-vende-cesarea-diz-pesquisadora-2/

AbouZahr, C., J. Cleland, F. Coullare, S. B. Macfarlane, et al. 2007. "The Way Forward." *The Lancet*, 370 (9601): 1791–1799, https://doi.org/10.1016/S0140-6736(07)61310-5.

Abraham-van der Mark, Eva. 1996. "Introduction to the Dutch System of Home Birth and Midwifery." In *Successful Home Birth and Midwifery*, edited by Eva Abraham-van der Mark, 1–18. Amsterdam: Het Spinhuis.

ACNM, MANA, NACPM. 2012. "Supporting Healthy and Normal Physiologic Childbirth: A Consensus Statement by the American College of Nurse-Midwives, Midwives Alliance of North America, and the National Association of Certified Professional Midwives." *Journal of Midwifery & Women's Health* 57 (5): 529–532.

ACOG. 2017. "Planned Home Birth." *Committee Opinion No. 697*. American College of Obstetricians and Gynecologists. https://www.acog.org/-/media/Committee-Opinions/Committee-on-Obstetric-Practice/co697.pdf?dmc=1&ts=20181207T1619246002

Adi, A. E., T. Abdu, A. Khan, M. H. Rashid, U. E. Ebri, A. Cockcroft, and N. Andersson. 2015. "Understanding Whose Births Get Registered: A Cross Sectional Study in Bauchi and Cross River States, Nigeria." *BMC Research Notes* 8 (1): 79.

AGOTA, Association of Gynecologists and Obstetricians of Tanzania. 2017. http:// www.agota.or.tz/index.php?option=com_content&view=article&id=6&Itemid=7

Aguiar, Janaina Marques de, and Ana Flávia Pires Lucas d'Oliveira. 2011. "Violência institucional em maternidades públicas sob a ótica das usuárias." *Interface* 15 (36): 79–91, http:// dx.doi.org/10.1590/S1414-32832010005000035.

Aitink, M., B. Goodarzi, and L. Marijn. 2014. *Beroepsprofiel verloskundige* (*Professional Profile of Midwives*). Utrecht, the Netherlands: The Royal Dutch Organisation of Midwives.

Allen, D. R. 2002. *Managing Motherhood, Managing Risk: Fertility and Danger in West Central Tanzania*. Ann Arbor: The University of Michigan Press.

Amaral, Marivaldo Cruz do. 2008. "Mulheres, imprensa e higiene: A medicalização do parto na Bahia (1910–1927)." *História, Ciências, Saúde* 15 (4): 927–944.

Amelink-Verburg, Marianne Paulina, and Simone Elisabeth Buitendijk. 2010. "Pregnancy and Labour in the Dutch Maternity Care System: What Is Normal? The Role Division between Midwives and Obstetricians." *Journal of Midwifery & Women's Health* 55 (3): 216–225.

Amo-Adjei, J., and S. K. Annim. 2015. "Socioeconomic Determinants of Birth Registration in Ghana." *BMC International Health and Human Rights* 15 (1): 14.

Anderson, David, Betty-Anne Daviss, and Ken Johnson. forthcoming. "What If 10% More Women Delivered at Home or in a Birth Center? The Economics and Politics of Out-of-Hospital Birth in the United States." In *Childbirth Models on the Human Rights Frontier: Speaking Truth to Power*, edited by Betty-Anne Daviss and Robbie Davis-Floyd. New York: Routledge.

Asociación Mexicana De Partería. 2014. "Foro de ética y valores." http://www.Asociacionmexicanadeparteria.Org/Wp-Content/Uploads/2015/06/Documento-Final-Amp-%C3%89tica-Y-Valores.Doc.Pdf

Austin, A., et al. 2014 "Approaches to Improve the Quality of Maternal and Newborn Health Care: An Overview of the Evidence." *Reproductive Health* 11 (2): S1.

Barbosa, Gisele Peixoto, Karen Giffin, Antonia Angulo-Tuesta, Andrea de Souza Gama, et al. 2003. "Parto cesáreo: quem o deseja? Em quais circunstâncias?" *Cadernos de Saúde Pública* 19 (6): 1611–1620.

Barclay et al. 2016. "Reconceptualising Risk: Perceptions of Risk in Rural and Remote Maternity Service Planning. *Midwifery* 38: 63–70, http://dx.doi.org/10.1016/j.midw.2016.04.007.

Barros, F. C., C. G. Victora, J. P. Vaughan, and S. R. A. Huttly. 1991. "Epidemic of Caesarean Sections in Brazil." *Lancet* 338 (8760): 167–169, https://doi.org/10.1016/0140-6736(91)90149-J.

Bedasa, H. 2016, November 7. "Advancing the Birth Registration System in Tanzania: Providing under-Five Children Their Right to Protection." *Unicef connect.* https://blogs.unicef.org/innovation/advancing-birth-registration-system-tanzania-providing-five-children-right-protection/

Beech, Beverley, and Jean Robinson. 1994. *Ultrasound? Unsound.* Springfield, MO: AIMS Press.

Beekman, J. P. 1836. *Verzameling van wetten, besluiten en reglementen, betrekkelijk de burgerlijke geneeskundige dienst in het Koninkrijk der Nederlanden.* Den Haag.

Béhague, Dominique P. 2002. "Beyond the Simple Economics of Cesarean Section Birthing: Women's Resistance to Social Inequality." *Culture, Medicine and Psychiatry* 26: 473–507.

Berry, N. 2006. "Kaqchikel Midwives, Homebirths and Emergency Obstetric Referrals: Contextualizing the Choice to Stay at Home" *Social Science & Medicine* 62: 1958–1969.

Berry, N. 2010. *Unsafe Motherhood: Maternal Mortality & Transformations in Kaqchikel Mayan Subjectivity in Post-War Guatemala.* New York: Berghahn Books.

Bhutta, Z. A., R. A. Salam, Z. S. Lassi, A. Austin, and A. Langer. 2014. "Approaches to Improve Quality of Care (QoC) for Women and Newborns: Conclusions, Evidence Gaps and Research Priorities." *Reproductive Health* 11 (Suppl. 2): S5.

Bonsel Gouke, J., et al. 2010. *Lijnen in de perinatale sterfte. Signalementstudie Zwangerschap en Geboorte 2010.* Rotterdam, the Netherlands: Erasmus MC. https://www.google.nl/url?sa=t&rct=j&q=&esrc=s&source=web&cd=1&cad=rja&uact=8&ved=0ahUKEwjyxrPrjdjSAhVFvRoKHYNBD8wQFggjMAA&url=https%3A%2F%2Frepub.eur.nl%2Fpub%2F23454%2FSignalementstudie%2520Zwangerschap%2520en%2520Geboorte%2520(JC%2520%252005-07-2010).pdf&usg=AFQjCNG0nxDcAV0rOxhKF-mO38rmyfwfaQ

Bourdieu, Pierre. 1972. *Outline of a Theory of Practice.* Cambridge: Cambridge University Press.

Bourdieu, Pierre. 2010 [1984]. *Distinction.* Cambridge, MA: Harvard University Press.

Bowser, Diana, and Kathleen Hill. 2010. *Exploring Evidence for Disrespect and Abuse in Facility-Based Childbirth.* USAID-TRAction Project, Harvard School of Public Health. http://www.mhtf.org/wp-content/uploads/sites/17/2013/02/Respectful_Care_at_Birth_9-20-101_Final.pdf

Brasil. 2016, April 8. "Governo quer reduzir cesarianas desencessárias." *Governo do Brasil.* http://www.brasil.gov.br/noticias/saude/2016/04/governo-federal-quer-reduzir-cesariana-desnecessaria

Brennan Center for Justice. 2006, November 28. *Citizens without Proof.* New York: NYU School of Law. https://www.brennancenter.org/analysis/citizens-without-proof

Brownell, M., N. D. Nickel, M. Chartier, J. E. Enns, et al. 2018. "An Unconditional Prenatal Income Supplement Reduces Population Inequities in Birth Outcomes." *Health Affairs* 37 (3): 447–455.

Bunkle, Phillida, 1988. *Second Opinion: The Politics of Women's Health in New Zealand.* Melbourne: Oxford University Press.

Calzada Martínez, H. 2009. *Veracruz, Primer estado que tipifica como delito la violencia obstétrica: IVM, al calor político.* http://www.alcalorpolitico.com/informacion/veracruz-primer-estado-que-tipifica-como-delito-la-violencia-obstetrica-ivm- 44406.html#.UhJekWSDR7M

Caraveli, Anna. 1986. "The Bitter Wounding: The Lament as Social Protest in Rural Greece." In *Gender and Power in Rural Greece*, edited by Jill Dubisch, 169–194. Princeton: Princeton University Press.

Carneiro, Rosamaria Giatti. 2015. *Cenas de parto e políticas do corpo*. Rio de Janeiro: Fiocruz. Print.

Carrillo, Ana María. 1999. "Nacimiento y muerte de una profesión. Las parteras tituladas en México." *Dynamis: Acta Hispanica ad Medicinae Scientiarumque Historiam Illustrandam* 19: 167–190.

Carvalho, I., A. S. Chacham, and P. Viana. 1998. "Traditional Birth Attendants and Their Practices in the State of Pernambuco Rural Area, Brazil, 1996." *International Journal of Gynecology & Obstetrics* 63 (Suppl. 1): S53–S60.

Cassidy, Tina. 2007. *Birth: The Surprising History of How We Are Born*. New York: Grove Press.

Castañeda Núñez, Imelda. 1988. "Síntesis histórica de la partera en el Valle de México." *Revista de Enfermería, Instituto Mexicano Del Seguro Social* (México) 1 (1): 35–39.

Caughey, A. B., A. G. Cahill, J. M. Guise, D. J. Rouse, and American College of Obstetricians and Gynecologists. 2014. "Safe Prevention of the Primary Cesarean Delivery." *American Journal of Obstetrics and Gynecology* 210 (3): 179–193.

CEDAW (Committee on the Elimination of Discrimination against Women). 2013. "Concluding Observations on the Seventh Periodic Report of Greece Adopted by the Committee at its Fifty Fourth Session (11 February–March 2013)." www2.ohchr.org/english/bodies/cedaw/docs/co/cedaw.c.grc.co.7.doc

Centrale Raad voor de Volksgezondheid. 1972. *Advies inzake de verstrekking van verloskundige hulp* (*Advice on Provision of Maternity Assistance*). Gravenhage, the Netherlands: Centrale Raad voor de Volksgezondheid.

Chacham, Alessandra Sampaio. 2012. "Médicos, mulheres e cesáreas: A construção do parto normal como um 'risco' e a medicalização do parto no Brasil." In *Diálogos em psicologia social*, edited by Ana Maria Jacó-Vilela and Leny Sato. Rio de Janeiro: Centro Edelstein de Pesquisas Sociais. http://books.scielo.org/id/vfgfh/27

Chang, Shiow-Ru, Kuang-Ho Chen, Ho-Hsiung Lin, Yu-Mei Y. Chao, and Yeur-Hur Lai. 2011. "Comparison of the Effects of Episiotomy and No Episiotomy on Pain, Urinary Incontinence, and Sexual Function 3 Months Postpartum: A Prospective Follow-up Study." *International Journal of Nursing Studies* 48 (4): 409–418.

Cheliotis, Leonidas. 2017. "Punitive Inclusion: The Political Economy of Irregular Migration on the Margins of Europe." *European Journal of Criminology* 14 (1): 1–22.

Cheng, Ching-Yu, Eileen R. Fowles, and Lorraine O. Walker. 2006. "Postpartum Maternal Health Care in the United States: A Critical Review." *The Journal of Perinatal Education* 15 (3): 34–42.

Chervenak, Frank A., et al. 2013. "Planned Home Birth in the United States and Professionalism: A Critical Assessment." *The Journal of Clinical Ethics* 24 (3): 184–191.

Cheyney, Melissa 2008. "Homebirth as Systems-Challenging Praxis: Knowledge, Power, and Intimacy in the Birthplace." *Qualitative Health Research*, 18 (2): 254–267.

Cheyney, Melissa. 2010. *Born at Home: The Biological, Cultural and Political Dimensions of Maternity Care in the United States*. Scarborough, Ontario: Nelson Education.

Cheyney, Melissa. 2011. "Reinscribing the Birthing Body: Homebirth as Ritual Performance." *Medical Anthropology Quarterly* 25 (4): 519–542.

Cheyney, M., M. Bovbjerg, L. Leeman, and S. Vedam. 2019. "Community versus Out-of-Hospital Birth: What's in a Name?" *Journal of Midwifery and Women's Health*.

Cheyney, Melissa, Paul Burcher, and Saraswathi Vedam. 2014. "A Crusade against Home Birth." *Birth* 41 (1): 1–4.

Cheyney, Melissa, Courtney Everson, and Paul Burcher. 2014. "Homebirth Transfers in the United States: Narratives of Risk, Fear and Mutual Accommodation." *Qualitative Health Research* 24 (4): 443–456, https://doi.org/10.1177/1049732314524028.

Cheyney, Melissa, et al. 2014a. "Development and Validation of a National Data Registry for Midwife-Led Births: The Midwives Alliance of North America Statistics Project 2.0 Dataset." *Journal of Midwifery & Women's Health* 59 (1): 8–16.

Cheyney, Melissa, et al. 2014b. "Outcomes of Care for 16,924 Planned Home Births in the United States: The Midwives Alliance of North America Statistics Project, 2004 to 2009." *Journal of Midwifery & Women's Health* 59 (1): 17–27.

Cheyney, Melissa, et al. 2015a. "Practitioner and Practice Characteristics of Certified Professional Midwives in the United States: Results of the 2011 North American Registry of Midwives Survey." *Journal of Midwifery & Women's Health* 60 (5): 534–545.

Cheyney, Melissa, et al. 2015b. "Home Birth Is Unsafe: AGAINST: Safe for Whom?" *BJOG: An International Journal of Obstetrics & Gynaecology* 122 (9): 1235–1235.

Clark, Helen. 1990 "Opening Address." *New Zealand College of Midwives Conference Proceedings.* Dunedin: New Zealand College of Midwives.

Clarke, A. 2012. *Born to a Changing World: Childbirth in Nineteenth-Century New Zealand.* Wellington, New Zealand: Bridget Williams Books.

Coimbra, Carlos E. A., et al. 2013. "The First National Survey of Indigenous People's Health and Nutrition in Brazil: Rationale, Methodology, and Overview of Results." *BMC Public Health* 13 (52), https://doi.org/10.1186/1471-2458-13-52.

Collins, John. 2015. *Revolt of the Saints: Memory and Redemption in the Twilight of Brazilian Racial Democracy.* Durham, NC: Duke University Press.

Colombotos, John, and Fakiolas, Nikos. 1993. "The Power of Organized Medicine in Greece." In *The Changing Medical Profession: An International Perspective*, edited by F. Hafferty and J. McKinlay, 138–149. New York: Oxford University Press.

Comissão Nacional de Incorporação de Tecnologias no SUS (CONITEC). 2016. *Diretrizes de atenção à gestante: A operação cesárea.* Brasília, Brasil: Comissão Nacional de Incorporação de Tecnologias no SUS. http://conitec.gov.br/images/Consultas/Relatorios/2016/Relatorio_Diretrizes_Cesariana_N179.pdf

Commissie Verloskunde CVZ. 2003, November. *Verloskundig Vademecum 2003.* Available at: http://www.knov.nl/fms/file/knov.nl/knov_downloads/769/file/Verloskundig%20Vademecum%202003.pdf?download_category=richtlijnen-praktijkkaarten (accessed March 15, 2017).

Congresso em Foco. 2013, July 11. "Íntegra da lei do ato médico," *UOL Notícias.* http://m.congressoemfoco.uol.com.br/noticias/a-integra-da-lei-do-ato-medico/

Cragin, Leslie, Lisa M. DeMaria, Lourdes Campero, and Dilys M. Walker. 2007. "Educating Skilled Birth Attendants in Mexico: Do the Curricula Meet International Confederation of Midwives Standards?" *Reproductive Health Matters* 15 (30): 50–60.

Craven, Christa. 2010. *Pushing for Midwives: Homebirth Mothers and the Reproductive Rights Movement.* Philadelphia: Temple University Press.

Crawford, Patricia. 1990. "The Construction and Experience of Maternity Care in Seventeenth-Century England." *Women as Mothers in Pre-industrial England*, edited by Valerie Fildes, 3–38. London: Routledge.

Cruz, Elaine Patricia. 2015, October 27. "Projeto consegue reduzir cesarianas em 42 hospitais do país." *Agência Brasil.* http://www.ebc.com.br/noticias/2015/10/em-seis-meses-projeto-consegue-reduzir-cesarianas-em-42-hospitais-do-pais

D'Gregorio, R. P. 2010. "Obstetric Violence: A New Legal Term Introduced in Venezuela." *International Journal of Gynecology & Obstetrics* 111: 201–202.

D'Oliveira, Ana Flávia Pires Lucas, Simone Grilo Diniz, and Lilia Blima Schraiber. 2002. "Violence against Women in Health-Care Institutions: An Emerging Problem." *The Lancet* 359 (9318): 1681–1685, https://doi.org/10.1016/S0140-6736(02)08592-6.

d'Orsi, Eleonora, et al. 2014. "Desigualdades sociais e satisfação das mulheres com o atendimento ao parto no Brasil: Estudo nacional de base hospitalar." *Cadernos de Saúde Pública* 30: S154–168, http://dx.doi.org/10.1590/0102-311X00087813.

Daellenbach, R. (1999). "The Paradox of Success and the Challenge of Change: Home Birth Associations of Aotearoa/New Zealand." PhD Thesis, University of Canterbury, Christchurch, New Zealand. https://ir.canterbury.ac.nz/handle/10092/6525

Daemers, Darie O. A., et al. 2017. "Factors Influencing the Clinical Decision-Making of Midwives: A Qualitative Study." *BMC Pregnancy and Childbirth* 17: 345, https://doi.org/10.1186/s12884-017-1511-5

Dalsgaard, Anne L. 2004. *Matters of Life and Longing: Female Sterilisation in Northeast Brazil.* Copenhagen: Museum Tusculanum Press, University of Copenhagen.

DaMatta, Roberto. 1984. *O que faz o Brasil, Brasil?* Rio de Janeiro: Rocco.

Damstra-Wijmenga, Sonja M. I. 1984. "Home Confinement: The Positive Results in Holland." *The Journal of the Royal College of General Practitioners* 34 (265): 425–430.

Danforth, E. J., et al. 2009. "Household Decision-making about Delivery in Health Facilities: Evidence from Tanzania." *Journal of Health, Population, and Nutrition* 27 (5): 696–703.

Davis, D., and K. Walker. 2010. "Case-Loading Midwifery in New Zealand: Making Space for Childbirth." *Midwifery* 26: 603–608.

Davis, D., et al. 2011. "Planned Place of Birth in New Zealand: Does It Affect Mode of Birth and Intervention Rates among Low-Risk Women?" *Birth* 38: 111–119, https://doi.org/10.1111/j.1523-536X.2010.00458.x.

Davis, K., A. Fisher, B. Kingsbury, and S. E. Merry. 2012. *Governance by Indicators: Global Power through Quantification and Rankings.* Oxford: Oxford University Press.

Davis-Floyd, Robbie E. 2001a. "The Technocratic, Humanistic, and Holistic Models of Birth." *International Journal of Gynecology & Obstetrics* 75 (Suppl. 1): S5–S23.

Davis-Floyd, Robbie E. 2001b. "*La Partera Profesional:* Articulating Identity and Cultural Space for a New Kind of Midwife in Mexico." *Medical Anthropology* 20 (2-3):185–243.

Davis-Floyd, Robbie. 2003 [1992]. *Birth as an American Rite of Passage.* 2nd ed. Berkeley: University of California Press.

Davis-Floyd, Robbie. 2018a. "The Technocratic, Humanistic, and Holistic Paradigms of Birth and Health Care." In *Ways of Knowing about Birth: Mothers, Midwives, Medicine, and Birth Activism.* Long Grove IL: Waveland Press.

Davis-Floyd, Robbie. 2018b. "The Rituals of Hospital Birth." In *Ways of Knowing about Birth: Mothers, Midwives, Medicine, and Birth Activism.* Long Grove IL: Waveland Press.

Davis-Floyd, Robbie. 2018c. "The Midwifery Model of Care: Anthropological Perspectives." In *Ways of Knowing about Birth: Mothers, Midwives, Medicine, and Birth Activism.* Long Grove IL: Waveland Press.

Davis-Floyd, Robbie. 2018d. "Creating the International MotherBaby Childbirth Initiative (IMBCI): Anthropologically Informed Activism." In *Ways of Knowing about Birth: Mothers, Midwives, Medicine, and Birth Activism.* Long Grove IL: Waveland Press.

Davis-Floyd, Robbie. 2018e. "American Midwifery: A Brief Anthropological Overview." In *Ways of Knowing about Birth: Mothers, Midwives, Medicine, and Birth* Activism. Long Grove IL: Waveland Press.

Davis-Floyd, Robbie. 2018f. "Daughter of Time: The Postmodern Midwife." In *Ways of Knowing about Birth: Mothers, Midwives, Medicine, and Birth Activism.* Long Grove IL: Waveland Press.

Davis-Floyd, Robbie. 2018g. "Intuition as Authoritative Knowledge in Midwifery and Homebirth." In *Ways of Knowing about Birth: Mothers, Midwives, Medicine, and Birth Activism.* Long Grove, IL: Waveland Press.

Davis-Floyd, Robbie. 2018h. "Homebirth Emergencies in the U.S. and Mexico: The Trouble with Transport." In *Ways of Knowing About Birth: Mothers, Midwives, Medicine and Birth Activism.* Long Grove, IL: Waveland Press.

Davis-Floyd, Robbie, and Melissa Cheyney. 2009. "Birth and the Big Bad Wolf: An Evolutionary Perspective." In *Childbirth across Cultures: Ideas and Practices of Pregnancy, Childbirth, and the Postpartum,* edited by Helaine Selin and Pamela K. Stone, 1–22. New York: Springer.

Davis-Floyd, Robbie, and Betty-Anne Daviss. forthcoming. *Birthing Models on the Human Rights Frontier: Speaking Truth to Power.* New York: Routledge.

Davis-Floyd, Robbie, and Eugenia Georges. 2018. "The Paradigm Shift of Holistic Obstetricians: Brazil's 'Good Guys and Girls.'" In *Ways of Knowing about Birth: Mothers, Midwives, Medicine, and Birth Activism.* Long Grove, IL: Waveland Press.

Davis-Floyd, Robbie, and Christine Barbara Johnson. 2018 [2005]. "Renegade Midwives: Assets or Liabilities?" In *Ways of Knowing About Birth: Mothers, Midwives, Medicine and Birth Activism.* Long Grove, IL: Waveland Press.

Davis-Floyd, Robbie, and Charles Laughlin. 2016. *The Power of Ritual.* Brisbane, Australia: Daily Grail Press.

Davis-Floyd, Robbie, et al. 2011. "The International MotherBaby Childbirth Initiative: Working to Create Optimal Maternity Care worldwide." *International Journal of Childbirth* 1 (3): 196–212.

Daviss, Betty-Anne. 1977. "Heeding Warnings from the Canary, the Whale, and the Inuit: A Framework for Analyzing Competing Types of Knowledge about Childbirth." In *Childbirth and Authoritative Knowledge: Cross-Cultural Perspectives*, edited by Robbie Davis-Floyd and Carolyn Sargent, 441–473. Berkeley: University of California Press.

de Jonge, Ank, et al. 2009. "Perinatal Mortality and Morbidity in a Nationwide Cohort of 529,688 Low-Risk Planned Home and Hospital Births." *BJOG: An International Journal of Obstetrics & Gynaecology* 116 (9): 1177–1184, https://doi.org/10.1111/j.1471-0528.2009.02175.x.

de Jonge, A., et al. 2015. "Perinatal Mortality and Morbidity up to 28 Days after Birth among 743,070 Low-Risk Planned Home and Hospital Births: A Cohort Study Based on Three Merged National Perinatal Databases." *BJOG An International Journal of Obstetrics & Gynaecology* 122 (5): 720–728.

De Vries, Cecelia Benoit, Edwin Van Teijlingen, and Sirpa Wrede (eds.). 2001. *Birth by Design: Pregnancy, Maternity Care, and Midwifery in North America and Europe*. London: Routledge.

De Vries, Raymond. 2004. *A Pleasing Birth*. Amsterdam: Amsterdam University Press.

De Vries, Raymond, et al. 2009. "The Dutch Obstetrical System." In *Birth Models that Work*, edited by Robbie Davis-Floyd, Lesley Barclay, Jan Tritten, and Betty-Anne Daviss. Berkeley: University of California Press.

de Vrieze, J. 2018. "Maakt de doorzettingsmacht het verschil als partijen er niet uitkomen?" ("Does Persistence Make the Difference When Parties Involved Cannot Reach Agreement?"). *Nederlands Tijdschrift Voor Geneeskunde* 162: C3774–C3776.

Declercq, Eugene R., et al. 2007. "Listening to Mothers II: Report of the Second National US Survey of Women's Childbearing Experiences." *The Journal of Perinatal Education* 16 (4): 9–14.

DelVecchio Good, Mary Jo, 1995. "Cultural Studies of Biomedicine: An Agenda for Research." *Social Science & Medicine* 41 (4): 461–473.

Diário Catarinense. 2017, January 19. "Lei contra a violência obstétrica é sancionada em Santa Catarina." *Diário Catarinense*. http://dc.clicrbs.com.br/sc/estilo-de-vida/noticia/2017/01/lei-contra-a-violencia-obstetrica-e-sancionada-em-santa-catarina-9461034.html

Dias, Marcos Augusto Bastos, and Suely Ferreira Deslandes. 2004. "Cesarean Sections: Risk Perception and Indication by Attending Obstetricians in a Public Maternity Hospital in Rio de Janeiro." *Cadernos de Saúde Pública* 20 (1): 109–116.

Diniz, Carmen Simone Grilo. 2005. "Humanização da assistência ao parto no Brasil: os muitos sentidos de um movimento." *Ciência & Saúde Coletiva* 10 (3): 627–37, http://dx.doi.org/10.1590/S1413-81232005000300019.

Diniz, Carmen Simone Grilo. 2009. "Gênero, saúde materna e o paradoxo perinatal." *Revista Brasileira de Crescimento e Desenvolvimento Humano* 19 (2): 313–26. https://ediscplinas.usp.br/pluginfile.php/204921/mod_resource/content/1/genero_saude_materna.pdf

Diniz, Carmen Simone Grilo, and Alessandra S. Chacham. 2004. "'The Cut Above' and 'the Cut Below': the Abuse of Caesareans and Episiotomy in São Paulo, Brazil." *Reproductive Health Matters* 12 (23): 100–110.

Diniz, Carmen Simone Grilo, and A. F. d'Oliveira. 1998. "Gender Violence and Reproductive Health." *International Journal of Gynecology and Obstetrics* 63 (Suppl. 1): S33–S42.

Diniz, Carmen Simone Grilo, et al. 2015. "Abuse and Disrespect in Childbirth Care as a Public Health Issue in Brazil: Origins, Definitions, Impacts on Maternal Health, and Proposals for Its Prevention." *Journal of Human Growth and Development* 25 (3): 377–382.

Diniz, Carmen Simone Grilo, et al. 2016. "A vagina-escola: seminário interdisciplinar sobre violência contra a mulher no ensino das profissões de saúde." *Interface* 20 (56): 253–59, http://dx.doi.org/10.1590/1807-57622015.0736.

DiVenere, Lucia. 2012. "Lay Midwives and the ObGyn: Is Collaboration Risky?" *OBG Management* 24 (5): 21.

Dixon, L., G. Preleszky, K. Guilliand, S. Miller, and J. Anderson. 2014. "Place of Birth and Outcomes for a Cohort of Low Risk Women in New Zealand: A Comparison with the Birthplace England." *New Zealand College of Midwives Journal* 50: 11–23

Dixon, Lydia Zacher. 2015. "Delivering Health: In Search of an Appropriate Model for Institutionalized Midwifery in Mexico." Doctoral Dissertation, University of California, Irvine.

Dixon, Lydia, Mounia El Kotni, and Veronica Miranda. forthcoming. "A Tale of Three Midwives: Inconsistent Policies and the Marginalization of Midwifery in Mexico." *Journal of Latin American and Caribbean Anthropology.*

Domingues, Rosa Maria Soares Madeira, et al. 2014. "Processo de decisão pelo tipo de parto no Brasil: da preferência inicial das mulheres à via de parto final." *Cadernos de Saúde Pública* 30 (Suppl.): S101–116, http://dx.doi.org/10.1590/0102-311X00105113.

Donley, Joan. 1986. *Save the Midwife.* Auckland, New Zealand: New Women's Press.

Dow, U. 1998. "Birth Registration: The First Right." *The Progress of Nations.* New York: Unicef.

Downe, Soo, Kenny Finlayson, and Anita Fleming. 2010. "Creating a Collaborative Culture in Maternity Care." *Journal of Midwifery & Women's Health* 55 (3): 250–254.

Drenth, P. 1998. *1898/1998; 100 jaar vroedvrouwen verenigd (1898–1998: 100 years of Midwives United).* Bilthoven, Nederlandse: Vereniging van Verloskundigen.

Dubisch, Jill. 1991. "Gender, Kinship and Religion: 'Reconstructing' the Anthropology of Greece." In *Contested Identities: Gender and Kinship in Modern Greece,* edited by P. Loizos and E. Papataxiarchis, 29–46. Princeton, NJ: Princeton University Press.

Durie, M. (1998). *Whaiora: Māori Health Development.* 2nd ed. Auckland, New Zealand: Oxford University Press.

Edmonds, Alexander. 2010. *Pretty Modern: Beauty, Sex, and Plastic Surgery in Brazil.* Durham and London: Duke University Press. Print.

Ehrenriech, Barbara, and Deirdre English. 2010. *Witches, Midwives, and Nurses: A History of Women Healer.* 2nd ed. New York: The Feminist Press at CUNY.

ekathimerini.com. 2015, December 13. "Six in Ten Births in Greece Are via C-section." http://www.ekathimerini.com/204289/article/ekathimerini/news/six-in-10-births-in-greece-are-via-c-section

El Kotni, Mounia. 2018. "Regulating Traditional Mexican Midwifery: Practices of Control, Strategies of Resistance." *Medical Anthropology,* online ahead of print https://www.tandfonline.com/doi/abs/10.1080/01459740.2018.1539974

ELSTAT. 2017. "Single–Multiple Births by Status of the Newborn (Alive–Dead) 1956–2017." http://www.statistics.gr/en/statistics/-/publication/SPO03/2017

Epoo, Brenda, Kim Moorhouse, Maggie Tayara, Jennie Stonier, and Betty Anne-Daviss. forthcoming. "'To Bring Back Birth Is to Bring Back Life': The Nunavik Story." In *Childbirth Models on the Human Rights Frontier: Speaking Truth to Power,* edited by Betty-Anne Daviss and Robbie Davis-Floyd. New York: Routledge.

Epstein, Randi Hutter. 2010. *Get Me Out: A History of Childbirth from the Garden of Eden to the Sperm Bank.* New York: W. W. Norton.

Eskes, Martine, Dick Van Alten, and Pieter. E. Treffers. 1993. "The Wormerveer Study: Perinatal Mortality and Non-Optimal Management in a Practice of Independent Midwives." *European Journal of Obstetrics & Gynecology and Reproductive Biology* 51 (2): 91–95.

Euro-Peristat Project, with SCPE, EUROCAT, EURONEOSTAT. 2008. *European Perinatal Health Report.* http://www.europeristat.com/images/doc/EPHR/european-perinatal-health-report.pdf

Euro-Peristat Project. 2013. *Health and Care of Pregnant Women and Babies in Europe in 2010.* http://www.europeristat.com/reports/european-perinatal-health-report-2010.html

Evers, Annemieke C., et al. 2010. "Perinatal Mortality and Severe Morbidity in Low and High Risk Term Pregnancies in the Netherlands: Prospective Cohort Study." *BMJ* 341: c5639.

Faneite, J., A. Feo, and J. Toro Merlo. 2012. "Grado de conocimiento de violencia obstétrica por el personal de salud." *Revista de Obstetricia y Ginecología de Venezuela* 72: 4–12.

Fannin, M. (2003). "Domesticating Birth in the Hospital: 'Family-Centered' Birth and the Emergence of 'Homelike' Birthing Rooms." *Antipode* 35: 513–535, https://doi.org/10.1111/1467-8330.00337.

Farmer, P. E., B. Nizeye, S. Stulac, and S. Keshavjee. 2006. "Structural Violence and Clinical Medicine." *PLoS Medicine* 3 (10): 1686–1691.

Faubion, James. 1991. *Modern Greek Lessons: A Primer in Historical Constructivism.* Princeton: Princeton University Press.

Faúndes, Aníbal, and José Guilherme Cecatti. 1991. "A operação cesárea no Brasil: incidência, tendências, causas, conseqüências e propostas de ação." *Cadernos de Saúde Pública* 7 (2): 150–173, http://dx.doi.org/10.1590/S0102-311X1991000200003.

Faúndes, Anibal, Karla Simônia de Pádua, Maria Duarte Osis, José Guilherme Cecatti, and Maria Helena de Sousa. 2004. "Brazilian women and physicians' viewpoints on their preferred route of delivery." *Revista de Saúde Pública* 38 (4): 488–494.

FCI, Family Care International. 2007. *Safe Motherhood: A Review.* New York: Family Care International. http://www.familycareintl.org/UserFiles/File/SM%20A%20Review_%20Full_Report_FINAL.pdf

Finkler, K. 2004. "Biomedicine Globalized and Localized: Western Medical Practices in an Outpatient Clinic of a Mexican Hospital." *Social Science & Medicine* 59: 2037–2051

Fleischer, Soraya. 2007. "Parteiras, buchudas e aperreios: uma etnografia do atendimento obstétrico não oficial na cidade de Melgaço, Pará." Doctoral dissertation, Universidade Federal do Rio Grande do Sul. http://www.lume.ufrgs.br/handle/10183/10246

Fraser, Gertrude Jacinta. 2009. *African American Midwifery in the South: Dialogues of Birth, Race, and Memory.* Cambridge: Harvard University Press.

Freedman, L. P., and M. E. Kruk. 2014. "Disrespect and Abuse of Women in Childbirth: Challenging the Global Quality and Accountability Agendas." *The Lancet* 384.

Freyermuth Enciso, M. G., and M. Luna Contreras. 2014. "Muerte materna y muertes evitables en exceso: Propuesta metodológica para evaluar la política pública en salud." *Revista Internacional de Estadística y Geografía* 5 (3): 44–61.

Friedman, A. M., C. V. Ananth, E. Prendergast, M. E. D'alton, and J. D. Wright. 2015. "Variation in and Factors Associated with Use of Episiotomy." *Jama* 313 (2): 197–199.

Fundação Perseu Abramo. 2013, March 25. "Violência no parto: na hora de fazer não gritou." https://fpabramo.org.br/2013/03/25/violencia-no-parto-na-hora-de-fazer-nao-gritou/

Gabrysch, S., and O. M. R. Campbell. 2009. "Still Too Far to Walk: Literature Review of the Determinants of Delivery Service Use." *BMC Pregnancy and Childbirth* 9: 34.

Gaines, Atwood D., and Robbie Davis-Floyd. 2004. "Biomedicine." In *Encyclopedia of Medical Anthropology* (pp. 95–109). New York: Springer.

Galtung, Johan. 1969. "Violence, Peace, and Peace Research." *Journal of Peace Research* 6 (3): 167–191.

Gama, Silvana Granado Nogueira da, et al. 2016. "Labor and Birth Care by Nurse with Midwifery Skills in Brazil." *Reproductive Health* 13 (Suppl. 3), https://doi.org/10.1186/s12978-016-0236-7.

García Vázquez, Iskra, Sandra E. Moncayo Cuagliotti, and Benjamín Sánchez Trocino. 2012. "El parto en México, reflexiones para su atención integral." *Ide@s CONCYTEG* 7 (84): 811–844.

Gaskin, Ina May. 2002. *Spiritual Midwifery.* 4th ed. Summertown TN: The Book Publishing Company.

Georges, Eugenia, and Robbie Davis-Floyd. 2017. "New Health Socialities in Brazil: The Movement to 'Humanize' Childbirth." In *Vital Signs: Medical Anthropology for the 21st Century*, edited by Lenore Manderson, Anita Hardon, and Elisabeth Cartwright. New York: Routledge.

Gibbons L., et al. 2010. "The Global Numbers and Costs of Additionally Needed and Unnecessary Caesarean Sections Performed per Year: Overuse as a Barrier to Universal Coverage." *World Health Report (2010): Background paper 30.* http://www.who.int/healthsystems/topics/financing/healthreport/30C-sectioncosts.pdf

Ginsburg, Faye, and Rayna Rapp. 1995. "Introduction: Conceiving the New World Order." In *Conceiving the New World Order: The Global Politics of Reproduction*, edited by Faye Ginsburg and Rayna Rapp, 1–17. Berkeley: University of California Press.

Goer, Henci. 1999. *The Thinking Woman's Guide to a Better Birth.* New York: Penguin.

Gomes, Annatália Meneses de Amorim, Marilyn K. Nations, and Madel Therezinha Luz. 2008. "Pisada como pano de chão: Experiência de violência hospitalar no Nordeste brasileiro." *Saúde e Sociedade* 17 (1): 61–72, http://dx.doi.org/10.1590/S0104-12902008000100006.

Goodarzi, B., et al. 2018. "Risk and the Politics of Boundary Work: Preserving Autonomous Midwifery in the Netherlands. *Health Risk and Society*, https://doi.org/10.1080/13698575.2018.1558182.

Green, Maia. 2000. "Public Reform and the Privatization of Property: Some Institutional Determinants of Health Seeking Behavior in Southern Tanzania." *Culture, Medicine, and Psychiatry* 24: 403–430.

Grigg, C., and S. Tracy. 2013. "New Zealand's Unique Maternity System." *Women and Birth* 26 (1) e59-64, https://doi.org/10.1016/j.wombi.2012.09.006.

Grigg, C., S. Tracy, R. Daellenbach, M. Kensington, and V. Schmied. 2014. "An Exploration of Influences on Women's Birthplace Decision-Making in New Zealand: A Mixed Methods Prospective Cohort within the Evaluating Maternity Units Study." *BMC Pregnancy and Childbirth* 14: 210. https://bmcpregnancychildbirth.biomedcentral.com/articles/10.1186/1471-2393-14-210

Grigg, C., S. Tracy, M. Tracy, R. Daellenbach, M. Kensington, A. Monk, and V. Schmied. 2017. "Evaluating Maternity Units: A Prospective Cohort Study of Freestanding Midwife-Led Primary Maternity Units in New Zealand—Clinical Outcomes." *BMJ Open* 7: e016288. https://bmjopen.bmj.com/content/bmjopen/7/8/e016288.full.pdf

Grigg, C., S. Tracy, V. Schmied, R. Daellenbach, and M. Kensington. 2015. "Women's Birthplace Decision-Making, the Role of Confidence: Part of the Evaluating Maternity Units Study, New Zealand." *Midwifery 31* (6): 597–605, https://doi.org/10.1016/j.midw.2015.02.00.

Grünebaum, Amos, et al. 2015. "Home Birth Is Unsafe: FOR: The Safety of Planned Homebirths: A Clinical Fiction." *BJOG: An International Journal of Obstetrics & Gynaecology* 122 (9): 1235–1235.

Guilliland, Karen. 2018. "Working to Keep a Great System Great: Our Struggle For Sustainability." Unpublished MS.

Guilliland, Karen, and Sally Pairman. 1995. *The Midwifery Partnership: A Model for Practice*. Monograph Series 95/1. Department of Nursing and Midwifery, Victoria University, Wellington, New Zealand.

Guilliland, Karen, and Sally Pairman. 2010. *Women's Business: The Story of the New Zealand College of Midwives 1986–2010*. Christchurch, New Zealand: NZ College of Midwives.

Gupta, J. K., G. J. Hofmeyr, and M. Shehmar. 2012. "Position for Women during Second Stage of Labour." *Cochrane Database System Review* 16 (5).

Hafferty, Frederic W. 1998. "Beyond Curriculum Reform: Confronting Medicine's Hidden Curriculum." *Academic Medicine* 73 (4): 403–407.

Hall, W. A., J. Tomkinson, and M. C. Klein. 2012. "'Canadian Care Providers' and Pregnant Women's Approaches to Managing Birth: Minimizing Risk while Maximizing Integrity." *Qualitative Health Research* 22 (5): 575–586, 10.1177/1049732311424292.

Hansen, D. A., R. J. Measom, and B. Scott. 2017. "Epidural Analgesia in Hispanic Parturients: A Single-Blinded Prospective Cohort Study on the Effects of an Educational Intervention on Epidural Analgesia Utilization." *Journal of Obstetric Anaesthesia and Critical Care* 7 (2): 90.

Harrington, J. 2016. "Refusal of Birth Certificates to Children of Undocumented Parents in Texas." *Texas Hispanic Journal of Law and Policy* 22 (41): 41–55.

Hay, Carla. 2002. "Childbirth in America: A Historical Perspective," In *Who's Having This Baby? Perspectives on Birthing*, edited by Helen M. Sterk, et al., 9–42. Lansing: Michigan State University Press.

Healy S., E. Humphreys, C. Kennedy. 2016. "Midwives' and Obstetricians' Perceptions of Risk and Its Impact on Clinical Practice and Decision-Making in Labour: An Integrative Review." *Women and Birth* 29: 107–116. https://www.sciencedirect.com/science/article/pii/S1871519215002917?via%3Dihub

Hermus, M. A. A., et al. 2015. "The Dutch Birth Centre Study: Study Design of a Programmatic Evaluation of the Effect of Birth Centre Care in the Netherlands." *BMC Pregnancy and Childbirth* 15 (1): 148.

Hermus, M. A. A., et al. 2017. "Defining and Describing Birth Centres in the Netherlands—A Component Study of the Dutch Birth Centre Study." *BMC Pregnancy and Childbirth* 17 (1): 210.

Hitzert M., et al. 2017. "Cost-Effectiveness of Planned Birth in a Birth Centre Compared with Alternative Planned Places of Birth: Results of the Dutch Birth Centre Study." *BMJ Open* 7: e016960, doi: 10.1136/bmjopen-2017-016960.

Hodnett, Ellen D. 2001. "Caregiver Support for Women During Childbirth." *Cochrane Library,* Issue 4. *Cochrane Database Syst. Rev.* CD000199.

Hodnette, Ellen D. 2002. "Pain and Women's Satisfaction with the Experience of Childbirth: A Systematic Review." *American Journal of Obstetrics and Gynecology* 186 (5): S160–S172.

Hofmeyr, G., J. P. Vogel, A. Cuthbert, and M. Singata. 2017. "Fundal Pressure during the Second Stage of Labour." *Cochrane Database of Syst. Rev.* (CD006067).

Hollander, M. H., and J. van Dillen. 2017. "Zorg op maar in de verloskunde, verklaard vanuit de geschiedenis." *Nederlands Tijdschrift voor Obstetrie en Gynaecologie* (130): 327–329.

Holmer, Albert, et al. 1956. *Leerboek der verloskunde,* Amsterdam,the Netherlands: van Holkema & Warendorf.

Holmes, S. M. 2013. *Fresh Fruit, Broken Bodies: Migrant Farmworkers in the United States.* Berkeley: University of California Press.

Homer, C. S, et al. 2014. "The Projected Effect of Scaling up Midwifery." *The Lancet* 384 (9948): 1146–1157, http://dx.doi.org/10.1016/S0140-6736(14)60790-X.

Hopkins, Kristine. 2000. "Are Brazilian Women Really Choosing to Deliver by Cesarean?" *Social Science & Medicine* 51: 725–740.

Hospital Intelligence Agency. 2015. "Number of Births per Annum by Hospitals and Clinics." http://hospia.jp/wp/archives/255

Ichikawa, Kimie. 2017a. "Hokkaido niokeru mukaijo-bunben no genjo" ("The Present Situations Concerning Unassisted Childbirth in Hokkaido"). *Boseieisei (Japanese Journal of Maternal Health)* 57 (4): 760–768.

Ichikawa, Kimie. 2017b. "Gendai no shisetsuka sareta shussan kannkyouka niokeru puraibeto shussan no tokuchou: puraibeto shussan taikensha no intabyu o motoni" ("Characteristics of Private Birth in Contemporary Japan : An Analysis Based on Interviews of Women with Private Birth Experience"). *Nara Joshidaigaku Shakaigaku Ronshu (Nara women's University Sociological Studies)* 24: 20–36. http://nwudir.lib.nara-wu.ac.jp/dspace/handle/10935/4436

Instituto Brasileiro de Geografia e Estatística (IBGE). n.d. "2010 Population Census: Results of the Universe—Municipal Social Indicators: Salvador, Bahia." *Instituto Brasileiro de Geografia e Estatística.* http://cidades.ibge.gov.br/xtras/temas.php?lang=_EN&codmun=292740&idtema= 79&search=bahia|salvador|2010-population-census:-results-of-the-universe-municipal-social-indicators

Instituto de Pesquisa Econômica Aplicada (IPEA). 2017. "Retrato das desigualdades de gênero e raça—1995 a 2015." http://www.ipea.gov.br/portal/images/stories/PDFs/170306_ retrato_das_desigualdades_de_genero_raca.pdf

Instituto Nacional de Estadística y Geografia (INEGI) 2015. *Encuesta nacional de la dinámica demográfica 2014.* http://www.inegi.org.mx/saladeprensa/boletines/2015/especiales/ especiales2015_07_1.pdf

International Childbirth Initiative (ICI): 12 Steps to Safe and Respectful MotherBaby-Family Maternity Care. 2018, September. https://www.internationalchildbirth.com/uploads/8/0/2/6/ 8026178/ici_full_color.pdf

International Federation of Gynecology and Obstetrics (FIGO) et al. 2014. "Mother-baby friendly birthing facilities." *International Journal of Gynecology and Obstetrics,* http://dx.doi.org/10.1016/j.jigo.2014.10.013.

Ivry, Tsipy. 2010. *Embodying Culture: Pregnancy in Japan and Israel.* New Brunswick, NJ: Rutgers University Press.

Ivry, Tsipy. n.d. "Unsettling Childbirth: Time, Space, and Gratitude in Japanese Women's Experiences of Giving Birth during the Disasters of 11 March 2011." Unpublished MS.

Japan Medical Journal. 2017, August 24. "Rate of Painless Delivery 6.1%—Research by Japan Association of Obstetricians and Gynecologists" (in Japanese).

Jewkes, R., and K. Wood. 1998. "Competing Discourses of Vital Registration and Personhood: Perspectives from Rural South Africa." *Social Science & Medicine* 46 (8): 1043–1056.

Jones, Ricardo. 2009. "Teamwork: An Obstetrician, a Midwife, and a Doula." In *Birth Models That Work*, edited by Robbie Davis-Floyd, Lesley Barclay, Betty-Anne Daviss, and Jan Tritten, 271–304. Berkeley: University of California Press.

Jordan, Brigitte. 1993. *Birth in Four Cultures: A Cross-Cultural Investigation of Childbirth in Yucatan, Sweden, Holland and the United States.* Long Grove, IL: Waveland Press.

Jordan, Brigitte. 1997. "Authoritative Knowledge and Its Construction." In *Childbirth and Authoritative Knowledge: Cross-Cultural Perspectives*, edited by Robbie E. Davis-Floyd and Carolyn Sargent, 55–79. Berkeley: University of California Press.

Joseph, Jennie. forthcoming. "'There's Something Wrong Here': African American Women and Their Babies Are at Greatest Risk in the U.S.A." In *Childbirth Models on the Human Rights Frontier: Speaking Truth to Power*, edited by Betty-Anne Daviss and Robbie Davis-Floyd. New York: Routledge.

Jusdanis, Gregory. 2001. *Belated Modernity and Aesthetic Culture: Inventing National Literature.* Minneapolis and Oxford: University of Minneapolis Press.

Kalyvas, Stathis N. 2015. *Modern Greece: What Everyone Needs to Know.* New York: Oxford University Press.

Karaçam, Z., and K. Eroğlu. 2003. "Effects of Episiotomy on Bonding and Mothers' Health." *Journal of Advanced Nursing* 13 (4): 384–394.

Kassebaum, Nicholas J., et al. 2016. "Global, Regional, and National Levels of Maternal Mortality, 1990–2015: A Systematic Analysis for the Global Burden of Disease Study 2015." *The Lancet* 388 (10053): 1775.

Kedgley, S. 1996. *Mum's the Word: The Untold Story of Motherhood in New Zealand.* Auckland, New Zealand: Random House.

Kennedy, H. P., et al. 2018. "Asking Different Questions: A Call to Action for Research to Improve the Quality of Care for Every Woman, Every Child." *Birth* 45 (3): 222–231, https://doi.org/10.1111/birt.12361.

Kenney, Christine. 2011. "Midwives, Women and Their Families: A Māori Gaze." *AlterNative: An International Journal of Indigenous Peoples* 7 (2): 123–137.

King, Tekoa L., Russell K. Laros, and Julian T. Parer. 2012. "Interprofessional Collaborative Practice in Obstetrics and Midwifery." *Obstetrics and Gynecology Clinics of North America* 39 (3): 411–422.

Klinkert, J. J. 1980. *Verloskundigen en artsen: verleden en heden van enkele professionele beroepen in de gezondheidszorg* (*Midwives and Doctors: The Past and the Present of Several Professions in Healthcare*). Amsterdam, the Netherlands: Vrije Universiteit van Amsterdam.

Klomp Trudy. 2015. *Management of Labour Pain in Midwifery Care.* Dissertation, Radboud Universiteit Nijmegen. http://repository.ubn.ru.nl/bitstream/handle/2066/139520/139520.pdf?sequence=1

Kloosterman. G. J. 1973. *De voortplanting van de mens leerboek voor Obstetrie en gynaecologie.* Bussum, the Netherlands: Uitgeverijmaatschappij Centen.

Knaul, Felicia, Héctor Arreola-Ornelas, Oscar Méndez, and Alejandra Martínez. 2005. "Justicia financiera y gastos catastróficos en salud: Impacto del seguro popular de salud en México." *Salud Pública de México* 47 (1): 54–65.

KNOV & NVOG. 2015. *Leidraad "verloskundige zorg buiten de richtlijnen."* Versie 1.0. Utrecht. Available at: http://www.knov.nl/fms/file/knov.nl/knov_downloads/2414/file/KNOV_en_NVOG_Leidraad_Verloskundige_zorg_buiten_richtlijnen_ek.pdf?download_category=overig (accessed February 8, 2017).

Kothari, C. L., C. Romph, T. Bautista, and D. Lenz. 2017. "Perinatal Periods of Risk Analysis: Disentangling Race and Socioeconomic Status to Inform a Black Infant Mortality Community Action Initiative." *Maternal and Child Health Journal* 21 (1): 49–58.

Kruk, M. E., et al. 2014. "Disrespectful and Abusive Treatment during Facility Delivery in Tanzania: A Facility and Community Survey." *Health Policy and Planning* 33 (1): e26–e33.

Langwick, Stacey A. 2011. *Bodies, Politics, and African Healing: The Matter of Maladies in Tanzania.* Bloomington: Indiana University Press.

Langwick, Stacey A. 2012. "The Choreography of Global Subjection: The Traditional Birth Attendant in Contemporary Configurations of Global Health." In *Medicine, Mobility, and*

Power in Global Africa: Transnational Health and Healing, edited by H. J. Dilger, A. Kane, and S. A. Langwick. Bloomington: Indiana University Press.

Lansky, Sônia, et al. 2014. "Birth in Brazil Survey: Neonatal Mortality, Pregnancy and Childbirth Quality of Care." *Cadernos de Saúde Pública* 30 (Suppl. 1): S192–S207, http://dx.doi.org/10.1590/0102-311X00133213.

Lappen, Justin R., and Dana R. Gossett. 2010. "Changes in Episiotomy Practice: Evidence-Based Medicine in Action." *Expert Review of Obstetrics & Gynecology* 5 (3): 301–309.

Laschinger, H. K. S. 2012. "Conditions for Work Effectiveness: Questionnaire I and II." Western University, Canada. https://www.uwo.ca/fhs/hkl/cweq.html

Latour, B. 2010. "Networks, Societies, Spheres: Reflections of an Actor-network Theorist." Keynote speech at the International Seminar on Network Theory: Network Multidimensionality in the Digital Age. Los Angeles, California, February 19.

Lauren, Michaela, Konstantine Petrogiannis, Eleni Valassi-Adam, and Tjeerd Tymstra. 2001. "Prenatal Diagnosis in Lay Press and Professional Journals in Finland, Greece and the Netherlands." In *Before Birth: Understanding Prenatal Screening*, edited by Elizabeth Ettorre, 17–37. Hampshire: Ashgate Publishing.

Lawrence, Christopher M. 2007. *Blood and Oranges: Immigrant Labor and European Markets in Rural Greece.* New York and Oxford: Berghahn Books.

Leal, Maria do Carmo, et al. 2012. "Birth in Brazil: National Survey into Labour and Birth." *Reproductive Health Matters* 9 (15): 1–8, https://doi.org/10.1186/1742-4755-9-15.

Leal, Maria do Carmo, et al. 2014. "Intervenções obstétricas durante o trabalho de parto e parto em mulheres brasileiras de risco habitual." *Cadernos de Saúde Pública* 30 (Suppl. 1): S17–S32, doi:10.1590/0102-311X00151513.

Leal, Maria do Carmo, et al. 2016. "Prevalence and Risk Factors Related to Preterm Birth in Brazil." *Reproductive Health* 13 (Suppl. 3): 163–74, https://doi.org/10.1186/s12978-016-0230-0.

Leis Municipais. 2012, December 5. "Lei no 7851, de 25 de maio de 2010." *Secretaria de Saúde do Estado da Bahia.* http://www.saude.ba.gov.br/novoportal/images/stories/PDF/Lei% 20Ordinaria%207851%202010%20de%20Salvador%20BA.pdf

León, Nicolás. 1910. *La obstetricia en México.* Mexico: Mexico, Tip. de la vda. de F. Diaz de Leon, sucrs.

Lindenbaum, Shirley, and Margaret Lock. 1993. *Knowledge, Power and Practice: The Anthropology of Medicine and Everyday Life.* Berkeley and Los Angeles: University of California Press.

Lock, Margaret. 2001. "The Tempering of Medical Anthropology: Troubling Natural Categories." *Medical Anthropology Quarterly* 15: 478–492.

Lock, Margaret. 2002. *Twice Dead: Organ Transplants and the Reinvention of Death.* Berkeley: University of California Press.

Lock, Margaret, and Vinh-Kim Ngyyen. 2010. *An Anthropology of Biomedicine.* Oxford: Wiley-Blackwell.

MacDorman, Marian F., and Eugene Declercq. 2016. "Trends and Characteristics of United States Out-of-Hospital Births 2004–2014: New Information on Risk Status and Access to Care." *Birth* 43 (2): 116–124.

Maia, Mônica Bara. 2010. *Humanização do parto: política pública, comportamento organizacional e ethos profissional.* Rio de Janeiro: Editora Fiocruz.

Malat, J., F. Jacquez, and G. M. Slavich. 2017. "Measuring Lifetime Stress Exposure and Protective Factors in Life Course Research on Racial Inequality and Birth Outcomes." *Stress* 20 (4): 379–385.

Malatest International. 2013. *Comparative Study of Maternity Systems.* Wellington: Ministry of Health.

Mander, Rosemary. 2007. *Cesarean: Just Another Way of Birth?* New York: Routledge.

Marcus, George E. 1995. "Ethnography in/of the World System: The Emergence of Multi-Sited Ethnography." *Annual Review of Anthropology* 24 (1): 95–117.

Martin, E. 2001. *The Woman in the Body: A Cultural Analysis of Reproduction.* Boston: Beacon Press.

Martins, Alaerte Leandro. 2006. "Mortalidade materna de mulheres negras no Brasil." *Cadernos de Saúde Pública* 22 (11): 2473–2479.

Matsuoka, Etsuko. 1995. "Is Hospital the Safest Place for Birth?" In *Gebären: ethnomedizinische perspektiven und neue wege*, edited by Wulf Schiefenhövel, Dorthea Sich, and Christine Gott-schalk-Batschkus, 293–304. Berlin: Verlag für Wissenschaft und Bildung.

Matsuoka, Etsuko. 2014. *Ninshin to shussan no jinruigaku: ripurodakushon o toinaosu.* Kyoto: Sekaishisosha.

Matsuoka, E., and F. Hinokuma. 2009. "Maternity Homes in Japan: Reservoir of Normal Child-birth." In *Birth Models That Work*, edited by Robbie Davis-Floyd, Lesley Barclay, Betty-Anne Daviss, and Jan Tritten, 213–237. Berkley: University of California Press.

May, Maureen. 2017. *Epiduralized Birth and Nurse-Midwifery: Childbirth in the United States. A Medical Ethnography.* Sampson Book Publishing.

Mayo Clinic. n.d. "Episiotomy: When It's Needed, When It's Not." Mayo Foundation for Medical Education and Research. www.mayoclinic.org/health-lifestyle/labor-and-delivery/in-depth/episiotomy/art-20047282

McCallum, Cecilia. 2005. "Explaining Caesarean Section in Salvador da Bahia, Brazil." *Sociology of Health & Illness* 27 (2): 215–242.

McCallum, Cecilia. 2016. "Technobirth in 21st Century Brazil." Working paper, Instituto de Saúde Coletiva, Universidade Federal da Bahia.

McCallum, Cecilia, and Ana Paula dos Reis. 2005. "Childbirth as Ritual in Brazil: Young Mothers' Experiences." *Ethnos* 70 (3): 335–60, https://doi.org/10.1080/00141840500294417.

McGarry, J., K. Hinsliff-Smith, K. Watts, P. McCloskey, and C. Evans. 2017. "Experiences and Impact of Mistreatment and Obstetric Violence on Women during Childbearing: A Systematic Review Protocol." *JBI Database of Systematic Reviews and Implementation Reports* 15 (3): 620–627.

McKinney, J., L. Keyser, S. Clinton, and C. Pagliano. 2018. "ACOG Committee Opinion No. 736: Optimizing Postpartum Care." *Obstetrics & Gynecology* 132 (3): 784–785.

Mehra, R., L. M. Boyd, and J. R. Ickovics. 2017. "Racial Residential Segregation and Adverse Birth Outcomes: A Systematic Review and Meta-Analysis." *Social Science & Medicine* 191: 237–250, https://doi.org/10.1016/j.socscimed.2017.09.018.

Menezes, Paula Fernanda Almeida de, Sandra Dutra Cabral Portella, and Tânia Christiane Ferreira Bispo. 2012. "A Situação do parto domiciliar no Brasil." *Revista Enfermagem Contemporânea* 1 (1): 3–43.

Merry, S. E. 2011. "Measuring the World: Indicators, Human Rights, and Global Governance." *Current Anthropology* 52 (S3): S83–S95.

Michalec, Barret, and W. Frederic. 2013. "Stunting Professionalism: The Potency and Durability of the Hidden Curriculum within Medical Education." *Social Theory & Health* 11 (4): 388–406.

Midwifery Council of New Zealand. 2007. *The Competencies for Entry to the Register of Midwives.* https://www.midwiferycouncil.health.nz/sites/default/files/professional-standards/Competencies%20for%20Entry%20to%20the%20register%20of%20Midwives%202007%20new%20form.pdf

Midwifery Council of New Zealand. 2010. *The Midwifery Scope of Practice.* https://www.midwiferycouncil.health.nz/sites/default/files/for-midwives/Gazette%20Notice%202010%20-scope%20%26%20quals%20new%20form.pdf

Midwifery Council of New Zealand. 2012. *Statement on Cultural Competence for Midwives.* https://www.midwiferycouncil.health.nz/sites/default/files/documents/PDF%20cultural%20compctence.pdf

Midwifery Council of New Zealand. 2017. *Workforce Survey 2016.* https://www.midwiferycouncil.health.nz/about-us/publications/midwifery-workforce-survey-2016

Midwifery Licensure and Discipline Program in Washington State: Economic Costs and Benefits. 2007, October. Produced by Health Management Associates for the State of Washington Department of Health. Available at: http://www.washingtonmidwives.org/documents/Midwifery_Cost_Study_10-31-07.pdf (accessed February 8, 2017).

Mikaere, Ani (2000). "Mai i te Kore kit e Ao Mārama: Māori Women as Whare Tangata." Proceedings of the New Zealand College of Midwives Conference, 28–30 September. Cambridge, New Zealand, pp. 371–386.

Miller S., et al. 2016. "Beyond Too Little, Too Late and Too Much, Too Soon: A Pathway towards Evidence-based, Respectful Maternity Care Worldwide." *The Lancet* 388 (10056): 2176–2192, https://doi.org/10.1016/S0140-6736(16)31472-6.

Miller, S., and A. Lalonde. 2015. "The Global Epidemic of Abuse and Disrespect during Childbirth: History, Evidence, Interventions, and FIGO's Mother–Baby Friendly Birthing Facilities Initiative." *International Journal of Gynecology & Obstetrics* 131 (S1).

Miller, S., and J. Skinner. 2012. "Are First-Time Mothers Who Plan Home Birth More Likely to Receive Evidence-Based Care? A Comparative Study of Home and Hospital Care Provided by the Same Midwives." *Birth* 39 (2): 135–144.

Miller, S., et al. 2003. "Quality of Care in Institutionalized Deliveries: The Paradox of the Dominican Republic." *International Journal of Gynecology & Obstetrics* 82 (1): 89–103.

Mills, Lisa, and Robbie Davis-Floyd. 2009. "The CASA Hospital and Professional Midwifery School." In *Birth Models That Work*, edited by Robbie Davis-Floyd, Lesley Barclay, Betty-Anne Daviss, and Jan Tritten, 305–335. Berkeley: University of California Press.

Ministerie van Volksgezondheid en Sport. 1993. "Wet op de beroepen in de individuele gezondheidszorg. Artikel 31." https://wetten.overheid.nl/BWBR0006251/2018-09-01#HoofdstukIII_Afdeling1

Ministerie van Volksgezondheid en Sport. 2014. *Besluit opleidingseisen deskundigheidsgebied verloskundige 2008.* http://wetten.overheid.nl/BWBR0024254/2014-09-01

Ministry of Health. 2007. *Primary Maternity Services Notice 2007.* Wellington, New Zealand: Ministry of Health. http://www.health.govt.nz/system/files/documents/publications/s88-primary-maternity-services-notice-gazetted-2007.pdf

Ministry of Health. 2012. *Guidelines for Consultation with Obstetric and Related Medical Services (Referral Guidelines).* Wellington: Ministry of Health. https://www.health.govt.nz/system/files/documents/publications/referral-glines-jan12.pdf

Ministry of Health. 2017. *Report on Maternity 2015.* Wellington: Ministry of Health.

Ministry of Health. 2018. "Third Stage of Labour." http://www.health.govt.nz/your-health/pregnancy-and-kids/birth-and-afterwards/labour-and-birth/third-stage-labour

Ministry of Health of Brazil. 2004. *Pacto nacional pela redução da mortalidade materna e neonatal.* Brasília, Brazil: Ministry of Health. http://portalarquivos.saude.gov.br/images/pdf/2016/junho/20/2.a%20Pacto%20redu%C3%A7%C3%A3o%20mortalidade.pdff

Ministry of Health of Brazil. 2017. *Diretrizes nacionais de assistência ao parto normal: Versão resumida.* Brasília, Brazil: Ministry of Health. http://conitec.gov.br/images/Relatorios/2017/Diretrizes_PartoNormal_Versao-Final.pdf

Ministry of Health, Labor and Welfare. 2009. *About In-Hospital Maternity Home and Midwifery Out-Patient Check-up.* https://www.mhlw.go.jp/shingi/2009/11/dl/s1104-3j.pdf

Ministry of Health and Social Welfare. 2013. *Human Resource for Health Country Profile 2012/2013.* Dar es Salaam, Tanzania. http://www.tzdpg.or.tz/fileadmin/documents/dpg_internal/dpg_working_groups_clusters/cluster_2/health/Key_Sector_Documents/HRH_Documents/Final_Country_Profile_2013.pdf

Mohri, T. 2001. "Nihon no josanpu ga dekitakoto, korekara dekirukoto" ("What Japanese Midwives Have Done and What They Can Do in the Future") *Josan zassi* (*The Japanese Journal for Midwives*) 55 (4): 52–57.

Mossialos, E., S. Allin, K. Karras, and K. Davaki. 2005. "An Investigation of Caesarean Sections in Three Greek Hospitals." *The European Journal of Public Health* 15 (3): 288–295.

Mott, Maria Lúcia. 2002. "Assistência ao parto: do domicílio ao hospital (1830–1960)." *Projeto História* 25: 197–219.

Mrisho, M., et al. 2007. "Factors Affecting Home Delivery in Rural Tanzania." *Tropical Medicine & International Health* 12 (7): 862–872.

Mselle, L.T., K. M. Moland, A. Mvungi, B. Evjen-Olsen, and T. W. Kohi. 2013. "Why Give Birth in Health Facility? Users' and Providers' Accounts of Poor Quality of Birth Care in Tanzania." *BMC Health Services Research* 13: 174–186.

Naisbitt, John. 1984. *Megatrends: Ten New Directions Transforming Our Lives.* New York: Warner Books.

Nederlandse Zorgautoriteit (NZa). 2012, June. *Advies bekostiging (integrale) zorg rondom zwangerschap en geboorte. Het stimuleren van samenwerking.* https://www.nza.nl/publicaties/1048188/Advies_Bekostiging_integrale_zorg_rondom_zwangerschap_en_geboorte

Neilson, Duncan. 2015. "Making Home Birth Safer in the United States through Strategic Collaboration: The Legacy Health System Experience." *Birth* 42 (4): 287–289.

New Zealand College of Midwives. 2009. *Consensus Statement: The role of Non-Regulated Support People in Maternity Services.* Christchurch: New Zealand College of Midwives. https://www.midwife.org.nz/quality-practice/nzcom-consensus-statements

Nigenda, Gustavo. 2013. "Social Service in Medicine in Mexico: An Urgent and Possible Reform." *Salud Pública de México* 55 (5): 519–527.

Nikolopoulos, Petros. 2010. "Tragic Flaw: Graft Feeds Greek Crisis." *Wall Street Journal*, April 17.

NIVEL, 2016. *Cijfers uit de registratie van verloskundigen.* Peiling 2015. https://www.nivel.nl/sites/default/files/bestanden/Cijfers-uit-de-registratie-van-verloskundigen-peiling-jan-2015.pdf

NIVEL. 2013. *Quickscan beroepen & opleidingen in de zorg, welzijn en kinderopvang. Hoofdrapport.* http://www.nivel.nl/sites/default/files/bestanden/Rapport-Quickscan-Beroepen-Opleidingen.pdf

Nursing Council of New Zealand. 1996. *Guidelines for the Cultural Safety Component of Nursing and Midwifery Education.* Wellington: Nursing Council of New Zealand.

Oberhelman, S. M., ed. 2016. *Dreams, Healing, and Medicine in Greece: From Antiquity to the Present.* New York: Routledge.

Objetivos de desarrollo del milenio en Mexico. 2015. http://www.objetivosdedesarrollodelmilenio.org.mx/Doctos/InfMex2015.pdf

OECD. 2017. "Fertility Rates." *OECD Library*, https://doi.org/10.1787/5f958f71-en.

Oladapo, O. T., et al. 2018. "Progression on the First State of Labor: A Prospective Cohort Study in two sub-Saharan African Countries." *PLOS Medicine.* https://www.ncbi.nlm.nih.gov/pmc/articles/PMC5770022/pdf/pmed.1002492.pdf

Olsen, Ole, and Jette A. Clausen. 2012. "Planned Hospital Birth versus Planned Home Birth." *The Cochrane Library*, doi: 10.1002/14651858.CD000352.pub2.

Otovo, Okezi T. 2016. *Progressive Mothers, Better Babies: Race, Public Health, and the State in Brazil, 1850–1945.* Austin, TX: University of Texas Press.

Out-of-Hospital Births in Oregon 2012. Public Health Division. Available at: https://public.health.oregon.gov/BirthDeathCertificates/VitalStatistics/birth/Pages/planned-birth-place.aspx017 (accessed June 27, 2017).

Page, Lesley Ann. 2001. "The Humanization of Birth." *International Journal of Gynecology & Obstetrics* 75 (November): S55–S58.

Paim, Jairnilson, Claudia Travassos, Celia Almeida, Ligia Bahia, and James Macinko. 2011. "The Brazilian Health System: History, Advances, and Challenges." *The Lancet* 377 (9779): 1778–1797, https://doi.org/10.1016/S0140-6736(11)60054-8.

Papagaroufali, Eleni. 1990. "Greek Women in Politics: Gender Ideology and Practice in Neighborhood Groups and Family." PhD Dissertation, Columbia University.

Papagaroufali, Eleni, and Eugenia Georges. 1993. "Greek Women in the Europe of 1992: Brokers of European Cargos and the Logic of the West." In *Perilous States: Conversations on Culture, Race and Nation*, edited by G. Marcus, 235–254. Chicago: University of Chicago Press.

Parto do Princípio. 2012. *Violência obstétrica: "Parirás com dor."* http://www.senado.gov.br/comissoes/documentos/SSCEPI/DOC%20VCM%20367.pdf

Paxson, Heather. 2004. *Making Modern Mothers: Ethics and Family Planning in Urban Greece.* Berkeley: University of California Press.

Pechlivani, Fani, and E. Adam. 1999. "Greek Midwives on Prenatal Screening." In *Prenatal Screening in Europe*, edited by Elizabeth Ettore. Commission of the European Union, unpublished report.

Pembe, A. B., et al. 2008. "Qualitative Study on Maternal Referrals in Rural Tanzania: Decision Making and Acceptance of Referral Advice." *African Journal of Reproductive Health* 12 (2): 120–131.

Penfold, S., et al. 2013. "Staff Experiences of Providing Maternity Services in Rural Southern Tanzania—A Focus on Equipment, Drug and Supply Issues." *BMC Health Services Research* 13: 61–70.

Penyak, Lee M. 2003. "Obstetrics and the Emergence of Women in Mexico's Medical Establishment." *The Americas* 60 (1): 59–85.

Pereira, C., and S. Bergström. forthcoming. "Where There Are No Doctors: Shifting Cesareans and Other Obstetric Surgeries to Mid-Level Providers of Care for Better Perinatal Outcomes in Mozambique and Tanzania." In *Childbirth Models on the Human Rights Frontier: Speaking Truth to Power*, edited by Betty-Anne Daviss and Robbie Davis-Floyd. New York: Routledge.

Perinatal and Maternal Mortality Review Committee. 2017. "Eleventh Annual Report of the Perinatal and Maternal Mortality Review Committee." Wellington, New Zealand: Health, Quality and Safety Commission. http://www.hqsc.govt.nz/our-programmes/mrc/pmmrc

Perined. 2015. *Perinatale Zorg in Nederland 2014.* https://assets.perined.nl/docs/353d9249-9875-4cb3-9c86-f078ae3f7aef.pdf

Perined. 2016. *Perinatale Zorg in Nederland 2015.* https://assets.perined.nl/docs/980021f9-6364-4dc1-9147-d976d6f4af8c.pdf

Perry, Keisha-Khan. 2013. *Black Women Against the Land Grab: The Fight for Racial Justice in Brazil.* Minneapolis: University of Minnesota Press.

Peters, L. L., et al. 2018. "The Effect of Medical and Operative Birth Interventions on Child Health Outcomes in the First 28 Days and up to 5 Years of Age: A Linked Data Population-based Cohort Study." *Birth Issues in Perinatal Care.* Hoboken, NJ: Wiley Periodicals, https://doi.org/10.1111/birt.12348.

Peterson, Gayle. 1984. *Birthing Normally: A Personal Growth Approach to Childbirth.* Berkeley, CA: Shadow and Light.

Petronzio, M. 2017, April 15. "How an 'Uber for Pregnant Women' Is Saving Lives in Tanzania." http://mashable.com/2017/04/15/vodafone-maternal-health-uber-ambulance/#mzkx074arEqq

Pollock, Linda A. 1990. "Embarking on a Rough Passage: The Experience of Pregnancy in Early Modern Society." In *Women as Mothers in Pre-Industrial England*, edited by Valerie Fildes, 39–67. New York: Routledge.

Portal da Saúde. 2017, March 10. "Pela primeira vez número de cesáreas não cresce no país." Ministério da Saúde. http://portalsaude.saude.gov.br/index.php/cidadao/principal/agencia-saude/27782-pela-primeira-vez-numero-de-cesarianas-nao-cresce-no-pais

Portela, Jaqueline Cardoso. 2018. "'Via de parto não é mãezímetro!': Tensões entre parto, maternidade e feminilidade em um grupo virtual pró-cesárea." Master's thesis, Universidade Federal da Bahia.

Porter, Roy, and Dorothy Porter. 1988. *In Sickness and in Health: The British Experience 1650–1850.* New York: Blackwell.

Potter, Joseph E., Kristine Hopkins, Anibal Faúndes, and Ignez Perpétuo. 2008. "Women's Autonomy and Scheduled Cesarean Sections in Brazil: A Cautionary Tale." *Birth* 35 (1): 33–40.

Prenatal Care Fact Sheet. 2017. Available at: https://www.womenshealth.gov/publications/our-publications/fact-sheet/prenatal-care.html (accessed February 5, 2017).

Quesada, J., L. K. Hart, and P. Bourgois. 2011. "Structural Vulnerability and Health: Latino Migrant Laborers in the United States." *Medical Anthropology* 30 (4): 339–362, https://doi.org/10.1080/01459740.2011.576725.

Ramsden, Irihapeti Merenia. 2002. "Cultural Safety and Nursing Education in Aotearoa and Te Waipounamu." PhD in Nursing Thesis, Victoria University, Wellington, New Zealand. https://www.nzno.org.nz/Portals/0/Files/Documents/Services/Library/2002%20RAMSDEN%20I%20Cultural%20Safety_Full.pdf210

Rasella, Davide, Rosana Aquino, and Maurício Lima Barreto. 2013. "Impact of Income Inequality on Life Expectancy in a Highly Unequal Developing Country: The Case of Brazil." *Journal of Epidemiology & Community Health* 67: 661–666.

Rattner, Daphne. 2010. "Humanizing Childbirth Care: A Brief Theoretical Framework." *Tempus Actas de Saúde Coletiva* 4 (4): 41–49.

Reerink, Antoinette. 2010, November 3. "Don't Try This at Home." *NRCnext*. https://
www.nrc.nl/nieuws/2010/11/03/dont-try-this-at-home-11964558-a1140923

Reynolds, Peter C. 1991. *Stealing Fire: The Atomic Bomb as Symbolic Body*. Palo Alto, CA: Iconic Anthropology Press.

Rijksinstituut voor Volksgezondheid en Milieu. 2015. Available at: http://www.rivm.nl/ (accessed February 8, 2017).

Roome, S., et al. 2015. "Why Such Differing Stances? A Review of Position Statements on Home Birth from Professional Colleges." *BJOG: An International Journal of Obstetrics & Gynaecology* 123 (3): 376–382.

Rose, Nikolas. 2007. *The Politics of Life Itself: Biomedicine, Power, and Subjectivity in the Twenty-First Century*. Princeton: Princeton University Press.

Rothman, Barbara Katz. 2016. *A Bun in the Oven: How the Food and Birth Movements Resist Industrialization*. London and New York: New York University Press.

Ruder, B., M. Cheyney, and A. A. Emasu. 2018. "Too Long to Wait: Obstetric Fistula and the Sociopolitical Dynamics of the Fourth Delay in Soroti, Uganda." *Qualitative Health Research* 28 (5): 721–732.

Rydahl, E., L. Eriksen, and M. Juhl. 2018. "Effects of Induction of Labor Prior to Post-Term in Low-Risk Pregnancies: A Systematic Review." *JBI Database of Systematic Reviews and Implementation Reports*, doi: 10.11124/JBISRIR-2017-003587.

Sanabria, Emilia. 2015. *Plastic Bodies: Sex Hormones and Menstrual Suppression in Brazil*. Durham, NC: Duke University Press.

Scamell, Mandie, and Andy Alaszewski. 2012. "Fateful Moments and the Categorisation of Risk: Midwifery Practice and the Ever-Narrowing Window of Normality during Childbirth." *Health, Risk & Society* 14 (2): 207–221.

Schmied, Virginia, et al. 2011. "Women's Perceptions and Experiences of Breastfeeding Support: A Metasynthesis." *Birth* 38 (1): 49–60.

Schultz, E. C. 2013. *Nederlandse verloskundigen, hun historie en verloskundig erfgoed: een veronachtzaamd gebied*. https://dspace.library.uu.nl/bitstream/handle/1874/281660/Gs%202013% 20MasterUU%20scriptie%20Erfgoed%20veronachtzaamd%20versie%20Igitur.pdf? sequence=1&isAllowed=y

Schut, Aischa. 2014. "Trust and Mistrust in Salvador, Brazil: Homebirth in a Country of Cesareans." Master's thesis, Universiteit van Amsterdam.

Secretaría de Gobernación. 2012. "Norma Oficial Mexicana PROY-NOM-007-SSA2-2010, Para la atención de la mujer durante el embarazo, parto y puerperio, y del recién nacido." *Diario Oficial de la Nación*, 5 of November. https://dof.gob.mx/nota_detalle.php?codigo= 5276550&fecha=05/11/2012

Secretaria de Vigilância em Saúde. n.d. Painel de Monitoramento da Mortalidade Materna; Óbitos maternos declarados, 2011 and 2015. http://svs.aids.gov.br/dantps/centrais-de-conteudos/paineis-de-monitoramento/mortalidade/materna/

Seijmonsbergen-Schermers, et al. 2018. "Regional Variations in Childbirth Interventions in the Netherlands: A Nationwide Explorative Study." *BMC Pregnancy and Childbirth* 18 (1): 192.

Seo, B. K. 2016. "The Work of Inscription: Antenatal Care, Birth Documents, and Shan Migrant Women in Chiang Mai." *Medical Anthropology Quarterly* 31 (4): 481–498, https://doi.org/ 10.1111/maq.12342.

Setel, P., et al. 2007. "A Scandal of Invisibility: Making Everyone Count by Counting Everyone." *The Lancet*, 370, 1569–1577.

Shanley, Laura Kaplan. 1994. *Unassisted Childbirth*. Westport, CT: Bergin & Garvey.

Shore, C., and S. Wright. 2011. "Conceptualising Policy: Technologies of Governance and the Politics of Visibility." In *Policy Worlds*, edited by C. Shore, S. Wright, and D. Pero. New York: Berghahn Books.

Simmonds, Naomi (2018). "The Spaces Between: The Inextricability of the Spiritual and Physical in Māori Women's Birthing Experiences in Aotearoa, New Zealand." In *Childbirth and Spirituality in the Modern to Contemporary World: A Reader*, edited by Marianne Delaporte and Morag Martin. Lanham MD: Lakewood Press.

Sluijs, A. M., M. P. Cleiren, S. A. Scherjon, and K. Wijma. 2015. "Does Fear of Childbirth or Family History Affect whether Pregnant Dutch Women Prefer a Home- or Hospital Birth?" *Midwifery* 31 (12): 1143–1148, doi: 10.1016/j.midw.2015.08.002.

Smith, Christen A. 2016. *Afro-Paradise: Blackness, Violence, and Performance in Brazil.* Champaign, IL: University of Illinois Press.

Smith-Oka, Vania. 2013a. *Shaping the Motherhood of Indigenous Mexico.* Nashville: Vanderbilt University Press.

Smith-Oka, Vania. 2013b. "Managing Labor and Delivery among Impoverished Populations in Mexico: Cervical Exams as Bureaucratic Practice." *American Anthropologist* 115 (4): 595–607.

Snowden, Jonathan M., et al. 2015. "Planned Out-of-Hospital Birth and Birth Outcomes." *New England Journal of Medicine* 373 (27): 2642–2653.

Soliday, E. (2012). *Childbirth in a Technocratic Age: The Documentation of Women's Expectations and Experiences.* Amherst, NY: Cambria Press.

Sosa-Rubí, Sandra G., et al. 2011. "Impacto del seguro popular en el gasto catastrófico y de bolsillo en el México rural y urbano, 2005–2008." *Salud Pública de México* 53 (4): 425–435.

Spangler, S. A. 2011. "'To Open Oneself Is a Poor Woman's Trouble': Embodied Inequality and Childbirth in South–Central Tanzania." *Medical Anthropology Quarterly* 25 (4): 479–498.

Staatsblad van het Koninkrijk der Nederlanden. 1818. Lijst der wetten en besluiten, vervat in het staatsblad van het Koninkrijk der Nederlanden. No 16. Wet, ter regeling van hetgene betrekkelijk is tot de uitoefening van verschillende takken der geneeskunde. Brussel Weissenburch. Available at: https://books.google.be/books?id=r7BbAAAAQAAJ&printsec=frontcover&hl=nl&source=gbs_ge_summary_r&cad=0#v=onepage&q&f=false (accessed February 8, 2017).

Staatsblad van het Koninkrijk der Nederlanden. 1986. No. 60. Wet regelde de uitoefening der geneeskunst. Available at: http://www.kwakzalverij.nl/assets/importeddownloads/1255372754thorbecke1.pdf (accessed February 8, 2017).

Stahnisch, F. W., and M. Verhoef. 2012. "The Flexner Report of 1910 and Its Impact on Complementary and Alternative Medicine and Psychiatry in North America in the 20th Century." *Evidence-based Complementary and Alternative Medicine,* http://dx.doi.org/10.1155/2012/647896.

Stapleton, Susan Rutledge, Cara Osborne, and Jessica Illuzzi. 2013. "Outcomes of Care in Birth Centers: Demonstration of a Durable Model." *Journal of Midwifery & Women's Health* 58 (1): 3–14.

Stewart, Charles. 1991. *Demons and the Devil: Moral Imagination in Modern Greek Culture.* Princeton: Princeton University Press.

Stichting Perinatale Registratie Nederland 1999–2012 (The Netherlands Perinatal Registry Trends 1999–2012). n.d. Pages 64–65. Available at: https://assets.perined.nl/docs/6f9eb6f1-f40c-4fb6-92b7-55787f230704.pdf.

Stone, P. K. 2009. "A History of Western Medicine, Labor, and Birth." In *Childbirth Across Cultures,* edited by Helaine Selin and Pamela K. Stone, 41–53. Dordrecht, the Netherlands: Springer.

Strong, A. E. 2017. "Working in Scarcity: 'Effects on Social Interactions at a Tanzanian Hospital.'" *Social Science & Medicine* 187: 217–224, https://doi.org/10.1016/j.socscimed.2017.02.010.

Sugimoto, Yoshio. 2014. *An Introduction to Japanese Society.* 4th ed. Melbourne: Cambridge University Press.

Suzui, Emiko. 2016. "Chouonpa shindan to josan" ("Ultrasound Diagnosis and Midwifery"). In *Umisodate to josan no rekishi (History of Childbirth/ Childcare and Midwifery),* edited by Chiaki Shirai, 183–205. Tokyo: Igaku-shoin. (in Japanese).

Szwarcwald, Celia Landmann, et al. 2014. "Estimação da razão de mortalidade materna no Brasil, 2008-2011." *Cadernos de Saúde Pública* 30 (Suppl. 1): S71–S83.

Szwarcwald, Célia Landmann, et al. 2016. "Inequalities in Healthy Life Expectancy by Brazilian Geographic Regions: Findings from the National Health Survey, 2013." *International Journal for Equity in Health* 15: 141–150.

Tanzania Ministry of Health. 1990. *National Health Policy.* Dar es Salaam: United Republic of Tanzania Ministry of Health.

Tanzania Ministry of Health. 2008. *The National Road Map Strategic Plan to Accelerate Reduction of Maternal, Newborn, and Child Deaths in Tanzania, 2008–2015.* http://www.who.int/pmnch/countries/tanzaniamapstrategic.pdf

TDHS-MIS. 2016. *Tanzania Demographic and Health Survey and Malaria Indicator Survey (TDHS-MIS) 2015–16.* Dar es Salaam, Tanzania, and Rockville, Maryland, USA: Ministry of Health, Community Development, Gender, Elderly and Children (MoHCDGEC) [Tanzania Mainland], Ministry of Health (MoH) [Zanzibar], National Bureau of Statistics (NBS), Office of the Chief Government Statistician (OCGS), and ICF.

Tilden, Ellen, Jonathan Snowden, Aaron Caughey, and Melissa Cheyney. 2016. "Making US Out-of-Hospital Birth Safer Requires Systems Change." *Medscape* (May 18): 106.

Tornquist, Carmen Susana. 2004. "Parto e poder: O movimento pela humanização do parto no Brasil." PhD dissertation, Universidade Federal de Santa Catarina. http://repositorio.ufsc.br/bitstream/handle/123456789/86639/207876.pdf?sequence=1

Turner, Victor. 1967. *The Forest of Symbols: Aspects of Ndembu Ritual.* Vol. 101. Ithaca, NY: Cornell University Press.

Tweede Kamer.1988–1989. Kamersstuk 201800 hoofstuk XVI ondernumme 163. Regerings-standpunt Adviescommissie Kloosterman. Available at: http://www.statengeneraaldigi-taal.nl/document?id=sgd%3A19881989%3A0005188&zoekopdracht%5Bkamer%5D%5B1%5D=Tweede+Kamer&zoekopdracht%5Bzoekwoorden%5D=regeringsstandpunt+adviescommissie+kloosterman&zoekopdracht%5Bvergaderjaar%5D%5Bvan%5D=1814+-+1815&zoekopdracht%5Bvergaderjaar%5D%5Btot%5D=1994+-+1995&zoekopdracht%5BdocumentType%5D=Alle+document+types&zoekopdracht%5Bpagina%5D=1&zoekopdracht%5Bsortering%5D=relevantie (accessed March 15, 2017).

Ulrich, Laurel Thatcher. 1990. *A Midwife's Tale: The Life of Martha Ballard, Based on her Diary, 1785–1812.* New York: Alfred A. Knopf.

UN/WHO. 2015. *Survive, Thrive, Transform The Global Strategy for Women's, Children's and Adolescents' Health (2016–2030).* http://www.who.int/life-course/partners/global-strategy/globalstrategyreport2016-2030-lowres.pdf

UNICEF. 2013. *Every Child's Birth Right: Inequities and Trends in Birth Registration.* https://www.un.org/ruleoflaw/files/Embargoed_11_Dec_Birth_Registration_report_low_res.pdf

UNICEF. 2014. "In the United Republic of Tanzania, a New Solution for Birth Registration." http://unicefstories.org/2014/02/06/in-the-united-republic-of-tanzania-a-new-solution-for-birth-registration/

UNICEF. 2016. UNICEF Statistics by Topic: Child Protection. http://data.unicef.org/topic/child-protection/birth-registration/

United Nations.2016. "Sustainable Development Goals." http://www.un.org/sustainabledevelopment/development-agenda/

US MERA Representatives. 2014. US MERA Meeting: A Summary Report. Available at: http://mana.org/us-midwifery-era-us-mera (accessed February 10, 2017).

Van Daalen, Rineke. 1988. "De groei van de ziekenhuisbevalling. Nederland en het buitenland" ("The Growth of Hospital Delivery: The Netherlands Compared to Other Countries"). *Amsterdams Sociologisch Tijdschrift* 15 (3): 414–445.

Van Lerberghe, W., et al. 2014. "Country Experience with Strengthening of Health Systems and Deployment of Midwives in Countries with High Maternal Mortality." *The Lancet* 384 (9949):1215–1225, http://dx.doi.org/10.1016/S0140-6736(14)60919-3.

van Lieburg, M. J., and H. Marland. 1989. "Midwife Regulation, Education and Practice in the Netherlands during the Nineteenth Century." *Medical History* 33 (3): 296–317.

Vedam, S., et al. 2014a. "The Canadian Birth Place Study: Examining Attitudes and Interprofessional Conflict." *BMC Pregnancy and Childbirth* 14: 353

Vedam, S., et al. 2014b. "Home Birth in North America: Attitudes and Practice of American Certified Nurse-Midwives and Canadian Registered Midwives." *Journal of Midwifery and Women's Health* 59(2):141–152.

Vedam, S., et al. 2014c. "Transfer from Planned Home Birth to Hospital: Improving Interprofessional Collaboration." *Journal of Midwifery & Women's Health* 59 (6): 624–634.

Vedam, S., et al. 2018. "Mapping Integration of Midwives across the United States: Impact on Access, Equity, and Outcomes." *PloS One* 13 (2): e0192523.

Victora, Cesar G., et al. 2011. "Maternal and Child Health in Brazil: Progress and Challenges." *The Lancet* 377 (9780): 1863–1876, https://doi.org/10.1016/S0140-6736(11)60138-4.

Villalonga-Olives, E., I. Kawachi, and N. von Steinbüchel. 2017. "Pregnancy and Birth Outcomes among Immigrant Women in the US and Europe: A Systematic Review." *Journal of Immigrant and Minority Health* 19 (6): 1469–1487.

Visscher, Marty O., et al. 2005. "Vernix Caseosa in Neonatal Adaptation." *Journal of Perinatology* 25: 440–446, https://doi.org/10.1038/sj.jp.7211305.

Vital Statistics Figure. 2016. *e-Stat: Statistics of Japan.* https://www.e-stat.go.jp/en/stat-search/files?page=1&layout=normal&toukei=00450011&tstat=000001028897&second=1

Vodafone Foundation. 2017. "Mobilising Maternal Health in Tanzania." http://www.vodafone.com/content/foundation/mobilising-maternal-health.html

Waldman, Richard, Holly Powell Kennedy, and Susan Kendig. "Collaboration in Maternity Care: Possibilities and Challenges." *Obstetrics and Gynecology Clinics of North America* 39 (3): 435–444.

Walker, Dilys, Lisa DeMaria, Gonzalez-Hernandez, Padron-Salas, Minerva Romero-Alvarez, and Suarez. 2013. "Are All Skilled Birth Attendants Created Equal? A Cluster Randomised Controlled Study of Non-Physician Based Obstetric Care in Primary Health Care Clinics in Mexico." *Midwifery, Midwives' Contribution to the Millennium Development Goals* 29 (10): 1199–1205.

Walker, Tai. 2011. "'Whānau—Māori and Family—Contemporary Understandings of Whānau,' Te Ara—The Encyclopedia of New Zealand." http://www.TeAra.govt.nz/en/whanau-maori-and-family/page-1

Wendland, C. 2016. "Estimating Death: A Close Reading of Maternal Mortality Metrics in Malawi." In *Metrics: What Counts in Global Health*, edited by V. Adams. Durham, NC: Duke University Press.

Werkgroep Bijstelling Kloostermanlijst. 1987. *Eindrapport van de Werkgroep Bijstelling Kloostermanlijst.* Amstelveen, the Netherlands: Ziekenfondsraad.

Werkgroep Geneeskundige Hoofdinspectie. 1969. *Rapport van de werkgroep "verloskunidge zorg" (Report of the Committee "Maternal and Newborn Care")*. Leidschendam, the Netherlands: Geneeskundige Hoofdinspectie van de Gezondheidszorg.

Wertz, Richard W., and Dorothy C. Wertz. 1989. *Lying-in: A History of Childbirth in America*. New Haven, CT: Yale University Press.

Wiegers, Trees, Hanneke de Graaf, and Karin van der Pal. 2012. "De opkomst van geboortecentra en hun rol in de zorg." *TSG* 90 (8). http://www.google.nl/url?sa=t&rct=j&q=&esrc=s&source=web&cd=1&cad=rja&uact=8&ved=0ahUKEwii7MXGi9jSAhVFSRoKHQz0Ad0QFgghMAA&url=http%3A%2F%2Fpublications.tno.nl%2Fpublication%2F34622526%2FROk8cv%2Fwiegers-2012-opkomst.pdf&usg=AFQjCNHFCitxdJKIsu73WpJxjJtQM98V_w

Wiegers, Therese A., Lammert Hingstman, and Jouke van der Zee. 2000. "Thuisbevalling in gevaar." *Medisch Contact* 55 (19). https://www.google.nl/url?sa=t&rct=j&q=&esrc=s&source=web&cd=1&ved=0ahUKEwi8zvT1itjSAhWKVhoKHS7MCcwQFggjMAA&url=https%3A%2F%2Fwww.medischcontact.nl%2Fweb%2Ffile%3Fuuid%3D44b9ceed-a23c-4c0e-be86-45e53beca534%26owner%3D369ebf1c-2b31-4028-9ac9-fb78303da853&usg=AFQjCNFNDFQXHjjqPItW0MU0eRKMePxCbw

Wiegers, Therese A., Marc Keirse, Jouke van der Zee, and Geert A. Berghs. 1996. "Outcome of Planned Home and Planned Hospital Births in Low Risk Pregnancies: Prospective Study in Midwifery Practices in the Netherlands." *BMJ Clinical Research* 313 (7068): 1309–1313.

Wiegers, T. A., C. J. Warmelink, E. R. Spelten, T. Klomp, and E. K. Hutton. 2013. "Work and Workload of Dutch Primary Care Midwives in 2010." *Midwifery*. Available online August 27, 2013. Final version published online: August 9, 2014: *Midwifery* 30 (9): 991–997, doi: 10.1016/j.midw.2014.08.010.

Williams, C. R., C. Jerez, K. Klein, M. Correa, J. M. Belizán, and G. Cormick. 2018. "Obstetric Violence: A Latin American Legal Response to Mistreatment during Childbirth." *BJOG:*

An International Journal of Obstetrics & Gynaecology 125 (10): 1208–1211, https://doi.org/ 10.1111/1471-0528.15270.

Witz, Anne. 1992. *Professions and Patriarchy*. New York: Routledge.

World Bank. 2017. "Population, Total." http://data.worldbank.org/indicator/SP.POP.TOTL

World Health Organization. 1996. *Care in Normal Birth: a Practical Guide*. Geneva: World Health Organization.

World Health Organization. 2014. "The Prevention and Elimination of Disrespect and Abuse during Facility-based Childbirth." http://apps.who.int/iris/bitstream/10665/134588/1/ WHO_RHR_14.23_eng.pdf?ua=1&ua=1

World Health Organization. 2015. "WHO Statement on Cesarean Section Rates." http://apps.who.int/iris/bitstream/10665/161442/1/WHO_RHR_15.02_eng.pdf

World Health Organization. 2016. *World Health Statistics 2016: Monitoring Health for the SDGs Sustainable Development Goals*. http://www.who.int/gho/publications/world_health_ statistics/2016/en/

World Health Organization. 2018. *WHO Recommendations: Intrapartum Care for a Positive Childbirth Experience*. http://apps.who.int/iris/bitstream/handle/10665/260178/ 9789241550215-eng.pdf;jsessionid=ECF0DC1646B2AB30345C668CC6290FD2?sequence=1.

Xie, Ri-Hua, et al. 2009. "Prenatal Social Support, Postnatal Social Support, and Postpartum Depression." *Annals of Epidemiology* 19 (9): 637–643.

Yamana, Kanami. 2016. "In-nai josan ni okeru bunbenji iryo-kainyuu ni tsuiteno bunken rebyu" ("Literature Review of Medical Intervention during Delivery at In-Hospital Midwifery"). *Bulletin of Faculty of Nursing, School of Medicine, Nara Medical University* 12: 45–54 (in Japanese).

Yoder, H., and L. R. Hardy. 2018. "Midwifery and Antenatal Care for Black Women: A Narrative Review." *SAGE Open*, https://doi.org/10.1177/2158244017752220

Zacher Dixon, Lydia 2015. "Obstetrics in a Time of Violence: Mexican Midwives Critique Routine Hospital Practices." *Medical Anthropology Quarterly* 29 (4): 437–454, https://doi.org/ 10.1111/maq.12174.

Ziekenfondsraad. 1999, January. *Vademecum Verloskunde: Eindrapport van het werkoverleg verloskunde van de Ziekenfondsraad (Final Report of the Sick Fund Council Work Group on Obstetrics)*. Amstelveen, the Netherlands: Inspectie voor de Gezondheidszorg.

Zielinski, R., K. Ackerson, and L. K. Low. 2015. "Planned Home Birth: Benefits, Risks, and Opportunities." *International Journal of Women's Health* 7: 361.

Zordo, Silvia de. 2012. "Programming the Body, Planning Reproduction, Governing Life: The '(Ir-) Rationality' of Family Planning and the Embodiment of Social Inequalities in Salvador da Bahia (Brazil)." *Anthropology & Medicine* 19 (2): 207–223, https://doi.org/10.1080/ 13648470.2012.675049.

Editors and Contributors

Editors

Robbie Davis-Floyd, PhD, Adjunct Professor, Department of Anthropology, Rice University, Houston, Texas, and Fellow of the Society for Applied Anthropology, is a well-known cultural/medical anthropologist, international speaker, and researcher in transformational models in childbirth, midwifery, and obstetrics. Much of her research on midwifery in the US and Mexico was funded by the Wenner-Gren Foundation for Anthropological Research. She is author of over 80 articles and of *Birth as an American Rite of Passage* (1992, 2003) and of an anthology of her most popular works, all revised and updated for publication in *Ways of Knowing about Birth: Mothers, Midwives, Medicine, and Birth Activism* (2018). She is also coauthor of *From Doctor to Healer: The Transformative Journey* (1998) and *The Power of Ritual* (2016) and lead editor of 11 collections, including *Childbirth and Authoritative Knowledge: Cross-Cultural Perspectives* (1997); *Cyborg Babies: From Techno-Sex to Techno-Tots* (1998); *Mainstreaming Midwives: The Politics of Change* (2006); and *Birth Models That Work* (2009), which highlights optimal models of birth care around the world. *Birthing Models on the Human Rights Frontier: Speaking Truth to Power,* coedited with Betty-Anne Daviss, is in process, as is *Sustainable Birth in Disruptive Times,* coedited with Kim Gutschow, and *The Global Witch Hunt: Practitioner Persecution and Restorative Resistance,* coedited with Betty-Anne Daviss and Hermine Hayes-Klein. Robbie serves as Senior Advisor to the Council on Anthropology and Reproduction and as Board Member of the International MotherBaby Childbirth Organization (IMBCO). In that capacity, she serves as Lead Editor for the *International Childbirth Initiative: 12 Steps to MotherBaby-Family Friendly Maternity Care*—the result of a merger of the IMBCI and the *FIGO Guidelines to MotherBaby-Friendly Birthing Facilities,* which Robbie "wordsmithed." Most of her published articles are freely available on her website www.davis-floyd.com. She can be reached at davis-floyd@outlook.com

Melissa Cheyney, PhD, CPM, LDM is Associate Professor of Clinical Medical Anthropology at Oregon State University (OSU) with additional appointments in Public Health and Women, Gender, and Sexuality Studies. She is also a Certified Professional Midwife in active practice and the Chair of the Division of Research for the Midwives Alliance of North America, where she directs the MANA Statistics Project, managing the largest registry of community births (home and birth center) in the United States. Missy currently also directs the International Reproductive Health Laboratory at Oregon State University, where she serves as the primary investigator for more than 30 maternal and infant health-related research projects in nine countries. She is the author of an ethnography entitled *Born at Home* (2010), along with dozens of peer-reviewed articles that examine the cultural beliefs and clinical outcomes associated with midwife-led birth at home in the United States. Dr. Cheyney is an award-winning professor, and in 2014 was given Oregon State University's prestigious Scholarship Impact Award for her work in the International Reproductive Health Laboratory and with the MANA Statistics Project. She is the mother of a daughter born at home on the International Day of the Midwife in 2009. cheyneym@oregonstate.edu

Contributors

Megan Cogburn is a doctoral candidate in cultural anthropology at the University of Florida. Her dissertation research, funded by the Fulbright-Hays program, examines the intended and unintended consequences of global maternal health policies and what counts as pregnancy and childbirth care in rural communities in Tanzania today. Megan has been active in development and maternal health projects and research in Tanzania since 2009. Most recently she worked as an ethnographer for the Harvard Kennedy School Transparency for Development Project in Mpwapwa District, Tanzania, in 2016. She has published in *Health Policy and Planning*, and can be reached at megandcogburn@ufl.edu

Rea Daellenbach, PhD is a Senior Lecturer in the Bachelor of Midwifery Program at the Ara Institute of Canterbury in Christchurch, New Zealand. Rea completed a PhD in sociology (University of Canterbury) in 1999; her dissertation addressed the growth and impact of the homebirth movement in New Zealand. Rea became involved in childbirth/homebirth activism after the births of her first two children in the mid-1980s. In the 1990s, she was an active consumer member of the New Zealand College of Midwives and was appointed as a lay member of the inaugural Midwifery Council of New Zealand, 2004–2009. Since completing her PhD, she has been part of several research teams looking at various aspects of midwifery practice and midwifery education. She is a coeditor of the book *Sustainability, Midwifery & Birth* (2011). She has also been involved in a team conducting research on women's birthplace choices (EMU study) in New Zealand, utilizing a concur-rent quantitative and qualitative methodology. Rea.Daellenbach@ara.ac.nz

Lydia Dixon, PhD is a cultural and medical anthropologist. She has worked in the field of women's health in Mexico since 2002 as a researcher, volunteer, and educator. Her article, "Obstetrics in a Time of Violence: Mexi-can Midwives Critique Routine Hospital Practices," was published in *Medical Anthropology Quarterly* in 2015, and she continues to research, write, and pub-lish about midwifery and women's health in Mexico and worldwide. Lydia currently works as a research associate with UCLA and Los Angeles County, evaluating a community health worker program that aims to reduce health inequalities in Los Angeles. lydiazacherdixon@gmail.com

Mounia El Kotni, PhD is a French-Moroccan cultural and medical anthropologist (PhD, SUNY Albany, 2016). Her research analyzes the multi-faceted impacts of global maternal health policies on Indigenous midwives' practices and women's reproductive care access in Chiapas, Mexico, where she has been conducting fieldwork since 2009. She is a Fondation de France Fellow (2019–2021) and postdoctoral researcher at the EHESS-CEMS in Paris, France. She has worked on different research projects involving women's health and human rights in France, the United States, Mexico, and Guatemala, and is an international consultant on gender equality. She has published her research results in journal articles, book chapters, and blog posts, in French, English, and Spanish. More information on her work can be found on her website www.mouniaelkotni.com. She can be reached at mounia.elkotni@gmail.com

Eugenia Georges, PhD is Professor and Chair of the Department of Anthropology at Rice University in Houston, Texas. She has conducted research on the implications of transnational migration for gender and class hierarchies in the Dominican Republic and on the political mobilization of Dominican immigrants in New York City. Her research in Greece examines the medicalization of reproduction, with a focus on the historical processes through which pregnancy and Greek obstetrical practice have been shaped in interaction with a range of reproductive technologies. Her research in Brazil examines the ethical and political strategies of a network of obstetricians-activ-ists who have organized to demedicalize childbirth on the national level and redefine a range of choices in maternity care as a woman's human right. She is the author of *Bodies of Knowledge: The Medicalization of Reproduction in Greece* (2008) and *The Making of a Transnational Community: Migration, Development and Cultural Change in the Dominican Republic* (1990). Her numerous articles have appeared in *Medical Anthropology Quarterly, Social Science and Medicine, Feminist Studies, Journal of Mediterranean Studies,* and other journals. nia@rice.edu

Bahareh Goodarzi, MSc, Midwife, Lecturer, and PhD student, Amsterdam UMC, Vrije Universiteit Amsterdam, Midwifery Science, AVAGM–Amsterdam Public Health research institute. Goodarzi qualified as a midwife in 2007 and worked as a primary care midwife from 2007 to 2012. During that time, she obtained a Master's in Health Management at the Erasmus University Rotterdam. From 2012 to 2015, she worked as a policy advisor at the Royal Dutch Collage of Midwives. Since 2011, she has also been working as a lecturer at the Midwifery Academy in Amsterdam. Her field of expertise is the physiology of the mechanisms and dynamics of birth, skills training, simulation training, and emergency training. Currently she is working on her PhD dissertation, which she started in 2015 at the Amsterdam UMC, Vrije Universiteit Amsterdam, Midwifery Science, AVAGM–Amsterdam Public Health research institute. Her research topic is risk selection in maternal and newborn care, on which she published an article in *Health, Risk & Society.* b.goodarzi@vumc.nl

Etsuko Matsuoka, PhD, Professor, Faculty of Human Life and Environment, Nara Women's University, Japan, is an anthropologist specializing in childbirth and midwifery studies in different parts of the world. Her works in English cover such topics as "The Interpretation of Fox-Possession: Illness as Metaphor" (*Culture, Medicine and Psychiatry* 1991), "Is Hospital the Safest Place for Birth? (*Curare* 1995), "Postmodern Midwives in Japan: The Offspring of Modern Hospital Birth (*Medical Anthropology* 2001), "Maternity Homes in Japan: Reservoirs of Normal Childbirth" (coauthored with Fumiko Hinokuma, in *Birth Models that Work* 2009), *Challenges to Women's Reproductive Health and Rights in Asia* (coedited by Pande Made Kutanegara, Gadjah Mada University Press 2015), and "The Gendered Body in Family Planning in Indonesia" (*Culture and Gender in Asia* 2017). She is a member of the Editorial Board of the *International Journal of Childbirth.* Currently she is conducting research in Asia comparing differing patterns of the modernizing process with regard to childbirth and midwifery. matsuokae1@gmail.com

Vania Smith-Oka, PhD is Associate Professor of Anthropology at the University of Notre Dame. Since 2008 she has engaged in research investigating birth practices in hospitals in urban Mexico, specifically Puebla. She has focused on the birth experiences of marginalized women, on notions of risk and responsibility, and on obstetric violence. Currently she is working on a collaborative project in Nairobi, Kenya, exploring the disrespectful intrapartum care inflicted on impoverished women. She is the author of one book, *Shaping the Reproduction of Indigenous Mexico* (2013) and numerous articles published in journals such as *American Anthropologist, Medical Anthropology Quarterly,* and *Social Science and Medicine.* Her current research also explores how medical students acquire the knowledge, skills, and attitudes of medicine from their peers and mentors. Vania.Smith-Oka.1@nd.edu

Adrienne Strong, PhD is Assistant Professor of Anthropology at the University of Florida. Adrienne completed a joint PhD in cultural anthropology at Washington University in St. Louis and the Universiteit van Amsterdam in 2017. Her research centers on ethnographic, political, economic, and historical investigations of maternal mortality in Tanzania, particularly the pathways leading to deaths in biomedical health facilities. Adrienne has received funding from the NSF, Fulbright, Fulbright-Hays, and a P.E.O. Scholar Award. She is published in *Social Science & Medicine, Health Care for Women International,* and *Human Organization.* A book about Adrienne's work on maternal death at Mawingu Hospital will be published by University of California Press in 2020. More information about her work is available on her website www.adrienne-strong.com, and she can be reached at adrienne.strong@ufl.edu

Saraswathi Vedam, RM, FACNM, SciD (hc) is Lead Investigator of the Birth Place Lab at University of British Columbia. For over 35 years, she has been a midwife, educator, and researcher. Saraswathi has been active in setting international policy on place of birth and interprofessional collaboration. She convened three national Home Birth Summits that catalyzed transdisciplinary imagination in the US to address equity and access to high-quality care among marginalized communities. Her community-based participatory studies, Changing Childbirth in BC and the Giving Voice to Mothers, led to new quality measures: the Mothers' Autonomy in Decision Making (MADM) scale and the Mothers on Respect (MORi) index, which assess quality and safety as defined by the service user. Saraswathi also coordinated multidisciplinary teams for the Access and Integration Maternity Care Mapping Study on the impact of integration of midwives on outcomes, and the Canadian Birth Place Study that examined attitudes to homebirth among midwives and physicians. saraswathi.vedam@ubc.ca

Therese A. Wiegers, PhD is a psychologist, epidemiologist, and Senior Researcher at the Netherlands Institute for Health Services Research (NIVEL). She qualified as an occupational therapist in 1976, studied psychology at the University of Utrecht, received her Master's degree in 1986, completed the postacademic study of epidemiology at the VU/EMGO in Amsterdam in 1995, and received her PhD from the University of Leiden in 1997 with a dissertation called *Home or Hospital Birth. A Prospective Study of Midwifery Care in the Netherlands.* She has been working as a researcher at NIVEL since 1988, where her main interest has always been midwifery and maternity care. T.Wiegers@nivel.nl

K. Eliza Williamson is a doctoral candidate in cultural anthropology at Rice University. Her dissertation research examines maternal and child health policy that aims to "humanize" birth care in Brazil's public health system. Eliza has received funding from the Wenner-Gren Foundation, Fulbright, and Fulbright-Hays and achieved Honorable Mention for the NSF Graduate Research Fellowship Program. She was also awarded the Rice Center for the Study of Women, Gender, and Sexuality Visionary Partners' Dissertation Fellowship, and the Association for Feminist Anthropology Dissertation Award. She has conducted fieldwork in South America since 2011 (Argentina and Brazil), focusing on grassroots and government efforts to improve birth care and combat obstetric violence. Since 2016 she has also worked with families raising disabled children with congenital Zika syndrome in the state of Bahia and has published "Care in the Time of Zika: Notes on the 'Afterlife' of the Epidemic in Salvador (Bahia), Brazil" in *Interface (Botucatu)*. She has also published in *Anthropology News* and *Medical Anthropology Quarterly*. elizawilliamson@gmail.com

Summer Wood, PhD, MPH is a researcher in the fields of public health and medical anthropology. She completed graduate training in public health at the University of Michigan, and in medical anthropology and legal anthropology at New York University. Summer has been active in health research in Tanzania since 2004 on topics including HIV/AIDS prevention and treatment, health and human rights, maternal and child health, health indicators, and health systems reform. Her dissertation (2016) is an ethnographic study of the issue of birth registration in Dar es Salaam, Tanzania, exploring the cultural, medical, legal, and political aspects of birth registration from the perspectives of both families and government officials. This research has been funded by the National Science Foundation and the Wenner-Gren Foundation for Anthropological Research. sjwood@nyu.edu